Political Science Today

To my colleagues and friends at Cameron University:
You have made life and lunches more entertaining,
and I am the better person for it.

Political Science Today

Wendy N. Whitman Cobb

*US Air Force School of Advanced Air and
Space Studies (SAASS)*

FOR INFORMATION:

CQ Press, an Imprint of SAGE Publications, Inc.

2455 Teller Road

Thousand Oaks, California 91320

E-mail: order@sagepub.com

SAGE Publications Ltd.

1 Oliver's Yard

55 City Road

London, EC1Y 1SP

United Kingdom

SAGE Publications India Pvt. Ltd.

B 1/I 1 Mohan Cooperative Industrial Area

Mathura Road, New Delhi 110 044

India

SAGE Publications Asia-Pacific Pte. Ltd.

18 Cross Street #10-10/11/12

China Square Central

Singapore 048423

Printed in the United States of America

Library of Congress Cataloging-in-Publication Data

Names: Whitman Cobb, Wendy N., author.

Title: Political science today / Wendy N. Whitman Cobb.

Description: Washington, DC : SAGE ; CQ Press, [2020] | Includes bibliographical references and index.

Identifiers: LCCN 2019003577 | ISBN 9781544336442 (pbk. : alk. paper)

Subjects: LCSH: Political science–Textbooks.

Classification: LCC JA66 .W455 2020 | DDC 320–dc23 LC record available at https://lccn.loc.gov/2019003577

This book is printed on acid-free paper.

Acquisitions Editor: Scott Greenan

Editorial Assistant: Lauren Younker

Content Development Editors: Elise Frasier, Scott Harris

Production Editor: Tracy Buyan

Copy Editor: Megan Markanich

Typesetter: Cenveo Publisher Services

Proofreader: Annie Lubinsky

Indexer: Robie Grant

Cover Designer: Scott Van Atta

Marketing Manager: Jennifer Jones

SUSTAINABLE FORESTRY INITIATIVE

Certified Chain of Custody
At Least 10% Certified Forest Content
www.sfiprogram.org
SFI-01028

19 20 21 22 23 10 9 8 7 6 5 4 3 2 1

Brief Contents

Detailed Contents

PART III SUBFIELDS

Chapter 7 American Politics 142

Preface

As of this writing, I have spent more than a decade teaching political science to undergraduates in different schools and in very different situations. My experience has spanned from massive lecture halls to the online classroom and everywhere in between. While not every student has been excited to sit in one of my classes (particularly in the required general education courses), I hope that they have all at least come away with a basic understanding of how politics—any kind of politics—affects their everyday lives. I also hope that my students have gained some insight into the study of politics, political science, itself. While today's political environment is often characterized by polarization, mistrust, frustration, and apathy, political science is a means through which we can study and understand the situation as it is and why it came to be. With political science, we achieve a sort of understanding that eludes commentators and talking heads who focus on the current news cycle in favor of context and explanation.

When I began studying political science as an undergraduate, I did not have the benefit of a book such as this. My choice of major was stimulated not so much by an interest in politics writ large but rather by my fascination with a certain public policy area. No one sat down with me to explain the *field* of political science and the vast breadth of topic areas that political scientists study. I don't think I'm alone; many political science majors and potential majors who find their way into my office and classes have little knowledge about the field itself. And while many colleges and universities offer introductory classes in political science, I believe that a field-based approach offers more of an introduction to political science itself than concepts alone. Concepts and ideas provide a valuable foundation, no doubt, but to understand the field, the job, the profession of political science requires an understanding of how political scientists view their career and its approaches. To that end, this book is an attempt at synthesizing those approaches, not only to talk about concepts but to organize them in such a way that students come away with a better understanding of political science as profession.

The title for this book, *Political Science Today*, went through a number of iterations before I settled on it. However, I believe it succinctly sums up the purpose of this book: to introduce students to what the field of political science looks like in the late 2010s. To that end, it is not a book about current events but a book about the state of political science research with today's students in mind. It balances an appreciation of history and past research findings with the current thinking on a wide variety of research questions and inquiries. To understand the field today (as well as how we got here), we must have an understanding and appreciation of what has come before. No political scientist performs research on a topic that has never been discussed before. All of our research is based on something someone else has already done. In the case of this book, the various subfields have not reached their current state of knowledge out of nowhere. Understanding political science today requires an understanding of, if not history, at least contextual background. In my classes, I call this background and previous research the "fruits and vegetables." No one really likes to eat them (or in this case read and know about them), but they are essential to understanding more recent research and findings.

Political science today also means confronting the political environment as we find it. As the political environment has worsened—both domestically and around the world—I find that it has gotten harder to teach. Students (and professors) are constantly on the lookout for bias or perceived bias. The moment a political position is even hinted at, tribalist politics lead us to defensive postures that preclude valuable discussion and exchange. *Political Science Today* does not shy away from discussing these topics although they are certainly not the focus. Instead, we can use controversial topics and policies as teaching opportunities, as ways to show students the difference between politics and political science and the leverage that political science can bring toward understanding our differences.

Approach to the Book

It's hard to write a book about political science when political scientists themselves have a hard time agreeing about the shape of the field. For some, methodology is a distinct subfield, whereas others might argue that American politics is not a specialization but a form of comparative politics; a graduate school professor once said that Americanists are simply comparativists without a passport. In any case, there will be disagreements about what is covered and how in *Political Science Today*. However, I believe that the subjects and subfields covered here are a good representation of how American political scientists (that is, those located in America, not those who study American politics) view the field and therefore how political science is taught. Again, there will be quibbling on the details, but my hope is that most political scientists will find something of value in this approach and the material.

In combining both a conceptual and subfield approach, *Political Science Today* is organized around three parts: Part I: Foundations, Part II: Institutions and Behavior, and Part III: Subfields. Part I: Foundations encompasses the introduction to political science, research methods, and political theory. Chapter 1 is not just an introduction to political science, including a discussion of what it is, but it briefly details the history of the field, including whether political science is truly a science. Finally, Chapter 1 introduces students to key ideas that are discussed throughout the text, including states, governments, power, and representation, among others. Continuing on with the idea of political science as a science, Chapter 2: Research Methods examines the ways in which political scientists study politics. This easy introduction to both qualitative and quantitative methods provides students with a methodological foundation from which to approach the study of politics, including a discussion of the advantages and disadvantages of different methodological tools and how the quantitative and qualitative debate has influenced political science. Finally, Chapter 3 discusses political theory. While political theory itself is considered its own subfield (and could thus rightly be included in Part III), questions about the role and nature of government and governing are essential in understanding politics and therefore political science.

Part II builds on the basic conceptual ideas outlined in Part I by focusing on larger ideas about political institutions and behavior. Chapter 4: Constitutions, Law, and Justice, takes many of the ideas outlined in Chapter 3 and puts them into practice. For example, the nature of justice and a just government and society are some of the most often tackled questions in political theory; constitutions take those notions and create functioning governmental systems that are intended to put words into action. Topics covered in this chapter include constitutions, systems of law, and court systems. Similarly, Chapter 5 expands on constitutions and systems of governance in detailing different governmental and electoral systems. The chapter compares presidential and parliamentary systems and the political parties that form to help organize the various electoral systems. Finally, Chapter 6 examines political communications and the media. While the nature of media and news is different around the world, there are basic commonalities in how an active media supports (or inhibits) governance and democratic government. Taking these three chapters together, Part II builds a framework on top of Part I's foundation, which is built out in Part III.

Part III represents a real and significant innovation in this book with chapters on specific subfields of political science. To reiterate, there is certainly disagreement over what constitutes a specific subfield, but I believe that a majority of political scientists can agree on the five included here. Chapter 7 presents American politics with the chapter split between institutions and political behavior. Any summary of such a complex topic necessarily leaves out some components, although this is one of the more extensive chapters in the book. If it is more exhaustive than other chapters, it is a bias toward explaining political situations that students most commonly confront in their everyday lives. It is a bias toward helping students understand political science through a lens that is most familiar to them. Chapter 8 introduces comparative politics, beginning with a discussion of the comparative method. In America, comparative politics include studies of global politics, so this chapter examines different themes in comparative politics including globalization, development, nationalism and ethnic conflict, and authoritarianism. International relations, a subfield that focuses on the relationship among and between states, is addressed in Chapter 9. International relations is a subfield that is dominated by grand theories that attempt to explain how states interact, and as such, Chapter 9 briefly outlines some of these theories along with theories about war and peace in the international domain. The relationship between economics and politics is taken up in Chapter 10: Political Economy. Although economics is considered a different field of study altogether, the connections between economics and politics are deep and intertwined. To fully comprehend the activities of government, we must also understand its influence on domestic and global economies. Finally,

Chapter 11 discusses public policy and public administration. Some political scientists would argue that each topic warrants its own chapter, but the relationship between policy and implementing and administering it is a fuzzy one and can thus be considered together here.

Given this brief outline, it is clear that *Political Science Today* is not comprehensive or all-encompassing; its purpose is to provide breadth over depth. It is also meant as an introduction for students to some topics and concepts that can be difficult to understand at first. Definitions of complex concepts are somewhat simplified to achieve this. In order to provide some supplementary resources, at the end of each chapter are additional readings that instructors and/or students can reference to get a deeper understanding of some of the topics discussed. Additionally, case studies throughout the chapters connect the material to real-life events that students can use to explore issues in more detail.

Support for Instructors and Students

SAGE edge offers a robust online environment featuring an impressive array of free tools and resources for review, study, and further exploration, keeping both instructors and students on the cutting edge of teaching and learning. Learn more at **edge.sagepub.com/whitmancobb**.

SAGE edge for Students provides a personalized approach to help students accomplish their coursework goals in an easy-to-use learning environment.

- Mobile-friendly **eFlashcards** strengthen understanding of key terms and concepts.

- Mobile-friendly practice **quizzes** allow for independent assessment by students of their mastery of course material.

- Links to meaningful **multimedia** facilitate student use of Internet resources and further exploration of topics.

- **Learning objectives** reinforce the most important material.

SAGE edge for Instructors supports your teaching by making it easy to integrate quality content and create a rich learning environment for students.

- **Test banks** provide a diverse range of pre-written options as well as the opportunity to edit any question and/or insert your own personalized questions to effectively assess students' progress and understanding.

- Editable, chapter-specific **PowerPoint® slides** offer complete flexibility for creating a multimedia presentation for your course.

- **Instructor Manual** for each chapter includes a chapter summary, outline, learning objectives, discussion questions, and in-class activities.

- All **tables and figures** from the textbook are included.

ⓈSAGE coursepacks

SAGE coursepacks makes it easy to import our quality instructor and student resource content into your school's learning management system (LMS). Intuitive and simple to use, **SAGE coursepacks** gives you the control to focus on what really matters: customizing course content to meet your students' needs.

Customized and curated for use in:

Blackboard

Canvas

Desire2Learn (D2L)

Moodle

Created specifically for *Political Science Today* by Wendy Whitman Cobb, SAGE coursepacks is included FREE! *Instructors*, **contact your sales representative** to request a brief demonstration or additional information. Learning and teaching has never been easier!

SAGE coursepacks for INSTRUCTORS supports teaching with quality content and easy-to-integrate course management tools, featuring:

- Our content delivered **directly into your LMS**

- **Intuitive and easy-to-use format** that makes it easy to integrate **SAGE coursepacks** into your course with minimal effort

- **Pedagogically robust assessment tools** that foster review, practice, and critical thinking, and offer a better, more complete way to measure student engagement, including:

  o **Instructions** on how to use and integrate the comprehensive assessments and resources provided

  o **Chapter tests** that identify opportunities for student improvement, track student progress, and ensure mastery of key learning objectives

  o **Test banks** built on Bloom's taxonomy that provide a diverse range of test items

  o **Activity and quiz options** that allow you to choose only the assignments and tests you want

- Access to all the resources offered on **SAGE edge**, including **PowerPoints, Instructor's Manual**, and **tables and figures**

SAGE coursepacks for STUDENTS enhances learning in an easy-to-use environment that offers all the resources provided on **SAGE edge**, including mobile-friendly **eFlashcards** and **practice quizzes**, links to meaningful **multimedia**, and chapter **learning objectives**.

Acknowledgments

Political Science Today has been a project several years in the making, so I have the opportunity to be grateful to a number of people who have been instrumental in that process. I'd first like to thank the editors and team at CQ Press who have helped shepherd the book through the writing, review, and production process, specifically Monica Eckman and Scott Greenan. The book has been helped significantly by their comments and assistance. I would also like to extend my appreciation to my colleagues at Cameron University, some of whom have read and provided helpful comments on portions of the book, including Travis Childs, Lance Janda, Sarah Janda, Jeff Metzger, Edris Montalvo, and the rest of the Department of Social Sciences. I am lucky beyond belief to be able to work with such amazing colleagues and friends; my work and my life are significantly better for it, and this book is dedicated to them. My students at Cameron also deserve my thanks as many of them got (or were assigned) the opportunity to read and comment on various chapters along the way.

I was fortunate throughout my political science training to be broadly trained. Although my specialization is in American institutions and policy, I have taken classes (sometimes multiple) in every subfield discussed here. I thank the wonderful political science faculty at both the University of Central Florida and the University of Florida for providing that education to me in the first place.

As always, I would not be where I am without the support of family along the way. Although my parents let me choose my own path, their insistence on high standards whether it was on the baseball field or in the classroom has been something that has stuck with me. I am grateful to my husband, Josh, who has been unfailingly supportive of my work even though it often keeps us apart. Ironically, it is often the time spent away from each other (Josh is an officer in the US Army and is often stationed away from me) that gives me the space to complete major projects such as this. In his absence, our dog, Gus, and cat, Bean, have kept me company during the process (and perhaps caused some chaos of their own). As always, any errors that remain are my own. CQ Press would like to thank the following instructors who participated in review for this book:

Manuel Balan, McGill University

Richard P. Farkas, DePaul University

Michael Huelshoff, University of New Orleans

George Kaloudis, Rivier University

Noel A. D. Thompson, Tuskegee University

John Zumbrunnen, University of Wisconsin–Madison

Jolly A. Emrey, University of Wisconsin–Whitewater

Marie A. Eisenstein, Indiana University Northwest

Lolita D. Gray, Jackson State University

Jill Lane, North Seattle College

H. Ege Ozen, College of Staten Island, CUNY

Andrew Dzeguze, Whittier College

Sterling Recker, North Central Missouri College

About the Author

Wendy N. Whitman Cobb is associate professor at the US Air Force School of Advanced Air and Space Studies (SAASS) in Montgomery, Alabama. She earned her PhD in political science from the University of Florida following undergraduate work at the University of Central Florida. Her work focuses on institutions and public policy, particularly as it concerns space exploration policy. Before joining the faculty at SAASS, she was associate professor of political science at Cameron University in Lawton, Oklahoma. Previous books include *Unbroken Government: Success and the Illusion of Failure in Policymaking*, *The Politics of Cancer: Malignant Indifference*, and *The CQ Press Career Guide for Political Science Students*.

Sara Miller McCune founded SAGE Publishing in 1965 to support the dissemination of usable knowledge and educate a global community. SAGE publishes more than 1000 journals and over 800 new books each year, spanning a wide range of subject areas. Our growing selection of library products includes archives, data, case studies and video. SAGE remains majority owned by our founder and after her lifetime will become owned by a charitable trust that secures the company's continued independence.

Los Angeles | London | New Delhi | Singapore | Washington DC | Melbourne

Foundations

Political science is the systematic and scientific study of politics, including institutions, behaviors, and processes.

Source: ©iStockphoto.com/designer491

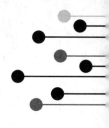

CHAPTER 1

What Is Political Science?

Politics, and American politics in particular, has become far more polarizing and uncivil over the past several decades. Political parties, whose bases have become more extreme, have little incentive to work together and more incentive to demonize the ideas of the other side. Social media and the Internet have made the process even more acute; online trolls harass other Internet users and leave nasty comments on Facebook sites and online news articles. And the accusations go both ways: Republicans claim Democrats are being un-American. Democrats claim that Republicans are ruining the country. The phenomenon has even occurred within political parties. A recent Senate candidate in the West Virginia primary, Don Blankenship, called Senate majority leader and fellow Republican Mitch McConnell "not an American" and "cocaine Mitch" all in response to the lack of support he got in the race from the Republican Party.[1] (Blankenship had also spent a year in jail following his role in a mine explosion.) *New York Times* reporter Amy Chozick writes in her account of reporting on the 2016 election of the nasty e-mails, comments, and even death threats that she received whenever she published a story that was critical of one of the major candidates.[2] This type of rhetoric has led to a growing discontentment with politics as they are—perhaps contributing to Donald Trump's presidential win in 2016 where he promised to "drain the swamp" of Washington and politics as usual.

The language used by politicians and their supporters today can certainly be disheartening—even to political scientists. The good news is that political science is not nearly the whirlwind of conflict, scandal, and frustration that is often, though not always, the object of its study. **Politics** is defined as the authoritative distribution of resources or rather the determining of who gets what, when, and how.

Chapter Objectives

1. Distinguish between politics and political science.

2. Develop an understanding and appreciation of the history of political science.

3. Examine the extent to which political science is a science.

4. Identify and discuss major concepts in political science, including the state, government, power, and ideology

Political science is the systematic and scientific study of politics, including institutions, behaviors, and processes. To that extent, political science is somewhat removed from the day-to-day chaos that is often reflected on our television screens.

Political science is a different animal altogether from what you usually hear on cable news channels with bright breaking news headlines. You would be forgiven, then, for being very confused about what political science is and means. Some students decide to major in it because they want to go to law school or into the military or because they already know they want to be a politician. Others won't even go near a political science class unless it's required because they "know" they won't like it. In any case, that's what this book is for—to clear up the misconceptions about what political science is and what's involved in it. This chapter introduces the field of political science, first by distinguishing it from what politics is and then by looking at its history and what makes political science a science. Secondly, the chapter explores some of the fundamental concepts of political science, including public goods, states, government, ideology, and representation. Finally, Chapter 1 discusses the layout of the book and the road ahead.

Differences between Politics and Political Science

Perhaps the easiest way to talk about the differences between politics and political science is to look at a few examples. Take immigration, something we often hear about in the news. Some politicians complain about illegal immigration and express a desire to build a wall on the Mexican American border, while former president Barack Obama issued sweeping executive orders dealing with immigration. The rhetoric, particularly as it is portrayed in the media, often shows Republicans and Democrats arguing over things like whether illegal immigrants who are already in the United States should be allowed to stay and perhaps made citizens, or forced to leave. Of course, immigration is not nearly as simple as that; illegal immigrants make up a significant portion of labor-intensive work in the US economy, and many come to the United States to escape dangerous conditions in their home countries.

Political scientists move beyond the media rhetoric. Political scientists study this issue by looking at the factors that go into making immigration policy like the economy, political ideology, and public opinion. Others compare US immigration policy to policy in other countries to examine the differences and why they arise. Still others will examine the politics of executive orders, including former president Obama's to allow some illegal immigrants to stay in the United States. Issues like sanctuary cities, federalism and state politics, and international relations are all aspects of immigration that political scientists study.

Yet another controversial policy in politics today is health care. With the passage of the Patient Protection and Affordable Care Act in 2010, those both for and against health care reforms have had much to talk about. Republicans have consistently derided the act and derisively nicknamed it Obamacare. Democrats have defended it while acknowledging that improvements can be made. Republicans in the House of Representatives have voted more than fifty times to repeal the Affordable Care Act.

Political scientists study health care policy in an analytical, less political way. One major question has been why the United States didn't act on health reform earlier than 2010 and, perhaps even more importantly, why the United States hasn't followed the lead of most other Western democracies to implement a single-payer system. Hacker, among others, has published several articles looking at the history and politics of health care reform in the United States beginning in the early twentieth century. Hacker argues in "National Health Care Reform: An Idea Whose Time Came and Went" that things such as structural changes in Congress, the interest group community, changes in the health care industry, and public opinion, among others, finally coalesced and allowed health care reform to be considered by the Clinton administration in 1993 and 1994.[3] Other studies examining health care have looked at the adoption of children's health care policies across the states and the role of interest groups like the AARP and the American Medical Association (AMA). The AMA, for example, has traditionally been against major government involvement in health care practices, fearing that the doctors they represent could be hurt or even that the government might dictate to doctors how to treat patients. In this sense, it is the political context that has helped to shape health care reform, including policy considerations that are ongoing in the United States.

In these two examples, we see how political scientists move beyond shallow political issues and examine patterns of politics: what factors allow bills to be passed, patterns in how states adopt different policies, how the development of Congress or of the executive branch makes things easier or harder to accomplish. These questions might not be sexy enough to capture the attention of political pundits on television, but they are arguably more interesting, informative, and important as they address the underlying questions of how and why things happen in politics.

It might be hard to see how these issues affect you; immigration may not affect you directly, and being young, you may not appreciate the need for health insurance let alone reform. However, most things in society can be connected to politics and political science in some way. Interested in sports? One way to explore sports in politics might be how Congress has involved itself in issues from steroids in baseball to concussions in football. Additionally, when local municipalities build stadiums or arenas for their local teams, politics is involved. Interested in the fine arts? Think about education policies that have placed a greater emphasis on science, math, and reading, and drawn money and attention away from theater, arts, and music. Have a passion for space? You can study the politics of NASA and human spaceflight or even broader contours of science policy like climate change.

The bottom line of this discussion is that political science is more than what we often think it is or can be. It is also more thorough, deliberate, and objective than the politics we see on TV or read about on the Internet. In that sense, even those who might be turned off by the nasty rhetoric or negative commercials might be interested in the actual dynamics of explaining why bills are passed or why the public feels the way they do.

History

Debates over the history and nature of political science are not new. (For readings on these topics, see the For Further Reading section at the end of this chapter.) Most everyone can agree that the roots of the discipline go back to ancient Greece with the philosophy of Socrates, Plato, and Aristotle. While Socrates himself is well known for his approach to teaching (the so-called Socratic method), his writings, if ever there were any, do not survive today. What we know about Socrates and his philosophy comes to us through his student Plato. Plato's writings, most importantly for us, *The Republic*, present his thoughts as a series of discussions between Socrates and his students. Many of these discussions centered on concepts like justice, government, morals, and what proper city-states should look like. Ironically, students are often taught that the origins of democracy come from ancient Greece quite literally: *demos* means "people" and *kratos* means "rule." However, among other discussions in *The Republic*, Plato classifies democracy as being an unjust government along with timocracy,[4] oligarchy, and tyranny. His reason for this is that democracy, allowing the people to rule, could lead to what is called tyranny of the majority. The danger, according to Plato, is that the majority could run roughshod over the rights of the minority and therefore devolve into a tyrannical, unjust government.

Aristotle continued this tradition in his work *Politics*. In it, Aristotle discusses what the best government is, arguing that the city is the natural community and the only just community. These three Greek philosophers left an indelible mark on political philosophy that would not be questioned nor significantly added to until the medieval period when philosophers like St. Augustine and St. Thomas Aquinas wrote treatises on the nature and purpose of law. These writings will be explored further in Chapter 3.

As Europe moved from the medieval period into the sixteenth century, religion and its role in government came to the forefront of European political matters. The first prominent treatise that appeared at this time was Niccolò Machiavelli's *The Prince*. With its oft-heard exhortations like "the ends justify the means" and "It is much safer to be feared than loved," Machiavelli's name is sometimes used as an adjective to mean cunning and deceitful. The real purpose of *The Prince*, however, was to win Machiavelli favor with the powerful Medici family out of which had come popes and royalty. Machiavelli thus represented a real attempt at synthesizing advice for rulers that would make them not only successful but powerful. This focus on the practical applications of politics represents a shift in political theory, considering not just the fundamental building blocks of society but demonstrating how they could be put into practice. This tradition can also be seen in Sir Thomas More's 1516 book *Utopia*, describing an ideal society and its religious, governmental, and cultural practices.

Ironically, in More's England, a massive government upheaval was in the works. In 1534, King Henry VIII of England declared the Church in England to be independent of the Roman Catholic Church because he desired a divorce from his first wife. The religious upheaval generated by this one move helped lead to the English Civil War in the 1600s. During this period, a new generation of political philosophers arose, questioning the original purposes of the governments under which they lived. What gave the king the right to rule over his people? Was the divine right of kings, the idea that God divinely inspired and supported monarchy and therefore implicitly supported the actions and decisions of kings, justifiable? Particularly given the religious reformation of the time, what role should religion play in forming a government?

A new generation of philosophers arose from the ashes of the English Civil War to try to provide answers to the now pressing questions. And while much of this will be discussed further in Chapter 3, we will briefly describe some of the innovations here. The philosophers Thomas Hobbes and John Locke separately proposed to begin from a thought experiment called the **state of nature**, imagining what life and human behavior might look like in the absence of government, society, and culture. Based on this, both Locke and Hobbes agreed that individuals are granted certain **natural rights** that all people have, but at some point, this state of nature begins to break down. Hobbes, believing that human nature is suspect, saw a breakdown among the people leading to a life that is "nasty, brutish, and short." Locke, on the other hand, believed that the state of nature can be more pleasant, arguing that people are naturally good; it is only the introduction of property and money that causes disputes among the people. In any case, once the state of nature breaks down, people, in need of safety, agree to enter into **social contracts** wherein everyone gives up some of their natural rights to a government in return for order and protection from one another. These ideas dramatically changed political theory. No longer did rule need to be divinely ordained; no longer was there justification to keep the common people from being involved in the operations of government. The age of Enlightenment had begun.

These social contract theorists greatly influenced views on the role and responsibilities of government moving into the eighteenth century. For example, the principles of consent of the governed, natural rights, and social contract theory are widely apparent in the founding documents of the United States. Jefferson readily admits to "certain unalienable rights" in the Declaration of Independence, along with "their right, it is their duty, to throw off such Government and to provide new Guards for their future security." Other influential theorists such as Montesquieu explicated ideas such as separation of powers that Americans like John Adams expounded on and advocated for the adoption of in a new American government.

Establishing a Discipline

Given the importance of such ideas to movements including the American and French revolutions, no one could deny the significance of political philosophy and theory. However, as the nineteenth century progressed and the role of the state grew, there was a clamor in the American academy to establish some sort of area of study that encompassed not only political philosophy but areas such as law and administration. This was also reflected in the changes in the American university system as it moved from a classical curriculum broadly focused on the classics, religion, and ethics to a curriculum dominated by specialized fields of study.[5]

This conception of political science as a field would soon come into conflict with the idea of developing a science of politics. The second influence on the development of political science was the very idea of developing a systematic and scientific view of the political world. Woodrow Wilson, before becoming president of the United States, was one of the first political scientists in America and in 1887 wrote, "I suppose that no practical science is ever studied where there is no need to know it. The very fact, therefore, that the eminently practical science of administration is finding its way into college courses in this country would prove that this country needs to know more about administration."[6] Implicit in this idea is that political science can inform public officials and the government of ways to improve. The roots of later debates within political science about its purpose and methods are also implied in Wilson's perception of the growth of political science.

Twentieth-Century Political Science

Most of the political science research carried out in the first half of the twentieth century was primarily observational, comparative, and categorizing in its intent. But as political scientists watched other social sciences, particularly psychology, develop (this was the time of Freud, after all), a movement arose to bring more scientifically based methods to the field. This movement came to fruition with the behavioral revolution in political science at the midcentury mark. Behind the concept of **behavioralism** was the idea that all human action, and therefore political action, can be observed, quantified, and explained in an objective, scientific way.

Proponents of behavioralism argue that the only way to uncover and explain political behavior is in a way that is value neutral, objective, and replicable. In this sense, political scientists can use the model of the natural sciences to improve their field and contribute scientifically to a basic body of knowledge. However, behavioralism is not without its critics. People are people, after all; much of what they do is not objective and is not replicable, especially when it comes to politics. How can political scientists expect to be objective and value neutral when their subjects are not? Additionally, the reasons people behave the way they do are varied, and often individuals are not even aware of why they behave in certain ways; what makes political scientists believe that they can distinguish these behaviors? While behavioralism has been discussed and debated within political science since the 1950s, many of its precepts abound today. Most political scientists seek to be objective, thorough, analytical, and explanatory. They use quantified data and statistical methods, and lacking that, they are methodical and precise in their analyses. Most political scientists are inculcated in statistical methodology and learn how to scientifically analyze data. Chapter 2 will discuss some of the ways in which statistics and quantitative analysis are used by political scientists to answer difficult questions.

Behavioralism is a view that political behavior can be explained through a focus on individual behavior; not everything in politics, however, is directed through individuals. Some things, such as laws and institutions, cannot necessarily be explained through a focus on the individual. **Institutionalism** and its proponents in the 1960s and 1970s sought to refocus the discipline on an analysis of institutions, their development, and their effects on politics. One way to think about the difference between institutions and individuals is to think about the rules of the game and the playing of a game. Any game has rules; those rules shape how individuals play the game. When those rules change, for whatever reason, it affects how the game is played. For institutionalists, the way political institutions are designed is like the rules in a game. Applied to something like Congress, institutionalists would focus on how things like committees are set up or how much power leaders have and the types of effects that might have on congressional productivity or power structures.

Institutionalists in the 1960s and 1970s brought to the field techniques that borrowed from the field of economics. Things like rational choice theory and game theory allowed institutions to be modeled in a formal way. These models also led to predictions, another hallmark of the push for a natural science approach in political science. Perhaps one of the most well-known game theoretic models in political science from this period was Downs's book *An Economic Theory of Democracy*.[7] In it, Downs builds a formal model of political behavior working from the assumption of rationality—that people and institutions make decisions based on what their preferences are. One of the results that comes from his analysis is that the likely number of major political parties in a country is a result of the distribution of voters and what they believe. Political parties also have an incentive to make their platforms vague and rarely change them to appear stable and attract as many voters as possible.

The difference between institutionalism and behavioralism is one of where the origins of political behavior lie: Is it with individual people or with the institutions and rules of the game that shape people's behaviors? Like many of the conflicts inherent in political science, there isn't necessarily a right or wrong answer; it's merely a reflection of where political scientists believe is the appropriate area for study.

The Role of Political Theory

The history of political science, detailed here, began with a discussion of political philosophy ranging from Plato to Montesquieu with Machiavelli and St. Augustine in between. Once political science as a discipline was formed, it would appear to a casual observer that political theory had been relegated to the dustbin of history. It is certainly true that since the late nineteenth century, the role of political theory and philosophy had been downgraded to an extent, but it has not disappeared entirely. Beginning in the mid-twentieth century, political theory experienced a resurgence of sorts with theorists reconsidering the role and purpose of the state. Theorists such as John Rawls published *A Theory of Justice*, exploring the shape that a truly just state would take.[8] Meanwhile, Nozick contributed to a critique of *A Theory of Justice* from a libertarian perspective (libertarians believe in as little government involvement in life as possible).[9] Political theory has increasingly explored the values of marginalized communities such as women, minorities, and the LGBTQ+ community. Books such as Pateman's *The Sexual Contract* and Mills's *The Racial Contract* take on the very ideas of what a social contract might mean in today's society.[10] There have even been political theorists exploring the role of multiculturalism in politics.

Despite this renaissance of political theory in the past fifty years, some political scientists and even some political theorists have argued for a separation between the two fields. Grant explores the relationship between political theory and political science in her article for *Political Theory* titled "Political Theory, Political Science, and Politics." She writes that political scientists see no place for political theory because it discusses normative questions—questions that by their very nature have no real answer. Further, theorists, political scientists argue, "lack meaningful standards for assessing what constitutes good research." On the other hand, "Political theorists, on their part, find their work evaluated by people who believe that research must have a 'cutting edge' and that its aim is to produce new knowledge, beliefs that they often do not share."[11]

The debate, then, goes to the heart of whether the purpose of political science is to produce scientific knowledge or knowledge of what is good or bad, just or unjust. It is indeed ironic that political theory is at the very roots of what political science is, and yet today, some argue it does not belong. This book approaches political theory as not only a subfield but as a foundational part of political science that will be taken up further in Chapter 3.

Is Political Science a Science?

One of the basic questions of political science that permeates the field today is whether political science is a science or can ever be a science. **Science** is defined as a systematic search for knowledge through observation, experiments, and tests and is associated with the scientific method. The **scientific method** (see box) is a series of steps that, when followed, allows scientists to thoroughly and methodically ask a question and answer it using observational evidence.

If we take this as the basic meaning of science, then political science is clearly science. Practitioners ask questions, make hypotheses, and systematically test the hypotheses. Even qualitative analyses follow the same pattern of asking a question and very carefully testing and analyzing the evidence. But the deeper meaning of the question is whether political science can ever build a body of knowledge that can be used to better government and politics or at least predict what will happen.

The idea of prediction is built into the natural sciences. Physicists can predict the behavior of molecules on the tiniest scale; astrophysicists can predict the movement of the planets. Biologists can discuss evolution, genetics, and the appearance of different physical characteristics. Medical professionals can predict how the human body will respond to various sorts of treatments for various sorts of ailments. Perhaps one of the greatest stories of predictions is on the part of physicists, who, on the basis of what's called the standard model, predicted the existence of something called a Higgs boson, otherwise known as "the God particle." According to physicists, the Higgs boson is what gives mass to all other particles. While the existence of such a

Scientific Method

The scientific method is a series of steps through which researchers can systematically study and analyze a given topic or question. While some scholars would add to the following steps that follow, the basic steps of the scientific method are these:

1. Form a research question.

2. Formulate a hypothesis, a reasonable guess as to what the answer to the question is.

3. Do background research.

4. Design a test through which to answer the question.

5. Perform the analysis, and gather the results.

6. Make conclusions based on your data. Was your hypothesis right or wrong?

particle has been predicted for some time, it was not until 2012 that scientists at the Large Hadron Collider in Switzerland confirmed its existence through physical tests.

It is hard to name one thing that political scientists can predict with certainty on the scale of the Higgs (at least in terms of importance). There are any number of studies analyzing congressional voting patterns on policies varying from health care to immigration; however, just because members of Congress behaved a certain way in the past does not guarantee they will behave the same in the future. A good way to think about this is in how political parties change over time. Following the Civil War, the Republican Party, the party of Lincoln, was known (at least in the North) to be more supportive of freed slaves, whereas the Democrats (the party of the South) were not. Just 100 years later, this disposition had shifted; Democrats were the party of civil rights and Republicans were not. If there had been any voting studies of how Republicans during the 1800s had voted on civil rights issues, the findings would not hold in voting studies in the twentieth century.

The question thus becomes whether the findings of political scientists are contingent on history. By contingent, we mean dependent on historical circumstances of the type noted previously. For example, given our current state of political polarization, perhaps any findings political scientists have about politics today might be contingent on the polarization that already exists. This historical contingency is apparent when political scientists claim unique historical factors for why something happens in politics. For example, both historians and political scientists have argued that President Lyndon B. Johnson's passage of the Civil Rights Act of 1964 and other elements of the Great Society agenda were only possible in the wake of President John F. Kennedy's assassination and the Democratic landslide that it helped contribute to in the 1964 elections.

To be sure, there is nothing wrong with historical contingency; if accidents of history have helped contribute to certain political events, it would be malpractice to ignore or deny it. The problem is that historical contingency often prohibits political scientists from making sweeping pronouncements that allow for future prediction. And if we cannot make predictions, then what is the purpose of political science? Is it all right for the purpose of political science to be simply the discovery of new knowledge or does it need to go further to justify its own existence? Again, these are existential questions built into the very foundation of what political science is as a discipline and again, the answers to the question do not lie in the category of right or wrong but in the mind of individual political scientists.

One way we use predictions in political science is in presidential elections. For the past four presidential election cycles, the political science journal *PS: Political Science and Politics* has published the results of several predictive models of the presidential election. Each model takes different factors into account, ranging from the economy to public opinion. The models take data from previous election cycles and combine it with current data to predict which candidate is more likely to win the presidential election. However, issues of data availability and contingent historical events are also important. Campbell notes that "an implicit assumption of election forecasting is that no *major* idiosyncratic events intervene between the forecast and the vote that divert the election's results from what would be historically expected by the fundamentals incorporated in the models." Should an "October surprise" happen, an unexpected event or announcement that can interrupt political campaigns, those forecasts may lose their predictive power.[12]

In the end, human nature and the confluence of history conspire to make prediction difficult. Human brains cannot be looked at and taken apart in petri dishes in some lab; they are real and living and able to change. In fact, a well-known phenomenon known as the observer effect acknowledges the idea that when people are told how they act or how they may act in the future, they will likely change their behavior. Applying the observer effect to politics, it could be possible that once members of Congress are told the factors that make them likely to vote for a bill (political party, salience, importance to their constituents), they may in fact change their behavior confounding any possible prediction that may have once come about.

So is political science a science? It is insofar as political scientists adhere to the scientific method, but attempts to make predictions, while admittedly few and far between, are far more difficult to model than the natural sciences. Recognizing the difficulties in predictions, it does not mean that political scientists do not try to learn and understand why politics happens the way it does, it just means that we are cautious in making any long-term predictions.

Major Concepts of Political Science

Before moving on to look at the individual fields of study that can be found within political science, we will examine some of the primary ideas and concepts that are found throughout. These include things such as states, forms of government, civil liberties and civil rights, power, representation, political culture, and ideology. While there are certainly many others that can be added to this list, these concepts can be found throughout the study of political science regardless of subfield.

Public Goods, the Tragedy of the Commons, and Free Riders

One of the key reasons often cited for the need for a government is the provision and protection of what are called public goods. **Public goods** are goods that are "available for, and consumed by, all individuals. Their consumption by any one person does not diminish their consumption by others. People cannot (easily) be excluded from sharing in their consumption and at times have no other choice."[13] Public goods include things like roads, schools, police, and the military—these are all things that everyone can partake in and cannot be excluded from.

To further understand what happens when these goods and services are provided, political scientists use the concept of the **tragedy of the commons**. Imagine a small village with no government to speak of and imagine that in the middle of this village is an open field. This open field can be used for farming or for animals to graze on. While this field is available to all, if too many people use it for too many purposes, its value to animals and crops will be limited. In other words, private individuals may abuse the common goods for private gain without thinking about the needs of others. A more modern example of this tragedy of the commons is in overfishing. With seas and oceans being openly available resources, private businesses will often overfish to their own gain. However, when fish populations become sufficiently limited as a result, it ruins the opportunities for others to use that public good and even eventually for the business that overfished in the first place. Since nobody can be excluded from the field or the seas, everybody uses the good so that at some point it is overused, thereby reducing the benefit to everyone. In this sense, governments are needed not only to provide public goods that may not be otherwise provided by the group but to protect the public goods that do exist.

If part of the purpose of a government is to regulate and provide these public goods, how can that government assemble the necessary resources to do so? Roads must be built, and police and military must be trained and fielded. If citizens know that they will receive these public goods no matter what, what incentive do they have to participate and/or pay for them? This concept is often called the **free rider problem**; if public goods cannot be exclusive to only the people who pay for them, there are bound to be those who seek to cheat the system and not pay. In terms of the government, this problem is circumvented by the requirement of taxes through which public goods can be provided.

The free rider problem can also be applied to smaller groups and associations like interest groups. In interest groups that are organized around the public interest, the benefits they pursue cannot be provided solely to the group members. For example, one of the missions of the American Cancer Society (ACS) is to support research looking for a cure for cancer. If a cure was ever found, the ACS cannot keep nonmembers from accessing that cure. What is the incentive, then, for people to join the ACS if they know they will receive the benefits anyway? Olson addressed this very problem in his book *The Logic of Collective Action*.[14] He theorized that groups like the ACS must use selective benefits in order to entice people to join their groups, things like material benefits (discounts, T-shirts, magazines, etc.), purposive benefits, or solidarity benefits. In sum, then, the government can overcome the free rider problem through its power to require taxes, but other groups must find some other incentive to cause people to want to join.

States

When we think of the term *state* in America, we usually also think of the fact that the country is called the United *States* of America. Although some political scientists may debate the true meaning or conceptualization of the term *state*, in general, **states** refer to groups of people living under a single governmental system.[15] Often, the term denotes sovereign states in the sense that those states have complete control over what happens to them, their government, and their people in the same way that the United States of America is a single group of people who have control over their political lives. The origins of the name *United States of America* comes from the period following the Declaration of Independence when each of the former colonies truly was sovereign, or all powerful, within its territory. Despite the existence of the Articles of Confederation, power resided with these thirteen states, and no central body had authority over them. When the Constitution was created and ratified, those thirteen formerly independent and sovereign entities became the *United* States of America.

States are often the main subject of study in political science. Political scientists study patterns of governmental or political behavior within a single state or compare such behaviors across multiple states or regions. Some try to understand the philosophy and reasoning behind the governmental structures of a state. Still, others seek to understand what makes states succeed, thrive, and prosper and others fail. In fact, the question of failed states is one that perplexes political scientists today; failed states are those entities that lose power and authority over their territory or people. Whether that is because those states have been overthrown by invaders or their own people, because of war or famine, or simply because the government did not operate as effectively as it could have are all up for debate. What is not up for debate is the effect that these failed states can have throughout the world; for example, Somalia, located in the Horn of Africa, is a failed state, and the lack of any control over the territory has allowed terrorist groups like al-Qaeda to thrive and for pirates to operate off its coasts. These effects, therefore, are not simply local but of a global nature. The topic of states, while important in establishing constitutions and governments, is an important part of the comparative politics subfield and will be addressed in Chapter 8.

One way of understanding what a state is is to know what a state is not. Many people confuse states with nations or even governments. This is natural, and we hear it all the time—particularly from people who may argue this or that about the "nation of the United States." While country is often (correctly) used as a synonym for state, it is not necessarily appropriate to use the term *nation* in this way. A **nation** refers to a group of people who have a common background, history, culture, language, etc. For example, the Native American nation of the Sioux represents a distinct cultural heritage, yet they do not have their own state in the sense that they have a piece of territory that they solely have control over. Some may argue that the United States comprises a single people brought together in a melting pot of immigration; others still see the United States as a multicultural entity with separate groups of Hispanics, Irish, Chinese, Middle Eastern, etc. For most of history, the main actors in global politics were called nation-states, representing a state that also encapsulated one group of nationals or peoples. For this, we can think of historical Europe, where England represented a single cultural group and the French another. In turn, each of these peoples managed to establish states in their territories earning the label of nation-state.

Government

Where states are groups of people living under one governmental system, the very term *government* means the style and structure of the institutions that make authoritative decisions for a society. Governments come in many different styles, from democratic republics of the American type or authoritarian regimes under dictators. One way to think about these different types of governments or regimes is to categorize them by how many people are involved in making decisions for society, from the one to the many (see Figure 1.1). We can begin with those governments in which only one person has the ultimate authority, and in this case, there are two potential styles of government: monarchy and authoritarian dictatorships.

In a monarchy, the highest authority is the king or queen. While the United Kingdom immediately comes to mind as an example of a monarchical system, today the United Kingdom is actually a constitutional monarchy where power resides with Parliament, an elected legislative body, and the ruling monarch is merely a figurehead. A better modern example of this style of government is the kingdom of Saudi Arabia, which is currently ruled by the House of Saud. These differences are important; for a system to be a true monarchy, the king or queen must have final say; this is not the case in the United Kingdom but is true for Saudi Arabia.

An authoritarian dictatorship, on the other hand, is rule by one individual with no constraints of law, institutions, or custom. When we use the term, it generally infers a malevolent nature, invoking the tenures of dictators like Hitler, Stalin, or Mao. However, that doesn't necessarily have to be the case as the term could potentially be used in a more positive manner—for instance, in what might be called a

Figure 1.1   Types of Government by Number of People in Power

One Person	Some People		All People
←			→
Monarchy, Authoritarian	Oligarchy	Indirect Democracy	Direct Democracy

benevolent dictatorship. While we have never witnessed such a regime in history, the fact remains that a dictatorship or government of one does not automatically imply either the intentions or the ideology supporting it. For example, Hitler's regime was one that operated under a fascist ideology, or a belief that the state came before all. On the other hand, Stalin's dictatorship utilized communist ideology, and as such, Hitler and Stalin intensely disliked each other. Thus, despite them being fellow dictators, they could not cooperate nor respect one another because of differing positions on ideology. This is all a means of illustrating how the structure of government (dictatorship) can be separated out from ideology (a consistent set of beliefs about how the world or government should work, discussed later in this chapter).

It might also appear easy to confuse a monarchy with a dictatorship; after all, one country's king could be another's dictator. Under a monarchical government, power is traditionally passed on by family ties; however, in dictatorships, this is not an absolute. When Stalin died in the Soviet Union, there was no clear successor to his duties; Nikita Khrushchev eventually came to power but was unable to secure it for more than a few years. In the authoritarian regime of North Korea, leadership has been passed down in the Kim family from the founder of the Democratic People's Republic of Korea, Kim Il-sung, to his son, Kim Jong-il, and finally to his son, Kim Jong-un.

Some states, instead of being ruled by one, may be ruled by a few; this is called oligarchy. In these situations, oligarchs usually represent the most prosperous or most powerful individuals in a state, and it is among these people where power is brokered and decisions are made. Following the signing of the Magna Carta in 1215, England went from an absolute monarchy to what could be arguably termed an *oligarchy*, where the king's power came from the landed aristocracy who could control some of what the king intended to do. The Soviet Union following Stalin and then Khrushchev could also be considered an oligarchy with the Soviet Politburo, the top communist organization in the state, controlling much of what went on in the country and replacing leaders when necessary. Today's modern Russia can also be seen as an oligarchy as Russian president Vladimir Putin is backed in his position by a small group of oil barons who have made billions of dollars from Russian oil reserves.

As more and more people gain power and the ability to contribute to decisions in a government, the type of government changes. This is where we may begin to think about democratic governments. There are two main types of democracies: indirect and direct. Indirect democracy is where citizens vote on people to represent them in the halls of government; this is called a republic and is the type of government that we have in the United States. In this sense, even though it is a democracy, *all* people do *not* have direct input in decisions; they exercise this power only indirectly through elected officials. If all people are involved in all decisions, this would be a direct democracy.

What good is understanding different types of governments, or rather, what type of analytical leverage can this gain us in political science? The concept of government can be quite helpful not only when comparing different governments but can also give political theorists a sense of the best form of government or even the worst. This was the subject of Plato, Socrates, and Aristotle in their early studies of government. Being able to recognize and identify different types of governments also helps us to explain why states behave the way they do. How do dictators preserve their power? How do voters vote? What constraints are placed on a state's leadership? Thus, the concept of government has significant value in understanding and explaining behavior in a global context and many of these types of governments are further explored in Chapter 8.

Power

In both of the previously given concepts, the idea of power is central to defining a state and a government. Both have the authority and legitimacy to wield power over their citizens, yet the concept of power is not easily defined or measured. Many scholars define **power** as the ability to get one to do something they otherwise would not do. For example, making citizens pay taxes or obey laws they would otherwise not pay or obey is the exercise of power. In these examples, this power is legitimate in the sense that the government has the privilege and ability to do these things. But how do we know power when we see it? And are there different types or forms of power? These questions are far more complicated than simply defining a word.

One of the most popular conceptions of power, at least in American politics, is from Neustadt, who argued that power is persuasion, or the ability to convince someone that they want to do this on their own, not simply because an individual is forcing them to do it.[16] Neustadt's argument, while appearing similar to the description of power that was just given is subtly different in the sense that you would be convincing someone that what you want them to do is in *their* best interest, not just yours. Therefore, Neustadt, who was writing this with respect to the US president, adds another layer to the power equation: not only making someone do what you want them to but do it because *they* want to.

Power is also a key concept in the realm of international relations where Barnett and Duval have defined it as "the ability of states to use material resources to get others to do what they otherwise would not."[17] Again, this definition, while appearing similar, invokes a different layer of interpretation. States are using their military, economic, and diplomatic resources to force others to act in a particular way. Theoretically, these assets might not be needed in a more general conception of power, but for international relations theorists, the fact that different means of persuasion, to use Neustadt's term, are being used is key. Nye has identified different types of power in global politics, differentiating between hard and soft power. Hard power represents the military and economic resources that a country possesses that can make countries respond in a positive way to what a country wants. However, soft power encompasses the values, example, prosperity, and openness that Nye says can "co-opt people rather than coerce them."[18] Nye, then, makes a distinct difference between force and persuasion of the Neustadt type.

In any case, it is quite difficult to measure power or to see it in action. Sometimes, for example, diplomatic negotiations or negotiations among policymakers may take place in public view, through public statements, news reports, and an interplay with public opinion. When this happens, it is somewhat easy to identify who is powerful and who is successfully using their power. However, far more often these types of actions take place hidden from public view, which makes it much harder to discern what is happening.

Much of politics is a game of power, getting people to agree, to act in a particular way, or to make something happen; this makes power an important element of political analysis and helps to explain political outcomes. Take health care reform, for example. When former president Bill Clinton attempted policy change in 1993 through his wife and first lady Hillary Clinton, he could not muster the support needed to get the reform he desired passed by Congress. However, President Barack Obama was far more successful in 2009; a fair question, then, is what made Barack Obama more powerful in regard to health care reform than Bill Clinton? While both were Democratic presidents with Democratic majorities in the House and Senate, Clinton could not wield his power in a way that would induce Congress to pass reform while Obama could. While the answers to this conundrum are out of the scope of this text, the question is nonetheless an excellent example of how the concept of power is often used in political science to help understand and explain outcomes.

Ideology

In the same way state, nation, and country are often confused, so are the ideas of ideology and government, and political party. An **ideology** is a consistent and coherent set of ideas concerning any number of things from religion and morals to theories about politics and how states should be run. Some of the ideologies that interest us most include liberalism, conservatism, and even communism. The reason that ideology is often confusing is that ideologies are often conflated with types of government—for example, communist dictatorship or liberal democracy. And while it is completely appropriate to use these terms together to signify a dictatorship that is run under a communist ideology or a democracy that is run under a liberal ideology, all too often the terms are taken to mean the same thing. Ideologies are not forms of government or *how* states are run, they are the theoretical underpinnings as to what the government should do or how they do it.

Two of the major ideologies that are often discussed today are liberalism and conservatism, although these ideas as ideologies may be quite different from the way you have heard them discussed by politicians or the news media.

Liberalism as an ideology developed out of the Enlightenment period—the same moment when Locke and Hobbes debated the rationales of government and natural rights. Classical liberals, in fact, based many of their beliefs on Locke's philosophy, including a belief in natural rights, a social contract view of government, and the values of liberty and individualism. This early view of liberalism emphasized limited government as the best means of protecting these values; however, modern liberals have evolved to endorse a more active role for government in society. Modern liberal ideology espouses the belief that government can and should be used to enforce the equality and liberty of all people, including racial and gender equality.[19] They also believe that government can be more broadly used to better the overall condition of society.

Because of the philosophical and political upheaval of the 1600s, many in Britain were concerned about the pace of political change and urged a slower movement toward it. They believed in order and tradition and, at least in Britain, felt that there was a place for the monarchy and the aristocracy. These early conservative proponents would give rise to the conservative ideology that we are more familiar with in the United States today. Modern conservatives also value law and order, but they believe that rather than slowing down change, change in government should be sped up. Specifically, they believe that that change should be toward reducing the scope of government and what government is asked to do and instead allow private and community organizations to take the place of the services that government currently provides. Thus, while liberals maintain that government involvement in society is desirable, necessary, and proper to better all of society, conservatives believe that the government should be limited and that it is this type of situation that best serves society as a whole.

Based on these two descriptions, it is easy to see the difference between ideology and government; government provides the vehicle, whereas ideology provides the direction. In many ways, central tenets of ideology refer specifically to government and to ideas about the proper size and scope of it. Despite the possibility for confusion, ideology plays a key role in political science. Not only does it form the central questions of political theory—a subfield of political science to be discussed in Chapter 3—but it helps to explain why political actors behave as they do. If an ideology becomes dominant across a country or region, this too can explain the ultimate actions of these players. People and countries do not act simply to act; there is a cause and an underpinning as to why they are behaving the way they are, and in this sense, ideology can form the basis of those justifications.

Another pair of ideas that is too often confused is ideology and political party. Because political parties also put forward their own ideas about how government should work and what it should do, it is easy to see how this mistake may be made. However, these two concepts are quite different in one major respect: Where ideologies represent consistent and coherent beliefs (one belief does not contradict another), political parties do not. Take, for example, the Republican Party. Many Republicans believe in the need for smaller government—something that conservatives would also agree with. But many Republicans also call for a larger military or a government that is more involved with social choices like abortion. The belief in the need for a smaller government and the belief in a larger military are contradictory; you cannot have a smaller government while having a larger defense force. Political parties, as the aggregate representation of a large group of people, have these sorts of contradictions built into their platforms. Because of this, their beliefs are not coherent and consistent and are thus not ideologies.

This does not make political parties any more or less worthwhile. Indeed, they are an intrinsic part of political science and understanding group political behavior. Now more than ever, the political party is an important concept in political science. Following the contentious presidential primary battle that ultimately led to the matchup between Hillary Clinton and Donald Trump, many were asking how the Democrats and Republicans, respectively, came to nominate such disliked candidates. Understanding how and why political parties behave and operate are key to answering this puzzle. These types of questions will be taken up in Chapter 5, which focuses on electoral and party systems.

Civil Liberties, Civil Rights, and Human Rights

The twin concepts of civil liberties and civil rights are inherent in the ideologies of liberalism and conservatism; they are the natural rights of which liberals speak and believe government should expand to enforce, particularly when it comes to civil rights. They are also those rights and liberties that conservatives believe are best protected when the government is small. **Civil liberties** encompass these natural rights or our ability to do certain things that must be protected *from* government. These include freedom of speech, thought, and action; freedom of religion; the ability to own and possess firearms; and the right to be free from unwarranted search and seizure. While we often call these things "rights," they are more properly termed *civil liberties*. One of the original concerns over the Constitution was that it did not contain a listing of these rights that many believed should be protected and that government should never be allowed to infringe on. As a compromise between those who supported the Constitution, the Federalists, and those who did not, the Anti-Federalists, the Federalists agreed to draft a Bill of Rights that would be amendments to the Constitution; this is where most of our American civil liberties are enshrined.

Civil rights, on the other hand, are our freedoms to be treated fairly and equally, and all too often these rights must be *enforced* by government rather than protected from it. Civil rights include the right to vote and have that vote count just as much as the next person's and the freedom from discrimination by law. Over time, the application of civil rights has greatly expanded to include minorities such as African Americans, women, and more recently individuals from the LGBTQ+ community.

These ideas can be divisive in a global environment. While many in America may believe in the right to freedom of religion or equality of women, these are not universally accepted beliefs. Following the end of World War II and the discovery of the atrocities committed by the Germans in the Holocaust, efforts were made at the international level to establish a set of human rights that could be agreed to across the world and, ultimately, ideally, enforced. The result of this effort was the Universal Declaration of Human Rights (UDHR), which delineated many of the civil liberties and rights we find in our own Constitution as well as some that go above and beyond it, including a right to an education and an explicit right to privacy. Many of the rights, however, that we find in the UDHR are not actively implemented in some of the countries that originally voted for it, including Pakistan and Egypt. Other countries with significant Muslim populations have also decided not to sign on to it. The question quickly becomes, then, what should be done about countries that refuse to endorse or implement the idea of human rights, that all people should have certain civil liberties and civil rights regardless of who they are or where they are? This is a major question for international relations scholars today and will be taken up in further detail in Chapter 9.

Representation

Particularly for democratic countries, representation is a key concept through which we can view how the government operates. **Representation** is the idea that even though they are not there, the views of all the people in a society are considered when decisions are being made. The wishes and desires of those people may not always win out, but to be truly represented, they must at least have been thought about and considered. The extent to which all are represented in government is important when asking whether a country is democratic or not or even how democratic a country is; these two questions are especially relevant in the field of comparative politics, which is discussed in Chapter 8.

To better understand the idea of representation, let's consider a few examples here in the United States. David Mayhew posits that elected officials in Congress behave the way they do because they desire reelection more than anything else.[20] If this is the case, those members of Congress will want to please their constituents, but therein we run into a problem: Not everyone votes. It would not be rational for the member of Congress to try and please everyone—just those who vote. Who is being represented then: all constituents or just those who vote? Given that voter turnout in the 2016 presidential election was 61.4 percent of the voting age population, just how representative is our resulting government?[21] And if we're not representing everyone, just how democratic is the United States? This example also demonstrates that there are different types of representation. While elected officials may be technically representing *all* people in their district even though some of them didn't vote, we can say that those who didn't vote may only have *symbolic* representation and those who did vote have *substantive* representation. A key theoretical question is what effect there may be of having people both symbolically and substantively represented—for example, to which group of people will the legislator respond? Are those who are symbolically represented ignored in the political process? What are the ramifications of these differences?

We can further consider a different type of representation that many political scientists find important: descriptive representation. Descriptive representation is the idea that those we elect *look* like us. Again, consider the US Congress. In 2015, less than 20 percent of the members of Congress were female while over 50 percent of the people of the United States are female.[22] While the gap has closed with 127 women serving in Congress after the 2018 elections (women now make up 23.7 percent of the Congress), this still-significant shortfall in the number of women in the United States and the number of women representing people in the United States demonstrates a lack of descriptive representation. Proponents of descriptive representation argue that when bodies of elected officials mirror proportions found in society, that government can better represent the ideas, beliefs, and desires of everyone involved. To this end, some Western European countries have instituted quotas in their legislatures to ensure that descriptive representation is better achieved. Again, some comparativists, those that study comparative politics, find these concepts quite useful in understanding the operations of governments around the world and what makes them better or worse or more or less democratic. Chapter 8, for instance, explores different definitions of democracy and considers how democratic governments around the world actually are.

Political Culture

Many of the ideas that we have discussed thus far contribute to this final concept to be discussed: political culture. Just as culture is the set of values, beliefs, behaviors, and norms that a society holds in common, a **political culture** consists of those *political* ideas, norms, beliefs, and actions in which a group of people generally believes. Think about the things we as Americans generally believe; we believe in civil liberties and civil rights, in a liberal democratic government, in the idea of the American dream. Granted, these are somewhat general and amorphous in nature; therefore, it is often more useful to look at different regions or areas of the globe or the United States to better understand political culture and categorize and define it.

The most well-known study of political culture was published in 1965 by Almond and Verba. *The Civic Culture* identified three subtypes of political culture based on how much people were involved in the political process: parochial, subject, and participant.[23] In a parochial political culture, people don't pay much attention to a central government if they are aware of it at all; as such, they are rarely involved in governmental decisions interested in them. In a subject culture, people are more aware of the government and its decisions but are relatively helpless at influencing or changing them. Finally, a participant culture is one in which people are aware of and can participate in the processes of government.

While Almond and Verba's study of political culture defines it based on the amount that citizens can participate in government, an alternative classification scheme is that of Elazar. In studying the United States, Elazar argues that instead of one political culture, there are actually several that vary largely by region.[24] A moral political culture generally refers to regions where people believe society is more important than the individual and that government is generally good and can be used to benefit that society as a whole. Communities are more important than individuals, so individual rights or abilities may often be sacrificed for the good of the whole. In regions with an individual political culture, government is used for practical concerns even though it may be corrupt or seen as "dirty." Governments are in place to serve individual needs, and individuals are placed above community. In the final type, traditional, politics follows a natural social order, where there is a hierarchy among families and groups and those at the top run the government. While limited government is the dominant idea, those in a traditional political culture see it as a way to perpetuate the traditional order and hierarchy.

Elazar identifies states where these political cultures are dominant and those states that may have a mixture of ideas.[25] In any case, what these conceptions of political culture allow us as political scientists to do is compare and contrast dominant attitudes about politics and government and what effects those attitudes have on political outcomes. They are a means of analyzing both the structure of government—particularly at the state and local levels and explaining what those governments may or may not do. For example, if we wish to compare the state of politics in California and Texas, the differing political culture may be one fruitful explanation to explore.

Plan of the Book

In the coming chapters, many of these concepts will continue to be essential in understanding the state of study in political science. For example, the nature and structures of things such as states and governments is further considered in Chapters 4, 5, and 8. While the ideas outlined previously are meant to provide you with a starting point from which to embark, this book is also structured in a way to provide you with a solid foundation about the field of political science and the state of research today. It is thus divided into three parts. Part I: Foundations, encompasses this chapter and the next two: Chapter 2 takes up how political scientists study politics or, in other words, the science in political science. Chapter 3 discusses political theory, which, as discussed previously, is the historical basis for today's political science. Part II examines common institutions and political behavior. Chapter 4 discusses constitutions and their writing and systems of law and justice. Chapter 5, meanwhile, examines types of electoral and party systems—most specifically presidential and parliamentary systems. Chapter 6 examines the role of the media, which is vital in both democracies and nondemocracies alike.

Finally, Part III focuses on the subfields of political science. Much like medicine, the study of political science can be subdivided into different fields of interest and specializations; in graduate education, and sometimes for your undergraduate degree, students in political science choose a particular subfield to concentrate most of their time in. Chapters 7 through 11 serve as introductions to some of the more commonly recognized subfields in political science, including American politics, comparative politics, international relations, and public policy and administration, and political economy. To be sure, political scientists often disagree about whether one particular area or not should be elevated to subfield status, but it is reasonable to consider the ones discussed here as most, if not all, of the major subfields of political science.

Taken in total, then, Part I will provide you with common theoretical and methodological foundations while Part II fills in some of the operational details that apply across political science. Part III introduces you to how the concepts and ideas discussed in the previous two parts are put into practice in the various fields of political science. Given that *Political Science Today* is an introduction to a wide and diverse field, it is necessary to limit discussion of key issues and debates; however, at the end of each chapter, you will find resources that can help you build on what is presented here, including additional readings and resources and critical thinking questions. Case studies throughout the chapter will also allow you to see how political scientists see and think about current issues. Thus, *Political Science Today* is a book about the state of political science in the late 2010s—where we've been, where we are, and where we're going.

STUDENT STUDY SITE

Visit https://edge.sagepub.com/whitmancobb

CHAPTER SUMMARY

- Political science is the scientific study, analysis, and understanding of political processes and behavior.

- People have been studying politics since ancient Greek and Roman times. Only in the nineteenth century did political science become a formal field of study.

- Political scientists can study politics from a variety of angles, including from the perspective of individual actions (behavioralism) or institutions of governments (institutionalism).

- Political scientists use the tools of science and the scientific method to systematically study politics.

- No matter the subfield, political scientists across the discipline utilize common ideas or concepts to understand politics around the globe, including public goods, states, governments, power, ideology, representation, and political culture.

KEY TERMS

behavioralism: The concept that all human action, and therefore political action, can be observed, quantified, and explained in an objective, scientific way

civil liberties: Natural rights or our ability to do certain things that must be protected from government

civil rights: Freedoms to be treated fairly and equally, which must be enforced by government

free rider problem: The idea that people will not pay to participate in achieving a public good or to participate in a public interest group

government: The style and structure of the institutions that make authoritative decisions for a society

ideology: A consistent and coherent set of ideas concerning any number of things from religion and morals to theories about politics and how states should be run

institutionalism: The study of political institutions and how they influence individual behavior

nation: A group of people who have a common background, history, culture, language, etc.

natural rights: A set of rights that all humans have

political culture: A set of political ideas, norms, beliefs, and actions in which a group of people generally believes

political science: The systematic and scientific study of politics, including institutions, behaviors, and processes

politics: The authoritative allocation of resources

power: The ability to get one to do something they otherwise would not do

public goods: Goods that are nonexclusive and whose use does not reduce the availability of the good to others

representation: The practice of all views being considered in governmental decisions

science: The systematic search for knowledge through observation, experiments, and tests

scientific method: A series of steps scientists use to systematically ask and answer a question

social contracts: Agreement entered into by members of a society agreeing to give up some rights in return for a governing structure

state of nature: A thought experiment imagining what life and human behavior might look like in the absence of government, society, and culture

states: Groups of people living under a single governmental system

tragedy of the commons: Describes a situation where people, acting rationally, overuse a common good thereby depleting it for all

DISCUSSION QUESTIONS

1. What does political science mean to you? Can you think of any real-life examples of political science that you've encountered?

2. Come up with a research question that relates a topic you're interested in to politics. How might everyday interests be translated into political science questions?

3. What is the relationship of political theory to political science today? Do you believe that political theory should be treated as a

separate subject area or remain embedded within political science?

4. What are some historical impacts that influence the practice of political science?

5. Do you believe political science is or could possibly be a science? Why or why not?

FOR FURTHER READING

Farr, James. "The History of Political Science." *American Journal of Political Science* 32, no. 4 (1988): 1175–1195.

Morgenthau, Hans J. "Reflections on the State of Political Science." *The Review of Politics* 17, no. 4 (1955): 431–460.

Ricci, David M. *The Tragedy of Political Science: Politics, Scholarship, and Democracy*. New Haven, CT: Yale University Press, 1984.

American Political Science Association (APSA): www.apsanet.org

UN Universal Declaration of Human Rights (UDHR): www.un.org/en/universal-declaration-human-rights

NOTES

1. Ali Vitali, "Blankenship Blames Trump in Open Letter: You Spread 'Fake News' against Me," *NBC News*, May 9, 2018, https://www.nbcnews.com/politics/politics-news/failed-candidate-blankenship-attacks-mcconnell-brings-china-again-n872796.

2. Amy Chozick, *Chasing Hillary: Ten Years, Two Presidential Campaigns, and One Intact Glass Ceiling* (New York: HarperCollins, 2018).

3. Jacob Hacker, "National Health Care Reform: An Idea Whose Time Came and Went," *Journal of Health Politics, Policy, and Law* 21, no. 4 (1996): 647–696.

4. A form of government where only property owners participate in government.

5. David M. Ricci, *The Tragedy of Political Science: Politics, Scholarship, and Democracy* (New Haven, CT: Yale University Press, 1984); Timothy V. Kaufman-Osborn, "Dividing the Domain of Political Science: On the Fetishism of Subfields," *Polity* 38, no. 1 (2006): 41–71.

6. Woodrow Wilson, "The Study of Administration," *Political Science Quarterly* 2, no. 2 (1887): 197–222.

7. Anthony Downs, *An Economic Theory of Democracy* (New York: Harper, 1957).

8. John Rawls, *A Theory of Justice* (Cambridge, MA: Harvard University Press, 1971).

9. Robert Nozick, *Anarchy, State, and Utopia* (New York: Basic Books, 1974).

10. Carole Pateman, *The Sexual Contract* (Stanford, CA: Stanford University Press, CA, 1988); Charles W. Mills, *The Racial Contract* (Ithaca, NY: Cornell University Press, 1997).

11. Ruth W. Grant, "Political Theory, Political Science, and Politics," *Political Theory* 30, no. 4 (2002): 577–595.

12. James E. Campbell, "Editor's Introduction," *PS: Political Science and Politics* 45, no. 4 (2012): 610–613.

13. John E. Jackson and David C. King, "Public Goods, Private Interests, and Representation," *American Political Science Review* 83, no. 4 (1989): 1144.

14. Mancur Olson, *The Logic of Collective Action: Public Goods and the Theory of Groups* (Cambridge, MA: Harvard University Press, 1971).

15. For a greater discussion of this, see Bert A. Rockman, "Minding the State—or a State of Mind? Issues in the Comparative Conceptualization of the State," *Comparative Political Studies* 23, no. 1 (1990): 22–55.

16. Richard E. Neustadt, *Presidential Power and the Modern Presidents* (New York: Free Press, 1990).

17. Michael Barnett and Raymond Duvall, "Power in International Politics," *International Organization* 59, no. 1 (2005): 40.

18. Joseph S. Nye, *The Paradox of American Power: Why the World's Only Superpower Can't Go It Alone* (Oxford: Oxford University Press, 2002): 9.

19. Timothy O. Lenz and Mirya Holman, *American Government* (Gainesville: University Press of Florida, 2013).

20. David Mayhew, *Congress: The Electoral Connection* (New Haven, CT: Yale University Press, 1974).

21. Thom File, "Voting in America: A Look at the 2016 Presidential Election," *US Census Bureau*, May 10, 2017, https://www.census.gov/newsroom/blogs/random-samplings/2017/05/voting_in_america.html.

22. Center for American Women and Politics, "Women in US Congress 2015," *Rutgers Eagleton Institute of Politics*, www.cawp.rutgers.edu/women-us-congress-2015.

23. Gabriel A. Almond and Sidney Verba, *The Civic Culture: Political Attitudes and Democracy in Five Nations* (Princeton, NJ: Princeton University Press, 1963).

24. Daniel Elazar, *American Federalism: A View from the South* (New York: Crowell, 1966).

25. Ibid.

Political scientists utilize a wide variety of methods to understand political events.

Source: ©iStockphoto.com/Steve Debenport

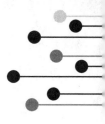

CHAPTER 2

Research Methods

I f you're new or relatively new to college, you've surely experienced the dreaded standardized test in high school. In many states, students must pass a rigorous set of examinations in order to be promoted from grade to grade or even to graduate. One of the significant criticisms of such an approach is either that teachers end up teaching to the test and neglect other important topics and skills that should be taught in the classroom or that the tests themselves don't adequately measure how much a student has learned or what kinds of capabilities students already possess. But in lieu of detailed observations and analyses of individual students and their knowledge, performance, and skills, what else do educators have to measure and assess student performance? In other words, what's more important in understanding student progress: The grade you receive on a test or an overall qualitative assessment done by those who know you best? Even if the best answer is a combination of both the test score and detailed observation of your knowledge and classroom performance, where will the resources come from for those observations? In an educational system that is already hard pressed for money and teachers, there is no ability to collect such data.

Similar questions plague political science research. How do we best grasp the information that already exists in the world: through numbers or through words? What is a better indicator of what's happening in the world that we want to analyze: words, actions, or numbers? This chapter introduces two of the major ways in which political scientists attempt to answer major research questions. To do so, however, requires a bit of explanation of the research process, which is what this chapter begins with. First, it details the process of moving from

Chapter Objectives

1. Describe basic research concepts, including hypothesis, causality, and variables.

2. Define *quantitative methods* and *qualitative methods* and the differences between them.

3. Describe basic research methods, including correlation and regression analysis, case studies, and contextual analysis.

4. Understand the strengths and weaknesses of both the quantitative and qualitative approaches.

5. Delineate the importance of research methods in the study of political science.

questions and answers to preparing to test your hypotheses. Afterward, it introduces both quantitative and qualitative methods while giving some examples of the different procedures that each uses. After comparing the two approaches, the chapter discusses why there is a debate in political science over the two methodological approaches and suggests some ways of, if not settling the question, how you might choose between the two.

A key caveat is in order before we begin. Some political scientists will argue that research methodology comprises an entirely different subfield of political science in the way American politics or international relations are. This chapter does not purport to cover in detail every aspect of this debate or every detail of research methods; that task is best left to the multitude of books and classes on research methods. The aim in this chapter is merely to introduce some of the major ways political scientists undertake their research.

Questions and Answers

Most of this book will focus on familiarizing you with the state of political science research today, but perhaps you would also like to ask questions that you can find answers to about politics. This is what the research process is for. In brief, political scientists tend to follow the scientific method of asking questions, forming hypotheses, defining tests, examining the evidence, and making conclusions. The first two steps, in particular, are crucial to the question of what methods you can use or should use.

Framing Questions and Hypotheses

All good research begins with a good question. By a good question, we usually mean something that is not amorphous or nonspecific but something that narrows down the topic you're looking at and specifies precisely the area that you're interested in. Let's take a few examples:

> Why does Russia behave the way it does?
>
> What influences immigration policy?
>
> Why can't Congress get anything done?

What do you think is wrong with these questions? The one thing they all have in common is that they are not nearly specific enough: What Russian behavior are we talking about and toward whom? Are you talking about immigration policy in the United States or elsewhere? What tasks specifically should Congress be doing that they aren't? Research questions need to be far more specific, or you're likely to end up on a wild-goose chase looking for potential answers. Here's how those three questions could possibly be narrowed down:

What motivations does Russia have in invading eastern Ukraine?

What influences immigration policy in America in the twenty-first century?

Why has there been a downturn in the frequency of laws passed in the US Congress?

These questions are far more detailed and point us in a more particular direction.

Once you've developed an appropriate research question, the next step is to come up with a **hypothesis**—a reasonable guess as to what the answer might be to your question. You should base your hypothesis on what you may already know or suspect about the topic, and the hypothesis should be specific as well. The following might serve as potential hypotheses to the previous research question:

Russia was motivated to invade eastern Ukraine because of a fear of European meddling in supposedly Russian affairs.

Immigration policy in America is influenced by economic and political factors.

Congress has passed fewer laws because party polarization has increased.

In all of these cases, the hypotheses direct your research in a particular way. Without questions and hypotheses, your research is likely to lack focus.

Once you have identified a question and hypothesis, the next step is to start researching! But don't skip to analyzing data just yet; most political science research starts with what scholars call a **literature review**. Quite literally, it is a summary and analysis of the research that has been done previously on your topic. It's important to include this because what people have already discovered can help you rule out and rule in potential variables in the relationship you are examining. The research of others can also help support your hypothesis; if other people are finding the same thing that you do, it makes your conclusions that much stronger. Don't worry if you still don't quite understand these early steps. It often takes practice and guidance to come to good questions and answers. Most colleges and universities offer specialized classes in research methods where these topics are covered, and you can work on making your questions specific and answerable.

Variables and Concepts

At this point in the process, you'll be preparing to perform your own independent research to attempt to answer your research question, and this is where the issue of methods come into play. Physicists or biologists in labs have this part relatively easy; they can perform experiments in petri dishes and controlled areas. This is the ideal method in which to answer research questions. All conditions can be controlled, and you can look through a microscope or even a telescope to understand exactly what is happening and why. Political scientists and other social scientists aren't so lucky; we must deal with the messiness and uncontrollability that we call life. Political scientists can't control peoples' actions or the conditions that might influence them; plus, it would be very hard to manipulate something like Russian policy or congressional action just to try and prove your hypothesis. Because of this, scholars must turn to nonexperimental methods to test our questions.

When we break our hypothesis down to its very basics, the hypothesis usually says that A causes B or A, B, and C cause D. Those letters, those causes and effects, are **variables**, they are ideas or concepts that can vary over time. When talking about research, there are two general types of variables, independent and dependent. **Independent variables** are your suspected causes while **dependent variables** are the effect. At the end of the day, our research is trying to show what independent variables cause the dependent variables.

Variables are discrete categories of data: number of Democrats or Republicans, number of presidential statements, type of ruling handed down. And while our research questions sometimes naturally suggest which variables to use, more often than not, our hypotheses give us concepts that we then have to define. For example, if the hypothesis is that presidential power increases when congressional power decreases, the two variables are presidential power and congressional power. But what is power? What is it? How do we know what it is? Defining what we mean by these concepts is what political scientists call **conceptualization**. Once we have a working definition, we can then turn our concepts into variables, a process called **operationalization**. Operationalization looks at the definition of the concept and says this is how we will measure the concept. Through these steps we go from general ideas to concepts to variables that we can study. No matter the methods we use to study our hypotheses, we almost always use this same process to clearly and specifically identify what we are studying and what we are expecting to find.

Let's work through an example using the earlier immigration policy hypothesis. What do we mean by "immigration policy"? The first step is conceptualizing or defining the concept. For our purposes, we may take immigration policy to mean the overriding paradigm or policy aim that the US federal government has adopted in regard to both legal and illegal immigration. Note that the conceptualization includes both illegal and legal immigration; this is important because depending on how another researcher may conceptualize immigration policy, they may or may not include both. This demonstrates just how important conceptualization can be to the research process—researchers may come to different conclusions on the same topic simply because they disagree on the meaning of a concept.

Once we have defined our concept, the next step is operationalization, taking the definition and turning it into a working variable. The result of this stage may vary slightly depending on the methodology you utilize (discussed in the next section). If you use qualitative methods, you may argue that presidential policy statements would be an indicator as to the direction of immigration policy in the United States. But what if you are using quantitative methods? How can you turn "immigration policy" into a numerical value? Depending on the researcher, you may go through immigration law and presidential statements to identify whether immigration policy is more or less stringent, perhaps on a scale of one to ten. Or maybe you can count the number of immigration regulations present in each year. Often, there is no tried, true, and correct way of operationalizing a variable, but the researcher must be able to justify why that particular operationalization is being chosen over another. This is another key role that literature reviews can serve in informing you as to what other scholars have chosen as their conceptualizations and operationalizations.

Once you have identified your concepts and turned them into workable variables, you can turn to testing whether your hypothesis is correct or not, and this is where the choice of methods becomes significant.

Quantitative Methods

As should be obvious by now, the word *quantitative* invokes the use of numbers, math, and statistics in working to answer a given research question. As a broad topic, there are many ways in which numbers can be used or in which words or concepts can be turned into numbers or quantified. You can count the frequency of particular actions like executive orders or legislative hearings. You can track those data over time to see if there are any patterns. And then, you can get data on multiple items to decode whether there is a correlation, or relationship, between two variables. In other words, **quantitative methods** can be used to describe patterns or understand statistical relationships between concepts and/or variables.

In turning to statistical methods, political scientists use these to approximate to the best of our ability an experiment. We attempt to show that an independent variable happens to coincide with a dependent variable or that multiple different independent variables influence whether the dependent variable goes up or down. Depending on your question and your data, there is a whole suite of different statistical tests and methods that can be used on your data. To explore these ideas just a bit more, let's consider just two: correlations and regression analyses.

A **correlation** happens when two things happen at the same time (see Figure 2.1). This does not necessarily mean that one causes the other, but it does give some evidence that a relationship does exist between the two variables you're examining. For example, refer back to the question and hypothesis about congressional activity. The hypothesis is that as party polarization increases, the rate at which Congress passes laws goes down. The hypothesis suggests that party polarization is causing fewer laws to be passed; therefore, party polarization is our independent variable and laws being passed is our dependent variable. Both of these variables can be quantified with party polarization being measured through DW-NOMINATE scores (discussed in Chapter 7) and laws passed as a simple frequency of how many laws Congress passes in a given year.

For quantitative methods, we want to have enough data where we can see patterns of change over time; if the data simply stayed the same or there were only five data points, there would not be any variance to quantify. For this example, we could gather both DW-NOMINATE scores and how many laws are passed per year for

Figure 2.1 Causation and Correlation

Source: xkcd.com.

fifty years and using a statistical program, we can calculate a score showing us if the two variables are correlated and how strong the relationship is (this score is called a Pearson's *r* and can be hand calculated as well). The correlation score, the Pearson's *r*, falls between 0 and 1 with a score closer to 1 indicating a stronger correlation and a score closer to 0 indicating a weak correlation.

But what if there are other variables that could be causing Congress to be less productive? Could it be something about the makeup of Congress itself? The parties that are in charge? The issues that they're dealing with? We can deal with these scenarios as well but not in the form of a correlation. A more advanced method of determining this relationship is something called a **regression analysis**. And while this exploration won't go into exacting detail on how this works, you can gather data on multiple independent variables and again, using a statistical program, calculate how much each variable affects the overall relationship while holding all of the others constant. In a sense, this method is about controlling all of the possible conditions that may affect the core relationship you're trying to find. It's a statistical version of laboratory control that hard scientists use in a sterile environment.

There are many other quantitative methods that can be used depending on the data you have. A Pearson's *r* can only be used with two interval variables; if you have a combination of different variables—say an interval and an ordinal or a nominal and ordinal—different statistical measures would be used. Depending on what the data looks like and what you're trying to discern from it, different models other than regression may be appropriate. Again, don't get too stuck in the weeds now; if you're interested in methods, more specialized classes are available. What's important to understand from this is that quantitative methods take hypotheses and turn them into research problems where we can measure numerically the variables and the relationship between them.

Costs and Benefits of Using Quantitative Methods

Like just about everything in this world, there are good and bad things about using quantitative methods to answer your research questions. First, short of a true experiment (which may be either impossible or unethical to perform), using statistical controls most nearly approximates the ideal laboratory setting. This claim holds as long as you're specifying what variables you're controlling for and including variables that you think may be contributing to the relationship. When done well and properly, statistical methods are powerful for demonstrating that a relationship exists between independent and dependent variables. But be careful: Statistics can also be done poorly; if you play with the data too much or use the wrong statistical test, quantitative methods can do as much harm as good. This is the root of the saying "damned lies and statistics." If you manipulate enough data enough times, you can make it say whatever you want.

A second pro about quantitative methods is that numbers and their significance are usually easy to understand. If there is more of one thing when there is less of another, numbers and quantities are something that is easily communicated and understood. Another saying that can also be brought to bear on this is that "numbers never lie." While we aren't here to debate the truthfulness of such a statement, when you quantify something, it does make it harder to argue about whether it is true or accurate. If we say that Congress passed fifty-five laws in one congressional session, not many people will be able to quibble about whether that is true or not.

Additionally, depending on the research project, quantitative data can usually be assembled with fewer resources than in more advanced qualitative methods. There are numerous data sets already available online, and the Internet can be used to assemble data on many different topics (some of these are listed in the For Further Reading section of this chapter). Where it used to be far more difficult in the past to find such information, the Internet has made researching far less of a hassle than it was in years and decades past. Once the data is assembled and you know the correct statistical tests to use and how to interpret them, completing an analysis is simply a matter of time.

But what about the possible pitfalls to such methods? For one, what do the numbers actually *mean*? What connection do they have to reality, to politics, to the phenomena we're trying to study? Lacking more information on the context or origins of the numbers, it's difficult to understand just what their significance and meaning are. What does it really mean if we say that congressional productivity decreases by a certain percentage when party polarization rises? Are DW-NOMINATE scores a true measure of party polarization? How do we know the numbers mean what we want them to say? This is a particularly sticky problem when we take broad concepts like success or power and try to put a number to them. How will we ever know that the number we assign or calculate really means what we think it does?

Another con to quantitative methods is that the person using them should have a sufficient level of knowledge and training to be able to understand what they are doing to the data and why. Another common saying is "garbage in, garbage out." For our purposes, this means that if you put bad data into the analysis, you won't get good conclusions; you'll just get faulty information and perhaps misinformed data. Quantitative scholars should be well versed in the methods that they use and be able to justify what they've done to the data and why their procedures make sense.

Qualitative Methods

Qualitative methods encompass several different types of methods, but what they all have in common is deep description and heavy textual and event analysis. While statistical analysis is used by quantitative scholars to approximate to the best of our ability an experiment, we can look at qualitative methods as approximating a microscope. These types of analyses dig deep into events and cases in an attempt to specifically trace the causes of a particular event. We put an event under a microscope to try and tease out what led to what and in what order. For our purposes here, we'll describe three types of qualitative methods that can be used either separately or together for a stronger type of analysis: case studies, process tracing, and the comparative method.

Case Studies

The basis of most qualitative methods is usually considered to be the **case study**. George and Bennett describe the case study approach as "the detailed examination of an aspect of a historical episode to develop or test historical explanations that may be generalizable to other events."[1] Researchers gather information on events and people and try to piece together the sequence of events that led to the ultimate outcome. If we return to one of the example questions and hypotheses we developed at the beginning of the chapter, we might wish to use the case study approach to examine what led to Russia's incursion into eastern Ukraine in 2014. In order to do so, we would gather news accounts, first person statements, and other data and lay out in detail the events that led up to the invasion. Based on this data, we may find evidence for or against our hypothesis that Russia and Russian leaders invaded Ukraine because of fear of European involvement in Russian affairs.

A caution is in order at this time. Clearly, it would be easy to bias the case study description and findings so that the only logical conclusion stemming from it is that our hypothesis is supported. You should take pains to avoid this possibility since, if it's done knowingly, it is highly unethical. As scientists, we want to look at *all* the evidence, including the evidence that might not support our hypotheses. Even if the data doesn't support our hypotheses, if we can draw conclusions from it, we can still say we learned something even if our original guess turns out to be wrong.

Process Tracing

When performing a case study, some qualitative scholars take special care to perform an analysis we call **process tracing**. Process tracing "attempts to trace the links between possible causes and observed outcomes. In process tracing, the researcher examines histories, archival documents, interview transcripts, and other sources to see whether the causal process a theory hypothesizes or implies in a case is in fact evident in the sequence and values of the intervening variables in that case."[2] You can think of process tracing as creating an outline of what causes something else; you look at the case very carefully so you can say that A leads to B, which leads to C, which leads to D. In doing so, we're taking a microscope to our case and watching an event unfold.

An obvious question at this point is how this differs from history. It is true that both history and qualitative political science often share common methods of archival research, interviews, and first person accounts, but there are subtle differences between the two disciplines. Political scientists tend to search for larger explanations of phenomena across time— for example, what causes revolutions? History, on the other hand, sees events as contextually and historically bound; they are not necessarily searching for overriding theories or models that can explain disparate events. At the end of the day, some political scientists will eventually conclude that certain events are time or history bound in the sense that they would not happen at any other given period, but many political scientists are searching for larger answers to the question of why.

Once we understand what a case study is, we can use it to build up our research repertoire. Rarely do we see a singular case study; often, political scientists combine multiple case studies in order to be able to generalize their findings a bit more broadly. To continue with our Russia example, in addition to the case study you might perform on Russian actions in Ukraine, you could combine that with a second case study on the Russian invasion of Georgia in 2008. You could see if the same explanation holds in both cases or whether the explanation differs and why. Being able to explain multiple cases with a single hypothesis is a good thing; it bolsters your certainty that your hypothesis is correct and it makes it easier to convince other people that you're right as well.

Another purpose that case studies fulfill is generating hypotheses. If a series of events are occurring and we're not sure exactly why, a set of case studies can be performed to give us some ideas about common causes across cases. What do the cases have in common? What is different? Was the chain of causation similar or different? We still have to understand that the hypotheses that are created out of such case studies might not be generalizable or applicable to other situations, but the knowledge created and detailed in such cases can point the way in future research.

Comparative Method

A third qualitative method that can be used with case studies as the main component is the **comparative method**. Using the comparative method, political scientists will select a series of cases to test their hypotheses through. Ragin, in his highly regarded book on the comparative method, says that "What distinguishes comparative social science is its use of attributes of macrosocial units in explanatory statements. This special usage is intimately linked to the twin goals of comparative social science—both to explain and to interpret macrosocial variation."[3] What Ragin means by macrosocial variation is that comparative social science compares what is going on between societies instead of within them. Comparativists can then use the similarities and differences at the societal level to explain, interpret, and understand causal processes.[4] Comparative politics and the comparative method are further examined in Chapter 8.

For such a comparative method to work, scholars must be very careful about picking their cases. In quantitative methods, this isn't so much of a problem because all applicable cases are studied, but case selection is crucial in qualitative methods. Let's take the immigration policy research question and hypothesis from earlier. As a reminder, our question asked what influences US immigration policy in the twenty-first century, and our hypothesis is that immigration policy in the United States is influenced by economic and political factors. If we were to do a comparative case study to examine this topic, we might pick two or three years in which immigration has been a hot-button issue in the United States. However, let's say that there's a case of immigration policymaking that you *know* does not fit your hypothesis. If you purposefully leave that out, you are making it more likely that you will prove your preferred hypothesis. This is called choosing cases on the dependent variable or selection bias. The comparative researcher must be especially careful in choosing their cases and should provide the reader with an explanation of why the cases that were included were chosen.

Costs and Benefits of Using Qualitative Methods

The pros and cons of choosing qualitative methods mirror those of quantitative methods. Using a qualitative method, you may be able to more precisely and specifically understand the causal mechanisms or the variables that contribute to the case you are trying to understand. Using a statistical method, the most you'll be able to say is that there is a correlation or a relationship among variables; you can never say for certain that A led to B. While this might not always be possible even with qualitative methods, getting in detail on a singular case will get you closer to the ability to say that.

That being said, although you may have a conclusion about one or a few cases, you may not be able to apply that to the whole universe of cases. Lacking experimental or statistical controls means that you won't be able to hold all possible variables constant so as to single out the one or two independent variables that you're most interested in. In choosing qualitative over quantitative, then, you're sacrificing breadth of explanation for depth of explanation.

Using qualitative methods, you can give numbers and variables meaning and context. Having such in-depth knowledge on your topic will give you, the researcher, the ability to determine whether those numbers and concepts are meaningful and important in the question you are researching. Telling someone that Congress has passed a certain amount of laws in one year is one thing, but is that number high, low, average, exceptionally high, or exceptionally low? The context often has more meaning than the number. The other side of this argument, however, is that people may be able to argue just what that context is. Rational people can and do disagree on what particular data points mean, and this is often the case even in qualitative research.

Qualitative research often requires more time and resources to get primary documents, do fieldwork, and piece together various pieces of evidence, but instead of general numbers, you will be able to understand exactly what happened in your cases. Both quantitative and qualitative methods involve some aspects of judgment on the part of the researcher, so both would require the knowledge of the particular skills needed to properly conduct research on your subject.

Quantitative and Qualitative Methods in Political Science

Quantitative methods involve turning concepts and variables into numbers and using that data to perform statistical or mathematical tests, and qualitative methods are more analytical, often involving deep description and causal tracing. Mahoney and Goertz perform an excellent comparison of the two on the basis of ten different criteria including how each method approaches explanation, how they conceive of causation, their scope and ability to generalize, and the impact of significant cases.[5] The following discussion draws from their examples and arguments.

Both quantitative and qualitative methods seek to explain why an independent variable or set of independent variables cause a dependent variable, but how they go about doing so is quite different. Qualitative research, because it is more in depth and detail oriented, simply does not have the ability to cover many cases at once; if we were to do an in-depth case study on all instances of Russian aggression, for example, we would run out of time and paper. As such, qualitative work tends to focus on just a handful of key cases. Mahoney and Goertz call this a "causes-of-effects" approach; qualitative research examines a few key cases and works backward to try and understand what caused the events to happen in the first place. On the other hand, quantitative methods can be used to examine a high number of cases all at once since the data is quantifiable and able to be analyzed in a statistical manner. When this is done, quantitative analysis can be used to find the "effects-of-causes" and pinpoint what variables are significant in determining a dependent variable.

But what about the significance of conclusions in each case? In the first instance, qualitative methods may only be able to speak with certainty about the causes of the particular cases chosen; the conclusions may not be generalizable to every possible instance. For quantitative methods, the results will be generalizable over all of the cases but may not fully explain any given case. Because of these differences, scholars are very careful about the types of conclusions they make about the data they have. According to Mahoney and Goertz, qualitative scholars will "adopt a narrow scope" to make sure their conclusions fit their data while quantitative scholars will be more broad in their findings.[6]

However, an important question arises out of this difference: Which type of conclusion is more significant or valuable? This falls under Mahoney and Goertz's criteria of causation. Is it better to be able to definitively say that A causes B in this one case only or that A has a tendency to influence B over a number of cases? This is a key difference between qualitative and quantitative political scientists, and there is no right or wrong answer; your position on it will hinge on what you believe to be more valuable to your research as a whole. Qualitative social scientists are more logical in trying to trace out a cause to effect; they use what we know as necessary and sufficient conditions to try and identify what causes a particular event and will often go into deep detail to support their conclusions. On the other side, quantitative analysts use statistics and probability to be able to say that A or B are *likely* or *not likely* to have caused the outcome under study.

Another comparison to be made, then, is the significance of individual cases or events under study. For quantitative researchers, all cases are equally important— even if there are what we call outliers. Outliers are particular cases that fall substantially above or below the average data point. For example, if Congress passes, on average, 50 laws per year and in one year they pass 200, this year would be considered an outlier. If we were studying this quantitatively, we might not be all that interested in this outlier, but if we were studying it qualitatively, this outlier would be incredibly important. Why was it so much higher in this particular year? What was special about the conditions Congress was operating in? What does it tell us about congressional productivity? Thus, in qualitative methods, outliers are very important and can change overall observations, analysis, and conclusions.

What's the Big Deal?

So what's the big deal? Why all the fuss in political science about which to use or which is better? As alluded to in Chapter 1, the debate between methods is one that is practically built into the discipline of political science. Where much of the early political science research was decidedly qualitative, the behavioral revolution after World War II changed the perspective of the discipline and reoriented it toward more quantitative, statistical methods in an effort to be more scientific and rigorous. Quantitative scholars will argue that qualitative research hardly stands up to scientific standards of examination, thereby relegating qualitatively derived findings to a lower status than those found quantitatively. This movement drove political science through much of the second half of the twentieth century, and many of the major political science publications reinforced the perspective in preferring or appearing to prefer quantitative research articles.

The debate comes down to the question of how do we know what we know, what data, what evidence can we trust? Quantitative scholars believe in a deductive approach to political science, generating hypotheses and testing them against available data. Because the statistical method is what comes closest to approximating the experimental gold standard, they believe that those sorts of findings should be more highly valued. On the other hand, qualitative scholars often rely on more of an inductive method, using selected cases to determine hypotheses that might cover all possible cases. Because qualitative analysis delves into details and context, findings developed through those methods, qualitative scholars believe, is more relevant and applicable than numbers that do not necessarily mean anything outside of a statistical program. Some political scientists will argue that if the political science field wants to be considered a true science, then it must be as rigorous and scientific as possible. For them, this means that quantitative methods are the only acceptable means of testing hypotheses.

How Do We Know What We Know?

The field of political science was also highly influenced in the mid-twentieth century by developments in the philosophical field of **epistemology** (how we know what we know) and histories of science. In particular, Kuhn, in a book originally published in 1962, lays out his theory of what science is and how it develops. In *The Structure of Scientific Revolutions*, Kuhn argues that "normal science" is "research firmly based upon one or more past scientific achievements, achievements that some particular scientific community acknowledges for a time as supplying the foundation for its further practice."[7] He goes on to argue that a sign of maturity in a field is the acquisition of a paradigm, or a tradition of practice. For political scientists who desperately wanted to make their field more scientific in the mid-twentieth century, the only way to become so was to follow Kuhn's prescription and adopt a tradition of quantitative studies of political science. However, adherence to this dictate does not abide by Kuhn's arguments as a whole. Elsewhere in the book, he states that "methodological directives, by themselves" are insufficient to generate conclusions.[8] Thus, adopting a methodological purity without some sort of guiding theory is itself insufficient for representing "normal science." This did not stop the focus on making political science a "better" science; the push for quantitative methods is itself demonstrative of that.

Another development in epistemology that greatly influenced midcentury political scientists was the idea of falsification of hypotheses rather than proving them. Karl Popper was a German philosopher who also worked on this question of what science is and what it isn't. For Popper, what was scientific and unscientific came down to a question of "demarcation." Instead of arguing that science is attempting to rigorously study and prove an idea, Popper argued that we can never truly *prove* something to be correct. We are not omniscient; we do not know of every possible situation that could possibly exist, so it is impossible for anyone to *prove* something. Instead, Popper defines science as being able to falsify or disprove hypotheses.[9] In order for a hypothesis to represent a scientific advance, it must be falsifiable; when we are testing a hypothesis, then, we are trying to disprove it.

We can never prove that we are correct; we can only say that to the extent of our knowledge, the hypothesis has not been disproved. Popper combined with Kuhn influenced political science as a field in their movement toward becoming more rigorous and scientific, which in the minds of a majority of political scientists at the time was quantitative in nature.

Smith argues that this debate is particularly meaningful in political science, whose "inquiry is undertaken to serve human interests" and whose findings necessarily affect those studying the question and those being studied.[10] Politics is personal for many people, so how we study it and the findings we make can become not only important for the researcher and the researcher's career but for the institution or the situations in which the findings may be applied. As Smith writes, "Political science is more likely to be seen as important and worth sustaining, and to be sustained, if it illuminates political topics that most people care about in comprehensible ways."[11] Because of this deep importance, the way we study politics becomes all the more important.

In reality, there is probably no real answer to which method is better; it is a highly personal question that often hinges on individual beliefs about the nature of reality and the nature of knowledge. But the problem, as many qualitative scholars have perceived it, is the monolithic way in which the political science establishment has preferred quantitative methods over qualitative and the edge that that has given quantitative researchers. When we talk about the "establishment" in political science, we are referring to the community of academic scholars who reside in universities and colleges throughout the country. One of the key things to understand about these professors is that for the vast majority of them, promotion in rank and acquisition of tenure is dependent on their ability to publish research in books and in political science journals. In fact, for many young scholars, the motto is that they must "publish or perish." If one set of methods is preferred by publishers and major journals over another, it privileges one set of scholars over the other.

Political Science's Perestroika

That is exactly the situation that political science found itself it as we moved into the twenty-first century. Qualitative scholars felt discriminated against because their work could not get published and they could not advance as quickly or as highly as the establishment quantitative scholars. Even books that purported to bridge the divide between the two methodologies seemed to favor quantitative methods. For example, one such book that attracted the attention of scholars of both stripes was *Designing Social Inquiry* by political scientists King, Keohane, and Verba, originally published in 1995. Reflecting a quantitative bias, King, Keohane, and Verba argue that qualitative scholars could benefit from adopting more of the logic and methods of quantitative scholars, thereby attempting a marriage of the two perspectives. In his review of the work, David Laitin claims that "the book contains a set of concepts, rules of inference, and methodological precepts that apply to all researchers who seek a generalized and systematic understanding of politics."[12] However, Tarrow does not buy their argument that the quantitative logic can be combined with qualitative methods, instead finding King, Keohane, and Verba's book somewhat patronizing to qualitative researchers. Even in attempts to bridge the two methodologies, quantitative work or logic still seemed to be preferred.[13]

The systematic disenfranchisement of qualitative research and the scholars who performed it resulted in a revolution of sorts in political science with the so-called Perestroika movement. In 2000, an anonymous political scientist writing under the name "Mr. Perestroika" sent an e-mail out to a political science LISTSERV listing out a number of questions about the state of the discipline. The e-mail questioned not only the overrepresentation of quantitative studies in the major political science journal the *American Political Science Review* (*APSR*) published by the American Political Science Association (APSA) but the orientation of both the *APSR* and the APSA toward diverse populations of scholars. Among the questions asked by Mr. Perestroika were the following:

> Why does a "coterie" of faculty dominate and control APSA and the editorial board of APSR—i (sic) scratch your back, you scratch mine. I give award to your student from Harvard and you give mine from Duke or Columbia. In short why do "East Coast Brahmins" control APSA?

> Have we learned any lesson from the thousands of pages of research that was funded by APSA in the name of political science to examine the former Soviet Union and make "predictive" models? What happened to those models and why did they fail? How is it that those esteemed colleagues failed to predict the collapse of the Soviet Empire while Sovietologists from Korea, Japan, India, and even one from Tanzania could predict the fall of the empire. Are we making the same mistake by ignoring diverse knowledges and methodologies present in the study of politics?

> Why are the overwhelming majority of Presidents of APSA or editorial board members of APSR, WHITE and MALE? Where are the African-Americans, Hispanics, Women, Gays, Asians—in short, where is the diversity of United States and the world that APSA "pretends" to study—is someone afraid that APSA will slip out of their hands??? (sic)

In short, Mr. Perestroika's e-mail was not just an assault centered around methodology but an out and out attack on the political science establishment.

While criticism about methodology made up only a part of the manifesto, the biggest discussion to result was one centering on the dominance of quantitative studies in the field of political science that was consistently denigrating the world of qualitative scholars. Efforts for greater methodological pluralism and opportunities for qualitative scholars and their work was expanded. Books about both methodologies abounded, many of them purporting to offer middle ways, solutions encompassing both qualitative and quantitative work. Studies of the extent to which the quantitative-qualitative divide penetrated political science were extensive. In one study of research methods texts that were used to teach young political scientists about research methods, Schwartz-Shea and Yanow find a distinct preference in favor of quantitative methods.[14] They argue that as a result, the indoctrination of political scientists into quantitative methodology is only continuing and being reinforced as a consequence of the types of texts that are being used to teach them. In another study, Schwartz-Shea compiled data on doctoral programs in political science only to find that what doctoral students are being taught is highly preferential toward quantitative methods.[15]

While there is a greater appreciation and acknowledgment of qualitative methods today as a result of the Perestroika movement, controversies still abound. Barkin argues that the very term *qualitative methods* is ill-defined and amorphous, especially compared to the specific tests and tools that quantitative methods have to answer a particular research question.[16] As a result, "Since there is no discrete set of methodologies, one cannot claim to have covered it comprehensively."[17] Students are thus not taught specific strategies and methods that they can use, instead filling their time with epistemology and philosophy of science.[18] Quantitative research continues to fill the pages of the top journals. And while the APSA itself has attempted to diversify its leadership and membership, there is still a propagation of senior and influential scholars compared to more junior, challenging professors.

So, is there an establishment answer to quantitative or qualitative? If there is one, it probably still leans toward the quantitative end of the spectrum, but it does not have to be that way. There is a growing education in and acceptance of qualitative methods; many scholars promote a multi-methods approach. While it does not take the side of either methodological approach, it argues that the better method is to select the right tool with which to answer your question.

Let Your Question Be Your Guide

Reminiscent of Jiminy Cricket's intonation to "let your conscience be your guide," the best answer to the question of which methods you should choose is that you should choose the method that best fits with the question you are asking. In other words, if your question and hypothesis necessarily lend themselves to a quantitative methodology, then that's what you should choose. If it calls for qualitative work, then go with that. To give some examples, let's return one more time to our research questions and hypotheses from earlier in this chapter.

Q: What motivations does Russia have in invading eastern Ukraine?
H: Russia was motivated to invade eastern Ukraine because of a fear of European meddling in supposedly Russian affairs.

Q: What influences immigration policy in the United States in the twenty-first century?

H: Immigration policy in the United States is influenced by economic and political factors.

Q: Why has there been a downturn in the frequency of laws passed in the US Congress?

H: Congress has passed fewer laws because party polarization has increased.

The first question and hypothesis have to do with Russia's incursion into eastern Ukraine. The best set of methods for answering such a question would most likely be a qualitative method based on case studies. The researcher would be able to gather primary documents, news reports, and interviews with key players to detail the chain of events that led to the Russian actions. As suggested previously, the study could even be enhanced with multiple case studies examining other Russian actions in the region, particularly in the case of Georgia. On the other hand, the third question and hypothesis on the frequency of laws passed in the United States would best be answered through quantitative methods. In fact, numbers are built into the question itself in terms of frequency and party polarization scores.

But what about the second question? What method best fits in that situation? This is where the skill and craft of the researcher comes into play. The independent variables in the second case include economics and politics while the dependent variable is immigration policy. If some way exists to quantitatively measure those three variables, a quantitative method might fit best. This can be done through measures such as GDP or inflation for the economy, political parties or other variables for the political part, and the number of immigration regulations for immigration policy. The researcher could then perform the requisite statistical tests to look for relationships between the variables. Alternatively, you could also perform case studies into some instances of immigration policymaking in the United States to look for the influence of economic and political variables. In reality, either approach is acceptable, or some scholars may even choose to *combine* both the quantitative and qualitative studies to enhance their research. If you can make the same or similar conclusions using different methods, this only enhances your conclusions (we call this **triangulation**).

The biggest problems with choosing the appropriate methods usually come when researchers try to pigeonhole a question into a particular method—for instance, a quantitative scholar wants to research something that is hard to put into numerical values. Some will try to force the issue, devise complicated means of measuring their concepts, all in the belief that their preferred method (in this case quantitative) is the best. This also can happen to qualitative researchers who refuse to use any numbers when those data may in fact make their research better. Both scholars find themselves slavishly devoted to their choice of method in the belief that that is the only way to truly prove their argument is correct.

CASE STUDY
Democracies and Conflict

One of the major questions that scholars in international relations and comparative politics seek to understand is this: When do countries go to war? Is it when they perceive their national interest to be at stake? If so, what is that interest? Is it in the interest of human rights' violations? Is it because of another belligerent country? While the question is fairly broad, we can make it more limited and specific by focusing on democracies: When do democracies go to war? The democratic peace theory suggests that, at a minimum, democracies will not go to war with each other, but we know that there are times the United States has entered into a conflict.

Before settling on a potential research design, a first step here would be to define our concepts—especially the ideas of democracy and war. As will be discussed in later chapters, there are a number of ways to define both. For our purposes here, we can utilize two commonly used definitions in the literature: a democratic government is one in which there are free, fair, and frequent elections, and war is a conflict between two entities with casualties numbering over 1,000. Given these definitions, what might be some hypotheses as to why democracies would go to war?

Once you have developed a hypothesis or hypotheses, you must decide on your research methods. While we should always let the question guide us, in this instance, either quantitative or qualitative methods will suffice. How might you design a quantitative study to answer the question and a qualitative one?

Quantitative: Create a database of all wars in the world since World War II and the countries involved in them (we call pairs of data points *dyads*). Variables to be included would not just be whether a country involved was democratic or not but other variables that could cause war, including economic indicators and ideology such as communism. Utilize statistical methods to determine if there are any patterns of circumstances when democracies go to war.

Qualitative: Select a small number of case studies of wars with some that involve democracies and some that do not. Examine in depth these cases to determine why the democratic countries went to war. Are there any generalizable conclusions that can be found across the cases?

Critical Thinking Questions

1. How do the quantitative and qualitative research designs differ?

2. What advantages does each have?

3. Are these two research designs complementary? Are there any benefits in combining them and doing both?

4. Are there additional methods you can think of to answer the research question?

STUDENT STUDY SITE

Visit https://edge.sagepub.com/whitmancobb

CHAPTER SUMMARY

- Research questions should be specific and tailored to the phenomenon you're trying to study. Hypotheses are proposed answers to these questions.

- Hypotheses identify the variables that are analyzed to determine if the hypothesized relationship exists or not.

- Hypotheses can be tested via quantitative or qualitative methods. Quantitative methods utilize statistical and mathematical tests while qualitative methods rely on deep description and analysis of primary and secondary documents.

- Quantitative and qualitative methods provide researchers different types of analytical leverage.

- Political scientists have historically preferred quantitative methods, but there has been a growing appreciation for the role qualitative methods can play.

KEY TERMS

case study: A detailed explanation and evaluation of one event or situation

comparative method: A research method based on comparing several cases to determine whether there are any commonalities or differences that can explain differing outcomes

conceptualization: The process of precisely defining what a concept means

correlation: A statistical tool that allows researchers to determine if there is a relationship between two numerical variables

dependent variable: The suspected effect; researchers look for changes in the dependent variable based on changes to the independent variable

epistemology: A field of philosophy that asks the question how do we know what we know

hypothesis: A reasonable guess as to the answer to your research question; a testable proposition

independent variable: The suspected cause of an effect; researchers can manipulate the independent variable to see the effects on the dependent variable

literature review: A summary and analysis of the research that has been done previously on a topic

operationalization: The process of turning the concept into a measurable variable

process tracing: A qualitative method that focuses on tracing the causes of an event step by step

qualitative methods: A set of methods that focus on deep description and heavy textual and event analysis

quantitative methods: Broad term denoting the use of mathematical and statistical tools to analyze the relationship between and among variables

regression analysis: A statistical method that tests if there is a relationship between multiple variables

triangulation: Using multiple types of methods to confirm the same results

variables: Ideas or concepts that can vary over time

DISCUSSION QUESTIONS

1. What is the difference between quantitative and qualitative methods? Why does it matter?

2. Come up with some possible research questions and hypotheses. Are they specific enough? Can you make them more specific?

3. What types of methods could you use to answer your research questions? Why?

4. Which methodology do you believe is the strongest for providing reliable evidence? Why?

5. Ask your professor about his or her training and experience in methods. What was he or she taught when a graduate student?

FOR FURTHER READING

Kuhn, Thomas, S. *The Structure of Scientific Revolutions*. Chicago: University of Chicago Press, 1996.

Mahoney, James, and Gary Goertz. "A Tale of Two Cultures: Contrasting Quantitative and Qualitative Research." *Political Analysis* 14 (2006): 227–249.

Smith, Rogers, M. 2002. "Should We Make Political Science More of a Science or More about Politics?" *PS: Political Science and Politics* 35, no. 2 (2002): 199–201.

American National Election Studies: www.electionstudies.org

General Social Survey: www.gss.norc.org

NOTES

1. Alexander L. George and Andrew Bennett, *Case Studies and Theory Development in the Social Sciences* (Cambridge, MA: MIT Press, 2005), 5.

2. Ibid., 6.

3. Charles C. Ragin, *The Comparative Method: Moving beyond Qualitative and Quantitative Strategies* (Berkeley: University of California Press, 1987), 5.

4. Ibid.

5. James Mahoney and Gary Goertz, "A Tale of Two Cultures: Contrasting Quantitative and Qualitative Research," *Political Analysis* 14 (2006): 227–249.

6. Ibid., 229.

7. Thomas S. Kuhn, *The Structure of Scientific Revolutions* (Chicago: University of Chicago Press, 1996), 10.

8. Ibid., 3.

9. Stephen Thornton, "Karl Popper," *The Stanford Encyclopedia of Philosophy*, ed. Edward N. Zalta, 2015, https://plato.stanford.edu/archives/win2015/entries/popper/.

10. Rogers M. Smith, "Should We Make Political Science More of Science of More about Politics?" *PS: Political Science and Politics*, 25, no. 2 (2002): 199.

11. Ibid., 200.

12. David D. Laitin, "Review: Disciplining Political Science," *American Political Science Review* 89, no. 2 (1995): 454.

13. Sydney Tarrow, "Review: Bridging the Quantitative-Qualitative Divide in Political Science," *American Political Science Review* 89, no. 2 (1995): 471–474.

14. Peregrine Schwartz-Shea and Dvora Yanow, "Reading 'Methods' Texts: How Research Methods Texts Construct Political Science," *Political Research Quarterly* 55, no. 2 (2002): 457–486.

15. Peregrine Schwartz-Shea, "Is This the Curriculum We Want? Doctoral Requirements and Offerings in Methods and Methodology," *PS: Political Science and Politics* 36, no. 3 (2003): 379–386.

16. Samuel Barkin, "What Defines Research as Qualitative?" *International Studies Review* 9, no. 4 (2007): 754–758.

17. Ibid., 755.

18. Ibid.

Plato's philosophy is an essential foundation of political science.

Source: ©iStockphoto.com/vasiliki

CHAPTER 3

Political Theory

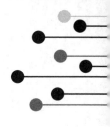

What is "good"? What is the "best"? It's usually easy for us to say what makes a burger "good" or "bad," but how do your definitions stack up against the definitions from somebody else? What makes your definition of a good or bad burger better than someone else's? A vegetarian might not agree with someone else's conception of good being a perfectly medium rare beef patty with all of the fixings. Political theory seeks to settle these types of arguments, but instead of arguing over what makes a burger good or bad, political theorists attempt to discern what makes society or government or even a person "good."

Political theory is one of several subfields in political science. It's not just society and government that are the proper topics for political theory. Many political theorists try to discover what makes for good behavior, ethics, law, justice, and even a good life. The problem in this search is that what is considered good or the best could be disputed from person to person. Therefore, embedded in this search for the good is the identification of what is good to begin with. We call these ideas **normative ideas**, meaning that there might not be any objective standards against which to measure the ideas as being good or bad. For example, the argument that democracy is the best form of government is a normative idea; there's no way to objectively prove that that assertion is correct.

This chapter focuses on just one aspect of theory in political science; theory can also refer to other types, including formal, empirical, and analytic. Formal theory utilizes mathematical models and techniques to deduce findings about political behavior. Formal theory is more closely associated with behavioralism and the scientific method as opposed to the types of normative questions taken up here. Similarly, empirical political theory looks at the world as it is, not as it perhaps should be. Studies examining real-world facts and situations and the theories

Chapter Objectives

1. Describe the basic arguments of early political theorists in ancient Greece, Rome, and later medieval Europe.

2. Understand the influence of religion, and in particular Christianity, on political theory and the origins of the Enlightenment.

3. Outline the political theory of liberalism, including its tenets, adherents, and contributors.

4. Summarize challenges to liberalism, including those of Karl Marx.

5. Describe modern political thought and its leading theorists and perspectives.

developed explaining them would fall under empirical theory. Finally, analytic theory has more in common with political thought as a whole. "It privileges the self-conscious search for clarity and precision of thesis and argument and has the ambition of presenting simple theories or principles of great power and application. It often uses abstract examples and simplified models, and favors quantitative over qualitative social science."[1]

Not only does political theory form the basis of the study of politics but many of its arguments form the logical underpinnings of politics around the world. For instance, what makes democratic societies so sure that their form of government is the best? Why do people believe that limited government is appropriate and that there should be controls on government abilities and powers? Many of the policy differences between today's Republicans and Democrats can be boiled down to beliefs about the role that government should play, which is itself political theory. This chapter, then, briefly traces the major lines of political thought from ancient Greece and Rome to the influence of the Enlightenment to political thought today. Given this brief treatment, the chapter does not purport to be comprehensive; there are many other areas of political theory that can be explored, including Eastern political thought. However, it provides a general overview of the philosophers who have had a major impact on political theory and politics.

The Ancients to the Enlightenment

As detailed in the first chapter, the origins of political theory date back to ancient Greece. While understanding some of the arguments Plato, Aristotle, and other ancient philosophers make is somewhat difficult, their early work provides the foundation for later generations of theorists. This section focuses on some of the more significant writers from the ancient period up until the early modern period in the 1500s and the Enlightenment.

Plato's *The Republic*

The earliest political thought and associated writings come to us through Plato, whose mentor was the philosopher Socrates. Although none of Socrates' writings exists today, the details we have of his philosophy come to us through Plato. While there is some scholarly discussion over which of Plato's writings best reflect Socrates' philosophy, scholars are generally sure that the earliest parts of Plato's writings are reflective of Socrates' teaching. Using the convention of a dialogue with Socrates, Plato's writings run the gamut from what we can conceive of as "true" knowledge to what the best form of the state is. It is from Plato's writings that we get the **allegory of the cave**, through which Plato explores the nature of truth and knowledge. In *The Republic*, Plato tells the story of a group of people who have lived their entire lives chained to the back of a cave where they can only see shadows on a wall. As the days go by, the cave dwellers see shadows moving on the wall and imagine them to be real people, and to the cave dwellers, they are real people. They give them names and stories, and because this life is all that they know, the cave dwellers believe them to be real. If, one day, one of those cave dwellers is released from their chains, they emerge into the real world and begin to see the shadows for what they really are: actual people. Plato compares this released person to a philosopher—someone who is able to emerge from the cave of ignorance and into the sunshine of real knowledge.

Plato's allegory of the cave suggests that for most people, what they see and believe to be true are merely shadows of what is actually real. This implies that what we see, hear, and feel may not be real at all; if this is the case, how can we believe anything that we see, anything that is told to us? From this, Plato develops the idea of "justified true belief"—that anything we believe, we should have a reasoned argument for believing it.

The allegory of the cave does not stop there, however. Plato describes what might happen if the released cave dweller should try to return to his fellow prisoners and attempt to enlighten them as to all that he has discovered. What happens to us when we suddenly enter a dark room from bright sunshine? We can't see anything! Then, can you imagine having to tell these same people you were chained in a cave with that there is a whole different world outside and that you don't know anything? Plato argues that if the budding philosopher were to return to try to enlighten the cave dwellers, they wouldn't believe him and would eventually kill him! There are two further lessons from the story. First, the cave dweller who can now understand the true nature of reality will find it difficult to see what the unenlightened see. He will be unable to think back to his days of ignorance and imagine what those people in the cave feel and believe. Second, those who are unenlightened will be frightened of the truth and attempt to suppress it; this makes the job of the philosopher even more heroic in knowing the truth and preaching it.

Coming out of the shadows of ignorance, one of the main tasks Plato undertakes is to understand the meaning of justice. Plato argues that justice can be found in the structure of the city, the government. In Book II of *The Republic*, he argues that a just city is one that provides for the basic needs of its society and that individuals are compelled to enter into such an arrangement because they cannot be completely self-sufficient. Entering into cooperation in a city, citizens can use their natural abilities to provide for one another. Here, however, Plato is challenged that such a city would not be a city worth living in. His reply is that a more "luxurious" city would require an educated army to guard it and that education would need to be carefully curated to ensure that the soldiers are properly educated in the aims and purposes of such a city. Other elements of a just city include leaders selected from the educated soldiers who are older and wiser, that the city should be just large enough to allow it to be stable, and to follow traditional Greek religion and customs. Because this city is just and has the virtues of wisdom, moderation, and courage, justice will naturally follow.

Plato recognizes, though, that a just city cannot remain forever and that change and decay are ultimately inevitable. From that, he argues that there are four unjust regime types: timocracy (pursuing success and honor rather than wisdom), oligarchy (emphasizing wealth), democracy, and dictatorship. These types of government that arise out of flawed individuals are similarly unjust. Therefore, for Plato and Socrates, individuals must have "balanced souls" who abide by reason and wisdom. This is connected with the argument that a just city is ruled over by philosophers who have exited the cave, become enlightened, and have the wisdom necessary to keep justice in mind. The "**Philosopher Kings**" (or queens; Socrates does not rule out women for the job) would have a special education that would prepare them for ruling, including an understanding of what "good" is. For this, he returns to the analogy of the cave and in particular the sun; as the sun illuminates and causes things to grow, so does the good.

Aristotle and Roman Developments

The work of Plato represents the first real attempt to specify a form of government that is good and just. While we might not necessarily agree with everything Plato argues (he also makes the argument that the families of the soldiers would be owned in common among them), he attempts to balance out the needs and happiness of individuals with the need for a just and fair society. Aristotle continues this effort in *Politics,* beginning again with the idea of a city. For Aristotle, much like Plato, the purpose of a city is to create a partnership of "persons who cannot exist without one another." Beginning first with a man and a woman who create a family that eventually expands into various communities or villages, this grouping eventually becomes large enough to be considered a city. This creation of a city, according to Aristotle, is a natural feature, with individuals naturally being "political animals." And while this all may happen rather automatically, Aristotle notes that just because we are by nature political animals, this does not mean that we automatically know how to behave in a just manner. Men in a city require just laws and structures to ensure that the partnership functions in an appropriate way.

Aristotle comes to a somewhat different conclusion about what types of governments would be the best kind. Monarchy, aristocracy, and polity (rule by the many but not *all*) are the most appropriate types of regimes as long as they are ruled in accordance with the common good. On the other hand, tyranny, oligarchy, and democracy (here defined as rule by many for their own interest) are identified as unjust regimes. Thus, the key difference in a just and unjust regime is the motivation behind the ruling: Are people acting on their own behalf or on behalf of all society including women and slaves who are not considered true citizens? Justice, then, is that all equal people should be treated equally. There are other elements to Aristotle's political theory, including the idea that a polity is the most "practical" regime and the need to pay attention to the economic conditions of a city in order to propagate itself. The common theme, however, in Greek political thought is the attention to the just or proper forms of government along with the types of virtues people must hold in order for the setup to be successful.

Several of these Greek ideas were incorporated later in the Roman civilization. After the overthrow of a king around 510 BCE, Rome instituted what is often referred to as a "mixed constitution" with two elected consuls: the Roman Senate and a series of popular assemblies to represent the people.[2]

Each element of the constitution exercised a distinctive form of power. The elected consuls wielded *imperium* or executive power; the Senate enjoyed the power to deliberate and consent to specific policies; and the popular assemblies served as the source of authoritative law, also electing the magistrates and the popular tribunes who exercised veto power over the Senate.[3]

While the Roman republic would eventually collapse into an imperial form of government, the very idea of a republic with a system of checks and balances would become an influential force in the founding of the United States. In sum, the significance of the first Greek political philosophy, handed down to and expressed in Rome, would prove important in how later generations conceived of and thought about ideas such as justice and just governing structures.

St. Augustine

A lot had changed in Europe from the times of Plato and Aristotle to the medieval age. Greek city-states lost much of their regional power while the Roman empire was on the upswing. In 313, the Roman emperor Constantine allowed the practice of Christianity and, as a result, the Christian religion was poised to grow in power over the next several centuries. Shortly following Constantine's moves and the official adoption of Christianity as the religion of the Empire, the Roman empire's long downswing came to a head with the fall of Rome and its split into western and eastern empires. The fall of Rome and the growth of Christianity allowed the new Roman Catholic Church to substantially grow and amass power that would be equal to and in some cases surpass the power of individual European states.

At about this same time, religious philosophers began to contemplate the role for religion in government. The most prominent of these philosophers included Augustine of Hippo, the erstwhile St. Augustine. Writing around the turn of the fifth century, Augustine contemplated the role of God and his followers in the creation of government. His formulation includes the idea of *The City of God* that includes those people whom God has chosen to save and are thus living in the state of grace, and an earthly city. Insofar as these two cities have consistent goals, the populations of the two can work in concert.

Augustine focuses much of his writings on the conception of good and virtue. Interestingly enough, Augustine does not argue that true evil exists, instead making the argument that evil is the absence of good or the choice of the less good. This leads directly into the aspect of political philosophy that Augustine may be most famous for: his conception of just war. God allowed the Israelites to engage in warfare and in some cases commanded it in the Old Testament, yet in the New Testament, Jesus encourages his followers along a more pacifist line with the lesson to "turn the other cheek." How to square these two conceptions of God? Should a Christian in engage in warfare or practice peace? Augustine's answer to this conundrum is that Christians may be permitted to engage in warfare so long as the conflict is just. And what is a **just war**? War pursued by government (Christian and non-Christian alike) to pursue peace and punish those who may benefit from such punishment (i.e., they have done wrong) may be considered just.

St. Thomas Aquinas

Augustine represents a melding of ancient political philosophy with the new religious ethos of Christianity. Particularly since the Roman Catholic Church would grow in power so as to practically encompass earthly cities and states, these new formulations of philosophy with religion represent a natural evolution with the times. A few hundred years later, the task would be picked up on and enlarged by St. Thomas Aquinas. Aquinas, a Roman Catholic priest, lived in the thirteenth century and melded Catholic and religious thought with Aristotle's conception of ethics and virtue. His major piece of work, *The Summa Theologiae,* delves into the ideas of God and ethics—with the first part attempting to provide proof of the existence of God. Koritansky notes that unlike Islam and Judaism which both have strict and comprehensive laws for everyday life in their theological texts, Christianity had no doctrine; as such, he argues that Aquinas never felt the need to reconcile Greek philosophy with religion leading to less of an emphasis on governing in Aquinas's work.[4]

Despite this, the second part of the *Summa* develops Aquinas's positions on ethics and government. According to Aquinas, law is the use of "reason for the common good" the function of which is to make men good.[5] Human law flows from divine law and reason, and humans can never know completely what the divine law is. However, "the participation of the eternal law in the rational creature is called the natural law."[6] What Aquinas is arguing for, then, is the recognition that natural law does exist through eternal and divine law or rather that God lays down certain laws and principles that we can all grasp. These laws can then be used to shape the nature of man, to prevent wicked, and to encourage good.[7] In particular, Aquinas's "first principle" of natural law states that "good is to be done and ensued and evil is to be avoided."[8] In many ways, this is similar to the Golden Rule: do unto others as you would have done unto you.

From these principles of divine and natural law, Aquinas says that we derive human law, an imperfect form of both. However, an important critique of Aquinas stems from this claim; Aquinas does not specify how we are to know the human from the natural law or even to recognize what natural law is.[9] Zuckert lays out four questions based on Aquinas's claims that highlight the difficulty of the analysis including how the first principles are self-evident and how Aquinas moves from practical reason to natural law.[10] Although these analyses can be quite in depth and daunting, the thing to keep in mind is the blending of the religious with the philosophical at the same time matters religious are dominating the state.

Although Aquinas doesn't address it himself, it is easy to see the concept of the divine right of kings in his arguments. If human law flows from the divine law—and there can be no law that does not flow from someone who cares about the community—it is only a small leap to the idea that the right to have dominion over earthly subjects flows from God himself.[11] This doctrine, with its origins in the medieval period, would come to have significant consequences for the politics of the Enlightenment.

The Enlightenment

Throughout the medieval period and into the 1500s, the Catholic Church continues to exert dominance over the governments of European states. This does not mean, however, that rulers in their own kingdoms did not exert an awesome amount of power but that these same rulers gave their obedience to Rome and the pope. By the early 1500s, though, cracks started to appear in the dominance and unity of the Catholic Church. Two movements, happening largely in separate countries but at the same time, combined to break the power of the Church and increase the amount of power that states and their rulers had.

The Reformation and the Establishment of the English Church

Beginning in the early 1500s, German theologian Martin Luther began developing critiques of the practices of the Church, including the practice of indulgences, the authority of the pope, corruption within the Church, and illiterate priests. It's no coincidence that the rise of the Reformation came after the development of the printing press in the late fifteenth century; the wider availability of the Bible and other works allowed Church critics access to the Bible, which previously had been restricted to clergy and Church officials. In general, these new Protestants encouraged a closer reading and interpretation of the Bible. For instance, although the pope was considered the head of the Church and God's representative on Earth, Luther and others claimed there was no biblical foundation for such a position and for such power. Similarly, they found little support for practices like the creation of saints or the reverence for the Virgin Mary. Luther made these criticisms public in his *Ninety-Five Theses,* which were nailed to a church door in Wittenberg, Germany. Luther's critiques of the Church's teachings and corruption helped lead to the wider **Protestant Reformation** that would rile Europe for decades to come and lead to a sharp decrease in the power of the Catholic Church.

Although the movement began in continental Europe, arguably one of the most influential legacies of Luther's criticisms came in England. King Henry VIII had taken the throne in 1509 upon the death of his brother at which time he married his brother's wife, Catherine of Aragon (they received a formal papal dispensation to do so since according to Church law, a man could not marry his brother's wife). Although Catherine gave birth to a girl in 1516, Henry desperately wanted a male heir who would inherit his throne. Like most prominent men of the period and since, Henry took up with various mistresses, including Anne Boleyn in 1525. By this time, the influence of the burgeoning Protestant Reformation and Martin Luther had spread to the British isle. Upset with Catherine's inability to produce a male heir and influenced by Anne, who told Henry of the Protestant teachings, Henry asked the Roman Catholic Church for a divorce from Catherine. When the Church denied him a divorce, Henry decided to declare England separate from the Roman Catholic Church and grant himself a divorce as head of the Church of England. The Reformation came to a head with the Thirty Years' War on the continent and the English Civil War. In particular, the English Civil War would come to have an out-sized influence on the developing political philosophy of the time.

The roots of the English Civil War were planted with Henry VIII. Although his daughters came to the throne after his death, Elizabeth did not marry and therefore produced no legitimate heir. Combined with the continuing clashes between Protestant and Catholic forces, many had come to question the right of the monarchy to rule, which had been traditionally supported by the precept of the divine right of kings. Some felt that Parliament, with its lower house elected by the people and the aristocracy represented in the House of Lords, was the more appropriate institution through which to govern, while others defended the role of the monarchy. This debate continued a centuries-long discussion about the rights and abilities of a monarch to rule over Britain. Beginning in the 1200s with the Magna Carta, British common law had begun to curtail the monarchy and their ability for total rule. By the time of the 1500s, the monarchy, while retaining much of their power, needed the support of Parliament for many of the routine tasks of governing, such as raising taxes.

Hobbes and Locke

Toward the end of the English Civil War, a piece of political philosophy appeared titled *Leviathan,* written by Thomas Hobbes. In it, the groundwork was laid for a new theory of government that stemmed from Hobbes's experience with and impressions of the English conflict. Instead of deriving government through the divine right of kings, Hobbes wants us to think back to what humans might be like in the absence of government and society, what life would be like in the so-called state of nature. In the state of nature, individuals have all the rights they want: their natural rights. The problem, however (and we can easily see how Hobbes might have thought this having just experienced the English Civil War), is that Hobbes believes that humans in the state of nature are not very good people. In the state of nature, it's a war of all against all, who will win, who will survive, who will live. In Hobbes's words, life in the state of nature is "nasty, brutish, and short." Eventually, though, people will come to realize that if they want to live and be able to exercise their natural rights, they're going to have to do something to stop everyone from threatening everyone else. Hobbes's solution is the idea of a social contract: People in the state of nature come together and agree to give up some of their natural rights to a ruler, a Leviathan, who would then ensure the safety and protection of those entering into the contract. Once the social contract was entered into, the Leviathan chosen and given power, there would be no leaving the new society. Hobbes would eventually go on to write more about what he believed to be the proper structure of society and government, but *Leviathan* would have an immediate effect. For starters, there is no role for the church or religion in this formulation; the leadership does not come to their position by dint of their association with any church or through the divine right of kings. Second, the book influenced and prompted John Locke later in the 1600s to compose a response in the form of Locke's *Two Treatises of Government*.

Locke begins his work from the same premise as Hobbes: What would humans be like in the state of nature? Contrary to Hobbes, however, Locke does not believe that humans are naturally terrible or, rather, singularly self-interested. Instead, they adhere to natural law and seek to live freely and equally among themselves. However, living in such a state can still be dangerous if people misbehave and laws are not equally enforced. As a result, those people would be willing to enter into a social contract, giving up some of their rights while retaining others. Unlike Hobbes's Leviathan, though, the people would retain a right to revolt against their leaders and leave the social contract should the contracted ruler infringe on their remaining rights.

The works of Hobbes and Locke along with other theorists of the 1600s collectively introduce the idea of a social contract or an agreement specifically laying out the government's responsibility to its people and the people's responsibilities toward their government. Thus, the idea of consent of the governed is introduced, and the idea of the divine right of kings to rule over their citizens is discredited. This can also be seen in the Puritans of the seventeenth century, who also engaged in the making of such a covenant among themselves and with God by leaving England to immigrate to the New World.

Scientific Enlightenment

While some Enlightenment thinkers focused their time and energy on the proper forms of government and rights, others sought to apply more scientific and logical principles to the pursuit of science. The works of Galileo, Newton, and countless others challenged the unscientific ideas of the so-called Dark Ages along with the teachings of the Church to declare that Earth was not flat and the sun did not revolve around Earth. While these are important findings in and of themselves, the type of scientific approach developed by these scientists heavily influenced other philosophers into thinking more logically, rationally, and scientifically. Further, the study of epistemology or of how we know what we know became a focus for both the natural philosophers and political philosophers and significantly influenced how we understand the nature of government and proper knowledge.

Later Enlightenment Writers

These ideas were quite influential in the lead-up to the American Revolution with many of them reflected in the Declaration of Independence itself. Not only is the idea of natural rights apparent—life, liberty, and the pursuit of happiness—but the concepts of consent of the government, a limited government, and a right to revolt are also included. (Incidentally, according to Locke, our natural rights included life, liberty, and property. Thomas Jefferson changed the formulation slightly for the Declaration.) Ideas developed by Jean-Jacques Rousseau written in the 1700s also had an impact on the construction of the Constitution in 1789.

Rousseau's philosophy also included the ideas of the state of nature, natural rights, and a social contract but he develops his ideas about the structure of a proper or good government further than Locke or Hobbes did. According to Rousseau, government should take the form of classical republicanism and endorsed the ideas of direct democracy in small city-states. Sovereignty and the rule of law would be vested with the people and voted on directly by them but exercised and enforced through government. Rousseau and his republican government were frequently cited by the American Founders and other writers of the period including Thomas Paine in his 1776 pamphlet *Common Sense*. Rousseau's writings are sometimes described as influencing the French Revolution in the late 1700s.

Other Enlightenment writers of the 1700s included Immanuel Kant, who combined scientific and natural philosophy with some emphasis on the political. Most important of his works was a paper titled "Perpetual Peace" in which he detailed how he believed all wars could be ended and states could live in peace. Not supporting the ideas of a true democracy for fear of a tyranny of a majority, Kant suggested that states reform themselves into constitutional republics after which states and their behavior would be constrained from entering too hastily into war. Combined with an international framework or organization, Kant's work represents one of the earliest formulations of a liberal foreign policy.

Moving into the 1800s, more complex and critical conceptions of government began to be developed. Where previous philosophers had proposed a republican-type government acting on behalf of all, Jeremy Bentham proposed a somewhat different formulation. Bentham introduced his fundamental axiom that became the heart of the idea of **utilitarianism**: "It is the greatest happiness of the greatest number that is the measure of right and wrong." Although this would seem to negate the need for a liberal government (i.e., a constitutional, limited government), Bentham was a strong advocate for liberty and the specification of law. To this point, it would be very difficult to scientifically know what the "best" or the "good" is. What Bentham was attempting to do was find a way to measure good and therefore be able to identify the best approach to take in each situation. He argued that when considering the best solution, we should take into account the amount of pain and pleasure that would be encountered but using specific factors including intensity, duration, certainty, proximity to action, the consequences, and the involvement of other emotions.

Bentham's student John Stuart Mill further elaborated on utilitarianism in his own writings. Although he agreed with many of Bentham's principles, he disagreed with him on the nature of happiness and whether all happiness is intrinsically the same. His major work of political philosophy, *On Liberty*, focuses on defining the boundaries between individuals and government, between liberty and authority. Mill defines *liberty* as "protection against the tyranny of the political rulers" and argues that the only reason people have for limiting liberty is to limit harm to others.[12] Otherwise, individuals should be as free as possible to conduct themselves however they see fit. This leads to Mill's support for women's rights, a lifting of laws against homosexuality, and generally what we would recognize as libertarian ideals today.

Challenges to Liberalism

Depending on the way you look at utilitarianism, it is either a critique of the traditional social contract philosophy or is a natural extension of applying scientific principles to governmental systems. Moving deeper into the 1800s, other approaches also arise, which, depending on your perspective, either take liberalism to its logical end points or challenge previous works. The first among these is Karl Marx with his writings on everything from religion to economics and history. Marx—with Friedrich Engels—is best known as the father of communism.

Karl Marx and Communism

Communism is a comprehensive doctrine that concerns itself not only with the proper forms of government but the patterns of history and economic disparities. Marx and Engels argue that all of history can be looked at as patterns of class struggles; the bourgeoisie own the means of production and therefore most of the capital, and they continually try to keep the majority, the proletariat, the workers, down. For Marx and Engels, this naturally creates a society where people are inherently *unequal*. If we want to create a society that is inherently *equal,* then a constitution and limited government are simply not enough. You must get rid of the system that creates the inequalities, the capitalist system. What communism imagines, then, is a system of society with no social classes to speak of, nor a government. In this sense, it is taking Enlightenment liberalism to a logical end point; if you want to create a society that is equal in status and rights, then you must remove the boundaries creating states and social classes.

Marx and Engels do not imagine that a transition to communism would happen overnight, nor do they think every society is as ready to accept such a move. In *The Communist Manifesto*, they argue that the proletariat will need to establish a certain amount of class consciousness, an awareness of how they as a class are being exploited by the bourgeoisie. Since those in power will not want to give it up freely,

Marx and Engels argue that a proletarian revolution will be needed to advance the communist agenda. The Communist Party would serve as mentor and organization to this emerging consciousness, encouraging and educating the proletariat as to the nature of their relationship with the rest of society.

Part of *The Communist Manifesto* addresses some of the objections Marx and Engels anticipate to communism such as the abolition of private property and the incentives of laborers to work in the absence of a capitalistic system. With regard to the abolition of private property, Marx and Engels argue that for most of the population, the proletariat, private property has already been abolished as the fruits of their labor are not used for the proletariat but are used by the bourgeoisie to exploit the workers. As for the rise of laziness, they assert that the bourgeoisie should have succumbed to this long ago, and the fact that they haven't demonstrates that this argument is simply not true. Of course, other critiques of *The Communist Manifesto* are less difficult to defend. One communist proposal is the abolition of the family as the family unit is also the tool of the bourgeoisie and simply propagates the current order of things. Marx and Engels freely admit to this desire in the quest for doing away with all barriers to a classless society.

Based on the Marxist theory of history as a struggle between classes, *The Communist Manifesto* does not call for an immediate movement to a communist state. Rather, they desire a proletarian revolution that results in the institutions of government being held by the working classes. At this stage, the proletarians would institute particular reforms such as the centralization of credit; the abolition of private property; a progressive income tax; and state control of industry, commerce, transportation, and communication. Once reforms are enacted, class distinctions will lose their significance, political power will no longer exist, and the former state will be replaced by a society with no need for a government, a society wherein everyone is free and equal.

It is important to note that the communist states that have existed in history (the Soviet Union and China still) have not existed in a state where communism as originally formulated by Marx and Engels truly exists. As discussed in previous chapters, both the Soviet Union and China took these principles and adopted them for their own purposes. It is hard to imagine a Chinese government today willingly giving up its power to further the communist agenda although that is the ultimate end called for in *The Communist Manifesto*.

The Communist Manifesto was hardly the only work that Karl Marx put forward. Perhaps one of the most interesting subjects that Marx wrote about was the role of religion in society. One of the major arguments that was being pursued in Marx's circle of philosophers in the mid-1800s was about the separation of church and state, particularly as it regarded the Jewish people. In "On the Jewish Question," Marx introduces a distinction between political emancipation (the ability of people to be free politically) and human emancipation (the ability of people to simply be free). Although religion may be a barrier to human emancipation, it is not a barrier for political emancipation; Marx argues that liberal rights, our political emancipation, are designed to protect people from one another, to protect them from someone else's interference. However, Marx argues that real freedom is not to be found in isolation but in community with one another—something that liberal rights may inhibit.[13] This argument previews his later statement that religion is "the opiate of the people"; it keeps them calm and content and unable to recognize their true freedom of self here on this earth.

Existentialism

Although it didn't come with a comprehensive political philosophy, it's also worth noting another nineteenth century challenge to liberalism and other Enlightenment philosophies. Much like Marx's focus on people and social groups, the existentialist school believed that philosophy had, to this point, focused too little on the individual in preference to the system of society. Existentialist authors wanted to bring the individual back into philosophy and recognize that the individual wasn't just some cog in the wheel of a larger machine but was a thinking and feeling person. "'**Existentialism**,' therefore, may be defined as the philosophical theory which holds that a further set of categories, governed by the norm of *authenticity*, is necessary to grasp human existence" (emphasis in the original).[14] In other words, existentialism gets to the central question of reality, why we exist, what we're here for, and the feelings and attitudes of individuals rather than the state. Existentialism would come into its own in the twentieth century and have a significant influence not just on philosophy but art and culture.

Contemporary Philosophy

With the beginning of the twentieth century, we begin to fall in line with the development of political science as a discipline. But at the same time, philosophy was beginning to diverge from political theory. Where political theory and philosophy engage with proper forms of government and society, philosophy writ large is more concerned with what is good and proper and understanding the world around us. There is some overlap, but as we move into twentieth century philosophy and political theory, theories and their theorists begin to construct more and more elaborate ideas and concepts about what makes the world go round.

The twentieth century is also a story about communism and reactions to it. As communism in its adapted form gets picked up in the Soviet Union and then China, democratic theorists found it to be important to respond to such movement. For example, the author Ayn Rand, who was born in Russia in 1902 and later moved to the United States, develops her theory of **objectivism** in books like *The Fountainhead* and *Atlas Shrugged*. Akin to libertarianism today, objectivism is built on the foundations of free market capitalism, limited government, and individual rights. In many ways, it is a direct response to the feared effects of communism, such as the abolition of private property and perhaps even the abolition of self.

John Rawls and *Justice as Fairness*

Perhaps one of the best known works of political theory in the twentieth century is John Rawls, whose work *A Theory of Justice* introduces his idea of justice as fairness.[15] Following in the liberal tradition of the Enlightenment, Rawls takes on the question of what is the best form of government and argues that the best type of society, or **basic state**, is one that enshrines the two principles of justice and fairness as their guiding values. For Rawls, the ideal society is one in which every person has the same equal basic liberties (the first principle of justice), and all positions are open to everyone under fair equality of opportunity and that all decisions should "be to the greatest benefit of the least-advantaged members of society (the difference principle)."[16] In both *A Theory of Justice* and his later *Justice as Fairness: A Restatement*, Rawls methodically traces the arguments for justice as fairness and outlines how such principles could be enacted.

Key to these ideas is the thought experiment Rawls develops called the **original position**. Much like the thought experiment of the state of nature that dates back to Hobbes and Locke, Rawls asks us to envision a situation wherein a number of representatives from society are all brought together and placed under what he calls the **veil of ignorance**. The veil of ignorance represents a limit on information these representatives can possess; they do not know who they represent or what position in society they themselves will have after the original position. They have a limited amount of information about their society and so must make decisions on what principles will guide their basic state in development and execution. Rawls argues that in such a situation, people will be motivated to make society as free and equal as possible since they do not know who they represent or even who they are out in the "real world." In this original position, the representatives will be given a list of possible principles around which their basic state can be structured. The representatives will then go through and select the principles they believe to be best suited for their situations. Of course, Rawls believes and argues that his two principles of justice will be the most appropriate for society and in *Justice as Fairness: A Restatement* lays out why this would be so.

While Rawls draws many of his ideas from traditional Enlightenment thought, he also includes some Marxist ideas such as the problems that class can play in making a society unequal and unfair. As such, he specifically lays out the difference principle that would require people and governments to make decisions with respect to the people whom Rawls identifies as the least advantaged, or the people who do not have the "various social conditions and all-purpose means that are generally necessary to enable citizens adequately to develop and fully exercise" their moral powers and conceptions of the good.[17] In the end, Rawls advocates that the only way to ensure a just society, a just government, is to make sure that everyone is not only treated fairly and equally but that everyone is fair and equal. Justice as fairness is really justice *is* fairness.

Know a Political Scientist

John Rawls

John Rawls's work has been quite influential in political theory and philosophy as well as in law and politics throughout the world. Rawls was born in 1921 and suffered dual tragedies in his childhood: Two of his brothers caught illnesses from Rawls and subsequently died. While an undergraduate at Princeton University, Rawls was often concerned with theology and religion. Following his graduation from Princeton in 1943, he enlisted in the US Army and was sent to fight in the Pacific, where he received the Bronze Star. His experiences in wartime caused a crisis of faith in Rawls; though he had been promoted, he refused an order to discipline a soldier, believing it to be unfair, and was demoted. He subsequently left the army in 1946 and returned to Princeton to work on his PhD.

Early in his career, Rawls taught at Cornell and MIT before joining the faculty at Harvard. There, he worked on his major work, *A Theory of Justice*, which was published in 1971. It was *A Theory of Justice* that laid out the basic principles that have been discussed in this chapter. He later went on to complete *Political Liberalism* (1993) and *The Law of the Peoples* (1999), which expanded his theory of fairness to the field of international relations. Rawls received the Schock Prize for Logic and Philosophy and the National Humanities Medal, which was awarded by then president Bill Clinton. At the awards ceremony, Clinton said this:

> John Rawls is perhaps the greatest political philosopher of the twentieth century.... Almost singlehandedly, John Rawls revived the disciplines of political and ethical philosophy with his argument that a society in which the most fortunate helped the least fortunate is not only a moral society but a logical one. Just as impressively, he has helped a whole generation of Americans revive their faith in democracy itself.[18]

After suffering several strokes in the late 1990s, John Rawls died in 2002.

Nozick's Response

As a means of ensuring such fairness, Rawls advocates for governments and decisions that are actively involved in ensuring that the background institutions of justice are followed and that decisions are made with regard to the benefit of the least advantaged. In a very real sense, such a government would be a very active one, one acting to ensure fairness and equality and making corrections if necessary. Three years after the release of *A Theory of Justice*, Robert Nozick published *Anarchy, State, and Utopia* wherein he argues against just such a government. For Nozick, the best type of government is the one that's the least developed and the least involved in individual affairs. Where they do agree, however, is on the importance of individual rights.

Nozick and his beliefs about anarchy and the possibility of anarchy do not come out of nowhere. The possibility of anarchy as a system of stateless and self-rule societies has a history dating back to the nineteenth century. Often associated with communist movements, there were strong anarchist leaders involved in many European conflicts in the early twentieth century. In America, anarchist philosophy played a strong role in the counterculture movement of the 1960s and 1970s.

Nozick proceeds in his analysis from the perspective of Locke and the state of nature. He acknowledges and claims that all individuals have a certain set of rights that exist independently of any institution, government, or social contract.[19] These natural, or moral, rights can never be infringed on or taken away. Nozick, then, is not asking the question of what kind of government protects these rights but if *any* government can protect these rights. Hence, as he suggests in the title, Nozick seriously considers the possibly of whether anarchy would better protect moral and natural rights than government would. In fact, Mack argues that "Nozick tells us that these rights may so extensively limit the permissible use of force that no room is left for a morally acceptable state."[20] If the existence of a social contract or a government itself violates natural rights, then none should exist.

This "individual anarchist" viewpoint is what Nozick sets out to disprove in *Anarchy, State, and Utopia*. Instead of an activist government of the sort recommended by Rawls, Nozick argues for what he calls a minimal state. The minimal state would be one that only acts to protect the individual rights of life, liberty, property, and contract. Nozick goes one step further than protecting individual rights but goes so far as to argue that when natural rights are curtailed for any reason, just compensation must be given to the individual or individuals whose rights have been curtailed.[21] Obviously, there is much more discussion and detail provided in Nozick's writings, but he provides the basis for a libertarian interpretation of the social contract wherein the best state is the smallest state with the smallest footprint possible.

One of Nozick's key natural rights is the right to contract. This means that individuals have the right and ability to fully enter into agreements with one another and have those agreements or contracts validated, supported, and enforced by the state. The term *contract* also references us back to the idea of a social contract that individuals freely enter into to create society. **Contractarianism** is a philosophy that argues that moral norms and political authority originate in contracts or agreements that we make with one another.[22] This doctrine deviates some from the traditional social contract theories of Hobbes and Locke in that contractarians are somewhat skeptical of the idea of natural rights or natural political authority. This is partly due to the inability of people to truly *know* where those rights originate and what those rights are. As such, contractarians argue that no rights exist until they are defined and laid out along with political structures and all people agree to them.

Social Contract Theory

Contractarian theory has led to two significant works examining modern social contracts and the influences in constructing them and their impact on politics today. First, Carole Pateman takes on sexual politics in *The Sexual Contract*.[23] In her book, Pateman argues that though it is never mentioned directly, "The sexual contract is a repressed dimension of contract theory" concerning "*patriarchal right* or sex-right, the power that men exercise over women."[24] Pateman, then, is arguing that in addition to a traditional social contract that lays out rights and the proper form of government for society, there is an implicit agreement in the original social contract that considers women as property to be owned by men. This has traditionally been a problem because when many of these social contracts were achieved (such as the one the United States entered into under the Constitution), women were not considered citizens and not afforded the same rights or privileges in ascribing to the social contract. This is continually perpetuated not only in the form of a social contract but in the marriage contract as well.

Pateman's work highlights the sexual inequalities that result from such a situation, including the comparison of wives to slaves and problems with the so-called marriage contract. It's not hard to see this dynamic at work in society today where women are still paid, on average, less than men and are still regarded as the primary keepers of house, home, and children. Pateman traces this situation back to the way in which the original social contract was structured. Pateman's solution is to end the silence over the law of male sex-right and bring to light the structural inequalities that have resulted from such an agreement.

> To retrieve the story of the sexual contract does not, in itself, provide a political programme or offer any short cuts in the hard task of deciding what, in any given circumstances, are the best course of action and policies for feminists to follow, or when and how feminists should form alliances with other political movements. Once the story has been told, however, a new perspective is available from which to assess political possibilities and to judge whether this path or that will aid or hinder (or both) the creation of a free society.[25]

In line with Pateman, Charles W. Mills takes on the racial aspect of contractarianism and the social contract. Like Pateman, Mills argues that included in the original social contract is an implicit acceptance of racism as a "political system, a particular power structure of formal or informal rule, socioeconomic privilege, and norms for the differential distribution of material wealth and opportunities, benefits and burdens, rights and duties."[26] Similarly, Mills argues that the social contract was made only between those people who "count," who are really people, which in his view eliminated an entire group of people from consideration. Not only does this allow for slavery to take place at the beginning of the American social contract but, Mills argues, the agreement has reached its tentacles into the politics of today.

> *White misunderstanding, misrepresentation, evasion, and self-deception on matters related to race* are among the most pervasive mental phenomena of the past few hundred years, a cognitive and moral economy psychically required for conquest, colonialization, and enslavement. And these phenomena are in no way *accidental*, but *prescribed* by the terms of *The Racial Contract*, which requires a certain schedule of structured blindnesses and opacities in order to establish and maintain the white polity.[27]

So what is the solution to a situation wherein a whole class of people are systematically derided and discriminated against? Again, like Pateman, Mills calls for a realization of the roots of the problem, for us to confront the situation we find ourselves in. In recognizing the problems, we can then understand just what it will take to solve them and point the way to the type of society we ultimately want to live in.

Multiculturalism

For both Pateman and Mills, the structure of the social contract and the underlying agreements about the status of blacks and women have influenced the world in which we live today. Our politicians look at both women and blacks in a particular way and attempt to impose policy based on those understandings. Fellow citizens look at one another through glasses colored by our societal understandings. But aren't there other groups for which we can say the same thing? Or what about groups that would like to maintain their group and social identity? How can they be integrated into the social contract? Are we all supposed to not only be treated the same but actually be the same? This is the subject that is taken up by Bhikhu Parekh in *Rethinking Multiculturalism*.[28] Parekh's issue with society today is the issue of forced assimilation, of forcing diverse cultural groups to give up their unique identities for the common good of society. In a sense, he is staking out a position on the social contract that identifies and appreciates differing groups, making them a part of the community without forcing them to give up their cultural and group heritage.

One aspect of this issue that Parekh identifies is that cultural subgroups may sometimes have ideologies or beliefs that do not easily mesh with the overarching beliefs of the society in which they live. A relevant example may be a Muslim community living in the United States who believe that women have a particular submissive role to play in society. While this does not equate with general principles in the United States today, that community nonetheless has a legitimate right to believe as they wish. Should they be forced to assimilate or give up their cultural heritage? Parekh argues that neither solution needs to be implemented; instead, the philosophy of multiculturalism directs us to create a society in which we can respect the practices and beliefs of different groups while maintaining a comprehensive and cohesive government for all. Indeed, Parekh goes above and beyond the conclusions of *The Sexual Contract* or *The Racial Contract* to actually outline and suggest approaches that could be adopted to encourage multiculturalism and to grease the wheels of government to allow that to happen. Suggestions such as teaching religion in schools, carving out special exceptions for religious organizations, and purposefully including such communities in political life are just some of the ways that Parekh suggests we can make our societies more multicultural.

The State of Political Theory Today

Three general comments can be made about what political theory looks like today. First, given the immense body of work that has only been partially outlined here, there is still so much work to be done considering what people have already written about political theory. This is one line of research that political theorists continue to pursue today: They engage and deconstruct the work of philosophers of this period and previous ones. For example, Saxonhouse engages with the texts of ancient Greece, including Plato's *Republic* and *Bacchae* from Euripedes to explore notions of the liberal argument of escaping from natural norms.[29] Herold examines Tocqueville's writings on religion and democracy in the context of the Enlightenment.[30] Herzog analyzes the economic writings of capitalist forefather Adam Smith and how his arguments might mesh with low or no growth in Western economies.[31] On issues like multiculturalism, Bejan identifies the ideas of evangelical toleration in the writings of Enlightenment thinkers like John Locke, recovering a liberal basis for what Parekh argues in his work on multiculturalism.[32]

A second line of research is expanding the ideas of philosophers to new areas and combining multiple approaches to highlight political problems. Lawrie Balfour combines racial and gender perspectives in examining the writing of Ida B. Wells, identifying strains of both feminism and racial thinking.[33] Bedi combines the approach of both Mills and Pateman in discussing issues of sexual racism.[34] Bedi argues that the very fact that people of particular ethnicities are less likely to be part of intimate relationships is itself a violation of the principle of justice. He writes, "Prioritizing individuals as romantic partners in a way that reinforces ideas of racial hierarchy or stereotypes is not just a private or moral wrong but an issue of social justice."[35] Ince attempts to better understand the character of modern capitalism through the works of both Karl Marx and Hannah Arendt.[36] International relations theorists are even attempting to expand some of these political theories to apply at the state level. In fact, Rawls himself explores in *A Theory of Justice* just such a prospect. All of these examples demonstrate the creative and philosophical project of bringing together multiple streams of thought to try and understand new dimensions of political thought.

Finally, there is confusion over where political theory belongs not just in political science but in academia at large. Since many of the works by political theorists seem to venture into notions of the good, should political theory be more properly aligned with philosophy? Within political science itself, political theory has been shunted to the side in a respect. Most major political science journals, while publishing work on political theory, tend to focus more heavily on the other subfields of political science. In many political science departments, political theory classes have been reduced or cut amid more and more students asking why they need to know this. There are no overarching conclusions to be made on this; even some political theorists believe that political theory classes belong with philosophy departments. However, political science and political scientists in general must realize that the roots of the discipline are deeply embedded in political theory and normative notions of the good and the just. To give just one example of how this plays a role in politics, when designing a new welfare policy, elected officials and policymakers will often try to consider not only what is fair and just but why the government should play a role in ensuring justice. The answers to these questions are not easily found anywhere, but political theory is a good place to begin looking for them.

As the saying goes, one of the two things you can definitely expect out of life is taxes. You likely pay some sort of tax almost every day whether it is a sales tax, the gas tax, a fee to register your car, or the payroll taxes that come out of your paycheck. Regardless of how much one pays, it almost always feels as if the amount of taxes we are paying is too high or unfair. But what is fair when it comes to taxes? Or in the words of John Rawls, what is just?

In large part, there are two major schemes of taxation: progressive taxes where the more you make, the more you pay and regressive taxes where the less you make, the more you pay. The income tax is an example of a progressive tax while the sales tax is a regressive example. The immediate question, then, is whether it is fair to make those who have less to pay more in the way of taxes? One argument to support such a contention is that those in the lower income brackets are more likely to need government benefits whether it's in the form of welfare, Medicaid, or federal grants or loans for higher education. If this is the group that is going to benefit the most from government actions, shouldn't they have to pay into the system? On the other hand, an argument for the progressive tax is that those who do not have much to start with should not be forced to pay more than those who make more money. They simply don't have as much to part ways with.

There are other means of determining whether a certain tax or mix of taxes is fair. The Urban-Brookings Tax Policy Center proposes three principles:

1. Equal justice or horizontal equity: Are people with equal ability to pay taxed equally?

2. Progressivity or vertical equity: Do those who are better off pay more tax than those who are less well off?

3. Individual equity: Are we entitled to keep the rewards of our own work? Is it unfair if we cannot?[37]

Critical Thinking Questions

1. Which tax system is more fair and just: a progressive income tax or a flat tax where everyone pays the same percentage of their income regardless of how much they make?

2. How well does a progressive income tax and a flat income tax meet the three principles of fairness put forward by the Tax Policy Center?

3. How well does each tax system meet Rawls's principles of justice?

CHAPTER SUMMARY

- Political theory has a long history. In ancient Greece, Plato was considering what made for a good government as well as a good society while Aristotle thought democracy would be an inappropriate form of government. As Christianity spread across Europe, several Christian thinkers including St. Augustine and St. Thomas Aquinas blended these early ideas with Christian ethics.

- The Enlightenment period led to a reconsideration of politics and political thinking. Hobbes and Locke introduced the notions of natural rights and social contract theory while other writers such as Rousseau and Kant expanded on these liberal ideas.

- Liberalism was not without its critics, including Karl Marx and his ideology of communism.

- Contemporary political thought has often returned to liberal notions of rights and social contract theory to consider ideas of justice and fairness in society.

- Political theorists today are often expanding upon these traditional ideas and expanding them in new and different ways to reflect an ever-changing society.

KEY TERMS

allegory of the cave: A story Plato utilizes to illustrate the nature of true knowledge and ignorance

basic state: A state that follows Rawls's two principles of justice: every person has the same equal basic liberties and all positions are open to everyone under fair equality of opportunity and that all decisions should "be to the greatest benefit of the least-advantaged members of society"

communism: Theory developed by Karl Marx and Fredrich Engels that argues that history is a series of conflicts between the proletariat and the bourgeoisie; eventually, the proletariat will overthrow the bourgeoisie and rid society of the causes of inequality

contractarianism: A philosophy that argues that moral norms and political authority originate in contracts or agreements that we make with one another

existentialism: Theory that philosophers had ignored what it meant to be a person in favor of categorization; need to focus on individuals rather than the state

just war: From St. Augustine, that war may be considered just if it is done to pursue peace and punish those who have done wrong

normative ideas: Ideas where there is no objective standards against which to measure the idea as being good or bad

objectivism: Political theory developed by Ayn Rand that focuses on free market capitalism, limited government, and individual rights

original position: In Rawls's *A Theory of Justice*, a time in which representatives of society are gathered together to consider the structure of their society and government

"philosopher kings": For Plato, enlightened rulers who would abide by reason and enlightenment in ruling over a society

Protestant Reformation: Movement started by Martin Luther in the sixteenth century that criticized the Catholic Church and led to a schism between Rome and the new sect of Protestants

utilitarianism: Theory put forward by Jeremy Bentham that what is right and wrong should be determined by what brings the most happiness or good to the most people

veil of ignorance: A limit to the information representatives would have in Rawls's original position; representatives would have no information about their future position or role in society

DISCUSSION QUESTIONS

1. What might be some ways in which you see early political philosophy reflected in politics and government today?

2. What role has the Christian religion had on the development of political theory?

3. What is the importance of the Enlightenment? What role has it had on the way we look at politics and government today?

4. How do people of today's generation view Marx and *The Communist Manifesto*? Why might this be the case?

5. Describe political theory in your own words. What is its purpose? Is it philosophy or politics?

FOR FURTHER READING

Mills, Charles, W. *The Racial Contract*. Ithaca, NY: Cornell University Press, 1997.

Nozick, Robert. *Anarchy, State, and Utopia*. New York: Basic Books, 1974.

Pateman, Carole. *The Sexual Contract*. Stanford, CA: Stanford University Press, 1988.

Rawls, John. *A Theory of Justice*. Cambridge, MA: Harvard University Press, 1971.

NOTES

1. Jonathan Wolff, "Analytic Political Philosophy," in *The Oxford Handbook of the History of Analytic Philosophy* (Oxford: Oxford University Press, 2013).

2. Melissa Lane, "Ancient Political Philosophy," in *The Stanford Encyclopedia of Philosophy*, ed. Edward N. Zalta, Summer 2017, https://plato.stanford.edu/entries/ancient-political/.

3. Ibid.

4. Peter Koritansky, "Thomas Aquinas: Political Philosophy," *Internet Encyclopedia of Philosophy*, www.iep.utm.edu/aqui-pol.

5. Jack Donnelly, "Natural Law and Right in Aquinas' Political Thought," *The Western Political Quarterly* 33, no. 4 (1980): 521.

6. Thomas Aquinas, *Summa Theologiae*, 91.2, www.newadvent.org/summa/2091.htm.

7. Donnelly, "Natural Law and Right in Aquinas's Political Thought," 521.

8. Thomas Aquinas, *Summa Theologiae*, 94.2, www.newadvent.org/summa/2094.htm

9. Donnelly, "Natural Law and Right in Aquinas's Political Thought," 521.

10. Michael Zuckert, "The Fullness of Being: Thomas Aquinas and the Modern Critique of Natural Law," *The Review of Politics* 69, no. 1 (2007): 28–47.

11. Koritansky, "Thomas Aquinas."

12. John Stuart Mill, *On Liberty* (London: Walter Scott Publishing, 1859), available at https://www.gutenberg.org/files/34901/34901-h/34901-h.htm.

13. Jonathan Wolff, "Karl Marx," in *The Stanford Encyclopedia of Philosophy*, ed. Edward N. Zalta, 2015, https://plato.stanford.edu/archives/win2015/entries/marx/.

14. Steven Crowell, "Existentialism," in *The Stanford Encyclopedia of Philosophy,* ed. Edward N. Zalta, 2017, https://plato.stanford.edu/archives/win2017/entries/existentialism/.

15. John Rawls, *A Theory of Justice* (Cambridge, MA: Harvard University Press, 1971).

16. Ibid., 42–43.

17. John Rawls, *Justice as Fairness: A Restatement* (Cambridge, MA: Belknap Press, 2001): 57.

18. Bill Clinton, "Remarks on Presenting the Arts and Humanities Awards," *Public Papers of the Presidents*, September 29, 1999, www.presidency.ucsb.edu/ws/?pid=56605.

19. Eric Mack, "Robert Nozick's Political Philosophy," *The Stanford Encyclopedia of Philosophy*, ed. Edward N. Zalta, 2015, https://plato.stanford.edu/archives/sum2015/entries/nozick-political/.

20. Ibid.

21. Robert Nozick, *Anarchy, State, and Utopia* (New York: Basic Books, 1974).

22. Ann Cudd, "Contractarianism," *The Stanford Encyclopedia of Philosophy*, ed. Edward N. Zalta, 2013, https://plato.stanford.edu/archives/win2013/entries/contractarianism/.

23. Carole Pateman, *The Sexual Contract* (Stanford, CA: Stanford University Press, 1988).

24. Ibid., ix, 1 (emphasis in the original).

25. Pateman, *The Sexual Contract,* 233.

26. Charles W. Mills, *The Racial Contract* (Ithaca, NY: Cornell University Press, 1997), 3.

27. Ibid.

28. Bhikhu Parekh, *Rethinking Multiculturalism: Cultural Diversity and Political Theory,* 2nd ed. (New York: Palgrave Macmillan, 2006).

29. Arlene Saxonhouse, "Freedom, Form, and Formlessness: Euripedes' *Bacchae* and Plato's *Republic*," *American Political Science Review* 108, no. 1 (2014): 88–99.

30. Aaron L. Herold, "Tocqueville on Religion, the Enlightenment, and the Democratic Soul," *American Political Science Review* 109, no. 3 (2015): 523–534.

31. Lisa Herzog, "The Normative Stakes of Economic Growth; Or Why Adam Smith Does Not Rely on 'Trickle Down,'" *The Journal of Politics* 78, no. 1 (2016): 50–62.

32. Teresa M. Bejan, "Evangelical Toleration," *The Journal of Politics* 77, no. 4 (2015): 1103–1114.

33. Lawrie Balfour, "Ida B. Well and 'Color Line Justice': Rethinking Reparations in Feminist Terms," *Perspectives on Politics* 13, no. 3 (2015): 680–696.

34. Sonu Bedi, "Sexual Racism: Intimacy as a Matter of Justice," *The Journal of Politics* 77, no. 4 (2015): 998–1011.

35. Ibid., 998.

36. Onur Ulas Ince, "Bringing the Economy Back In: Hannah Arendt, Karl Marx, and the Politics of Capitalism," *The Journal of Politics* 78, no. 2 (2016): 411–426.

37. Howard Gleckman, "Is the US Tax System Fair?" *Tax Policy Center,* May 3, 2012, www.taxpolicycenter.org/taxvox/us-tax-system-fair.

Institutions and Behavior

Philadelphia's State House witnessed the birth of both the Declaration of Independence and the Constitution.

Source: Bettmann/Getty Images

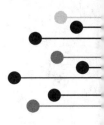

CHAPTER 4

Constitutions, Law, and Justice

When a group of representatives of the states met in Philadelphia in the summer of 1787, they made several key decisions as they began to consider revisions to the first constitution of the United States, the Articles of Confederation. First, they decided to keep all of their deliberations secret until the end, thereby freeing them from potentially damaging public opinion about what they were about to do. Second, they decided to scrap the Articles altogether instead of fulfilling their mission of amending them. As the Constitutional Convention took shape, the Framers took pains to create a document that would create a viable and functioning government while allowing room for the inevitable changes that time would surely bring. The result was a Constitution that specified a federal form of government with a presidential system of three branches that could check and balance each other's power. It is really quite an amazing feat that aside from the first ten amendments to the Constitution, the Bill of Rights, there have been only seventeen additional changes since the document took effect.

That is not to say that the Framers believed that this Constitution would be the last for the United States. Thomas Jefferson, although not a delegate at the Constitutional Convention, believed that there should be a constitutional convention every twenty years or so. In this way, each new generation would not only have a way of amending the Constitution but would also be able to participate in the act of consenting to be governed. Although Jefferson did not get his wish, the Constitution has essentially been updated as time has gone on through new interpretations of the Constitution that are occasioned by various court cases. For instance, the meaning of the Eighth Amendment's ban on "cruel and unusual punishment" is an example of how the Constitution has changed. In the late eighteenth

Chapter Objectives

1. Discuss the characteristics of constitutions, including their formality, vagueness, and ability to be amended.

2. Describe and compare systems of law, including English common law, civil code, and religious law.

3. Identify different types of law, such as constitutional, civil, and criminal.

4. Compare and contrast various definitions of justice and the role of judges in determining justice.

5. Define *judicial review*, and identify the purposes of judicial review in various types of governments.

century, hanging was certainly not considered cruel and unusual nor was the death penalty by firing squad. Today, neither of these execution methods would be deemed acceptable; in fact, lethal injection may someday be considered cruel and unusual.

There are problems, however, if the only updates to the Constitution come through the process of judicial review, to be discussed later in this chapter. If judges are making decisions about how to interpret the Constitution today, who's to say which judge's interpretation is correct—if any of them? How do we know when an interpretation needs to change or what it should be changed to? And, at least at the federal level, the judges who are making these decisions are unelected officials; how democratic is the process of changing the meaning of the Constitution when the people do not have a direct say?

To this end, there has been an increasing call for a new constitutional convention in the United States. One of the ways this would be accomplished is through the mechanisms provided by the Constitution itself: If two thirds of states call for a constitutional convention, one must be held to consider amendments. The legislatures of several states, including Florida, Georgia, and Tennessee, have taken the step of calling for a convention.[1] Several others have signed on to specific constitutional amendments, such as a balanced budget amendment, that they would like to see passed.[2] Although the prospects for a new constitutional convention are slim (the only way amendments have ever been added to the Constitution is through proposal by the Congress and approval by the states), constitution writers today would have a much more challenging time ahead of them. They likely would not be able to invoke a shield of secrecy in their deliberations, and the technical challenges would be far greater than those of the Constitutional Convention of 1787. Further, with the degree of political polarization that exists today, reasoned compromises and agreements would be far more difficult to attain.

While rewriting a constitution in the United States might not seem realistic, constitutions comprise an important part of every country's government, not only dictating the form of government the state will establish but laying out powers, duties, and responsibilities for the government and the governed. Newer countries have to engage in the writing of a constitution, and some are still being revised and rewritten. And while state constitutions might exist in some state of semipermanence, countries around the world are constantly engaged in lawmaking and law interpreting that are just as essential to states and citizens. Therefore, this chapter not only explores the characteristics of constitutions but also systems of law that exist and the judicial systems that serve to enforce and interpret.

Characteristics of Constitutions

Constitutions consist of basic ideas: the formal ways in which power will be distributed in a state, the relationship or relationships among those in power, and the special rules or procedures under which a government must operate. Not only does nearly every country have a constitution, but most businesses, organizations, and clubs have some sort of constitution or document organizing the entity. While constitutions can take many forms, there are some basic characteristics that most have.

Governments, Structure, and Power

First, constitutions specify what kind of government is to be established. Will it be a republic, a monarchy, a presidential system, a parliamentary system? Will it be a direct democracy or even a theocracy? Constitutions must lay out the ground rules for how a government is to operate. Once this has been specified, the document can then lay out other basic structures: Will the state be a unitary, federal, or confederal state? **Unitary states** are those in which the central government has almost all of the power with little to none reserved for lower-level governments such as cities and provinces. **Federal governments**, like the United States, split and share power between cities and states and the central, national government. Finally, **confederal states** are a loose alliance of states in which there is only a weak central government. The United States under the Articles of Confederation was a confederal state, and today's European Union can also be considered a confederation.

Detailing the structure of the government is important in writing a constitution, but so is the consideration of power structures and the distribution of power. This not only includes whether there will be separate branches, and if so, how many, but how much power each will have both individually and over the other. A distribution of power will also want to consider geography in deciding whether a state will be a federal or unitary one. Larger countries geographically may find it more difficult to have a unitary structure because of the time and distances that will separate outlying regions from a central authority. For example, Russia spans eleven different time zones and a wide swath of Asia; while the central government certainly has a fair amount of power, they are officially set up as a federal government.

As constitution writers consider the type of government they wish to establish, two things are also taken into account: the country's history and traditions. Establishing a government that is significantly different from what had previously been used or established will require a significant change among both leadership and citizens. For example, countries transitioning to democracy often find it difficult at first and sometimes even backslide into nondemocratic tendencies. Russia is just such a country. After the fall of the Soviet Union in 1991, the country rewrote its constitution to establish a democratic government. However, Russia had very little, if any, experience with democracy prior to the 1990s; before they were an authoritarian communist state, the country was ruled by an autocratic czar. While this does not make a democratic government impossible to establish, it did make it easier for authoritarian-like rulers like Vladimir Putin to establish power and take away many democratic features of the Russian government.

Specificity

Another idea constitution writers must think about is how specific they want to be in writing their constitution. Do you want a constitution that has many specific rules about the government and how power is distributed, or do you want a constitution that is perhaps more vague and open to interpretation? The US Constitution is one that is relatively short and vague; the Framers established the basic outlines of a government including the type of government and distribution of power, but other aspects were left intentionally vague or unknown. For example, Article 3, which establishes the judiciary, is very short and gives the Congress a lot of room to work with. It begins, "The judicial Power of the United States, shall be vested in one supreme Court, and in such inferior Courts as the Congress may from time to time ordain and establish." From this one clause, the Congress has designed and established a judicial system in the United States that consists of various districts, appeals courts, administrative law courts, and national security courts.

There are obviously pros and cons in considering how vague or how specific a constitution should be. The more specific a constitution is, the less room for interpretation there will be. For instance, what does the phrase "cruel and unusual" in the Eighth Amendment to the US Constitution mean? Further, there might be fewer questions about the types of power either the government or its citizens may have. There would also be fewer interpretations that people may claim to be authoritative. Vague portions of a constitution may lead to differing interpretations; who is to stay which one is the best or the one that accords the most with what the constitution says? On the other hand, if the constitution is designed to last for longer than a generation, constitution writers must consider how their country is likely to change. Will the specifics that they write in the constitution today be able to stand up to the situation of the country tomorrow? Or will the specificity lock future citizens into a government system that cannot be altered except in the most extreme circumstances?

Over time, constitutions appear to have gotten more specific, more formal, and therefore longer. Shively notes that the US Constitution, written in 1787, was originally 4,300 words long, whereas the German Basic Law, written in 1949, is approximately 19,700 words long.[3] More recently, the Iraqi constitution, approved in 2005, is approximately 11,400 words.

Guarantees of Rights

Another element that is often considered in constitution writing are guarantees of rights for citizens. One of the key elements of a democracy, according to a number of scholars, are citizen rights, also known as civil liberties. When the US Constitution was written in 1787, civil liberties, including those eventually enshrined in the Bill of Rights, were not included. Those who participated in the Constitutional Convention claimed they left guarantees of rights out for several reasons. One, the constitutions of the individual states already included civil liberties, including freedom of speech and religion. Two, some of the Framers were afraid that by listing out the specific rights that individuals had, later generations would believe that those were the *only* rights that citizens had— something which they did not intend. Finally, the writing of the Constitution itself had taken so long that most of the participants were just ready to go home.

In the debate over ratification of the Constitution, opponents argued that without a guarantee of rights, the federal government might be tempted to trample on civil liberties. As states held conventions to ratify the Constitution, one of the compromises that was agreed upon to satisfy these concerns was the addition of amendments that would establish limitations on government power. Once the federal government was established, one of the first things the Congress did was to propose several amendments—ten of which would be ratified by the states and make up the Bill of Rights. In other words, for some, the guarantee of civil liberties, which specifically says what the government cannot do and the rights that citizens fully retain, was and is an intrinsic part of limiting governmental power through a constitution.

Ease of Changes

That the Constitution was amended so quickly after its writing, highlights another element that constitution writers must consider: how and in what ways a constitution can be changed. Few people, and especially those involved in the mechanics of writing a constitution, would believe that their work is infallible, perfect, and therefore should not be changed. The ability to amend a constitution, then, is a significant part of a constitution. Constitution writers must consider the mechanisms through which amendments can be both proposed and approved; depending on the government type and features set out by a constitution, amendments could be added in a number of ways. In the United States, amendments can be proposed by the Congress and ratified by a three-fourths vote of the states; however, that is not the only way amendments can be added. Amendments can also be proposed when two thirds of states call for a convention to propose amendments and ratified by three fourths of the states or by state conventions called for the specific purpose of ratifying a constitutional amendment. Of course, formal amendment processes may look quite different than this. Proposals may come from the executive or even the judiciary in some states; in other states, a vote in the legislature may be all that is required.

Formal amendments are not the only way in which constitutions may be changed and adapted. Constitutions with vague or unclear provisions may be subject to differing interpretations over time. Courts, or other institutions charged with interpreting a constitution, may decide to change the meaning of different provisions or even change how they are applied. One way we can see this is in the application of the Fourth Amendment's protection from illegal search and seizure. The Fourth Amendment to the US Constitution states the following:

> The right of the people to be secure in their persons, houses, papers, and effects, against unreasonable searches and seizures, shall not be violated, and no Warrants shall issue, but upon probable cause, supported by Oath or affirmation, and particularly describing the place to be searched, and the persons or things to be seized.

When this was written, the Internet, cell phones, and electronics could hardly have been envisioned by the Framers. However, over time, courts have taken the Fourth Amendment and applied it to electronic data as well as "houses, papers, and effects."

Systems of Law

Laws, in whatever form they come, are some of the most fundamental requirements of society. Legal systems are laid out in the Old Testament with the Ten
Commandments comprising one of the oldest systems of law. Hammurabi's Code
is similarly ancient, dating back to approximately 1700 BCE. In the ancient East,
Confucianism provided not just a religious code but a legal code as well—one that
would be used throughout China for centuries. While these early legal systems were
based on religious ideas and principles, as the Western world developed through
the Middle Ages and especially in the Enlightenment, nonreligious systems of law
began to develop. This section describes several types of law as well as legal codes
that provide a basis for modern judicial systems.

Constitutional Law

A constitution, no matter how detailed or well designed it is, is merely a foundation
onto which other layers of policy decisions, laws, and precedents will be placed.
While it is certainly a foundation, a constitution also provides a higher level of law,
something we would call **constitutional law**. Those interested or concerned with
constitutional law examine the roles and powers of institutions as laid out by the
constitution as well as the interpretation and application of a constitution. This is
particularly important in countries whose constitutions can be somewhat vague and
therefore whose meanings and applications can change over time. Constitutional law
can be very influential as government institutions seek to expand their power or take
certain actions that might not be clearly defined in the Constitution. For example,
one of the major criticisms of 2010's Patient Protection and Affordable Care Act was
that it was unconstitutional; what in the Constitution gives the federal government
the power to tell a citizen that they *have* to do something, something like buy health
insurance? There are plenty of instances where the Constitution says what the government *cannot* do, but where does it say what it can legitimately force us to do? The
federal government put forward two major arguments about how they derive their
power to support the Affordable Care Act: one referenced the commerce clause,
which gives the federal government the power to regulate all interstate commerce,
and the second referred to the Sixteenth Amendment, which gives the federal government the power to tax. While the Supreme Court rejected the commerce clause
argument, it did find merit in the Sixteenth Amendment argument and thus upheld
the Affordable Care Act as a constitutional act.

Statutory and Administrative Law

While constitutional law and arguments over the meaning and interpretation of constitutions often consume talking heads in the media, there are two other types of
law that can be just as consequential in carrying out the everyday duties of a government. The first is statutory law. **Statutory law** is law derived from legislative acts

known as statutes. The key difference between statutory law and other types of law is that statutory law must be passed by a legislative body. Statutory laws generally define what is allowed and not allowed under the law and prescribe particular penalties for breaking that law, which courts can then adjudicate.

Another type of related law is often called **administrative law**. When a legislature passes a bill such as the Affordable Care Act, many provisions are often left vague; after the law is passed, it falls to government bureaucracies to add specifics to the law in order to put it into practice. Bureaucracies will then write a series of regulations that serve to implement laws that have been passed; these regulations make up administrative law. While it might at first appear that bureaucracies would have significant leeway to write regulations how they please, bureaucracies are typically limited either through the procedures that they must use to write and finalize regulations or through administrative law courts. For example, American bureaucracies, before a regulation is finalized, must create a detailed record supporting the regulation and go through several phases involving public comment. Even then, people can challenge a bureaucracy's interpretation of a law in an administrative law court where an administrative law judge will determine whether the bureaucracy acted within the scope of the power granted them by the legislature.

Although administrative law may appear technical and boring, governmental regulations and administrative law affect nearly every part of our lives. In the United States, the Environmental Protection Agency (EPA) writes regulations that protect the air we breathe and the water we drink, the Occupational Safety and Health Administration writes regulations so that employees are provided sufficient protections in the workplace, and the Food and Drug Administration oversees the process through which prescription medications are approved and regulated.

Career Guidance

If you are considering being a lawyer, be aware that lawyers can specialize in many different areas of the law, including constitutional, criminal, civil, labor, family, contracts, etc. When you are considering where to go to law school, also consider what type of law you may be interested in; different schools specialize in different types of law.

Case Law

A final type of law is what is often called **case law**. An important principle at work in case law is that of **stare decisis**, which is Latin for "to stand by things decided." Stare decisis means that decisions judges have made previously, called precedents, should continue to be followed by later judges. Therefore, case law is the body of precedents that have been built up over the years through judicial rulings and interpretations. Case law can be an important part of stabilizing a judicial system; if judges based their decisions on their own interpretations every time a new case came before them, there would be little certainty in how judges might rule. It would then be difficult for citizens to know how a law is being interpreted or applied. One judge in one part of the country may impose a stiffer penalty on someone for breaking a law than another judge somewhere else all because of differing interpretations of the law.

This does not mean that case law never changes; it certainly does. In his confirmation hearings for the Supreme Court in 2005, current Supreme Court chief justice John Roberts was asked about stare decisis and precedent and noted this:

> The principles of stare decisis look at a number of factors, settled expectations one of them... whether or not particular precedents have proven to be unworkable is another consideration. On the other side, whether the doctrinal bases of the decision have been eroded by subsequent developments. For example, if you have a case in which there are three precedents that lead and support that result and in the intervening period, two of them have been overruled, that may be a basis for reconsidering the prior precedent.[4]

In other words, if times have changed and previous precedents have been overruled for various reasons, judges may be justified in overturning precedent and going against the principle of stare decisis. Therefore, while case law helps keep the judicial rulings and interpretations somewhat consistent, it does not by any means mean that they cannot change due to other circumstances.

English Common Law

The common law system originated in England (later called the United Kingdom) in the late medieval and early modern periods.[5] Similar to the idea that the British constitution consists of a body of tradition, law, and decision, **common law** consisted of judge-made law that was developed by the courts, not the parliament or the king.[6] Though the parliament could pass new laws and thereby change the courts' decisions, it was accepted that the judiciary was something that existed independently of the government and could and should be involved in deciding law. Therefore, the basis of English common law was really case law or the body of decisions and precedents defined by judges.

Of course, judges could not just rule based on whim; they were expected to base their decisions on statute, precedent, and equity. Winfield notes that "its [common law] rules could be modified where they were harsh, and extended where they were defective, by 'equity.'"[7] That is, judges could essentially rule in ways that were considered equitable with the principle of equity overriding the previous decisions of common law.[8] Winfield continues, "Equity mitigates the rigor of law, where the words of the law are against justice and the commonwealth."[9]

Given the importance of the job that judges held in the English common law system, it was also expected that judges and lawyers would be specially trained not just in the university but under the tutelage of other lawyers. Judges were also expected to remain neutral arbiters in their cases, ruling on behalf of the law. Additionally, over time, certain legal protections were developed to further protect defendants in cases. This includes the idea that defendants should be considered innocent until proven guilty and the writ of habeas corpus, which means that individuals cannot and should not be jailed unless there is evidence that a crime has been committed.

Since the United States started out as a series of English colonies, it was only natural that common law would be adopted in the colonies and later on in the states. When the Constitution was ratified, it did not take away from this notion of common law but instead added to it a layer of constitutional law. Further, the Constitution permanently enshrined several rights of the accused that were developed in the common law courts.

Continental Law

Unlike English tradition and custom, laws developed somewhat differently in continental Europe. Where the English saw the courts as a somewhat separate institution of government that could be used to temper and limit the power of the monarchy, codified civil law was used as an expression of state power and limited the amount of discretion judges had. The key distinguishing characteristic between common law and civil or **continental law** is the fact that civil law is formally codified and known to all; specific crimes are described along with their punishments. Rather than relying on judicial precedent, judges would rely on the civil code law to render judgments.

The civil law developed in Europe out of the remains of the Roman law, which was formally codified by the emperor Justinian.[10] Further, the Catholic Church had developed a system of canon law, or church law, that related to the procedures and policies of the Church. Centuries later, various countries throughout Europe, including Italy and France, developed similar legal codes. The civil law "offered a store of legal principles and rules invested with the authority of ancient Rome and centuries of distinguished jurists, and it held out the possibility of a comprehensive legal code providing substantive and procedural law for all situations."[11] As a result, courts and judges were not seen as above the state but a part of the state, carrying out government policy as dictated by the code.

In France, Napoleon undertook an extensive effort to codify French law, which resulted in the Napoleonic Code issued in 1804. Napoleon's civil law not only took many of its cues from Justinian's Roman code but sought to include principles of the French Revolution. The resulting code took effect not just in France but in French colonies and territories including Louisiana. When Thomas Jefferson purchased the Louisiana Territory from France, the resulting state of Louisiana actually kept to the idea of civil law. As a result, Louisiana's court and judicial systems are still based on civil law today although certain principles derived from English common law and the US Constitution are integrated in it. Additionally, California, which had Spanish influence, has a civil code that contains principles of common law but is written in a way that reflects Roman civil law categories relating to persons, things, and actions.[12]

Religious Law

As mentioned at the beginning of this section, some of the oldest systems of law are rooted in religious practice. While most would be familiar with the contents of the Ten Commandments, the Old Testament contains a number of other laws and practices that the Jewish people were expected to observe. Even more so than the Jewish law developed in the Torah (the first five books of the Old Testament), Islamic law, known as **sharia**, represents the most formal codification of religious law. Part of the reasoning for the *sharia* is that Islam rejects the Christian notion of separation of church and state; *sharia*, as it was developed, was designed to include both religious and governmental aspects of the law, including crimes and their requisite punishment.

Before delving into *sharia* in a bit more detail, we can see how religious and secular laws often interact in the case of marriage and divorce. Historically, marriage and divorce law were determined and enforced not by the state but by various religious entities. In order for a couple to be considered married, the act had to be endorsed by the church, the rabbi, or other religious leader. Similarly, divorces were or were not allowed based on religious custom; even King Henry VIII of England was denied a divorce from his first wife because the Catholic Church does not recognize divorce. Since that early modern period, however, marriage and divorce has transitioned from a domain governed by religious law to one that is governed by secular law. Today, in most states, what makes a couple married is not necessarily a religious ceremony but the marriage license that is issued by the government. This does not mean, however, that religious law has not influenced secular law in this issue; Ireland, a predominantly Catholic country, prohibited divorce in its constitution until an amendment was passed in 1995 that finally allowed for it. While marriage and divorce are but one aspect of religious law whose influence we can see in secular law today, *sharia* law provides a far more comprehensive guide, consolidating both the government and religion.

Sharia was not something that was necessarily envisioned by the founder of the Islamic religion, the prophet Mohammed. Rather, "Since the Prophet Mohammed was considered the most pious of all believers, his life and ways became a model for all other Muslims and were collected by scholars into what is known as the *hadith*."[13] Combined with the Quran and local traditions, *sharia* law was developed by different communities throughout the Muslim world. For example, the two main branches of Islam, Shia and Sunni, while differing in who they believe should lead after the death of the prophet Mohammed, also differ on the weight that should be given to the hadith and other Muslim traditions. Shia Islam believe that "the true Sharia consists only of the Quran and the traditions and sayings of Prophet Mohammed. Sunni Islam... sees the *Sharia* as broader and somewhat more flexible" and can include the hadith and other interpretations of Mohammed's teachings.[14] Even beyond these two sects, different Muslim communities have adapted *sharia* based on their own historical teachings and traditions, thus making exactly what *sharia* contains difficult to nail down.

Sharia contains laws regarding both marriage and divorce and criminal acts. The *sharia* divides criminal behavior into three categories: those acts for which the Quran provides a specific punishment, those acts in which judges have discretion, and those acts that are punished through a tit-for-tat measure.[15] And while the punishments prescribed by the Quran can be quite harsh (flogging, stoning, amputation, execution), there are only five crimes to which they are applied, and in most states that incorporate *sharia* law, lesser penalties are acceptable. However, the public attention given to those situations where these punishments are inflicted or women are discriminated against is usually great and can strongly influence overall judgment about the appropriateness of *sharia*. Finally, these punishments are most often inflicted by terrorist groups seeking to purge Islam of what they see as impure influences and thus brings even greater attention to *sharia*.[16] It is important to note, though, that other religious codes, including Judaism, have similarly tough penalties.

Perhaps one of the most discussed aspects of *sharia* law has to do with its treatment of women. In stricter forms of *sharia*, women lack many legal rights, including participation in government or even in the financial system. Women can be required to follow Islamic dress codes and perhaps even be mandated to wear a veil. Women can be restricted in terms of their mobility, requiring men to give permission for women to travel. In Saudi Arabia, for example, women are not allowed to drive—although that provision is being considered for repeal. Aside from concerns about how these provisions limit equality and rights for women, they can also be detrimental economically; by banning half of a population from participating in the economic sphere, a significant amount of economic potential is being kept to the side.

While *sharia* is widely used in Iran and Saudi Arabia, other countries incorporate it to a greater or lesser extent. Some Muslim-majority countries have adopted completely secular (nonreligious) constitutions and law—for example, Turkey. Others have a dual legal system in which the government is secular, but some disputes, primarily family and financial, can be brought to *sharia* courts. Whether and to what extent *sharia* is used in a country, however, is often overshadowed by the critiques that have been brought about it in terms of women and the criminal code.

The Court System

At the heart of any type of law or system of law is a desire to create a just society—one that provides rights and protections for its citizens and punishments for when laws are broken. But what is just? What is the right punishment? And who are the people making these decisions? Throughout this chapter, we've made reference to courts, judges, and even implicitly justice, but just what do those ideas mean? This section examines in a bit more detail the institutions of the court, justice, and the way in which courts utilize their power to review and advance law.

Judicial Independence

Throughout the world, courts and judges are a vital part of governmental systems of all types. Two ways we can look at courts include how they are structured and how much independence is given to them. To begin with the second aspect, it is important to understand how insulated from the political process courts and judges (the terms can be used interchangeably) are. Too closely tied to the political organs of government and there could be accusations of bias in favor of the government. If judges are selected (or even elected) by the people, they may temper their decisions to the whims of the crowd. On the other hand, without some accountability, whether it's to a political process or the citizenry, judges may be tempted to assert too much power or go too far in interpreting and applying the law. Thus, "the institutional arrangements governing the selection and retention of... judges frequently reflect contradictory strains... in political thought concerning the role of courts."[17]

In the United States, at the federal level, judges are appointed by the president and approved by the Senate before serving lifetime terms. While some certainly criticize the long-term lengths for judges, their life tenure is expected to provide some distance from politics so that judges will be able to interpret and rule based on the law and not appeasing some political master. Critics, however, argue that the lack of accountability over time can lead to activist judges who pursue their own desired policy goals rather than the fulfillment of justice. By means of comparison, in many states in the United States, judges are elected by the citizens. This can lead to the strange situation of judges altering their decisions based on their electoral cycle; some research has found that judges who are up for reelection tend to make harsher rulings in the months prior to the election. Additionally, the need to raise campaign funds can lead to a situation where judges are asking lawyers who might appear before them in the courtroom for donations. As a result of these pitfalls, some states utilize merit-based systems wherein judges are appointed from a list that has been approved by the state bar or judicial qualifications committee; at a certain interval of years following that, judges go up for a retention election, which asks voters if they wish to retain that judge.

The United Kingdom has changed its method of judicial appointments fairly recently. Prior to 2006, judges were appointed solely by the lord chancellor, one of the oldest positions in British government. The lord chancellor was appointed by the monarch on the advice of the prime minister and was expected to head the judicial branch. Under the Constitutional Reform Act 2005, the job of appointing judges was given to a Judicial Appointments Commission with the goals of diversifying the judiciary and removing the appointment power from a single individual. Further, overall responsibility for the courts was shifted from the lord chancellor to the lord chief justice and a Judicial Executive Board, thereby reinforcing the judiciary's independence from the government.

In addition to the degree of independence or insularity from politics and government, we can also examine the structure of various court systems. Two ways in which courts are often organized are by topic and by function. In terms of topic, there may be different courts to deal with the different varieties of law; for example, one set of courts may deal only with civil law, one only with criminal law, and one only with constitutional law. In the United States, this is often broken down even further into family law courts, drug courts, youth courts, or even juvenile courts. In federal states like the United States or Germany, courts can exist at a variety of levels from county courts to state courts to federal courts with each one enforcing the laws of their own jurisdiction.

Courts can also be organized via their function or jurisdiction. For instance, lower courts (also variously called trial courts or courts of first instance) handle cases directly. They try cases, hear witnesses, declare guilt or innocence. While this would appear to contain the bulk of judicial work, in many states, citizens have the right to appeal rulings based on legal uncertainties or questions. When cases are appealed, they would typically go to an appeals court that specializes in hearing appeals from the lower courts. Trials are not typically conducted here; rather, a judge or panel of judges considers procedural questions in the case that went before the lower court. Finally, in some states, there is a supreme court or court of last resort that also serves an appellate function but above which there is no further recourse. Sometimes these supreme courts will also deal with questions about constitutional issues, whereas in other states there may be a completely separate constitutional court that handles constitutional disputes and undertakes judicial review.

Based only on this brief discussion, it is clear that the organization of courts can significantly vary across countries with many options for states to choose from when setting up the courts. While much of it typically depends on the system of law, the type of government, and beliefs about judicial independence and accountability, states can still avail themselves of a number of options when designing their judicial systems.

Justice

Courts and justices are intricately involved in the determination of justice. What does justice mean? What does it entail? What does it require? There are various conceptualizations of justice that we will consider, but at their heart, the idea of justice means that people receive the treatment they deserve. Obviously, the application of justice extends far beyond the courtroom. We can ask whether a certain governmental policy is just; is it just that tax revenue is redistributed to those who do not have a high income? Is it just to take money away from some to give it to some other? Is it just to restrict people from using certain drugs? For instance, if a drug is being developed and tested in clinical trials and it might possibly save someone's life, is it just that it be withheld from that person because some government agency has not approved it yet?

Philosophers have debated the notion of justice since ancient Greece and Rome. Plato, concerned with the apparent deterioration of Athenian society, determined that justice involved fulfilling the duties of your place in life and not interfering in the duties of others. Justice is therefore a social idea, an order, that keeps society in good working order.[18] Some mid-twentieth century philosophers, however, returned to this conception of justice to argue that Plato's justice actually supports the tenants of a totalitarian state in which what is good for individuals is what is good for the state.[19] Recall from Chapter 3 our discussion of John Rawls and his take on justice; Rawls argues that justice is fairness. The only way to ensure justice is to ensure that everyone is both treated fairly and equally but that everyone *is* fair and equal. To this end, governments should act in such ways that consider the needs of the least advantaged, providing resources to them in such a way that fairness is ensured.

While questions regarding the fairness or justness of a particular government policy or position can be political issues, what is important here for our discussion of the law and the courts is that judges are often key actors in determining what is just, what is fair, or what people deserve. To consider this further, we can discuss several particular types of justice: substantive, procedural, and retributive.

Substantive vs. Procedural Justice

Substantive justice involves questions of people getting what they deserve. Substantive laws are those that specify a crime or infraction and prescribe a specific penalty. For instance, laws regarding speeding that specify the fine that a driver should pay for going a certain speed above the speed limit are substantive laws. You are expected to know the law, and if you break it, you receive the penalty that is deserved.

While substantive justice seems simple on its face, what if the procedures used to determine the law in the first place were unfair? For instance, what if a certain element of the population was excluded from the legislative decision making? What if a law was designed to punish a certain group of people? What if different types of people are treated differently by the law? Those laws could hardly be said to be fair or just. **Procedural justice** focuses on the processes and procedures through which laws are made as well as the processes and procedures under which penalties are determined. In many ways, Rawls's argument regarding justice as fairness is a procedural one; people should be treated fairly and equally through institutions that are also created to ensure fairness. If the laws are not only designed in such a way as to promote justice but the institutions that create them are just, then the laws should be just as well.

Procedural justice can also be secured through the provision of special rights to citizens. For example, the Fifth Amendment to the US Constitution provides that citizens cannot be "deprived of life, liberty, or property, without due process of law." This principle is further expanded in the Fourteenth Amendment, which states that states must provide due process as well as "equal protection of the laws." Due process is the idea that every citizen is afforded the same procedures in court as everyone else; the same processes and standards must be used in every case and given to every citizen to avoid the problem of arbitrary decision making. Procedural justice, then, is ensured through the provision of due process and equal protection, providing another layer to a court system to ensure that everyone is treated justly and fairly.

Retributive Justice

Every court system has aspects of substantive and procedural justice worked into their fabric. There are some substantive laws that provide penalties for specific crimes. Every person is afforded the same rights and procedures. But still there are places where judges are granted broad discretionary authority not only to interpret law but to determine just punishment. It is in this case where the idea of **retributive justice** plays a role. Retributive justice is based on three elements:

1. Those who commit certain kinds of wrongful acts deserve to be punished proportionally to their crime.

2. It is morally good for a certain legitimate person to inflict the punishment on the individual.

3. It is morally wrong to punish the innocent or inflict harm out of proportion with the crime committed.[20]

In other words, retributive justice calls for punishments that fit the crime to be determined by some legitimate individual with the authority to decide, in this case, a judge.

There are a number of factors to consider when determining whether a punishment fits the crime; in court, these are called mitigating factors. Was the defendant of sound mind and body when they committed the crime? Was there some sort of extenuating circumstance that forced them to break the law? Was it their first offense? Their fifth? Did they utilize a deadly weapon? Judges are expected to consider both the law and mitigating factors in determining the appropriate punishment in each case.

In the United States over the past several decades, there was a push to enforce mandatory minimums or minimum sentences for offenders depending on the crime with no room for a judge's discretion. While mandatory minimums would certainly meet standards of substantive justice, they might not necessarily meet the standard of retributive justice. For instance, if a first-time offender is found with more than a certain level of cocaine on their person and is therefore considered a drug trafficker, is it just to sentence them to a mandatory jail term of a certain number of years? Many critics of mandatory minimums argue that in taking away a judge's discretion in sentencing, more people are ending up in jail and for longer terms than may otherwise occur.

Judicial Review

In addition to providing for justice and the enforcement of laws, a final element that some courts engage in is judicial review. **Judicial review** is the ability of courts and judges to overturn the decisions of other branches of government if they violate a country's constitution. For example, if a legislature passes a law that violates a constitutional principle, judicial review allows for a court to strike the law down. Similarly, if an action of the executive branch violates either law or the constitution, those actions can be reversed.

Judicial review is another means of checking and balancing government power. First, if there is a separate executive branch, there may be times in which the executive and the legislature conflict in how laws or the constitution should be interpreted or the amount of power each branch has. Courts utilizing judicial review can then step in to settle the disputes and provide an authoritative interpretation of law or the constitution. However, even if both the executive and legislative branches agree on a particular law, there is still a chance that the law may violate certain aspects of the constitution. Thus, another purpose of judicial review is to step in and restrain the other two branches from taking actions that may violate constitutional principles.

Judicial review can be organized in different ways depending on country. In the United States, federal courts have the power of judicial review up to and including the Supreme Court, which has the ultimate authority to interpret the Constitution. This may be especially important if different federal courts have interpreted the same part of the Constitution differently; the Supreme Court can step in and provide one ruling. While the US Supreme Court reviews constitutional, civil, and criminal cases, other countries may have a constitutional court whose sole purpose is to resolve disputes and rule on constitutionality. For example, in Germany, the Federal Constitutional Court can be asked to rule on the constitutionality of a law before or after it is passed. Some constitutional courts can even propose amendments to a country's constitution or must approve of constitutional amendments before they are considered further.

CASE STUDY
International Law and Courts

As globalization has quickened and states have more and more interaction with one another, there has been a movement to develop international norms of behavior that countries could or should be expected to adhere to. The concept of international law is not new; maritime law, which has to do with conflicts on the seas, has existed in some form for several centuries. Similarly, rules and laws regarding warfare developed over several centuries, eventually leading to the creation of the Geneva Convention. However, it is exceedingly difficult to design laws to which most or all countries can agree to, especially if there is no authority to oversee and enforce them. Additionally, most countries do not want an international authority with the ability to enforce international law because that would require them to give up an element of their own sovereignty, or a state's ability to control its own territory.

Following World War II, further efforts have been made to establish at least the outlines of international law, especially in the form of treaties under the auspices of the United Nations. For example, the United Nations developed the Universal Declaration of Human Rights (UDHR) in 1948 with the goal of creating a universal set of human rights that should apply globally. Enforcement of these human rights is difficult, though, because some countries culturally disagree with the stated rights (including equal rights for women) and because the treaty that established the United Nations itself recognizes state sovereignty and pledges that the United Nations will not involve itself in the actions of states within their own territories.

Part of the UN Charter did establish a court—the International Court of Justice (ICJ). The ICJ does not enforce international law or prosecute violations of it. Instead, it acts as a court of arbitration in which member states to the United Nations can choose to have disputes settled, and it can provide interpretations to UN bodies of applicable treaties. The ICJ is comprised of fifteen judges elected by the UN General Assembly and UN Security Council, who each serve nine-year terms. Because the ICJ only mediates disputes, an effort was made in the 1990s to establish an international tribunal that could try international criminal cases; the result was the Rome Statute, which established the International Criminal Court (ICC) in 2002 (the treaty was signed in 1998). The ICC can prosecute crimes related to genocide, crimes against humanity, and war crimes. However, one significant drawback is that not all states have agreed to the Rome Statute and thus refuse to recognize the ICC, including the United States. This has not stopped the ICC from prosecuting several cases related to genocide and war crimes.

While international law is certainly developing, the two hurdles noted previously—the ability of a majority of states to agree to particular principles and the unwillingness of states to give up their sovereignty—often preclude more comprehensive treaties and agreements. This does not mean the situation is impossible, however. The development of the European Union has meant that EU states have given up individual power in many economic areas including monetary policy. Further, the European Union itself has established a judicial system, the Court of Justice of the European Union. Thus, it may be possible for regional systems of law and regional courts to develop as a precursor to a larger international system.

Critical Thinking Questions

1. Given the different systems of law described in this chapter, do you believe it is possible to develop one system of international law?

2. What kinds of characteristics do you believe an international system of law should have?

3. What are some things that often prevent states from participating in international law and courts?

STUDENT STUDY SITE

Visit https://edge.sagepub.com/whitmancobb

CHAPTER SUMMARY

- Constitutions are fundamental documents that outline the government and power structures of a state. Constitutions often contain guarantees of rights for citizens, and writers must consider characteristics such as the possibility for amendments and specificity as they write their constitution.

- Historically, different systems of law have developed, including common law, the civil code, and religious law. Within each of

these systems exist types of law, including constitutional, statutory, and case law.

- Courts and judges have varying types of power to make independent determinations of law and justice. Depending on the state, judges may have more or less independence from the governing structures. Further, judges have significant power to determine penalties and constitutionality of laws.

KEY TERMS

administrative law: Regulations that serve to implement laws that have been passed

case law: The body of precedents that have been built up over the years through judicial rulings and interpretations

common law: Judge-made law that was developed by the courts

confederal states: Loose alliance of states in which there is only a weak central government

constitutional law: Type of law that examines the roles and powers of institutions as laid out by the constitution as well as the interpretation and application of a constitution

constitutions: Formal documents outlining governing structures, power arrangements, and basic operating procedures

continental law: Formally codified laws wherein specific crimes are described along with their punishments

federal governments: Types of government where power is split and shared between cities and states and the central, national government

judicial review: The ability of courts and judges to overturn the decisions of other branches of government if they violate a country's constitution

procedural justice: Focuses on the processes and procedures through which laws are made as well as the processes and procedures under which penalties are determined

retributive justice: Calls for punishments that fit the crime to be determined by a judge

sharia: Islamic religious law

stare decisis: The principle that precedents should continue to be followed by later judges

statutory law: Law derived from legislative acts known as statutes

substantive justice: A philosophy about justice in which the defendant is given the punishment they deserve

unitary states: Governments in which the central government has almost all of the power with little to none reserved for lower-level governments, such as cities and provinces

DISCUSSION QUESTIONS

1. What are the benefits of having a constitution that is somewhat vague?

2. How do the various systems of law (common law, civil code, religious law) promote the different types of justice (substantive, procedural, retributive)? For instance, does one system of law promote substantive justice more than the others? Procedural?

3. How can constitutions be used to further notions of justice?

4. How independent should judges and courts be from the political process?

FOR FURTHER READING

American Bar Association: www.americanbar.org

International Court of Justice (ICJ): www.icj-cij.org/en

NOTES

1. Chas Sisk, "Rewrite the Constitution? Several States Are Trying To," *NPR*, Feb. 4, 2016, https://www.npr.org/2016/02/04/465593798/rewrite-the-constitution-several-states-are-trying-to.

2. David Scharfenburg, "Time to Rewrite the Constitution?" *Boston Globe*, Oct. 6, 2017, https://www.bostonglobe.com/ideas/2017/10/06/time-rewrite-constitution/Pcad5XvcYwBatcCz2UUKNP/story.html.

3. W. Phillips Shively, *Power and Choice: An Introduction to Political Science*, 14th ed. (New York: McGraw-Hill, 2014), 206.

4. "John Roberts: Supreme Court Nomination Hearings from *PBS NewsHour* and EMK Institute," YouTube, June 25, 2010, https://www.youtube.com/watch?v=PNF_pwkP6gg.

5. Shively, *Power and Choice,* 376–377.

6. Munroe Smith, "State Statute and Common Law," *Political Science Quarterly* 2, no. 1 (1887): 105.

7. Percy H. Winfield, "Public Policy in the English Common Law," *Harvard Law Review* 42, no. 1 (1928): 77.

8. Smith, "State Statute and Common Law," 106.

9. Winfield, "Public Policy in the English Common Law," 78.

10. "The Common Law and Civil Law Traditions," School of Law, University of California at Berkeley, https://www.law.berkeley.edu/library/robbins/CommonLawCivilLawTraditions.html.

11. "The Common Law and Civil Law Traditions," 2.

12. "The Common Law and Civil Law Traditions," 4.

13. Toni Johnson and Mohammed Aly Sergie, "Islam: Governing under Sharia," *Council on Foreign Relations*, July 25, 2014, https://www.cfr.org/backgrounder/islam-governing-under-sharia.

14. Shively, *Power and Choice,* 382.

15. Johnson and Sergie, "Islam: Governing under Sharia."

16. Johnson and Sergie, "Islam: Governing under Sharia."

17. Philip L. Dubois, "Accountability, Independence, and the Selection of State Judges: The Role of Popular Judicial Elections," *Southwestern Law Journal* 40 (1986): 34.

18. D. R. Bhandari, "Plato's Concept of Justice: An Analysis," *World Congress of Philosophy*, https://www.bu.edu/wcp/Papers/Anci/AnciBhan.htm.

19. M. B. Foster, "On Plato's Conception of Justice in the Republic," *The Philosophical Quarterly* 1, no. 3 (1951): 206–217.

20. Alec Walen, "Retributive Justice," in *The Stanford Encyclopedia of Philosophy*, ed., Edward N. Zalta, Winter 2016, https://plato.stanford.edu/entries/justice-retributive/.

Republican nominee Donald Trump gestures as Democratic nominee Hillary Clinton looks on during the final presidential debate at the Thomas and Mack Center on the campus of the University of Nevada, Las Vegas, on October 19, 2016.

Source: ASFP/Stringer/Getty Images

Electoral and Party Systems

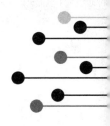

In the United States, one of the most persistent criticisms of political parties in the past several decades is the increasing level of acrimony and partisanship that colors American politics. Democrats have moved to the left of the ideological spectrum while Republicans have moved to the right, leaving a large space between them in which neither is prepared to compromise. Increased polarization has led to, among other things, longer confirmation times for judges, fewer bills passed in Congress, higher levels of deadlock between Congress and the president, budgetary difficulties, and an increasingly divisive rhetoric that threatens to shut down government on a regular basis. According to polling done by the Gallup Organization, Americans have increasingly viewed both the Republican and Democratic Parties with skepticism: in 1997, 60 percent of Americans held a favorable view of the Democratic Party, which, by 2017, had fallen to 44 percent. For Republicans, the high-water mark came in 2002 when 61 percent of Americans held a favorable view, compared to 36 percent in 2017.[1] A final notable figure from Gallup is this: in the weeks before the 2016 presidential election, Gallup found that 57 percent of Americans believed that a third party was needed.[2]

These figures present us with a sort of quandary. If Americans dislike political parties so much, why do we continue to use them and find them helpful? And two, if Americans are not satisfied with the political parties that exist, why not move to a third party? The answers to both of these questions can be found in the connections between state systems and elections. Although not directly mentioned in the US Constitution, political parties have become essential linkages between the voting public and elected representatives; they organize government, campaigns, and

Chapter Objectives

1. Identify and describe parliamentary systems.

2. Identify and describe presidential systems.

3. Identify the purposes of political parties.

4. Understand Duverger's law and the role of electoral systems in shaping political parties.

even voters. For all of the critiques that we have of them, government as it exists today would be practicably unimaginable. Further, the types of states that countries organize themselves into directly feeds into the role that political parties can play in government. Therefore, there is almost a symbiotic relationship between states and political parties—one always needing the other to exist if not succeed.

This chapter examines two types of state organizations: parliamentary and presidential systems along with the purposes and roles of political parties. Certainly, parliamentary and presidential governments are not the only types of government systems that exist, but they are the main types of democratic governments. In that sense, political parties play key roles in facilitating both types of governments, just in different ways. While both systems are undoubtedly democratic, they both operate in quite different ways, especially in terms of where political power lies and how unified or centralized it is.

Parliamentary Systems

While we in the United States are familiar with our system of separated branches sharing power, in states with a **parliamentary system**, the executive and legislative branches are fused with the executive functions also being carried out by the majority party or majority coalition in the legislature or parliament. Shiveley identifies four basic principles of a parliamentary system:

1. Citizens elect members of parliament, and it is the only elected body in a state.

2. The executive powers are carried out by a cabinet, chosen by the parliament and usually made up of members of the parliament.

3. The cabinet continues to function as long as it has the "confidence" of the majority party or majority coalition in the parliament.

4. The leader of the parliament (can be called various names, including prime minister or chancellor) can dissolve the cabinet and call for new elections at any time.[3]

One additional feature of parliamentary systems is that they almost always have a separate **head of state**, or ceremonial figure representing the country, where the prime minister, the head of the parliament's cabinet, is considered the **head of government**. In many European countries where parliamentary systems are used, the head of state is a member of the country's royal family and is considered king and/or queen. These heads of state have no formal responsibility beyond being a figurehead for the country and in some countries are legally prohibited from being involved in politics.

The obvious question, then, is if all the monarch does is represent a country, why have one at all? What is the need or purpose? In this, we can consider the United

Kingdom. Although the United Kingdom today comprises several different regions, including Great Britain, Scotland, and Northern Ireland, when Great Britain (then known as England) formed, it was a total monarchical system. Kings wielded absolute rule and authority through other nobles and aristocrats; however, over time and very gradually, more and more limits were placed on the king's authority. This began in 1215 with the signing of the Magna Carta, which placed some restrictions on the king (although neither side kept to the bargain for very long). As Great Britain continued to develop, different restrictions were placed on the monarchy to take away their power and plant it more firmly in the Parliament. Monarchs today still play a minor role in the British Parliament: the prime minister reports to the Queen about the actions of the government, the Queen (or her designee) goes to the Parliament annually to read out the majority party's plan for the coming year, and she even asks potential prime ministers to form governments, but this is only after it is clear that a majority has won out. The royal family must support whatever party is in power, whether they agree with them or not, and cannot make any political statements. Although the popularity of the monarchy has waxed and waned through the years, support for the British royal family remains high. They are looked to as figures of stability and a representation of a long British history that remains valuable to Britons.

Elections

To understand how a parliamentary government functions, we can begin with elections to the parliament. While this is by no means true of every parliamentary system, in most, a type of election known as **proportional representation** is used. In this system, when voters go to the ballot box, they do not vote for individual members of parliament but for a political party to represent them. Representation in the parliament is then divided proportionally based on the amount of votes each party received. For example, consider a parliament with 100 seats in it. In one election party A receives 55 percent of the vote, party B receives 30 percent, and party C receives 15 percent of the vote. As a result, party A is granted fifty-five seats, party B gets thirty seats, and party C gets fifteen seats. To determine who exactly gets to sit in those seats, each party, prior to the election, publishes a party list—a list of people who would serve in parliament if the party receives seats. In the previously given example, party A would take the first fifty-five people on their list to serve in parliament and so on.

If a party wins an outright majority of seats, as in the example previously given, they are given the right to form a government. The party can choose its prime minister and cabinet, who are charged with the executive functions of government. If, however, no party receives a majority, parties must negotiate to form a coalition to get to a majority. The coalition is then in charge of the government and of selecting key officials. If at any time the coalitions fail to agree on policy or different actions to take, the government can "fail" and is then dissolved, and new elections are held. In most parliamentary governments, there is no set timetable for when elections must be held although usually there is a maximum number of years after which elections must be held. For example, if the government does not fail and the prime minister does not call for elections in the meantime, in the United Kingdom, elections must be held at a minimum after five years. Sometimes, prime ministers will call for elections short of five years even if the government doesn't fail; this allows them to take advantage of favorable conditions for their own party and hold elections when their party is popular or on the upswing.

The preceding discussion has referred only to what are called lower houses of a parliament, but in many cases a parliament is bicameral, meaning it has two chambers. The upper chambers of parliament are often designed in different ways to represent different populations. In the British Parliament, the lower house is called the House of Commons while the upper house is the House of Lords. Again, this stems from a long historical tradition where the House of Commons represented the mass population and the House of Lords, the aristocracy. In Germany, however, the Bundesrat, the upper house, represents the different federal states (lander) in the country, and representatives sent to the Bundesrat represent the state governments themselves. These institutions can also have different amounts of power; today's House of Lords has very little power and serves more as a rubber stamp, whereas the German Bundesrat has more power in negotiating legislation and approving it, especially if it has to deal with Germany's Basic Law. However, the overriding principle behind a parliamentary system is a union of executive and legislative functions so as to make the exercise of power easier. Requiring consent of an upper house complicates that task, especially since the cabinet or majority party would not be able to exercise the same amount of control over members of the upper chamber. Therefore, typically, the powers of upper chambers are quite limited and circumscribed.

The Legislative Process

Theoretically, because a party or a coalition of parties holds all power in a parliament, they should be able to consider and pass legislation fairly easily. This does not mean, however, that the parliament is a rubber stamp. Depending on the balance of power between the parties or the coalitions, sometimes legislation has to be considered very carefully. Pieces of legislation begin in the cabinet where members write bills for further consideration. Once introduced, they may be sent to an ad hoc committee for further review (very rarely are there standing committees of the type used by the US Congress) or debated in the parliament. When the bill is ready to be voted on, the majority, which sent the bill to the parliament in the first place, can vote to approve it.

Majorities and coalitions can usually be assured of passage of legislation because of strict **party discipline**. Members of parliament are expected to vote with their party, especially on the most important policy issues of the day. Parties ensure that their members will do this because the parties get to choose who will serve in those seats to begin with and who can advance their careers in government. It would not be beneficial to the party to choose someone who may not vote with the party all the time. Party members would soon find themselves out of the parliament if they did so anyway. On some minor bills, parties may release their members to vote however they wish, but on major bills, if members do not vote with their party, the government fails and new elections must be held.

Once bills have been passed through the lower house, they often go to the upper house for their assent. In the United Kingdom, the House of Lords can delay legislation for only a year; after a year has passed, the House of Commons can pass a piece of legislation and bypass the Lords. In the German Bundesrat, the Bundestag (the lower house) must actually submit bills to them first, although they do not have to directly approve it. The Bundesrat's approval, however, is required on all bills having to do with constitutional or affecting the lander. There is a role as well for supreme or constitutional courts. These courts can step in at various points in the legislative process (depending on the country) to approve of significant laws or strike them down based on a country's constitution.

Parliaments also carry out important legislative functions such as oversight of government policy. Members of parliament from minority parties or coalitions can utilize their power to ensure that the majority is carrying out what it says it is. Since the prime minister or chancellor is drawn from the parliament, they can be questioned just like any other member of parliament. In the United Kingdom, this comes in the form of the prime minister's question time where he or she is questioned by all members of the House of Commons. In fact, question time is quite a unique characteristic of the British Parliament as other members hoot and holler and express their approval or disapproval of the questions and the prime minister's answers. C-SPAN often broadcasts the question time with the prime minister, and the broadcasts are easily accessible on YouTube. Finally, parliaments also provide the people who oversee the executive departments or portfolio.

Advantages and Disadvantages

Lawmaking is often easier in a parliamentary system than in a presidential system, which we will discuss shortly. Not only do parties exercise strict party loyalty, making it all but assured that their bills will pass, but the legislature and executive is fused and the executive has no ability to veto or stop legislation. This also makes it easier for the voting public to know who is or is not to blame for legislative or policy failures. In a fragmented system like the United States, blame can be placed on many actors: individual members of Congress, the president, or the parties themselves. But if there are significant policy failures, the public knows that the majority party or coalition was in charge and can vote them out in the next election.

However, this potential advantage also has its flip side. An argument could be made that too much power is centralized in the parliament and that there is no opportunity for dissent or minority views that may make the bills better. In the same vein, the majority could push through major legislative action without taking the time to seriously consider the ramifications of the bill, and there would be no executive authority to stop them. In the United States, we call these checks and balances, and in a strict parliamentary system, there are not very many checks on parliamentary authority. One of the reasons the founding fathers of the United States wanted checks and balances in our system of government was to avoid exactly this pitfall even though at the time of America's split from England the monarchy still held a fair amount of power.

Additionally, a parliamentary system, if it has to rely on minority coalitions, may prove unstable in the short term. If a coalition of parties comes together to form a government, that coalition must continue to agree on policy and legislation; if they do not, the government fails and new elections must be held. Parliamentary coalitions are in constant negotiation regarding who holds cabinet positions and what types of bills will be put forward. If governments are constantly failing and elections are constantly being held, it can spell constant upheaval for a country and little in the way of consistent policy direction. Italy, discussed in a moment, is an excellent example where governing coalitions are constantly forming and falling apart, leading to new parliamentary elections.

CASE STUDY
The Italian Parliament

The Italian parliament represents an interesting case of parliamentary government wherein the two chambers, the Senate and the Chamber of Deputies, have coequal powers. As such, each chamber also must approve of any and all legislation giving the Senate an equal say in the legislative process. The Chamber of Deputies, the "lower house," has a two-round proportional representation electoral system: If a party, in the first round, gets more than 40 percent of the vote, they receive 340 out of the 630 seats with the other seats being granted proportionally to the other parties. If no party or coalition wins 40 percent or more of the vote, a second round of voting is held between the top two parties with the winner receiving the 340 seats. There is an added layer of constituency, however, with the country divided into twenty electoral regions ensuring that at least one member is selected from each; voters can express a preference for a member of the party list when they vote, and the candidate with the most votes in the party wins from that region. There is one additional seat that is reserved to represent Italians living abroad. The Italian Senate consists of 315 elected seats divided among twenty different electoral regions of Italy. Seats are then assigned on a proportional basis based on election results. The Senate also has several appointed seats, and former presidents of Italy are considered ex officio members. Requirements to run for the Chamber of Deputies and the Senate as well as vote in their elections also differ. To vote for the Chamber of Deputies, you must be eighteen years old, while you have to wait until age twenty-five to vote in Senate elections.

The two chambers plus fifty-eight regional representatives select a president to serve as head of state in Italy for a term of seven years. However, as in most parliamentary systems, the real power resides with the prime minister as head of the Council of Ministers (the cabinet), which is then formally approved by the president. Italian presidents have several additional powers, including the ability to call for a referendum under certain circumstances, grant pardons, and dissolve one or both chambers of parliament. If a majority coalition fails, the president can appoint a new prime minister to attempt to form a new government or simply call for new elections.

Italian politics has been quite chaotic in recent years. Political parties have dissolved and reformed. A number of Italian political officials have been caught breaking the law or engaging in scandalous behavior. Perhaps most widely publicized was the case of former Italian prime minister Silvio Berlusconi, who was known for hosting "sex parties" and was eventually tried on tax fraud charges. Although he was sentenced to jail, under Italian law, his age allowed him to commute the prison sentence into time doing community service. Despite this, Berlusconi has remained on the Italian political scene and is perhaps angling for another stint as prime minister once he has served his two-year ban from public office. In the most recent Italian elections held in March 2018, two right-wing parties, Five Star Movement and Lega, together received more than 50 percent of the vote, but neither of them reached the 40 percent threshold. It took the major parties three months of negotiations before finally determining the makeup of their government and who the prime minister would be.

Critical Thinking Questions

1. Based on this description of Italy's parliament, what are the strengths of a parliamentary system?

2. What are some of the problems of parliamentary systems that the Italian parliament has experienced?

3. Are there any advantages to both chambers having coequal powers in terms of legislation?

Presidential Systems

Unlike the parliamentary system, a **presidential system** has the legislature and executive separated into two different branches or institutions that serve to check and balance the other. While the writers of the US Constitution were certainly influenced by British parliamentary politics and historical political theory, the creation of a separate executive was an altogether new innovation of the Founders. Never before in history had such a position been designed and attempted. The very idea that a president would willingly step down and hand over power following a term in office was a novel concept of which no one was sure would work. The only reason the Founders believed it would work at first was the involvement of George Washington, who they all assumed would be the first president. The success of the American presidential system has been copied by governments throughout the world who now use some version of it in their political system.

In presidential systems, the position of head of state and head of government is fused; the president is not only the ceremonial head of state but is also the head of government. The hallmark of a presidential system is that the executive, the president, is elected separately from the legislature. In general, all voters participate in the election of a president; in the United States, we utilize a form of indirect election called the Electoral College, but in many other states, citizens directly elect their president. Once in office, the president selects their own cabinet, which is wholly separate from the legislature. If the president would like a member of the legislature to serve in their cabinet, the member often has to resign first in order to do so. (In fact, there is a provision in the US Constitution that prohibits individuals from working for more than one branch of government at a time.) Often, the members of the president's cabinet must be approved by the legislature in some way as a means to check the executive's power.

In a presidential system, the legislature is often bicameral, meaning it has two houses. Depending on the country, the electoral requirements and setup of the two chambers can vary. In the United States, the House of Representatives is apportioned by population, meaning that larger states get more seats, and the members are directly elected by voters. The Senate, on the other hand, was originally designed to represent the interests of the states; each state gets two senators who were originally chosen by the state legislatures themselves. Today, senators are directly elected. Germany's parliament today utilizes a similar balance where the Bundestag (the lower house) is directly elected by the people through a proportional representation system, and the Bundesrat (the upper house) represents the Lander, the states. The two houses, unlike in a parliamentary system, often have coequal powers. In other words, both chambers must approve of legislation before it can be sent to the president.

Legislative-Executive Relations

In terms of legislative relations, the president or his or her cabinet have no formal means to introduce legislation. The president can propose legislation or ask that the legislature act to pass a bill, but presidents cannot propose or force the legislature to do anything. This is where the power of political party (discussed later in this chapter) often comes into play. Using their political allies, presidents can have bills introduced by members of the legislature and have their allies work to pass legislation. Of course, the opposite is also true; if the legislature passes a bill, they cannot force the president to sign it either. A president can sign a bill into law or veto it, although in some cases legislatures can override a presidential veto by a supermajority vote of both chambers.

The balance of power between a president and the legislature is constantly evolving. When the US Constitution was first written, the Founders envisioned a much stronger Congress than president; this was exemplified by the fact that the Congress was given many more enumerated powers than the president and many of the president's powers are circumscribed and checked by Congress. For example, while the president is commander in chief of the military, only the Congress has the ability to declare war and Congress ultimately holds the power of the purse if the president wants to pursue any major military action. Over time, however, the balance of power has changed. Scholars in the United States have identified crises, both military and economic, as causes of growth in presidential power. During crises, presidents are often empowered to act swiftly on behalf of the country as Congress can find it difficult to act quickly.

There is obviously a concern about how much power a president can amass. This led to charges of an **imperial presidency** in the United States in the 1960s and

1970s. The situation came to a head with the Nixon administration, with Nixon himself arguing that if presidents do something, it can't be illegal. Nixon took this to the extreme, attempting to cover up crimes using the CIA, and was eventually forced from office. Although legislatures cannot remove presidents easily, most legislatures in a presidential system have a means of removing a president, in the case of the United States, for "high crimes and misdemeanors." Nixon resigned before he could be impeached and removed from office, but Congress acted to take back power from the president that the executive had slowly amassed over time. This demonstrates that the balance of power between an executive and the legislature is constantly changing and evolving based on the needs of the country and even who is president and whether the legislature believes they are acting in good faith.

The relationship between an executive and legislature is obviously premised on the idea of **checks and balances** that each branch can check the powers of the other in some way. While this does institute a certain amount of conflict between the two branches, the writers of the US Constitution found it preferable to the fused executive-legislature in a parliamentary system that does allow for one party and its prime minister to amass a good deal of power. The more difficult question, then, is how much conflict and disagreement is good and productive and how much is too much.

The Special Role of the President

Even though most monarchs today have little to no constitutional power, a fair amount of attention is still paid to them and their royal families as symbols of a country and its traditions. In presidential systems, presidents are paid much more attention and are more well known outside of a country than leaders of the legislature. They combine the ceremonial head of state functions with the actual duties of a head of government. And given that they are often the only political figure elected by all citizens, presidents are often the focus of politics in a country.

First, presidents serve the symbolic function of a monarchy and therefore become a moral and ethical figure that citizens look to for guidance, especially in difficult times. One of the functions often assigned to the president of the United States is that of "comforter in chief." In times of crisis, Americans look to the president for decisive action and comforting words. This has been clearly on display with the recent spate of mass shootings, many of them taking place at schools. During President Obama's term in office, he took on the duty of consoling not only the nation but the victims and survivors of such incidents. In President Trump's first year in office, the country experienced several disastrous hurricanes after which the president and first lady often traveled to the affected locations to see firsthand the damage for themselves.

Presidents are often looked to as major agenda setters and sources of policy proposals. Even though presidents cannot force their proposals through the legislature, they still often set the agenda and help determine what the legislature does or doesn't do. Particularly since presidents are often the only nationally elected figure and responsible for many facets of national policy, they are confronted with a number of policy problems daily. That a president chooses to focus on two or three of them at a time can signal the rest of the political community that a president considers them worthy of concern and attention. This, in turn, will focus their attention on the issue. Presidents can use speeches and statements along with visits to certain places to draw attention to the issues they wish to deal with. In the United States, one of the most visible acts of presidential agenda setting takes place every year in the State of the Union address. Required by the Constitution, the president "shall from time to time give to the Congress Information of the State of the Union, and recommend to their Consideration such Measures as he shall deem just and necessary." This gives the president an opportunity to lay out their agenda before Congress and, today, before the public itself.

Advantages and Disadvantages

One of the obvious advantages to a presidential system is the added layer of checks and balances that exist. No one branch can move to act too swiftly or on their own without additional action from the other. However, just as in a parliamentary system, this can present additional policy hurdles, slowing down and possibly preventing altogether bills from getting passed. Added to this is the difficulty in determining which party or which branch is most responsible for policy failure. While presidents are certainly looked to for leadership and policy proposals, the legislature is equally empowered not to act. This also makes it more difficult, but not impossible, to pursue large-scale policy change.

If voters cannot determine who is to blame for policy failure, it makes it much harder to hold politicians accountable. In 1950, the American Political Science Association (APSA) convened a committee to consider the current state of the party system in the United States. The APSA committee argued that given the growing number of responsibilities of the US government, parties were an indispensable link to provide "for more effective formulation of general policies and programs and for better integration of all of the far-flung activities of modern government."[4] Without political parties that were strong enough to provide plans of government and then enact them once in power, the danger, warned the committee, was that the country would simply drift from one policy option to another, never considering an entire policy program or making choices without considering the whole set of government policies. In the eyes of the APSA committee, political parties were the means of providing guidance and that the political parties of the early twentieth century could not provide such guidance was a danger. The committee then called for a system of "responsible party government" so that voters could make a clear distinction between the policy directions offered by each party and then hold the party in power responsible if the platform was not carried out. While political parties have certainly become stronger in the United States since the 1950s (discussed further in the next section), it is still difficult in a presidential system to determine which party is to blame for policy failure in a situation of divided government.

Another advantage of a presidential system is that the head of state is effectively elected by the entire country, not passed on hereditarily or selected by the parliament. This is, arguably, a more democratic means of selecting a state's leader, the one person that all voters can look to and an election that voters can claim to have participated in (whether directly or indirectly). This can, in certain ways, endow a president with a greater amount of authority and leadership. However, it also creates a distinct separation between the legislature and the executive, especially compared to a parliamentary system. In a parliament, the executive reports to and is responsible to the legislature; this is notably absent in a presidential system. This can often create a scenario in a presidential system where the presidency operates quite apart from the legislature. One possible consequence is that presidents are often accused of being inward looking or existing within a bubble.[5] In situations of divided government, a somewhat antagonistic relationship between the president and the legislature can arise with each blaming the other for shortcomings or failures.

Given this discussion of what are supposedly both the advantages and disadvantages of a presidential system, one thing stands out: there seem to be more disadvantages than advantages. Shiveley summarizes the disadvantages of presidential systems as such:

- difficulty of locating responsibility for policies
- difficulty of making comprehensive policy
- a different pattern of recruitment for executive leaders
- special problems for review and control [of the executive]
- the inflexibility of fixed terms in presidential systems and the need for a vice president
- a merger of the symbolic and political aspects of the executive in a single person

Shiveley is right to ask the question, then, why any democracies might have presidential systems at all. To his list of pitfalls, we can similarly add a list of advantages:

- division of power between the executive and legislature so that the parliament and the majority party do not hold too much power
- checks and balances between the different branches of government
- one national elected leader who can claim to represent the whole country
- ability of the minority to check majority power
- predictability in terms of how long elected officials serve
- more room for input and debate on major policy questions; harder to enact policy quickly but that can perhaps make policy better

Following World War II, France experienced particular difficulties in recovering from the war. Not only had the country been destroyed by fighting but its government had been taken over by Nazi Germany. Thus, at the end of the war, French leaders faced the dual tasks of not only rebuilding their country but their state. The Fourth Republic, the form of constitutional government that existed in France between 1946 and 1958, was for all intents and purposes, a parliamentary system. However, so many political parties with very divergent views existed that it created a situation where the parliament was essentially paralyzed. Hauss and Haussman describe the situation as such:

> The French were never able to achieve anything like party government as it existed in Britain. Because the parties were so divided, elections never produced a majority. Instead, cabinets had to include members of three or four parties that had little or nothing in common… Virtually any issue of consequence would split the coalition so that every nine months or so the government would lose its majority and resign, almost always before a formal vote of no confidence was held. The ensuing cabinet crisis would last until the parties could resolve their differences on the issues that brought the old government down and then form a new one. That cabinet, in turn, would survive until it had to confront the next difficult issue.[6]

As a result of the indecisiveness of parliament and the cabinet, control on many issues devolved to the French bureaucracy, resulting in a high degree of centralization. Finally, with war breaking out in Algeria, a French colony, in 1958, the government once again fell, and Charles de Gaulle, hero of World War II, agreed to become prime minister only if he were given the ability to revise the constitution.

The resulting constitution, called the Fifth Republic, created a hybrid version of a parliamentary system with presidential leadership. The president is elected through a direct, majority vote for a five-year term (with the possibility for a second). The parliament is bicameral, consisting of the Senate and the National Assembly. The National Assembly has 577 directly elected seats whose members serve five-year terms, but the Senate's electoral setup is a bit different. The winners of the 348 seats are elected indirectly through an electoral college-like system. In both cases, however, to win a seat in the French parliament, individuals must win the majority of the vote; elections go to a second round if needed. The cabinet is officially appointed by the president but at the suggestion of the prime minister, who is selected by the president.

Critical Thinking Questions

1. In this hybrid system, who has more power: the head of state, the president, or the head of government, the prime minister?

2. How does the hybrid system solve some of the problems France experienced with a parliamentary system?

Political Parties and Duverger's Law

In both parliamentary and presidential systems, political parties are an essential part of forming governments and organizing what they do. Political scientist Aldrich writes that "democracy is *unworkable* save in terms of parties."[7] Throughout political history, there have been groups and coalitions that have come together and support or oppose political movements or policies. In the United States, however, the country's Founders were suspect of what they called factions. James Madison, in *Federalist No. 10*, identified factions as a significant danger in a republican style of government, writing that "the latent causes of faction are thus sown in the nature of man." Madison's solution was that a republican government of the type that was written into the US Constitution would cure the ailments of factions. George Washington even warned against the dangers of faction and party in his Farewell Address. Hofstadter, in his exploration of parties, *The Idea of a Party System,* notes the general American attitudes toward parties in the eighteenth and nineteenth centuries as "sores" that threatened government by consensus and unanimity.[8]

Despite these cautions and warnings, political parties, as Madison wrote, are seemingly baked into politics. People of like mind simply seem to gravitate toward one another and agree to work together toward some common goal. Even though political parties were not written into the US Constitution, they have become the backbone of how we organize government. In parliamentary systems, political parties are the means by which representatives are selected and governments organized. Even if not officially recognized in a country, political parties emerge as a strong glue through which governments are held together in various ways.

Why Parties Form

Political scientists have recognized various reasons for why political parties form. Aldrich argues that political parties form because politicians need them and the services they provide.[9] Given that the goal of partisan politicians is to seek office and hold it, an organization such as a political party is a valuable tool through which they can realize their goal. Parties connect the office seekers with the party activists who provide valuable support in terms of money, electioneering, and get-out-the-vote efforts. According to Aldrich, parties also solve several other problems politicians encounter in seeking office, including access to office, making decisions both for the party and the country, and collective action.[10] Recall from Chapter 1 that the collective action problem describes the difficulty of getting people to act together when the incentives to do so are low. Parties help to overcome those barriers and provide resources to politicians in return for them working together as a single-party organization. Running for office alone or as an independent requires more resources and effort on the part of the office seeker; by running as part of a party, there are certain advantages that parties can provide. Therefore, from Aldrich's perspective, political parties provide a set of incentives that encourage politicians to turn to political parties.

In another formulation of the purpose of political parties in democracy, Downs argues this: "Political parties in a democracy formulate policy strictly as a means of gaining votes. They do not seek to gain office in order to carry out certain preconceived policies or to serve any particular interest group; rather they formulate policies and serve interest groups in order to gain office."[11] This idea has clear parallels to Aldrich's later theory but places a larger emphasis on the success of the party, not the politician, of winning political races. Downs argues that in an imperfect world where perfect information is difficult if not impossible to come by, parties and the ideologies they represent provide useful guides in educating voters about the goals of each party; in turn, the party creates an ideology that they believe will help them succeed in gaining votes. Once those ideologies have been established, multiple parties cannot establish identical ideologies nor can a party radically alter or change their established platform.[12] While this makes intuitive sense, Downs advances a more controversial idea, however, about what might result from parties that behave as such:

> Stable government in a two-party democracy requires a distribution of voters roughly approximating a normal curve. When such a distribution exists, the two parties come to resemble each other closely. Thus when one replaces the other in office, no drastic policy changes occur, and most voters are located relatively close to the incumbent's position no matter which party is in power. But when the electorate is polarized... a change in parties causes a radical alteration in policy. And, regardless of which party is in office, half the electorate always feels that the other half is imposing policies upon it that are strongly repugnant to it. In this situation, if one party keeps getting re-elected, the disgruntled supporters of the other party will probably revolt; whereas if the two parties alternate in office, social chaos occurs, because government policy keeps changing from one extreme to the other. Thus democracy does not lead to effective, stable government when the electorate is polarized. Either the distribution must change or democracy will be replaced by tyranny in which one extreme imposes its will upon the other.[13]

This is a stunning conclusion about the theoretical political outcomes of a polarized electorate in a democracy. And on its face, it would appear as if current conditions in the United States meet the polarized criteria; with one party in power, a large portion of the other party feels put out and put upon. However, there is little cause for panic. Even though elite politicians may be polarized to a large extent, the general population of the United States is not nearly as polarized and, in fact, more closely resembles a normal distribution that Downs says leads to stable two-party democracy.[14]

The Functions of Political Parties

If political parties provide valuable services to politicians, as Aldrich argues, and to voters, as Downs argues, what exactly are these services? Political scientists often divide the functions of political parties into three different areas: parties in the electorate, parties in government, and party organization. The party as a means of organizing is a key element of both Downs's and Aldrich's arguments. Parties provide a means of organization from the local level to the national level. In the United States, party organizing often begins at the precinct level. Precincts are little sections of cities and towns in which people vote at a particular polling location. Going up the line, there is then often a city party committee, county party committee, state committee, and the national party committee. While these often act somewhat independent of each other, the connection from the national to the very local provides a ready-made system of communication and promotion of party ideals.

Party organizations can be described as either strong or weak; however, there are varying definitions of what party strength means. "Stronger parties would have larger budgets and more full-time, paid staff members."[15] What these resources give parties is the ability to register and rally voters, provide effective advertising during an election, and help the party enact its platform once in office. As Hershey puts it, "In order for a party to do these things... it needs money, staff, and other forms of organizational strength."[16] Party strength could also be conceptualized, though, as how significant an ability the party has to force members to conform to what the party wants. As discussed previously, in parliamentary systems, parties often extract strict party loyalty; otherwise, the government would fail. In the United States, parties today, while strong organizationally, are often considered weaker because they cannot force party members to adhere to the party line. It is for this reason that elections are often considered candidate-centered affairs with who the candidate is mattering far more than the party they are affiliated with. Even though American parties cannot enforce party discipline, both the Republican and Democratic Parties have significant services to provide candidates.

The role of political parties in the electorate touches upon some of what Downs was referencing: They provide voters, who often have imperfect information and the lack of time or inclination to find more information, a quick reference guide of sorts to what candidates may believe in. If a voter goes to the ballot box on election day and knows nothing about the candidates except the *D* or *R* next to their names, they have a general idea of the types of positions those candidates will take. In psychological terms, this is called an ideological shortcut. Further, political parties help to energize voters, register them to vote, organize elections, recruit candidates, and conduct get-out-the-vote efforts.

Finally, political parties play an important role in government. In presidential systems, since the executive is not chosen by the legislature, he or she owes no loyalty or accountability to them. What knits the two branches together so that they may be able to work together is the bond of political party. If the president and majorities in the legislature are of the same party, it is easier for them to cooperate to pass legislation and

Career Guidance

As political parties have strengthened over the last half of the twentieth century, opportunities to work with and for political parties have also increased. Political parties provide a number of services to candidates, and people are needed to coordinate and organize polling, media, commercials, and fund-raising. Since American political parties are organized on a local, state, and national basis, check with your local or state party organization on employment opportunities. Even if they are not currently hiring, you may wish to intern with them to get a sense of what working for a political party is like.

create policy. This is a situation known as unified government, and political scientists have often found that when this is the case, the government is able to do more in terms of passing laws. Members of the president's party in the legislature have a strong incentive to help their president succeed so that the president may be elected to another term or the president's partisans in the legislature may be reelected. This incentive to cooperate, though, is limited in a presidential system because often the bonds of party loyalty are neither strict nor required. However, in a situation of divided government, where a different party holds the legislature and the executive, the incentive to cooperate is lessened. Not only would the two parties hold different views of what needs to be done but each party has an incentive to make the other look bad so that they can capitalize on it in the next election.

As previously discussed, the role of political parties in parliamentary systems is even more centralized and important. They select candidates either at the local level or through the development of party lists; they create the party platforms that are then followed through on if the party achieves a majority in the government.

Duverger's Law

One of the more often asked questions about American politics is why there are only two major political parties. In other systems, particularly parliamentary systems with proportional representation, multiple major parties are involved in a country's politics. Maurice Duverger proposed an answer to the question of how many political parties exist in a political system. According to Duverger, winner-take-all (also known as first past the post) systems tend to create only two major political parties where proportional representation encourages the development of multiple major parties. Winner-take-all electoral systems are often used in presidential elections or elections where a single individual is being elected to represent a district (single-member districts). In these systems, the person who wins the most votes wins the election, even if they don't win a majority of votes. For example, three people may be running for a seat in the legislature with candidate A receiving 45 percent of the vote, candidate B receiving 15 percent of the vote, and candidate C receiving 40 percent of the vote. In this instance, candidate A would win even though they did not win a majority of the votes. Comparatively, in a proportional representation system, voters would be casting their ballots for a party, and each party would be rewarded with representation in the legislature.

According to Duverger, single-member, winner-take-all districts discourage the potential of third parties because weaker parties, with little potential of winning, are quickly eliminated from electoral competition by either dropping out or merging with other smaller parties. Further, individual voters will be discouraged from voting for smaller third parties because they know the candidate will have little chance of winning compared to the larger parties' candidates. On the other hand, in a proportional system, if a party receives a small amount of votes, they can still be rewarded with representation in the legislature. Countries with proportional representation, however, will often have a threshold percentage of votes that parties have to reach in order to receive seats in the legislature; for example, in Italy, parties must receive a minimum of 3 percent of the vote to receive seats in the parliament.

In the United States, **Duverger's law** is clearly at work; the single member, winner-take-all elections have led to the creation of and domination by the two major political parties, the Democratic and Republican Parties. However, the two major parties have also worked to pass laws to protect their partisan advantage. For example, the presidential nominee of each party automatically appears on the ballot in each of the states, but candidates running as independents do not get their names on the ballot in every state. Each state determines what minor party candidates must do to get on the ballot; in some instances, it requires a fee or a certain number of signatures on a petition. Some states, like Oklahoma, don't even recognize any parties other than the Republican and Democratic Parties, making it exceedingly hard for third-party candidates to get on the ballot. These various ballot access laws protect the position of the major parties in the United States and discourage third parties from running for office. Therefore, even though Duverger's law provides that in the United States, two major political parties will emerge, the two parties themselves have reinforced their position by passing laws that give them an even greater advantage.

Role and Influence of Third Parties

In countries where two parties are dominant, it by no means prevents the existence of third parties or minor parties. In fact, in the United States, there are several third parties, including the Libertarian Party and the Green Party. And historically, third parties serve valuable functions even in two-party systems. First, third parties can be a spoiler in that they take votes away from one of the two major parties or candidates and therefore throw the election to the other candidate. This situation happened in 1992 when Ross Perot, running as an independent, received 19 percent of the vote compared to George H. W. Bush's 37.7 percent of the vote, and Bill Clinton's 43.3 percent of the vote. Arguably, Perot drew enough votes from George H. W. Bush to throw the election to Bill Clinton. While the popular vote certainly doesn't determine who wins the presidency in the United States, the same situation happened in Florida in 2000 with Ralph Nader drawing enough votes from Al Gore to give the state's electoral votes to George W. Bush.

Third parties can also highlight and bring attention to issues that the major parties have previously ignored. In the United States, this was most clearly seen in the 1890s at the beginning of the Progressive Era. Due to price controls put in place by the railroad and industrial barons of the time, a number of farmers and others involved in agriculture banded together to form the Populist Party, which urged significant government and economic reform. In many ways, the populists represented traditional agrarian issues that its supporters believed had been ignored in American politics. While the populist candidate for president managed to win four states in the election of 1892, the Populist Party began to be subsumed into the Democratic Party, resulting in the double nomination of William Jennings Bryan by both the Democratic and Populist Parties in 1896. Thus, while the short-lived Populist Party drew attention to significant issues they felt had been ignored, they also suffered the fate of many third parties—being overtaken by one of the two major parties that adopts those issues as their own.

Finally, third parties can often be successful in smaller elections at the state or local level. Smaller elections do not require the type of resources and organizations that the two major parties can provide in a superior manner to small third parties. Often, these local elections have a much greater impact on the day-to-day lives of average citizens; thus, third-party candidates can often have a significant political influence.

STUDENT STUDY SITE

Visit https://edge.sagepub.com/whitmancobb

CHAPTER SUMMARY

- Governments in which the legislative and executive functions are fused in one branch of government are parliamentary systems. They typically feature elections with proportional representation and limited involvement from a head of state.

- Governments where the legislature and executive are split with a strong head of state are called presidential systems. While this can strengthen checks and balances on one branch's power, it can also hamper efficient policymaking and make it difficult to understand who is to be credited or blamed for government actions.

- Political parties are an essential part of politics, as they serve several functions including recruiting people for office, organizing elections and governments, and mobilizing voters.

- Duverger's law stipulates that electoral systems help to determine how many major political parties a state will have: proportional representation often leads to multiple major political parties while winner-take-all systems often leads to just two major political parties.

KEY TERMS

checks and balances: Describes ways in which a legislature and an executive can curtail each other's powers

Duverger's law: Theory wherein proportional representation systems lead to the establishment of multiple major political parties and winner-take-all systems lead to the creation of two major political parties

head of government: Political figure who is in charge of the functioning of a state's government

head of state: Political figure representing the entire country, sometimes a formal position with little power

imperial presidency: Describes a situation where a president has amassed too much power compared to the legislative branch

parliamentary system: Governmental system in which the executive and legislative functions are fused in one body

party discipline: The ability of political parties to force its members to vote a certain way in a legislature

presidential system: Governmental system in which the executive and legislative functions are carried out by separate branches of government

proportional representation: Electoral system in which parties receive representation in a legislature based on the proportion of votes they receive

DISCUSSION QUESTIONS

1. Compare and contrast a monarch to a president. What type of power does each have?

2. Describe proportional representation. What consequences flow both governmentally and electorally from having a proportional representation system?

3. What are the advantages of checks and balances in a presidential system? Are they worth the potential gridlock that they can create?

4. What purposes do political parties fulfill?

FOR FURTHER READING

Aldrich, John. *Why Parties? The Origin and Transformation of Political Parties in America.* Chicago: University of Chicago Press, 1995.

Dalton, Russell J. *Citizen Politics: Public Opinion and Political Parties in Advanced Industrial Democracies.* 5th ed. Washington, DC: CQ Press, 2008.

Downs, Anthony. "An Economic Theory of Political Action in a Democracy." *Journal of Political Economy* 65, no. 2 (1957).

Democratic National Committee: www.democrats.org

Republican National Committee: www.gop.org

UK Parliament: https://www.parliament.uk

NOTES

1. "Party Images," *Gallup*, http://news.gallup.com/poll/24655/party-images.aspx.

2. "Americans' Desire for Third Party Persists This Election Year," *Gallup*, Sept. 30, 2016, http://news.gallup.com/poll/195920/americans-desire- third-party-persists-election-year.aspx?g_source=link_ NEWSV9&g_

medium=tile_7&g_campaign=item_24655&g_content=Americans%27%2520Desire%2520for%2520Third%2520Party%2520Persists%2520This%2520Election%2520Year.

3. W. Phillips Shively, *Power and Choice: An Introduction to Political Science* (New York: McGraw-Hill, 2014), 315–317.

4. APSA Committee on Political Parties, "Toward a More Responsible Two-Party System," *American Political Science Association* (1950): 16 (emphasis in the original).

5. Shively, *Power and Choice*, 346.

6. Charles Hauss and Melissa Haussman, *Comparative Politics: Domestic Responses to Global Challenges*, 8th ed. (Boston: Wadsworth, 2013), 108–109.

7. John Aldrich, *Why Parties? The Origin and Transformation of Political Parties in America* (Chicago: University of Chicago Press, 1995), 3.

8. Richard Hofstadter, *The Idea of a Party System: The Rise of Legitimate Opposition in the United States, 1780–1840* (Berkeley: University of California Press, 1970).

9. Aldrich, *Why Parties?*

10. Ibid.

11. Anthony Downs, "An Economic Theory of Political Action in a Democracy," *Journal of Political Economy* 65, no. 2 (1957): 137.

12. Ibid.

13. Ibid., 143.

14. Morris P. Fiorina with Samuel J. Abrams and Jeremy C. Pope, *Culture War? The Myth of a Polarized America*, 3rd ed. (Boston: Longman, 2011).

15. Marjorie Randon Hershey, *Party Politics in America*, 16th ed. (Boston: Pearson, 2015), 51.

16. Ibid., 52.

Information is vital for a functioning democracy, and it is more plentiful and available than ever.

Source: ©iStockphoto.com/GoodLifeStudio

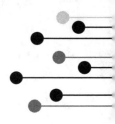

CHAPTER 6

Political Communications

For all of the things the Founders of the United States agreed on, there were quite a few disagreements among them that are often papered over. John Adams and Thomas Jefferson refused to speak to each other for over a decade. Jefferson and Alexander Hamilton traded pointed barbs against one another through the press. Aaron Burr would go on to kill Hamilton in a duel. While they didn't agree on everything, there was one thing on which they did: the value and importance of the First Amendment, including freedom of the press. Jefferson is quoted as having said, "Were it left to me to decide whether we should have a government without newspapers, or newspapers without a government, I should not hesitate a moment to prefer the later." Adams, Jefferson's "frenemy," concurred, writing, "The liberty of the press is essential to the security of the state." Benjamin Franklin, himself an author and printer, wrote, "Freedom of speech is a principal pillar of a free government. When this support is taken away, the constitution of a free society is dissolved."[1]

While this is certainly glowing praise from several of America's Founders, consider the following quotes, also about the media:

"Nothing can now be believed which is seen in a newspaper. Truth itself becomes suspicious by being put into the polluted vehicle."

"The press is your enemy. Enemies. Understand that?"[2]

"We hear so many loud and angry voices in America today whose sole goal seems to be to try

Chapter Objectives

1. Identify and discuss the various roles of the media in a democratic society.

2. Analyze the economic and social variables that influence modern media and their effects.

3. Explore the role of the media around the world, including the dangers that journalists often face.

4. Discuss the impact that fake news and social media can have on democracy.

to keep some people as paranoid as possible and the rest of us all torn up and upset with each other. They spread hate. They leave the impression that, by their very words, that violence is acceptable."[3]

These quotes, too, are from American presidents: the first from Thomas Jefferson, the second from Richard Nixon, and the third from Bill Clinton.

Since the beginning of the country, politicians have had a love-hate relationship with the media. Given that media has historically been the sole mechanism of informing and communicating with the public, politicians find the media important and valuable when it covers the stories they wish to see covered and an annoyance and dangerous when it works against them. But who is the media supposed to work for? In the ideal world of the First Amendment, it works for the people, providing information and a check on government power. However, media today does not operate in an ideal world; media outlets are owned by larger corporations that are beholden to shareholders. Twenty-four hour news channels seek out stories to fill their days with. The Internet provides an opportunity for democratization of the media along with outlets who pretend to be reporters but are instead pushing their own version of the truth.

This chapter examines some of the dynamics involved with the media today, including the roles that the media plays, the decisions that go into what to cover, the state of the press around the world, and the implications that new media such as social media have for democracy.

Roles of the Media

The media is often collectively called the fourth branch of government, but why? Aside from the First Amendment, the press is not discussed in the Constitution nor is there any formal role for the media in American government (this cannot be said for other countries where the government does often sponsor a television news network or newspaper). However, the media does serve as a conduit between the public and the government, providing the public with information as to the actions of government and checking the power of government at the same time. For these reasons, commentators often describe three roles for the media: education, watchdog, and socialization.

Education

The ideal of democracy or democratic participation in governing relies on an educated citizenry. Education about the structure, forms, and functions of government is only half of it; citizens should be knowledgeable and aware of what their government is currently doing. Without public awareness, it is quite possible for a government to take actions that its citizenry might not support. Further, elections are a voter's opportunity to reward elected officials for a job well done or punish them for the jobs they have failed to do. Voters could rely on the candidates and the political parties to inform them of what was happening in government, but the information itself may be biased and unreliable. The media thus serves the function of providing independent news and information to the citizenry so that they can made educated and informed decisions about whom to vote for.

Watchdog

In the course of educating the public about the actions of government, media can also serve a watchdog function. In this sense, the media can serve as a check on government power, bringing to light harmful government actions and those who are responsible for them. Upton Sinclair's *The Jungle* is an example of investigative journalism that blew the whistle on the practices of the Chicago meatpacking industry. Perhaps the greatest or most significant example of the media's watchdog function was Watergate. President Richard Nixon, who had a long, torturous relationship with the press to begin with, ordered a cover-up of a break-in at the Democratic National Committee's headquarters at the Watergate complex in Washington, D.C. The break-in had been undertaken by Nixon's Committee for the Reelection of the President (CREEP) to examine campaign documents. While Nixon and his administration denied any connection between the break-in and Nixon himself, it soon became clear that CREEP had sponsored the burglars, and several administration figures had tried to stop the investigation. Two young *Washington Post* reporters, Bob Woodward and Carl Bernstein, received several anonymous tips linking Nixon to the break-in; they continued to investigate the connection and broke the news to the public about the cover-up and the administration's role in it.

Woodward and Bernstein's coverage of Watergate would eventually help lead to a series of hearings in the House of Representatives, which sought to investigate the Nixon administration's connection to Watergate. It was there that the existence of a recording system within the White House was discovered and the tapes subpoenaed. Following the Supreme Court's ruling that the administration must hand over the tapes to Congress, the House began to draft articles of impeachment, which would have no doubt been passed. To avoid this fate, Nixon was forced to resign, the first American president in history to do so.

The reporting conducted by Woodward and Bernstein was vital to the watchdog function of the media. They were able to expose corruption at the highest ranks, and eventually Nixon was held to account for it in his own way: by resigning. Woodward and Bernstein, however, are by no means the only journalists who have been vital in holding government officials to account. In more recent years, reporters have broken stories about prisoner abuses at Abu Ghraib by American soldiers, the huge extent of government spying organizations, as well as the programs that were being used by the American government to spy on its own citizens. Reporters have also had a significant role in the recent #MeToo movement in which major figures, including politicians, have been accused of sexual assault and harassment.

Socialization

Finally, the media plays a role in socialization. Socialization is the process through which we acquire beliefs about the world around us; the media is a key way in which those ideals, values, and beliefs are communicated. In this sense, media can be seen as far more encompassing than just newspapers, news channels, or even news websites. Media can also include television shows, movies, magazines, books—any way through which ideas are communicated. For just one example, consider this study: Pautz and Warnement, in "Government on the Silver Screen," examine how movies portray government officials. They find that while films generally present a mixed assessment of governments and government officials, certain types of government officials were portrayed more positively than others: bureaucrats, police officers, soldiers, and, surprisingly, politicians.[4] Consider what might be the effect of such individuals being portrayed negatively in movies: people who watch movies and who may not keep up with politics might end up having a skewed idea about what these sorts of individuals do that could affect their assessment of the government as a whole.

Media and Democracy

A final potential role for the media is in promoting the idea of democracy itself. Although providing information and educating voters is a role in and of itself, some scholars have argued that freedom of the press specifically is not only a requisite characteristic of democracy but can promote democratic attitudes and ideas. This argument is what political scientists typically call a normative argument; there is not necessarily a right or wrong answer, but your answer is influenced about what you believe about democracy and its place in the world. However, there is some intriguing evidence about the relationship between democracy and the media. Muller analyzed the media in forty-seven different countries on two different dimensions: how well they performed their watchdog function and how well they represented the views of their citizenry. Not only does she find wide variation on these two indicators but she also finds a correlation with the state of democracy in each of those countries.[5] Younger democracies tended to score poorly on both indicators while Anglo-Saxon countries (including the United States), Scandinavian countries, and Japan performed best in providing political information and West Central Europe countries were better representatives of the views of the citizens. As a conclusion, Muller argues that "countries with a higher degree of media performance show higher levels of political participation and less corruption… These findings illustrate that media performance is clearly related to at least some aspects of the functioning of a democratic regime."[6]

In another study, Karlekar and Becker examine press freedom and how democratic a country is.[7] Not only did they find that democracy and press freedom were highly correlated but also found that when change occurred in one area, change quickly followed in the other. The correlation was found whether the change was positive (in the direction of more democracy or more press freedom) or negative (in the direction of less democracy and less press freedom). Despite the tight correlation between press freedom and democracy, as discussed in Chapter 2, correlation does not equal causation. Karlekar and Becker suggest four different ideas about the relationship between the two: one, press freedom could be an indicator of other freedoms essential to democracy; two, broader political freedoms could precede freedom of the press, "either because those broad political freedoms bring about media change or because they are conditions for change of freedom in the media"; three, democracy and freedom in the media change together because of some other condition; and four, that the data were an outlier and there is no relationship between the two.[8]

In summary, there is broad agreement for the role that the media plays in government, especially democratic government. They provide information, a check on government power, and the means through which socialization can occur. Given the strong connection of freedom of the press to democracy itself, a final role could be seen in promoting democratic ideals if not democracy itself.

Shaping and Making the News

While we hold the media up to certain ideals, unfortunately, there are a number of ways in which the media can fall short of what we need it to be. Media outlets today are owned by corporations who seek to make a profit. Individual reporters and editors, whether they do it on purpose or not, can introduce elements of bias into the news. Some of the information we receive may even be false or inaccurate. These elements of the media and how it affects coverage of government and politics are important to understand when looking at the relationship between government and media.

Political Economy of the News

If press freedom as well as the provision of information are essential to a well-functioning democracy, then one could argue that the media provides a public good. As discussed in Chapter 1, public goods are those things that the public cannot be excluded from partaking in and that the use of by one person does not decrease the value to another. Examples of public goods include the police, the military, clean air, clean water, etc. News and information can also be seen in that sense; certain individuals or groups cannot be excluded from gaining information from the news. Public goods, however, are subject to several types of limitations. First, since no one can be excluded from participating in them, often there is no private incentive to provide the good. Think about it this way: If the media had to provide all news for free and could not charge anything, would anyone want to report the news? Two, public goods are subject to the free rider problem that was discussed in Chapter 1. If everyone can access the news, why would anyone pay for it? This has become a particular problem for the media today.

Media corporations are just that—businesses. Businesses seek to make a profit while providing a service. In the nineteenth century, most newspapers, the main means through which citizens received their news, were sponsored by political parties who used them to publicize their activities and denigrate their opponents.[9] Even Thomas Jefferson and Alexander Hamilton partook in this practice with the newspaper that Alexander Hamilton founded, the *New York Post*, which is still in operation today. While newspapers supported through political parties often lacked control over what they covered and printed, they were essentially paid through the political party. Petrova finds that as the opportunities for advertising and their revenue increased in the late nineteenth century, newspapers were finally provided an independent revenue stream that allowed them to become independent of the political parties and their subsidies.[10] This, in turn, set the stage for the **muckraking journalists** of the late nineteenth and early twentieth century who sought to uncover and reveal political wrongdoing.

For most of the twentieth century, the media was able to rely on the same economic model. Advertising revenue was able to support the operations of the press—both in print and increasingly on television. One changing pattern, however, was the increase in **media consolidation**. In the early and mid-twentieth century, newspapers and local television channels were largely independently owned by individuals, families, or even a small business. Today, very few of these independent outlets continue to exist; most are owned by media chains that own multiple outlets, encompassing print, online, radio, and television. This pattern has only increased with some very large corporations owning several types of media outlets. For example, Disney not only has a theme park enterprise and movie and television studios but they also own ABC, ESPN, Freeform, and a number of other cable outlets. Comcast, which began as a cable provider, has expanded to encompass NBC, MSNBC, CNBC, and USA as well as Universal Studios theme parks.

Economically, the consolidation of media outlets can be a good thing for business. Producing good reporting can cost quite a bit with perhaps no economic return. Stories that seem promising might turn out otherwise, or there could be an opportunity cost in focusing on one story and not another. Larger corporations can bring to bear greater resources in terms of reporters, resources, and the ability to produce high-quality media. However, there is a danger in the loss of variety across the press. If news outlets are all owned by the same corporation, there is a chance that instead of providing different views of politics and government, they will provide the same or similar views.

Corporate ownership and consolidation also affect allegations of potential media bias—and not just partisan bias. In various studies, news channels such as Fox News and MSNBC have been singled out as providing slanted media coverage.[11] Fox News' corporate ownership is 21st Century Fox, owned by famous conservative Rupert Murdoch. Former New York City mayor Michael Bloomberg is the famous billionaire owner of Bloomberg L. P. When former mayor Bloomberg announced in January 2016 that he was considering an independent run at the White House, his news organization had to consider how to cover not only the man making the news but the man publishing the news. This ultimately led to the resignation of Bloomberg's Washington news editor over concerns about coverage of Bloomberg's run highlighting the immense pressure news organizations and reporters often face.[12]

Another challenge that the media faces is due to their reliance on advertising revenue. For advertising to be more expensive (and therefore produce a higher revenue), the outlet has to have more eyes watching or reading. In order to increase viewership and readership, mainstream media outlets have a tendency to focus on "entertainment news or other commercially appealing news items."[13] As a result, news about politics, elections, and global affairs is often minimized or avoided altogether. This effect is further magnified at a local level: although several national news outlets and twenty-four-hour news networks exist and spend a significant amount of time focusing on national politics, there is even greater scarcity of coverage for local news. Dunaway finds that corporate ownership of a newspaper is related to a significant decline in substantive political coverage.[14]

A final factor that has affected the economics of news is the birth of the Internet. The Internet has only upped the ante for traditional news outlets because individuals can find their news on the Internet for free instead of paying for a daily newspaper. The loss of revenue on the part of daily papers has significantly contributed to the tendency toward media consolidation as it is difficult for an independent newspaper to continue to publish on a daily basis, if at all, without reliable revenue sources. Some newspapers have experimented with content online that individuals must pay to access; in many cases, consumers will often find their news elsewhere instead of paying a fee. Of course, Internet news outlets face similar pressure to raise revenue for advertising on their websites by increasing the traffic through their sites. While news stories already tend to be sensationalized, some outlets have resorted to click-bait headlines, which entice the reader to click on the story even if the story is not exactly as the headline would have you believe.

These economic pressures have the potential of being significantly detrimental to the goals and ideals for the media in a democracy. If citizens cannot access the news in a timely, reliable way or if news is not provided for some reason, they could lack the knowledge needed to make good decisions about politics and particularly when it comes to voting. If the markets fail to provide a public good, the other option is often that the government steps in to provide it. However, publicly sponsored media could present some problems as well. If the government sponsors a media outlet, what guarantee is there that there will be no political interference? In other words, couldn't the government simply utilize the airwaves to produce government friendly stories or, at worst, propaganda? What if the outlet produces reporting that the government doesn't like? Reporters may feel an unspoken pressure not to dig too deeply into stories or produce reporting that is counter to the government line. Additionally, in an atmosphere of government budget cutting, budgets for public media are similarly likely to be cut. As a result, the resources that a public media outlet would have might be subject to the whims of budget appropriators from year to year.

Journalists and Journalism

Like any individual, journalists bring with them to their job their own individual ideas and predispositions. These along with their demographic characteristics, some argue, influence the types of stories that they are likely to pursue. Dunaway and Graber highlight some characteristics of journalists as a group:

- Eight percent of national journalists identified as conservative, one third identified as liberal, and more than half identified as moderate.

- They tend to be economically and socially liberal.

- They tend to have a preference for internationalist foreign policy but are cautious about military intervention.
- The majority are white and male.[15]

Given that the demographics of journalists tend to be significantly different from the mass public, then there is the potential that journalists may allow their own agendas to influence their coverage. In a survey of German journalists and the types of issues they felt were important, Peiser found that there was not a single agenda that journalists all seemed to be pursuing. Additionally, journalists seemed to assess significance to the types of issues that they were covering in their work.[16]

One area that does distinguish journalists from the mass public is in terms of education. "Education appears to be the single most important background characteristic that shapes newspeople's general philosophy of reporting."[17] A significant chunk of reporters, at least in the United States, have a humanities, social sciences, or liberal arts educational background. Perhaps one of the most fundamental elements of this educational background is a strong grounding in ethics, especially for those who have specialized in a journalism degree. Journalistic ethics are an important means through which the media is able to self-police. The potential for a story to be shown to be untrue or falsified and the consequences that come with it often keep journalists from going too far out on a ledge. In recent years, many reporters have been fired or resigned from their jobs because a story was proven to be false. One prominent example of this was *CBS Evening News* anchor Dan Rather in 2004. Relying on National Guard documentation that turned out to be falsified, Rather reported that then president George W. Bush had failed to fulfill his military service obligations in the 1970. More recently, NBC News anchor Brian Williams was suspended following revelations that he lied about several incidents, including being in Berlin on the day the Berlin Wall fell and meeting Pope John Paul II.[18] While these items never made it into news stories, the fact that Williams had lied severely damaged his journalistic credibility.

Gatekeeping, Agenda Setting, and the Potential for Bias

The explicit reason why the interests and characteristics of journalists might be important when discussing the press is that perhaps these traits influence the stories journalists cover and choose to highlight. In this sense, journalists, and especially their editors, serve as **gatekeepers**, determining what is covered and how it is covered. The gatekeepers, in choosing stories, are setting the agenda for what the media will cover. To see gatekeeping and **agenda setting** in action for yourself, conduct an experiment. Look at the website for

MSNBC News (www.msnbc.com), a more liberal-leaning news outlet. What stories are at the top of the page? Who or what are they focusing on? Now go to the website for Fox News (www.foxnews.com), a conservative outlet. What stories are they highlighting? Who is being talked about? Even if the two websites are talking about the same story or type of story, the way in which it is being covered is likely to be different. While that may not be all that surprising, consider this: If a person only ever got their news from one of those websites, what would be their impression of politics and government?

The differences between the two media outlets demonstrate the power of agenda setting. The types of stories and the way they are covered have the potential to influence how citizens see the world around them. So how do media gatekeepers choose the stories that will be covered? Several factors influence their choices—some of which we have already discussed. First, major events such as natural disasters, wars, or major presidential speeches will typically always be covered. Organizational factors may also influence news selection; each media organization may have a different idea of the types of news that should be covered and thus allow that to influence their choices. Some media outlets may also choose to cover stories that their competitors are also covering in order to compete for attention. Community interests will also be important—particularly for smaller, local outlets. Political pressure from politicians and representatives may also be significant. Finally, the economic pressures discussed previously will also influence media gatekeepers who have to satisfy the desires of their viewers but also attract viewership and readership.

If editors and reporters serve as gatekeepers and thus set the agenda for the American public, this obviously has the potential to lead to bias in the news. Accusations of media bias, though perhaps louder today, are nothing new. Most of these accusations have to do with perceived partisan bias. While there certainly are twenty-four-hour news outlets and Internet news outlets in which a liberal-conservative bias can be found, there is little evidence of one in mainstream news outlets such as the big three networks (ABC, NBC, and CBS) or major national newspapers (*New York Times*, *Wall Street Journal*, *Washington Post*, *USA Today*). Graber and Dunaway explain it this way: "Even though a majority of journalists rate themselves as more liberal than the general public and even though corporations have conservative interests, the simple fact is that many of the norms and routines of making the news prevent opportunities for individual journalists to systematically slant the news."[19] News gathering and reporting are not endeavors undertaken by a single individual but a large group. Combined with the ethical and reporting considerations, it is actually quite difficult to be continuously biased in favor of one ideology or party over the other.

One other element of bias in the news comes not from a partisan divide but from the perspective of positive and negative news. The saying, "If it bleeds, it leads" highlights the idea that negative stories seem to get far more attention than positive ones. Further study confirms this. In a study of *New York Times* coverage of the US economy across several presidents, Soroka finds a tendency toward news coverage that is more negative in tone.[20] More recently, Patterson examined news coverage of President Donald Trump's first 100 days in office finding that there was a striking emphasis on negative stories especially when compared to news coverage for other presidents. Comparing the tone of coverage between President Trump's first 100 days in office and the first 100 days of Barack Obama, George W. Bush, and Bill Clinton, Patterson found that 80 percent of Trump's coverage was negative compared to 41 percent for Obama, 57 percent for Bush, and 60 percent for Clinton.[21]

The trend toward negative news is accelerating. News stories are increasingly focusing on negative stories about the government, politicians, and especially elections without talking about substantive issues. This is also reflected in the growing prevalence toward negative attack ads used by candidates in the run-up to elections. Twenty-four hour news outlets, the Internet, and social media have also given opinion commentators (as distinct from journalists and reporters) a greater opportunity to publicly criticize their political opponents, thereby highlighting further negative coverage. Finally, negative coverage seemingly has a greater appeal to audiences, leaving a more memorable impression.[22]

Horse Race Journalism

Think about what makes your favorite sport exciting. It's probably not just watching the game, although that can be fun. Usually it's the excitement of watching your favorite team compete against its biggest rival and win. It's the competition and anticipation. In many ways, that is how many media organizations cover politics today; it's not as disinterested and objective as possible—it's the competition, it's who's winning and who's losing, whose tactics and strategies are working or not.

Know a Political Scientist

Doris Graber

Doris Graber was an influential researcher and writer in the field of political communication. Dr. Graber earned bachelor's and master's degrees from Washington University in St. Louis in political science and a PhD from Columbia University in international law and relations. She joined the faculty of the University of Illinois at Chicago and eventually held joint appointments with Harvard. In her career, Dr. Graber "conducted experimental research on mass media information processing based on brain psychology and behavioral data."[23] She was the founding editor of the journal *Political Communication* and wrote eighteen books as well as hundreds of book chapters and journal articles. Throughout her seventy plus-year career, she won several awards, including the 2003 Goldsmith Book Prize and awards from the American Political Science Association (APSA), the International Society of Political Psychology, and the National Communication Association. She is still one of the most cited scholars in political science, and her coauthored book *Mass Media and American Politics* is a staple of media classes across the country.

This adds to the thrill of watching politics, heightening the drama, increasing viewership, and thereby increasing profits.[24]

What are the characteristics of **horse race journalism**? Reporters focus on who's ahead and who's behind in the polls, highlighting the differences and disagreements between candidates and feature very shallow analysis rather than in-depth policy reporting. Such reporting can lead to serious deficits in voter and citizen information and can foster a belief that policy issues are not as important as personality or other easily understandable characteristics.

One very real result of the focus on the horse race is the phenomenon of news stations "calling" or predicting election outcomes based on incoming precinct and exit polling data. The infamous 2000 presidential election is an example of the consequences of calling elections. The state of Florida is located in two time zones, so when most of Florida's polls closed at 7:00 p.m. (EST), some of the news networks began predicting that Florida would go to Al Gore rather than George W. Bush. Anecdotal evidence suggests that voters in Florida's panhandle region, which lies in the central time zone and therefore had one more hour of voting left were less likely to go out and vote for Al Gore because they assumed he had already won the state. The rest is political history; the contested Florida election led to days of recounts, a visit to the US Supreme Court, and a George W. Bush victory.

And yet today, news stations continue to call elections but with attention to the issue of time zones and releasing information only after *all* the precincts have closed.[25] The reason for this emphasis on predicting election outcomes stems from the competition aspect of horse race journalism. Another example of this comes from fivethirtyeight.com, run by statistician Nate Silver. Prior to elections, utilizing all available polling data, Silver attempts to predict the likelihood of particular candidates winning. Ironically, his website also provides advanced statistical data for sports games—again highlighting this connection to electoral competition.

Political science research today focuses on the impacts of horse race journalism with respect to citizens' knowledge and views of politics,[26] elections,[27] gender,[28] public opinion,[29] and the influence of the Internet.[30] For example, Kahn and Kenney found evidence of bias in newspaper coverage of Senate candidates based on who the editorial page of the newspaper endorsed.[31] This suggests that even though most newspapers have a "wall of separation" policy between their editorial board and their journalists, there is some sort of partisan slant that appears to affect the type of news that is reported. However, for those who fear that political media might influence the views of voters too much, Smith reports that the impact of favorable press coverage of candidates is the highest in the early parts of a campaign when little is known about a candidate; the effect then wears off as the campaign goes on.[32]

Media Effects

A final element to consider in the making of news is how all of this impacts actual voters. Does media coverage actually change political behavior? The term

media effects refers to the observable changes that result from media coverage. In addition to the media's influence on political socialization, scholars have identified a number of other consequences of the media's coverage of politics. Media coverage of news issues has been shown to increase individuals' political knowledge.[33] In addition to basic political knowledge, media coverage has also been shown to influence various attitudes. For instance, Ridout, Grosse, and Appleton find that those who consume more media tend to have a higher perception of global threats such as terrorism.[34]

While the media's effects on knowledge and attitudes is well established, one area of research that has flourished in recent years is the effects of an increasingly partisan media on individuals. Over the past two decades, news outlets have emerged that espouse fairly partisan and polarized attitudes; Fox News tends toward the conservative side of the spectrum, whereas MSNBC, and to a lesser extent CNN, tend to be more liberal. This is in addition to the growth of the Internet and social media, which allows opinion commentators another outlet through which to reach consumers. On many of these channels, it is often difficult to distinguish between reporters and commentators who have a partisan opinion. Smith and Searles not only demonstrate that these polarized news outlets spend more time demonizing opposition candidates, as compared to focusing on their preferred candidate, but those who watch these opinion shows tend to have more extreme opinions of the channel's opposition candidates.[35] However, Smith, in a separate article, finds that these effects may be limited to early in the election cycle when not much is known about the presidential candidates.[36] Finally, Levendusky argues that partisan media has the effect of causing more extreme opinions in those who already tend to have extreme positions.[37] Although this group of people is relatively small, they have an outsize influence in elections through their participation in primary elections (where voter turnout is low to begin with) and their proclivity toward donating to political campaigns.

Consumption of particular types of media may also have an influence on voter turnout. One particular line of research has focused specifically on the utilization of attack ads during elections. In the 1990s, Ansolabehere and Iyengar advanced the theory that negative attack ads depress voter turnout in elections.[38] Not only did the two researchers focus on evidence from actual elections but they conducted a series of experiments through which they showed people both positive and negative political campaigns to determine the effects they might have on voter turnout. However, other researchers have questioned this connection with evidence showing otherwise.[39] In focusing on television advertising in general, especially during presidential elections, Krasno and Green argue that "televised presidential ads had little or no effect on turnout rates."[40] Since the early 2000s when much of this research was done, political advertising has shifted in some significant ways. First, people have the ability to record television shows and fast-forward through commercials, thus reducing their exposure to television commercials. However, the Internet has also become a significant place for political advertising, as recent elections in 2012 and 2016 have demonstrated.

Media around the World

While much of this chapter has examined media from an American perspective, many of the key ideas can be applied to media around the world. The relationship among media, press freedom, and democracy is often studied in comparative perspective as some of the findings highlighted previously show. Journalists around the world face serious dangers in pursuing the news. Reporters are regularly sent to war zones and areas where conflict is occurring. Additionally, some nondemocratic governments severely curtail reporters' access and ability to report. Given that access to information is a key component in the ability of people to participate in their governments, the role of the media is crucial for all countries. A Pew Research Center poll found that a median of 75 percent of respondents across thirty-eight different countries say "it is never acceptable for a news organization to favor one political party over others when reporting the news," but a median of 52 percent of respondents felt that the news outlets in their countries were doing a good job of reporting issues fairly.[41]

In 2017, Freedom House, an independent watchdog organization that analyzes and tracks freedom and democracy across the globe, released its latest "Freedom of the Press" rankings with several troubling findings about journalism around the world:

- Global press freedom has declined to its lowest point in thirteen years.

- Only 13 percent of the world's population has a free press; 45 percent of the world's population lives in countries where the press is considered not free.

- "Officials in more authoritarian settings such as Turkey, Ethiopia, and Venezuela used political or social unrest as a pretext for new crackdowns on independent or opposition-oriented outlets."

- "Authorities in several countries in Sub-Saharan Africa, the Middle East, and Asia extended restrictive laws to online speech, or simply shut down telecommunications services at crucial moments, such as before elections or during protests."[42]

The findings highlight a double-edged sword that is the media: while it can provide information and, perhaps more importantly, the ability to connect people, leaders with authoritarian streaks or tendencies can use the unrest that it spurs to crack down all that much harder on the media.

Take, for example, the Arab Spring movement. In 2010, a series of protests spread throughout North Africa and the Middle East, representing a challenge to the authoritarian leadership in many of those countries. In Egypt, in particular, protest leaders used social media like Facebook to connect to one another, in the process spurring huge demonstrations that would eventually lead to the ouster of Egypt's military leader. Kirkpatrick notes that this phenomenon was not limited to Egypt but spread to Syria, Yemen, Bahrain, Israel, India, and even the United States and the United Kingdom.[43] "Facebook is a common thread in all these movements—it has become the new infrastructure of protest."[44] Media, and increasingly social media, is making information and access to it more widely available than ever before—with surprising effects. However, a number of countries that have experienced such waves of protests have used the unrest to further crack down on freedom of the press. Officials in Egypt attempted to shut down the very Internet that was fueling the protests. In other countries like China, censors have been used to restrict information access or keep information from the web altogether. Global media companies also have a role to play. For example, large media corporations hoping to break into the Chinese market often have to carefully regulate their coverage of issues like Hong Kong and Taiwan. Facebook itself has been banned in China but has not ruled out working with censors should they eventually enter the Chinese market.[45]

China is but one country of many that heavily censor and restrict their press. The Committee to Protect Journalists (CPJ) ranks Eritrea, North Korea, Saudi Arabia, Ethiopia, Azerbaijan, Vietnam, and Iran all before China on a list of most censored countries. Noting the impact of the Arab Spring, the CPJ notes that Eritrea got rid of plans in 2011 to provide mobile Internet to its citizens and "although Internet is available, it is through slow dial-up communications, and fewer than 1 percent of the population goes online."[46] Another method many of these countries have used to limit press freedom is the imprisonment and intimidation of journalists. In 2017 alone, the CPJ reports that 262 journalists were imprisoned worldwide with 73 alone in Turkey and 41 in China.[47] Those numbers don't even take into account the 58 journalists who have gone missing since 1992 and the over 1,300 journalists who have been killed since 1992.[48] With such threats against their lives, many journalists are likely to restrict the information in their stories if not give up covering dangerous stories altogether.

CASE STUDY
Media in Russia

One country where many of these chilling trends have come together is Russia. While there are a large number of media outlets available along with Internet access, the increasing control exerted by Vladimir Putin and his ruling oligarchs have stifled the ability of reporters to do their job. In Freedom House's "Freedom of the Press 2017" report, they gave Russia a freedom of the press score of 83 out of 100 with 100 being not free. They also write that "the media are also expected to conform to official narratives on issues like Russia's occupation of Crimea and military intervention in Syria, and the dissemination of critical views on those topics can result in website blocking or prison sentences."[49]

Russia's government has also used intimidation and threats to limit press freedom. One recent incident is indicative of the approach that Russia takes: Nikolai Andrushchenko was a veteran journalist and critic of the Putin regime; he had focused his journalistic efforts on exposing corruption and human rights abuses.[50] Andrushchenko had been the victim of several beatings throughout his career, but in April 2017, he was severely beaten and left for dead in the streets of St. Petersburg. Six weeks later, he died of his injuries, and no assailant or assailants have been arrested. Since 1992, fifty-eight journalists have been killed in Russia, and in 2017 alone, five journalists have been imprisoned.

Russia's use of the press does not stop at their borders, however. In recent years, the Russian government established the channel Russia Today, or RT, within the United States and around the world. With a potential audience of 700 million people, "Russia Today was conceived as a soft-power tool to improve Russia's image abroad, to counter the anti-Russia bias the Kremlin saw in Western media."[51] RT has been used not only to push the Russian news narrative but has also provided more "soft news," entertainment programming that reaffirms the Russian line.[52]

Additionally, RT has been implicated in Russian efforts to influence the 2016 US presidential elections. Jim Rutenberg of the *New York Times* has noted that what makes RT particularly difficult to attack is that RT operates "on the stated terms of Western liberal democracy; they count themselves as news organizations, protected by the first amendment and the libertarian ethos of the internet."[53] Although actual viewership is quite small, it also takes advantage of social media networks like Twitter and Facebook to spread its news with several of its stories becoming viral in the process.

Critical Thinking Questions

1. How can threats and intimidation reduce the freedom of the press?

2. Is there a value or benefit in state-sponsored news broadcasts?

3. What are the possible effects of lack of press freedom in Russia?

The Internet, Social Media, and Democracy

One of the most notable changes in the media landscape over the past ten years has been the advent of social media. While outlets such as Facebook, Twitter, and Snapchat allow people around the world to connect more than ever, it has opened up new avenues, both good and bad, for people to communicate with politicians and get their news. Not only does social media and the Internet allow for faster communications but it also allows for cheaper dissemination of news and information to the point where most anyone can become a journalist or at least look like one online. While the media and freedom of the press are generally held to be beneficial to a democratic society, this darker side of the Internet and media freedom may come with significant drawbacks.

What Is Fake News? Its Effect on the 2016 Campaign

With all of the critiques of the media and concerns about its accuracy and intentions, a number of politicians have come to consider some news outlets and reports as **fake news**. This phenomenon is still relatively new and amorphous; what is fake news anyway? Does it depend on the source? Does it depend on the evidence? Is it fake simply because you disagree with it? Rather than appearing to be a single, definable concept, "The term 'fake news' itself has evolved into an all-purpose smear… to deride journalism they [politicians] don't like."[54] Allcott and Gentzkow, in their analysis of the influence of fake news in the 2016 election, define it as "news articles that are intentionally and verifiably false, and could mislead readers."[55] Even this definition of fake news can be problematic: How can someone tell if the article is *intentionally* false? What evidence can we get for the motivations of authors or news outlets? A story might turn out to be demonstrably false if new information is found or come to light, but that story might not have been intentionally wrong. Further, Allcott and Gentzkow acknowledge that their definition also includes satirical stories from websites like *The Onion,* which are demonstrably false but could be taken seriously—despite the fact that the authors of those articles probably did not mean for them to be taken seriously.

Importantly, the phenomenon of fake news is not new; consider the radio broadcast of H. G. Wells's *The War of the Worlds* in 1938. With many listeners tuning in late and not hearing the introduction, a panic swept many communities that believed that the alien invasion Wells described was actually happening. We can also consider the long list of conspiracy theories that some have taken to be true at some point or another including whether moon landing in 1969 was faked (it wasn't). However, Allcott and Gentzkow believe that fake news could be more dangerous now than ever. First, as noted previously, it is very easy to get into the "news" game on the Internet with a low cost of entry. Two, social media has made it easier for fake news to spread. And three, trust and confidence in the media in general has fallen, making it more likely for people to discount what they hear in traditional news outlets.[56]

But what effect, if any, did so-called fake news have on the 2016 election? Several studies have attempted to answer this question. Guess, Nyhan, and Reifler found that one in four Americans visited a website that could be classified as fake news; examples of such sites include bipartisanreport.com, redstatewatcher.com, usherald.com, dailywire.com, and worldnewspolitics.com.[57] Notably, many of these fake news websites have names that could be confused with actual media outlets, making it harder for news consumers to discriminate between fake and accurate news. Further, they find that most of the people who visited such sites were supporters of Donald Trump and that an even smaller subset of Trump supporters, about 10 percent, represented the most visits, about 60 percent, to fake news sites.[58] Allcott and Gentzkow find that the fake news sites they identified received 159 million visits in the month prior to the 2016 election.[59] Finally, both studies found that most fake news in the lead-up to the 2016 election was not only about Donald Trump but pro-Donald Trump in nature.

It is probably impossible to determine whether the onslaught of fake news in any direction affected the outcome of the 2016 election. A certain element of fake news was propagated by the Russian government through various mediums including RT, discussed previously, and on the Internet through their innocuously named Internet Research Agency, which was indicted for their actions during the 2016 campaign. US intelligence agencies have concluded that the intent of Russia in undertaking such actions was to influence the election in Donald Trump's favor, but even they could not, and would not, determine whether the efforts had any effect.

Social Media's Role

What we do know is that social media has propagated the flow of false and fake news. Not only does social media provide an outlet for posting fake news but with over 60 percent of Americans reporting that they get their news via social media, the opportunity for fake news to become viral and spread is greater than ever. Facebook, in particular, has come under fire since the 2016 election for their role in spreading fake news. Guess, Nyhan, and Reifler report that Facebook was "the most important mechanism facilitating the spread of fake news"; not only does Facebook allow its users to like and share news stories that could potentially be false with a simple click but it provides a platform for groups with bad intentions to spread false and misleading information.[60] Perhaps even more damning, another analysis showed that the best performing news stories (in terms of engagement) on Facebook in the three months prior to the election were from fake news.[61]

Facebook was also utilized by Russians in the Internet Research Agency to stir up discontent among Americans. Following the election, Facebook "revealed that an estimated 10 million people in the US have been served ads purchased by accounts linked to Russia, with approximately 44% appearing prior to the November 2016 presidential election. The majority focused on 'divisive social and political messages.'"[62] While Facebook closed the suspicious accounts, it also provided a tool for Facebook users to determine whether they had been exposed to the Russian ads but only did so nearly a year after the election.

Consequences for Democracy

Several elements of the preceding discussion are worthy of concern. First, the relative ease with which fake news can be disseminated could be harmful in terms of accuracy of information needed for citizens and voters to make good decisions in terms of voting and politics. As fake news becomes more prominent and as trust in the media has declined, the danger is in believing news that is actually fake and disbelieving news that is actually true.

A second concern is in the ability of foreign actors to utilize fake news and social media to involve themselves in American politics. The 2016 election was not a one-off. The Russian government, in particular, has sought previously to impact elections around the world and are continuing their efforts. Since the 2016 election, analysts have identified several events following which Russian agents perpetuated false information on the Internet, including after the Parkland school shooting. The Alliance for Securing Democracy tracks Russian influence efforts online and has identified over 600 Russia-connected Twitter accounts or bots in addition to Russian media and news outlets. While social media and the Internet make it easier for people to connect, it also makes it easier for bad actors to influence politics and society.

Facebook now provides fact-checking on news stories posted on the site and buries stories that they deem to be fake. However, this brings up another element involved not just with Facebook but with Google: Who is checking the checkers? Does filtering out news that is classified as fake take away a certain element of choice and discretion? In a 2018 blog post, Facebook noted the controversy:

> In the public debate over false news, many believe Facebook should use its own judgment to filter out misinformation. We've chosen not to do that

because we don't want to be the arbiters of truth, nor do we imagine this is a role the world would want for us.[63]

This makes it all the more incumbent on individual people to be media literate or have the ability to discern good reporting from bad. When people do not understand the news or the sources from which the news is coming, it can make it even easier for bad actors to influence a country's politics.

Finally, social media may be reinforcing some of our worst media habits. Research has shown that people tend to be selectively engaged with different media sources—that is, they choose which news sources to pay attention to and usually choose those sources that already agree with their own ideological or political bias. These sources thus tend to reinforce the biases people already have. Combine **selective engagement**, media bias, and social media together, and there is a recipe for disaster. Siegel argues that social networks can amplify the impact of media bias—particularly media bias that is away from the status quo. This can have significant effects in terms of making media bias not only more obvious but perhaps more consequential in terms of the number of people being exposed to it.[64] In other words, social media can amplify the bias that people are already engaging in. What results is a vicious circle of becoming so biased that it is easy to call news that doesn't agree with one's viewpoint fake and discount it altogether.

While the moniker of fake news is often bandied about, the fact remains that most journalists are committed to the work they do and to providing the best, most accurate, and timely information that they can. Journalists abide by a high standard of ethics and have often been fired or otherwise punished for violating them. To a certain extent, we must be able to trust journalists to do their job or risk having so little information, or so much wrong information, that democracy is ultimately undermined.

STUDENT STUDY SITE

Visit https://edge.sagepub.com/whitmancobb

CHAPTER SUMMARY

- The media can serve various functions in a democracy, including educating citizens, being a watchdog, and providing an avenue for political socialization.

- Many factors affect how journalists report the news. Economics and business practices significantly affect what news is reported and how. In turn, journalists and reporters can be gatekeepers in determining what the media will cover and how. These choices can ultimately affect political behavior of citizens.

- There is great variability in the amount of freedom of the press around the world. Journalists face danger not only in covering dangerous situations but from pressure and intimidation from governments as well.

- Fake news is difficult to define, but its effect, combined with increasing distrust of the media, can have particular consequences for the media and the general population alike.

KEY TERMS

agenda setting: Determining what gets covered, when, and how

fake news: News that is intentionally false and misleading

gatekeepers: Editors and journalists deciding what news makes it to the public

horse race journalism: Journalism that focuses on the contest of politics rather than the substance

media consolidation: Describes the pattern of small independent media outlets being bought by larger media corporations

media effects: Observable changes that result from media coverage

muckraking journalists: A journalistic practice of the late nineteenth and early twentieth century where journalists sought to uncover corruption in government institutions

selective engagement: Consumers choosing news stories and outlets that already conform with their political beliefs

DISCUSSION QUESTIONS

1. In your opinion, what is the most important role that the media plays? Why?

2. How do economic pressures impact the making of news? Is it a positive or negative impact?

3. Why do you think freedom of the press has been trending downward globally?

4. What is fake news? How do you know it when you see it?

5. Is social media a beneficial element in a democratic society or a detrimental one? Why?

FOR FURTHER READING

Allcott, Hunt, and Matthew Gentzkow. "Social Media and Fake News in the 2016 Election." *The Journal of Economic Perspectives* 31, no. 2 (2017): 213.

Patterson, Thomas. "News Coverage of Donald Trump's First 100 Days in Office." *Shorenstein Center on Media, Politics, and Public Policy*, May 2017, https://shorensteincenter.org/news-coverage-donald-trumps-first-100-days/.

Pautz, Michelle C., and Megan K. Warnement. "Government on the Silver Screen: Contemporary American Cinema's Depiction of Bureaucrats, Police, Officers, and Soldiers."

PS: Political Science and Politics 46, no. 3 (2013): 569–579.

Jim Rutenberg. "RT, Sputnik, and Russia's New Theory of War." New York Times Magazine, Sept. 13, 2017, https://www.nytimes.com/2017/09/13/magazine/rt-sputnik-and-russias-new-theory-of-war.html.

Committee to Protect Journalists (CPJ): www.cpj.org

NOTES

1. "Great American Thinkers on Free Speech," *Saturday Evening Post*, Jan. 16, 2015, www.saturdayeveningpost.com/2015/01/16/history/great-american-thinkers-free-speech.html.

2. Nancy Benac, "Remember Nixon? There's History behind Trump's Press Attacks," *Seattle Times*, Feb. 17, 2017, https://www.seattletimes.com/nation-world/remember-nixon-theres-history-behind-trumps-press-attacks/.

3. Todd S. Purdum, "Terror in Oklahoma: The President; Shifting Debate to the Political Climate, Clinton Condemns 'Promoters of Paranoia,'" *New York Times*, April 25, 1995, https://www.nytimes.com/1995/04/25/us/terror-oklahoma-president-shifting-debate-political-climate-clinton-condemns.html.

4. Michelle C. Pautz and Megan K. Warnement, "Government on the Silver Screen: Contemporary American Cinema's Depiction of Bureaucrats, Police, Officers, and Soldiers," *PS: Political Science and Politics* 46, no. 3 (2013): 569–579.

5. Lisa Muller, "The Impact of Mass Media on the Quality of Democracy within a State Remains a Much Overlooked Area of Study," *London School of Economics: Euro Crisis in the Press*, Dec. 10, 2014, http://blogs.lse.ac.uk/eurocrisispress/2014/12/10/the-impact-of-the-mass-media-on-the-quality-of-democracy-within-a-state-remains-a-much-overlooked-area-of-study/.

6. Ibid.

7. Karin Deutsch Karlekar and Lee B. Becker, "By the Numbers: Tracing the Statistical Correlation between Press Freedom and Democracy," *Center for International Media Assistance*, April 22, 2014, https://www.cima.ned.org/publication/by_the_numbers___tracing_the_statistical_correlation_between_press_freedom_and_democracy/.

8. Ibid., 5

9. Maria Petrova, "Newspapers and Parties: How Advertising Revenues Created an Independent Press," *American Political Science Review* 105, no. 4 (2011): 790–808.

10. Ibid.

11. Matthew S. Levendusky, "Why Do Partisan Media Polarize Viewers?" *American Journal of Political Science* 57, no. 3 (2013): 611–623.

12. Tom Kludt, "Bloomberg Editor Quits: We Can't Cover Michael Bloomberg Aggressively," *CNN Money*, Jan. 27, 2016, http://money.cnn.com/2016/01/27/media/michael-bloomberg-editor-kathy-kiely-quits/.

13. Johanna Dunaway, "Markets, Ownership, and the Quality of Campaign News Coverage," *The Journal of Politics* 70, no. 4 (2008): 1193.

14. Ibid.

15. Doris A. Graber and Johanna Dunaway, *Mass Media and American Politics*, 10th ed. (Washington, DC: CQ Press, 2018), 153–154.

16. Wolfram Peiser, "Setting the Journalist Agenda: Influences from Journalists' Individual Characteristics and from Media Factors," *Journalism and Mass Communication Quarterly* 77, no. 2 (2000): 243–257.

17. Graber and Dunaway, *Mass Media and American Politics*, 153.

18. Pamela Engel and Natasha Bertrand, "3 Events Brian Williams Is Suspected of Lying About," *Business Insider*, Feb. 3, 2015, http://www.businessinsider.com/what-brian-williams-has-lied-about-2015-2.

19. Graber and Dunaway, *Mass Media and American Politics*, 428.

20. Stuart N. Soroka, "The Gatekeeping Function: Distributions of Information in Media and the Real World," *The Journal of Politics* 74, no. 2 (2012): 514–528.

21. Thomas Patterson, "News Coverage of Donald Trump's First 100 Days in Office," *Shorenstein Center on Media, Politics, and Public Policy*, May 2017, https://shorensteincenter.org/news-coverage-donald-trumps-first-100-days/.

22. Graber and Dunaway, *Mass Media and American Politics*.

23. "Doris Graber, Professor Emerita," *UIC Communication*, https://comm.uic.edu/comm/people/affiliate-faculty/doris-graber.

24. Shanto Iyengar, Helmut Norpoth, and Kyu S. Hahn, "Consumer Demand for Election News: The Horserace Sells," *The Journal of Politics* 66, no. 1 (2004): 157–175.

25. Kathleen A. Frankovic, "News Organizations' Responses to the Mistakes of Election 2000: Why They Will Continue to Project Elections," *Public Opinion Quarterly* 67, no. 1 (2003): 19–31.

26. Kim Friedkin Kahn and Patrick J. Kenney, "The Slant of the News: How Editorial Endorsements Influence Campaign Coverage and Citizens' Views of Candidates," *American Political Science Review* 96, no. 2 (2002): 381–394. Susan A. Banducci and Jeffrey A. Karp, "How Elections Change the Way Citizens View the Political System: Campaigns, Media Effects, and Electoral Outcomes in Comparative Perspective, "*British Journal of Political Science* 33, no. 3 (2003): 443–467.

27. David A. M. Peterson and Paul A. Djupe, "When Primary Campaigns Go Negative: The Determinants of Campaign Negativity," *Political Research Quarterly* 58, no. 1 (2005): 45–54.

28. Lonna Raw Atkeson and Timothy B. Krebs, "Press Coverage of Mayoral Candidates: The Role of Gender in News Reporting and Campaign Issue Speech," *Political Research Quarterly* 61, no. 2 (2008): 239–252. Johanna Dunaway et al., "Traits versus Issues: How Female Candidates Shape Coverage of Senate and Gubernatorial Races," *Political Research Quarterly* 66, no. 3 (2013): 715–726.

29. Richard Forgette and Jonathan S. Morris, "High-Conflict Television News and Public Opinion," *Political Research Quarterly* 59, no. 3 (2006): 447–456.

30. Caroline J. Tolbert and Ramona S. McNeal, "Unraveling the Effects of the Internet on Political Participation," *Political Research Quarterly* 56, no. 2 (2003): 175–185.

31. Kahn and Kenney, "The Slant of the News."

32. Glen Smith, "The Timing of Partisan Media Effects during a Presidential Election," *Political Research Quarterly* 69, no. 4 (2016): 655–666.

33. Jason Barabas and Jennifer Jerit, "Estimating the Causal Effects of Media Coverage on Policy-Specific Knowledge," *American Journal of Political Science* 53, no. 1 (2009): 73–89.

34. Travis N. Ridout, Ashley C. Grosse, and Andrew M. Appleton, "News Media Use and Americans' Perceptions of Global Threat," *British Journal of Political Science* 38, no. 4 (2008): 575–593.

35. Glen Smith and Kathleen Searles, "Fair and Balanced News or a Difference of Opinion? Why Opinion Shows Matter for Media Effects," *Political Research Quarterly* 66, no. 3 (2013): 671–684.

36. Smith, "The Timing of Partisan Media Effects."

37. Matthew S. Levendusky, "Why Do Partisan Media Polarize Viewers?" *American Journal of Political Science* 57, no. 3 (2013): 611–623.

38. Stephen Ansolabehere and Shanto Iyengar, *Going Negative: How Political Advertisements Shrink and Polarize the Electorate* (New York: The Free Press, 1997).

39. Martin P. Wattenberg and Craig Leonard Brians, "Negative Campaign Advertising: Demobilizer or Mobilizer?" *American Political Science Review* 93, no. 4 (1999): 891–899.

40. Jonathan S. Krasno and Donald P. Green, "Do Televised Presidential Ads Increase Voter Turnout? Evidence from a Natural Experiment," *The Journal of Politics* 70, no. 1 (2008): 246.

41. Amy Mitchell, Katie Simmons, Katerina Eva Matsa, and Laura Silver, "Publics Globally Want Unbiased

News Coverage, but are Divided on Whether Their News Media Deliver," *Pew Research Center*, Jan. 11, 2018, www.pewglobal.org/2018/01/11/publics-globally-want-unbiased-news-coverage-but-are-divided-on-whether-their-news-media-deliver/.

42. Freedom House, "Press Freedom's Dark Horizon," *Freedom House*, https://freedomhouse.org/report/freedom-press/freedom-press-2017.

43. David Kirkpatrick, "Does Facebook Have a Foreign Policy?" *Foreign Policy* 190 (2011): 55.

44. Ibid.

45. Ibid.

46. Committee to Protect Journalists, "10 Most Censored Countries," *CPJ.org*, https://cpj.org/2015/04/10-most-censored-countries.php.

47. Committee to Protect Journalists, "Imprisoned in 2017," *CPJ.org*, https://cpj.org/data/imprisoned/2017/?status=Imprisoned&end_year=2017&group_by=location.

48. Committee to Protect Journalists, "1303 Journalists Killed," *CPJ.org*, https://cpj.org/data/killed/?status=Killed&motive Confirmed%5B%5D=Confirmed& type%5B%5D=Journalist&start_year=1992&end_year=2018&group_by=year.

49. Freedom House, "Freedom of the Press 2017: Russia Profile," *FreedomHouse.org*, https://freedomhouse.org/report/freedom-press/2017/russia.

50. Committee to Protect Journalists, "Nikolai Andrushchenko," *CPJ.org*, https://cpj.org/data/people/nikolai-andrushchenko/index.php.

51. Julia Ioffe, "What Is Russia Today?" *Columbia Journalism Review*, Sept./Oct. 2010, https://archives.cjr.org/feature/what_is_russia_today.php.

52. Vera Toltz and Precious N. Chatterje-Doody, "Four Things You Need to Know about Russian Media Manipulation Strategies," *The Conversation*, April 5, 2018, http://theconversation.com/four-things-you-need-to-know-about-russian-media-manipulation-strategies-94307.

53. Jim Rutenberg, "RT, Sputnik, and Russia's New Theory of War," *New York Times Magazine*, Sept.

13, 2017, https://www.nytimes.com/2017/09/13/magazine/rt-sputnik-and-russias-new-theory-of-war.html.

54. Benedict Carey, "'Fake News': Wide Reach but Little Impact, Study Suggests," *New York Times*, Jan. 2, 2018, https://www.nytimes.com/2018/01/02/health/fake-news-conservative-liberal.html.

55. Hunt Allcott and Matthew Gentzkow, "Social Media and Fake News in the 2016 Election," *The Journal of Economic Perspectives* 31, no. 2 (2017): 213.

56. Ibid.

57. Andrew Guess, Brendan Nyhan, and Jason Reifler, "Selective Exposure to Misinformation: Evidence from the Consumption of Fake News During the 2016 Presidential Campaign," *European Research Council*, Jan. 9, 2018, https://www.dartmouth.edu/~nyhan/fake-news-2016.pdf.

58. Ibid.

59. Allcott and Gentzkow, "Social Media and Fake News in the 2016 Election."

60. Guess, Nyhan, and Reifler, "Selection Exposure to Misinformation," 2.

61. Craig Silverman, "This Analysis Shows How Viral Fake Election News Stories Outperformed Real News on Facebook," *Buzzfeed News*, Nov. 16, 2016, https://www.buzzfeed.com/craigsilverman/viral-fake-election-news-outperformed-real-news-on-facebook?utm_term=.qk7D08LkkQ#.doydvBZ11V.

62. Jason Murdock, "What Is the Internet Research Agency? Facebook Shuts Hundreds of Accounts Linked to Russian Troll Factory," *Newsweek*, April 4, 2018, www.newsweek.com/what-internet-research-agency-facebook-shuts-hundreds-accounts-linked-russia-870889.

63. Samidh Chakrabarti, "Hard Questions: What Effect Does Social Media Have on Democracy?" *Facebook Newsroom*, Jan. 22, 2018, https://newsroom.fb.com/news/2018/01/effect-social-media-democracy/?frame-nonce=bd5e374778.

64. David A. Siegel, "Social Networks and the Mass Media," *American Political Science Review* 107, no. 4 (2013): 786–805.

Subfields

Senate majority leader Mitch McConnell of Kentucky (center) makes remarks after President Donald Trump's visit to Capitol Hill, as Sen. John Cornyn, R-TX (right), listens, November 28, 2017, in Washington, D.C. Trump attended the GOP weekly policy luncheon for talks on tax reform, among other issues.

Source: MIKE THEILER/UP/Newscom

American Politics

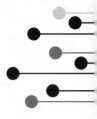

Many people do not take an interest in politics until it affects them directly. For some, it's too boring to take the time to understand, or they simply don't see how it affects them personally. In reality, politics affects all of us every day, practically from the moment we wake up. The government ensures the safety of the water we use to shower and brush our teeth with, the government determines the laws of the road that we drive on every day, and the government stipulates the conditions under which we work and what is considered a safe workplace environment. Although these facts can be pointed out to everyone, politics is still a confusing, messy, and difficult topic to master; understanding political science is one step to understanding why it should be that way.

Take, as an example, passing a law, an activity that involves two branches of government (and sometimes all three) and thousands of people. In December 2017, Congress passed and President Donald Trump signed into law a massive overhaul of the US tax code—something that had not been done since the 1980s. However, writing a complicated piece of legislation such as a tax bill involves not just the 535 elected members of Congress but hundreds of subject matter experts, lobbyists, public organizations, businesses, and—yes—citizens. Once the bill was written, it had to be negotiated and passed by a majority of both the House and the Senate, all abiding by strict rules under what's known as a budget reconciliation procedure. Only then could the bill be signed by the president and become law. If you watched this process in real time, it appeared messy, confusing, and complicated. But understanding the functions and responsibilities of the different branches of government and the motivations

Chapter Objectives

1. Describe the major functions and characteristics of Congress.

2. Understand the powers and functions of the presidency.

3. Examine the role and politics of the federal courts.

4. Examine patterns of political behavior in the United States.

and obligations of those who populate those organizations demonstrates a somewhat orderly, if not entirely, rational process to it.

American politics as a subfield of political science is a broad area of study. While it will not be possible to go into complete detail about every topic, this chapter takes up an examination of the institutions of American government as well as political behavior. Those who study political institutions generally believe that the rules of the game shape how individuals play it. Institutionalists like to study how things like Congress and the presidency develop over time or the factors that influence developments like the enlargement of the executive branch. **Political behavior** refers to the actions of individuals in a political system and includes things such as political parties and interest groups, public opinion, and voting. This chapter begins with a discussion of American institutions, including Congress, the presidency, and the courts (bureaucracy is left for Chapter 11) before delving into aspects of political behavior in the United States.

Congress

The Founders envisioned the Congress to be the center of American power, the branch of government in which the wishes and desires of the American public would be translated into public policy. To this end, they created a Congress that melded together different aspects of representation, power, and responsibility, along the way fashioning the House of Representatives and the Senate. Perhaps no other characteristic is as important to understanding the United States Congress as its bicameralism. The two chambers are incredibly different in size, scope, and powers, yet both must agree to any legislation that is intended to become law.

Differences between the House and Senate

To begin with, the House has 435 members divided proportionally across the states by population; every ten years, the US Census allows for a reapportionment of representatives based on current population numbers. Each member represents not an entire state but merely a small slice of a state, something called a district. This process of districting is redone every ten years, but, in many cases, is done in an incredibly partisan process known as **gerrymandering**. The resulting gerrymandered districts are often safe seats for Republicans or Democrats—with a majority of voters in the district intending to vote in a particular way. Gerrymandering has been blamed for everything from increased polarization in the Congress to a growing reelection rate.[1]

The Senate, on the other hand, consists of 100 senators: two from each state. Originally, senators were chosen by state legislatures; because of the Seventeenth Amendment to the Constitution, voters in each state were given the opportunity to directly choose their senators. Lee and Oppenheimer highlight the representational differences that their sizes introduce. In 2014, California had 38.8 million residents and still had two US senators. On the other hand, Alaska had fewer than 1 million at 736,732 residents and two US senators. The argument can be made, then, that Alaskans, and the residents of other small states, receive more representation in the Senate than large states like California; Lee and Oppenheimer show that these representational differences can have a significant impact on the policy outcomes of the Senate.[2] Specifically, smaller states tend to get federal dollars and benefits out of proportion with the amount of income taxes their citizens pay.

Another institutional difference between the House and Senate related to size is their ability to hone in (or not) on major issues of the day. With only 100 members in the Senate, senators must serve on more committees and subcommittees than their House counterparts. In the House, with more representatives, members do not have to divide their time as much. Thus, House members have more time to focus on issues that are related to their constituency as well as a greater opportunity to focus on those issues on a regular basis. Senators, instead, must divide their time much more and focus on more national and varied interests since their constituencies will almost always be larger than districts for the House.[3]

The difference in size between the House and the Senate contributes to the rules under which each chamber works. In the House, with its 435-member population, there are stricter rules about what goes on the House floor, how committees are operated, and the privileges of the majority and minority parties. These rules essentially define a majoritarian institution—an organization in which the majority party tends to have the most power and resources. Take, for example, the House Rules Committee, one of the most important and consequential committees in the body. It sets the rules for consideration of a bill, including the length of debate and whether any amendments may be considered and who those amendments may be offered by. The majority party in the House holds a supermajority of seats on the rules committee, thereby ensuring that the majority party gets favorable treatment for their legislating and oftentimes stopping legislation sponsored by the minority.

With the Senate's smaller size and traditions of greater individual power, the minority party is granted far more influence than in the House. The senatorial procedure of the **filibuster** has been portrayed in the classic film *Mr. Smith Goes to Washington,* but the reality is that the threat of the filibuster forces the Senate to operate in a supermajoritarian manner. The Senate, partially because of its small size, has a tradition of unlimited debate on most topics; in order to end debate on a bill and move toward voting procedures, senators must vote to invoke cloture, which requires the vote of sixty senators. When the split between Democrats and Republicans is as close as it has been in recent years, the sixty-vote requirement forces as least some of the minority party's members to vote to end debate—something that may be difficult to achieve. Many political scientists have examined the effects of the sixty-vote Senate, including Barbara Sinclair whose data demonstrate that the number of filibusters has increased over time. Frances Lee has argued that the sixty-vote threshold has become the norm in the Senate, unlike past periods of American history.[4] Still, others have examined the effect that this requirement has on judicial appointments, especially in regard to the rate at which they have been approved.[5]

Congressional Behavior

Political scientists have also explored the question of why members of Congress behave the way they do. In 1974, Mayhew published the classic *Congress: The Electoral Connection*. In it, Mayhew postulates that members act the way they do for one basic reason: they desire reelection. To demonstrate this idea, he explores the different types of activities members of Congress would focus on if indeed reelection is the ultimate goal: advertising, credit claiming, and position taking. Mayhew acknowledges that there could be other goals that members seek, such as future jobs, power, and good policy.[6] Mayhew's book has been an influential piece of research that has underlined much of the congressional literature that has come after it.

The Jobs of Congress

But what is it that members of Congress *do* or are supposed to do? In addition to representing the interests of their constituents, they are tasked with legislating, appropriating the nation's money, and providing oversight of the executive branch. Creating and passing laws is perhaps the single most significant job the American public expects Congress to do. Congress is expected to produce solutions to those problems that are the most pressing and to improve the lives of American citizens in doing so. A simple sketch of the legislative process can be boiled down to the following steps:

Know a Political Scientist

David Mayhew

David Mayhew, one of the most well-known congressional scholars, has left an indelible mark on political science. Mayhew earned his doctorate from Harvard in 1964 and joined the faculty at Yale University in 1968, where he remained until his retirement in 2015. Mayhew published the seminal work *Congress: The Electoral Connection* in 1974. The book argues that members of Congress behave the way they do because they pursue the goal of reelection. The theory has influenced a generation of congressional scholars for its simplicity and underlying rationality.

Mayhew has written seven other books on topics such as divided government, electoral realignments, and political parties.

In addition to his major works, he has authored numerous referred articles, made over 100 presentations of his work, participated in numerous sponsored panels and discussions, and has won seven prestigious awards, including the Richard E. Neustadt Award and the James Madison Award for career contributions.

1. A bill is introduced in either the House or the Senate.

2. The bill is referred to a standing committee that deals with the subject matter in the bill.

3. The committee holds hearings and revises the bill. The committee will vote on the bill.

4. In the House, the bill goes to the rules committee, which schedules floor debate and votes. It also creates "rules" under which the bill will be considered that specify the total debate time and the amount and type of amendments that may or may not be considered.

   a. The entire House considers the bill and votes.

5. In the Senate, the bill may be brought to the floor under a unanimous consent agreement (UCA) under which the entire Senate membership agrees to terms of debate, or it can be motioned to the floor.

   a. If the bill is brought under a UCA, debate proceeds and a vote is held. If the bill is brought as a motion, debate continues until cloture is invoked to end debate. The Senate then votes.

6. If there are any differences between the two bills, a conference committee may be created to deal with them. A conference committee is a temporary committee made up of both House and Senate members to work out a compromise bill.

7. The bill is then voted on again by both the House and Senate, and only then, if it passes both chambers in the same form, does it get sent to the president.

While these steps seem relatively simple, in real life, it can be anything but; as shown in Figure 7.1, the number of bills passed by Congress has fallen from a high of 804 in the 95th Congress (1977–1978) to just 284 in the 112th Congress (2011–2012).

In addition to legislating, Congress is also responsible for creating and passing a budget for the United States in accordance with the Constitution. Specifically, this process must begin with the House of Representatives, which was designed by the Founders to be the most direct voice of the people. Ideally, a budget is first passed by the House and then the Senate, all to be signed by the president by the beginning of each fiscal year. However, like legislating itself, the process has become all the more difficult as members of Congress disagree on both the levels of spending to give to various areas and the priority they should receive. These disagreements have often prevented Congress from passing a budget before the October 1 fiscal year, leading to the passage of **continuing resolutions**, which allow the government to continue operating until a certain date.

Figure 7.1   Bills Enacted by Congressional Session

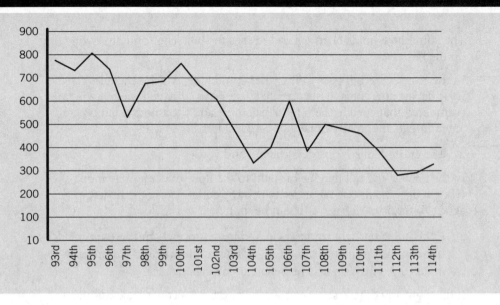

Source: Govtrack.us.

One of the most recent government shutdowns is instructive in today's budgetary politics. In the fall of 2013, with Republicans in the majority in the House and Democrats holding both the Senate and the presidency, the budget was held up over funding for the Patient Protection and Affordable Care Act—something Republicans wished to restrict and Democrats wanted included. In an attempt to create a budget that could pass both chambers, the House and the Senate traded different budget options, but none could muster a majority in both chambers, leading to a sixteen-day government shutdown. Today's budgetary conundrums continue to center around health care and entitlement funding, military spending, and other domestic priorities.

A final major task of members of Congress is oversight of the executive branch. This activity primarily takes place in the various committees into which members of Congress are divided. These standing committees are organized around policy areas and help to oversee those relevant agencies that deal with those policies. Committees will hold hearings and conduct investigations into the conduct of executive branch agencies and officials. While many investigations can be nonpolitical, or at least bipartisan, oftentimes committee investigations become very political acts. In the wake of both the *Challenger* and *Columbia* space shuttle disasters, for example, committees in both the House and the Senate investigated NASA and the immediate causes of the loss of the shuttles. More recently, however, the Intelligence committees in both the House and the Senate have been investigating the ties between the Russian government and the 2016 election.

The Presidency

It's hard to tease out the difference between the *president*, the person who inhabits the Oval Office at any given time, and the *presidency*, the office itself. Sometimes, we can't tell where one ends and the other begins; the office of the president becomes so much like the person of the president. However, the distinction between the two is important; there are characteristics and aspects of the office that political scientists wish to delve into above and apart from the politics of the man (or the woman). Although studies of individual presidents are worthwhile, for the most part, they contain mostly history. As such, political scientists try to look at the broader themes and patterns across different presidencies.

Presidential Power

For most of the history of the United States, the office of the president was so small that you could take the two to mean the same thing. It was not until Franklin Roosevelt's presidency that the size and scope of the executive office began to change. It is exactly this growth of the presidency that intrigues many political scientists; they examine the causes and consequences of the growth of the presidency that has accompanied modern life. Ragsdale and Theis, for example, explore the institutionalization of the presidency arguing that an increase in governmental activities led to the growth of the presidency.[7] This coincides with what government was being asked to do—particularly from the 1930s on; Roosevelt had to respond to the Great Depression with World War II coming quickly on its heels. On the other hand, Dickinson and Lebo find that the growth of the presidency was driven by changes in how the presidency relates to other institutions, particularly the Congress, the press, and the public, rather than what government was being asked to do.[8] In the end, many of the changes in the executive branch were probably influenced by all of these considerations as well as the crises America experienced in the 1930s and 1940s.

Presidential power has also increased over time. When the Constitution was first formulated, most of the Founders imagined that Congress would be the most powerful of the three branches, representing the will, and sometimes the whim, of the people. However, presidents have often sought to increase their own power over time, particularly during times of trouble. When we talk about power, particularly for the president, there are different types. First, there are the president's constitutional powers—the duties and responsibilities laid out for the position in the Constitution. These include the president's ability to execute the laws, make treaties and appointments (with the advice and consent of the Senate), sign and veto laws, be commander in chief of the armed forces, and issue pardons. Compared to the powers laid out for Congress in the Constitution, these are very limited indeed. On the other hand, presidents have far more power to exercise than this today. They can influence public opinion, the media, and Congress. They can carry out foreign policy with only limited influence from Congress. They can send troops wherever they would like for up to sixty days without congressional approval. They can issue executive orders and signing statements as well as interpret laws in particular ways.

Power is also the subject of one of the classic treatises on the presidency, Neustadt's *Presidential Power and the Modern Presidents*. Originally published in 1960, Neustadt examines the record of presidential accomplishment, looking to explain what increases and decreases presidential power. He theorizes that real presidential power is in the president's ability to persuade, in his ability to get other people to do things that they would not have otherwise done. For Neustadt, the president's power to persuade is contingent not only on his professional reputation inside Washington—how the Washington elite view his power—but also on the president's reputation with the public. When the president can manage these two reputations, he (or she) has more leverage to get what they want done.[9] Neustadt's book has left a long legacy. His description of the three branches of government as separated institutions sharing power (rather than separate institutions) has redefined how political scientists look at the exercise of power.

The President and the Other Branches

Of course, presidential power does not exist in a vacuum; presidents need power because they must work in a governmental system of separated institutions sharing power. In order for the president to get their way, they must have power. This leads to a discussion of not only where the presidency fits in the political system but of the relationships between the president and other parts of the system. The one relationship that has merited the most attention has been that of the president with Congress. Together, they are the heart and soul of the lawmaking and law executing part of government; one cannot do much without the other, though they try. Recent research, for example, has focused on the idea of presidential unilateralism, or the ability of presidents to operate independently of the Congress. Given the combination of divided government and increased party polarization in the last years of Barack Obama's presidency, then president Obama often resorted to the use of executive orders, further discussed in the next section. Bolton and Thrower find historical support for these types of presidential actions, arguing that presidents tend to issue more executive orders under periods of divided government and low congressional capacity.[10] While this might seem a usurpation of legislative and congressional power, Belco and Rottinghaus find that presidents may actually issue executive orders in order to support legislative efforts of their own party.[11] This pattern actually fits quite well with how President Donald Trump has utilized executive orders in his first term as president.

Unlike the president and Congress, there is little in the way of regular contact between the president and the courts. When there are vacancies either on the Supreme Court or elsewhere in the federal judiciary, the president can make judicial nominations. If the federal government or the president himself is a party to a lawsuit being heard in court, the president may be involved in shaping the arguments to be used through the position of the solicitor general. However, and perhaps more importantly, presidents, by virtue of their position, must carry out the decisions of the courts, particularly those that interpret laws in various ways. For instance, legend has it that after the Supreme Court handed down a ruling in the case *Worchester v. Georgia* in 1832, Andrew Jackson said, "John Marshall has made his decision; now let him enforce it!" This story (and it is a story as there is no hard evidence that he ever said this) reminds us that often presidents are asked to carry out laws they do not agree with when courts determine that it is right and constitutional.

By far, the bulk of the political science research into the relationship between the president and the courts has examined the nomination process that has become more contentious over the past half century. Whittington has noted that the partisan makeup of the Senate and the White House along with electoral timetables has impacted the president's ability to make a successful Supreme Court appointment.[12] Johnson and Roberts, building on Neustadt's idea of presidential power as the power to persuade, argue that presidents can overcome a reluctant Senate by going public and using their political capital to force the issue on Capitol Hill.[13] Finally, Shipan and Shannon find that the more ideological distance between the president and the Senate, the longer the nomination and confirmation process takes.[14]

If the president is going to take his case to the public regarding potential nominees to the Supreme Court or lower federal courts, we must also examine the relationship between the president and the press. Kernell, in his book *Going Public*, studies how presidents use the media as a mechanism of exerting influence and power. He argues that presidents **go public,** or try to influence public opinion on an issue so that the public will then influence their members of Congress to support the president.[15] Although the usefulness of such a strategy has been challenged, particularly by Edwards in *On Deaf Ears*, one look at a news station covering what the president has said that day demonstrates that this is a strategy that is often used by occupants of the Oval Office.[16] Other research into the relationship between the press and the president has focused on how the media covers the president,[17] the pattern of presidential press conferences,[18] and how the president can use the going public strategy to affect public opinion.[19]

An additional area of research is into the relationship between the president and the bureaucracy. As the bureaucracy comprises most of the executive branch, it would seem natural to subsume the administrative side in with the executive office. This is not necessarily the case. While the president is certainly the head of the executive branch, there is far more bureaucratic autonomy and discretion available to bureaucrats than most people believe. Thus, one area of research is into what is called the **administrative presidency**, denoting not only the political functions of the president but the executive and administrative functions involved with running the government.[20] Chapter 11 will deal more specifically with the bureaucracy and public administration, but when it comes to the president, political scientists have studied how presidents can influence and affect bureaucracy. Wood and Waterman, for instance, demonstrate that the president can have the biggest influence through the leadership appointment process.[21] Bertelli and Feldman suggest that presidents are best off when they select bureaucratic leaders who can offset the influence of entrenched interests such as business and interest groups.[22] Other ways in which the president can attempt to control and influence the bureaucracy is in the amount of control the White House has over certain areas such as budgets and regulations; it is in this way, Nathan argues, that presidents can have the most guidance over bureaucrats.

Policymaking

Despite this long list of topics, one major aspect that has yet to be touched on is how the president actually influences policymaking. This is perhaps one of the most important jobs a president has; in fact, it is even mentioned in the Constitution itself. Article 2, section 3 states, "He shall from time to time give to the Congress information of the State of the Union, and recommend to their consideration such measures as he shall judge necessary and expedient." Out of this one line stems the annual spectacle of the president going to Capitol Hill and giving the State of the Union address. The State of the Union is one of the most significant opportunities a president has to affect the policymaking environment. It signals to Congress and the rest of the political community what the president wants to work on in the coming year. It sets the agenda, a very powerful ability to shape what Washington and the rest of the country thinks about certain policy areas. Think about it for a moment; of all the possible things a president could talk about on the biggest stage of the year, if a president chooses to focus on something like foreign policy or criminal justice reform, it can signal to the country that the president is willing to spend time and political capital on the issue.

While the State of the Union is certainly the biggest agenda-shaping opportunity the president has, it is by no means the only one. Again, given the demands of the day, the act of merely choosing what topics to give speeches on or make appearances to highlight communicates to the public what the president wants to achieve. This directly connects with the going public literature noted previously; presidents can take their message to the public through speeches, appearances on television and in person, news conferences, interviews, and the like to use the Neustadtian power to persuade the public what is important and what should or should not be done.

If presidents cannot get their way through the traditional legislative process, there are some other options afforded to them. The use of executive orders has grown from 8 by George Washington to 291 by George W. Bush. **Executive orders** are used to direct government agencies to perform some task or interpret a law in a certain way. Found to be constitutional by the Supreme Court, political scientists have taken to examining the frequency and content of them for insights into the growth of presidential power and the executive branch itself. Another form of presidential power has been the use of **signing statements**. Signing statements are made when a president signs a bill into law and are used to praise the passage of the bill and to lay out the president's interpretation of the bill. In their study of the usage of signing statements, Ostrander and Sievert write that "Signing statements thus appear to be institutionally oriented and directed at reiterating the boundaries between Congress and the president rather than outlining policy disagreements between the branches."[23] Signing statements are often used to highlight disagreements about constitutional principles and therefore allow the president to shape the implementation of the law.

The Courts

Examining the institution of the judiciary is different than the previous two institutions we've discussed. Judges do not make decisions based on politics but law. Their decisions are supposed to be objective, based on facts and evidence as discussed in Chapter 4. Although it is not possible to squeeze every ounce of subjective bias from the court system, ideally politics should not play into decisions. As such, most study of judicial cases and rulings are left to legal scholars and lawyers. But there are some areas where politics bleeds into the court system, and these are areas of interest for political scientists.

Role of the Courts

The first area concerns what role the courts should play; should they be involved in making policy pronouncements from the bench or leave political questions to elected officials? An example of judicial policymaking is the classic case, *Brown v. Board of Education* in 1954. In it, the Supreme Court ruled that segregation in schools was inherently unequal and ordered the integration of schools. Whether to pursue segregation or desegregation is intrinsically a political question of which policy to follow. In *Brown v. Board*, the Supreme Court decided on a policy and expected the rest of the political system to enforce it. The same thing occurred with *Roe v. Wade* in 1973 when the Supreme Court ruled that women have a right to an abortion. Since, governments at every level have waded into abortion policy with the background always being the policy decision made by the Court.

Most cases of judicial policymaking occur through the courts' function of judicial review. Established by the case *Marbury v. Madison*, this doctrine allows federal courts to invalidate laws passed by the Congress and signed by the president if they are not constitutional—that is, not allowed by the Constitution. Opponents of judicial policymaking claim that any and all policy decisions should be decided on by elected officials in Congress and the executive branch, not by unelected judges who serve lifetime terms. On the other hand, proponents will argue that it is the place of the judicial branch to make the ultimate authoritative interpretations of what is legal and what is constitutional and therefore should be empowered to make policy from the bench.

In any case, political scientists have examined the circumstances under which judicial policymaking is most likely to occur. Because there are far more court cases at the state level (fifty different sets of courts and supreme courts versus one federal system and one federal Supreme Court), most of the research has taken advantage of the large number of cases to be able to draw firmer conclusions. In examining cases surrounding education policy in the states, Wilhelm found that courts often have the biggest impact in the policy introduction phase because the ideological makeup of the courts influences state legislatures as to the actions they believe courts may undertake.[24] Emmert identifies a host of different variables, including the type of constitutional arguments made, the lower court rulings, and the number of issues raised as contributing to the likelihood of whether a court decision engages in policymaking.[25] Staton and Vanberg, on the other hand, argue that courts realize the difficult position that judicial policymaking puts them in and tend to make very vague opinions that can mask judicial uncertainty about the reaction to judicial policy mandates.[26]

Ultimately, the question about whether judges should engage in policymaking from the bench is one of democratic principles. Given that judges are likely the most undemocratic position one can have in this country (unelected, selected for life, no opportunity for citizens to vote on them), why should they be given responsibility to make decisions about major policy directions? Certainly, Congress has often responded to judicial decisions, altering laws to make them constitutional following judicial review cases, but who are the ultimate arbiters of what we can or should do, the representatives, the citizens, or judges?

Judicial Nominations

The focus on the decisions and policy that can be made from the courts places a significant emphasis on who becomes a judge in the first place. Since this is a lifetime position, the issue of judicial nominations, especially in recent years, has become a polarizing hot topic. To demonstrate just how partisan this process has become, when Supreme Court justice Antonin Scalia died suddenly in 2016, the last year of the Obama administration, Republicans in the Senate immediately declared that they would not consider an Obama nominee to replace the conservative justice. An unprecedented move, the failure to fill Scalia's position on the Supreme Court left the Court with eight justices and the potential for tie votes. In holding out on considering Obama's eventual nominee, Merrick Garland, Republicans were making a bet that Republicans would win the White House in November 2016, thereby enabling a Republican president to nominate a justice who would be more to their liking. This is exactly what happened when Donald Trump won the election and nominated and saw confirmed Neil Gorsuch to the now-vacant Scalia seat.

Once presidents have nominated individuals to serve in the judiciary, the process moves to the Senate for its advice and consent function. Since 1996, the average length of time it takes for the Senate to consider and vote on a nomination has increased dramatically, reflecting the increasingly partisan nature of the battle.[27] Because confirmed judges will serve on the bench for years, and perhaps decades, to come, both the Senate and the president have a strong incentive to ensure that sitting judges reflect their partisan ideology so as to shape decisions long after many elected officials will leave office. Martinek, Kemper, and Van Winkle find that the quality of the nominee, the makeup of the judiciary committee, and other pending nominations all impact the length of time that it takes for the Senate to confirm judicial nominations.[28]

Senate politics have also contributed to the pace at which judicial nominations have been considered. Prior to 2013, all executive judicial nominees had to overcome the cloture vote, which required sixty senators to end debate on the nomination. With a Senate so sharply divided, this hurdle was one that was difficult to overcome leading to a significant backlog in judicial nominations. As a result of Republican recalcitrance, Senate Democrats enacted the nuclear option in 2013, lowering the cloture threshold for all judicial nominees except those for the Supreme Court to a majority rather than sixty. This allowed Democrats to push through a number of then president Obama's nominations. However, the nuclear option was also used by Republicans in 2017, who changed the rules once again to allow for a majority cloture vote on Supreme Court nominees, allowing them to confirm Neil Gorsuch to the Supreme Court without Democratic support (discussed earlier).

In most instances of judicial nominations, the Senate will vote to confirm the individual; however, this is not always the case. The high-profile failures of Ronald Reagan's Supreme Court nominee Robert Bork in 1987 and George W. Bush's nominee Harriet Miers in 2005, demonstrate that the Senate is sometimes unwilling to go along with the president. Krutz, Fleisher, and Bond argue that the failure of some nominations has very little to do with divided government, or a president of one party and a Senate majority of the other. Rather, they identify policy entrepreneurs as key players in providing negative information on a nominee and expanding the arena for conflict.[29] On the other hand, Whittington, following the failure of the Miers nomination, argues that divided party control does influence the success or failure of nominees but that its role is not constant over time.[30] It could well be the case that with the increased salience of partisanship in the twenty-first century, Krutz, Fleisher, and Bond's findings may not hold up anymore; if that is the case, it does not bode well for future nominations under divided government.

Public Opinion and the Courts

A final area ripe for study by political scientists is the role that public opinion plays in influencing judges and their decisions. As discussed previously and in Chapter 4, judges are supposed to make decisions based on law and objectivity. However, it is inevitable that public opinion and politics makes its way into the minds of judges. Why might this be the case? Because the courts have no independent means of enforcing their decisions, they must rely on other aspects of the government to do the enforcing for them. If the courts do not have the respect and approval of the public, there could come a time when the executive branch refuses to cooperate with a court order. In fact, this was a fear in 1974 when the Supreme Court ordered President Richard Nixon to hand over his secretly recorded audiotapes in connection with the Watergate investigation. As relayed by Woodward and Armstrong in *The Brethren*, the justices of the Supreme Court were worried that if their decision showed some dissension within their ranks, if the decision were not unanimous, that Nixon would be tempted to defy the Court and not hand over the tapes. If this did happen, the Court would have no way of enforcing their decision.[31]

As a result, the federal courts, and in particular, the Supreme Court, are concerned about their standing with the public. The need to maintain a high approval rating and public respect for the institution shapes some of the thinking of the judges. Research has borne this relationship out. In 1977, Cook found a significant relationship between the sentences federal judges handed down for draft dodgers during the Vietnam War and public opinion about the war. Others have suggested that the link between the courts and public opinion is perhaps more indirect, stemming from judicial retirements and replacements when a focus is put on nominees who conform to current public opinion.[32]

Political Behavior

At the heart of studies of political behavior is the belief that individuals are fundamental to the study of politics. Political behavioralists believe that the attitudes and actions of individual political actors are fundamental to understanding the political system. Figure 7.2 highlights this idea and provides an overview of two things: first, the chain of action from an individual person to how they behave. The intermediate level is the formation of attitudes, beliefs, and ideologies that then influence people to behave in a certain way. On the other side of the figure are the different topics that political scientists are interested in at each of these stages. At the individual level, we are interested in *how* people form their beliefs and *what* influences them. In addition to typical socialization influences like parents and family, friends, education, community, and religion, we can also examine how the media influences individual beliefs. Once people have formed their beliefs about politics, we can examine what those beliefs are. Here, political scientists study public opinion (along with how public opinion should be measured), patterns of beliefs, and the type and amount of political knowledge individuals have.

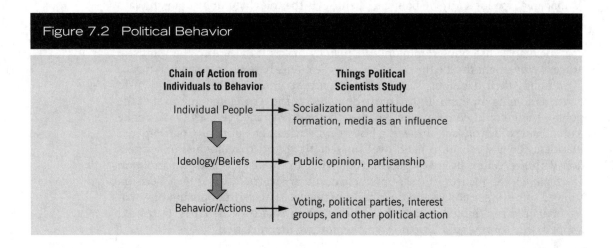

Figure 7.2 Political Behavior

Chain of Action from Individuals to Behavior

Individual People → **Things Political Scientists Study**: Socialization and attitude formation, media as an influence

Ideology/Beliefs → Public opinion, partisanship

Behavior/Actions → Voting, political parties, interest groups, and other political action

Ideally, people will behave in ways that are in accordance with what they believe. While this is not always true, we take this as a basic assumption with political behavior. At the bottom of Figure 7.2, then, we have how individuals behave politically. Political behavior can vary from how people vote to the parties and interest groups that they do (or do not) join, how much people pay attention to politics, and whether they participate in other ways (protests, letter writing, campaign donations).

In examining the thoughts and behaviors of individual people, we hope to understand the contours of American politics. For the rest of this chapter, then, we will take each of these concepts, in turn, and discuss not only what they are but some of the key findings that political scientists have made about them.

Socialization

Socialization is the process through which we acquire beliefs about the world around us. Why do you believe the things you do about the world around you? About politics? About America? The process of socialization, while it takes place throughout a lifetime, is concentrated in our childhood. Think about what you learned about America in elementary and middle school; they probably didn't teach much about the negative aspects of our collective history—things like treatment of the Native Americans or the widespread discrimination against African Americans. When we are young, we are taught to believe the good things about America and her government, to look up to American heroes like George Washington and Abraham Lincoln, and to believe that America is an exceptional country. While many American adults are skeptical about politics, in childhood, attitudes tend to be quite positive.[33]

Early research into socialization focused on these childhood experiences and learning. Much of our political socialization happens in school through what we are taught about our country and how. By the time we reach high school, many of our ideas about politics are fairly consistent.[34] However, this socialization experience can vary despite large groups of children being taught much of the same thing about America and its politics; race, family, personality, and even an individual's biology have been shown to impact how children develop their ideas about the American political process.[35] For example, African American children may come to see America quite differently from their white peers simply because of the environment in which they grow up.

A key set of ideas that is intrinsic to political socialization is that of political culture. Political culture, defined in Chapter 1 as a set of values, beliefs, behaviors, and norms that a society holds in common, is often transmitted precisely through the socialization process. Although defining the ideas and values that *most* Americans believe is obviously a difficult process, most Americans can agree that they value ideas like liberty, individualism, the American dream, and opportunity for all. Sometimes, these values can even conflict with one another. Following the terrorist attacks of 9/11, there was a greater need to focus on the security of the American homeland; however, some of the ways in which this was done could be seen as inimical to the American value of freedom and even privacy. Airport screenings, warrantless wiretaps, and the collection of Internet data do not seem to fit into the American political creed. Americans since then have struggled with the balance of privacy and freedom and safety and security, but that does not mean the American political culture values either of them any less. These ideas become a part of the American political canon precisely because they are transmitted from generation to generation by way of political socialization.

Public Opinion

Rarely a day goes by that the media, an entity that emphasizes competition and breaking news, publishes some sort of public opinion poll. Polls have become nearly ubiquitous in American politics today for their ability to give some insight as to how the public thinks and feels. Polls feed the need for competitive updates, to tell us who's ahead and who's behind. It is this very tool, the public opinion poll, that has shaped and molded research into public opinion. As Korzi writes, "The predominance of the poll as research tool would fundamentally change *how* and *what* researchers studied."[36]

One of the first comprehensive studies to take advantage of the growth of polling was *The American Voter*, published in 1960.[37] Its authors, using one of the first nationwide comprehensive surveys, tried to identify what caused people to vote the way they did. Out of this and work done independently by Converse (he also coauthored *The American Voter*), the authors developed what they called the **funnel of causality**, postulating that sociodemographics influenced party identification that in turn influenced individuals' positions on given issues and then candidates, which all led to the defining event: the vote. Further, the data generated demonstrate little in the way of true ideological beliefs among the American public, instead finding that many have inconsistent attitudes that do not represent true ideologies.

As computers and statistical processing software became more available, more detailed and mathematical analyses of public opinion became possible. Zaller took up the question of how individuals form opinions and how they change in *The Nature and Origins of Mass Opinion*. Acknowledging that most people don't really pay attention to government, Zaller took varying attention levels into account along with the role that elites play in mediating public opinion.[38] The result is a comprehensive test of his opinion formation model that shows how mass public opinion changes over time.

The pattern of greater data availability continues today. Stimson attempts to take a measure of public opinion on various subjects and combine them to form a measure of public mood.[39] A brand-new generation of scholars out of the University of Michigan (Lewis-Beck, Jacoby, Norpoth, and Weisberg) went back to *The American Voter* for *The American Voter Revisited* to explore how public opinion has or hasn't changed since 1960.[40] Many others take on patterns of polarization and partisanship. The bottom line is that as our tools for measuring public opinion have become more widely available, our ability to dig further into the contours of public opinion has expanded. In addition to understanding the patterns of public opinion development and change, other scholars have looked at how public opinion influences government. These studies include not only the president[41] or Congress but other institutions like the judiciary.[42] Others look at specific ethnic groups to explore differences in opinion.[43]

Despite this seeming obsession in both political science and political campaigns with public opinion polling, polls can still get it wrong as evidenced by the 2016 presidential election. Despite nearly every national poll predicting a Hillary Clinton win, by the time all the votes were counted, Donald Trump was declared the winner. How did the polls get it so wrong? To understand the limits of public opinion polling in both political science and popular politics, one must first understand how polls are taken. It is impossible to ask every American how they plan to vote; there is no way of contacting all of them. As such, researchers and pollsters rely on the math of inferential statistics: If you survey enough people properly, you'll be able to get a sense, within some margin of error, of how that group feels. Thus, national polls often survey only 1,000 to 1,500 people. However, it is still not enough simply to ask 1,500 random people who they plan on voting for; not all of those people may be able to vote, may be registered to vote, or even likely to vote. As such, modern-day pollsters have taken to "weighting" their sample to rely more heavily on the responses of "likely voters." But what constitutes a likely voter? This was a major problem of the pre-2016 election polls: they weighted their samples too heavily for minority voters and not enough for white rural voters.

Partisanship and Polarization

We're all familiar with partisanship and polarization today. Republicans criticize Democrats, Democrats criticize Republicans, polarization in Congress makes getting anything done incredibly difficult. For many college students, partisan polarization might be all they know; however, it isn't the case that partisanship is always as high as it is today. In fact, the level of partisanship in Washington tends to rise and fall in cycles over time.

Being **partisan** is the state of being in favor of one thing or another—in this case, a political party. To be partisan in politics is to be supportive of one party or another; this does not necessarily mean that those who are partisan are automatically disposed to not working with members of another party; it simply means they prefer one party or another. **Polarization**, on the other hand, means that the average beliefs of two political parties have moved so far apart that there is little to no overlap. We can easily visualize this in Figure 7.3. If we assume the horizontal line at the bottom represents political beliefs from the left to the right and the vertical line is the number of people with those beliefs, the first panel shows little polarization; the beliefs of each party somewhat overlap in the middle. In the second panel,

Career Guidance

One possible job option for political science majors is in public opinion polling. There are a number of organizations that continually provide polling information, including the Gallup Organization and the Pew Research Center. In addition to knowledge about politics and political science, pollsters should also have good working knowledge of statistics and sampling.

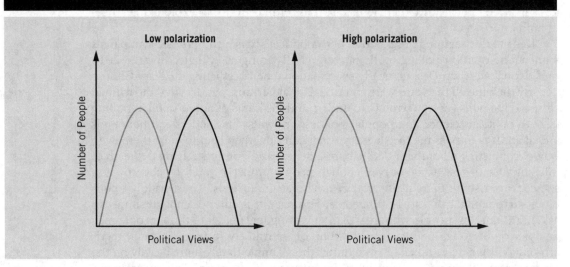

Figure 7.3 Polarization

however, the beliefs have moved more to the left and to the right so that there is no one left in the middle; this is a case of high polarization.

Political scientists have sought to quantify, measure, and understand partisanship and polarization. The most prominent effort toward this has been done by Poole and Rosenthal with what they call DW-NOMINATE scores. Poole and Rosenthal take every recorded vote in each Congress and standardize individual members on a scale of –2 to +2. The closer one is to –2, the more liberal their views, and the closer one is to +2, the more conservative their views. This procedure allows political scientists to put a number on how liberal or conservative a member of Congress is and to then look at all members and calculate how polarized Congress is. To measure polarization, Poole and Rosenthal take the score of the median Democratic member and the median Republican member and find the absolute difference; the larger the number, the more polarized a Congress is. Figure 7.4 plots this polarization measure for all Congresses.

Figure 7.4 demonstrates a fundamental pattern in American politics: Polarization rises and falls over time. What causes these cycles? Why do Americans become more partisan at some points and less at others? These are the types of questions that studies of partisanship and partisan behavior examine. Some of these studies were already noted previously; books like *The American Voter* and Zaller's *The Nature and Origins of Mass Opinion* have attempted to identify the ideology and partisan beliefs of the American public. Since partisanship has been identified as a key influence in how people ultimately vote, understanding feelings of partisanship remains a key task in political science.

Some of the most interesting research has been into what triggers individuals to become partisan or more polarized in their attitudes and beliefs. Gerber, Huber, and Washington show that something as simple as reminding voters that they need to be registered with a political party heightens their partisan attitudes.[44] Rapoport provides

Figure 7.4   Polarization in the House and Senate, 1871–2017

Source: Jeffrey B. Lewis, Keith Poole, Howard Rosenthal, Adam Boche, Aaron Rudkin, and Luke Sonnet, *Voteview: Congressional Roll Call Database*, https://voteview.com.

evidence that the extent to which people are partisan can be affected by the candidates who run for office—particularly since elections have become more candidate-centered.[45] Klar examines how social settings can impact an individual's partisanship.[46]

The relationship between partisanship and votes is not the only one that is important; the relationship between partisan attitudes and positions on issues is also significant. The theory laid out in *The American Voter* specifies that party identification influences the positions people have on issues like immigration, health care, and foreign policy. However, how do we know that it isn't people's positions on issues that influences their partisanship? Highton and Kam explore this question only to find that the causal direction is dependent on certain periods of time.[47] Other scholars have focused on the connections between specific policy areas like Souva and Rhode with partisanship and foreign policy and Milner and Judkins with trade policy.[48]

A final area of research into partisanship is the extent to which polarization is becoming more important. Poole and Rosenthal's DW-NOMINATE scores show an increasing level of polarization in Congress, but is the public equally polarized? Even if polarization is increasing, is it affecting voter behavior? Two distinct schools of thought have emerged. Scholars like Fiorina and Abrams and Pope contend that a supposed culture war between red and blue America doesn't exist.[49] Citing public opinion studies that show the mass public is rather moderate, what appears as polarization in the mass public is actually the public having to respond to more polarized choices at the ballot box. On the other hand, Abramowitz and Saunders argue that polarization is actually occurring in the American public. Utilizing data from the American National

Election Studies, they show that there are increasing differences between Republicans and Democrats and that increasing polarization is energizing the mass public.[50]

Voting and Other Political Behavior

All the concepts we've discussed thus far ultimately filter down to the ultimate political action: voting. Voting is the primary means through which American citizens have a voice in the political process, and electing a president is not the only important vote. Americans can vote for any number of state and local offices from governors and state legislators to county and city leaders, sheriffs, clerks, judges, and even dog catchers. Much of what we've discussed thus far influences how people vote at the ballot box: socialization and the media affect what people think about politics and their political ideology, which is a direct influence on how they vote. Ideally, citizens will vote for those representatives whom they believe will best represent their interests and views in government.

Given that voting is a cornerstone of our democracy and the fact that not many people take advantage of that singular act, one of the biggest questions political scientists can tackle is why people do or don't vote or even why people do or don't participate in politics. Traditionally, political scientists have identified certain characteristics of people who tend to show up to vote: They have more education, a greater income level, are older, and have strong partisan leanings. On the other hand, those who don't vote tend to be younger, less educated, and poorer. Often these people have low levels of political efficacy, the feeling that the political process works for them. Just taking these few characteristics into consideration, it's obvious that if this is truly the case, those who need and use government the most are probably not getting as much representation as they should.

But do people actually vote? Experience tells us not always. In the 2012 presidential election, only 54.9 percent of the voting-age population voted. And although this number has been trending upward for the past few presidential elections, turnout can still be abysmal at the state and local levels. State and local elections in Oklahoma are a case in point. During the 2014 gubernatorial election, only 29 percent of the voting-eligible population voted. At the local level, it's even worse; in some local elections in Lawton, Oklahoma, less than 10 percent of the voting-age population votes. That means in a city of approximately 100,000, fewer than 10,000 people show up to vote. The consequences of this low voter turnout can be stunning. In Florida in 2000, George W. Bush won by only 537 votes out of almost 6 million votes. If just 537 more people had shown up to vote for Al Gore, our recent history could have turned out much differently. In state and local elections, the low turnout can be even more important with the chance to swing local outcomes greatly based on who comes out to vote.

But there is some good news: Many states and localities have begun to experiment with new methods of voting. In the late 1990s, Oregon switched to a vote by mail system; other states have instituted and expanded early voting, a process that allows voters to show up before election day to vote. Some new research has shown that these "convenience" methods are encouraging more people to vote.[51] Others have shown more mixed results with Giammo and Brox finding only a temporary increase in turn-out once convenience voting has been introduced.[52] However, more people are routinely taking advantage of early and absentee voting—thereby reducing the time costs to vote. Making the act of voting easier could eliminate at least one barrier to voting.

In addition to the characteristics already listed that affect voting (all of which also affect wider political participation), researchers have found other factors that influence or increase political participation. When we are asked to participate by candidates or parties (this is often called voter mobilization or get-out-the-vote efforts), we are more likely to participate. For example, in a study of young people in Belgium (although this study uses data from Belgium, we should remember that young people everywhere are notorious for not voting or not participating in politics), Quintelier, Stolle, and Harell show that as the diversity of one's social network increased, the chances of an individual participating in politics increases.[53] Kam, on the other hand, presents data on the relationship between risk perception and political participation. Those who are more accepting of risk tend to participate more, excluding the act of voting itself. She hypothesizes that this is the case because those who are more risk accepting get into politics for the thrill and excitement of the unknown.[54]

Certainly, this news about voter turnout can be rather depressing. If Americans aren't showing up to exercise their basic right in a democracy, what makes our government a democracy? However, voting is not the only means by which we can participate in government. Other political activities include writing letters (or e-mails or tweets); volunteering for candidates, parties, or interest groups; signing a petition; raising or donating money; or even protesting. In many ways, these forms of participation may be even more meaningful to representatives than voting is; they can be done on a consistent basis and may even influence representatives to behave in a certain way.

Interest Groups

From partisanship to voting to political participation, there is another set of actors that is intrinsic to the political act: political parties and interest groups. Ironically, however, this was not the original plan of the Framers of the Constitution. Perhaps most famously, James Madison in *Federalist* No. 10 rails against the evils of factions: groups of people formed around special interests. Madison feared that the multiplication of factions would lead to the multiplication of conflict, tearing at the foundations of the new country. George Washington also warned against parties and factions in his Farewell Address, writing, "The common and continual mischiefs of the spirit of party are sufficient to make it the interest and duty of a wise people to discourage and restrain it." And yet everywhere we turn today, political parties are in the news, and interest groups are actively representing the interests of a wide variety of people in Washington, D.C., and state capitals everywhere.

Let's start with the difference between interest groups and political parties. Both represent groups of citizens but in different ways. **Political parties**, as discussed in Chapter 5, bring together large and diverse groups of people under a general umbrella of what they believe government is for and should look like. They have positions on a wide range of issues, and above all, they run people for office. Parties want to effect change from inside government, by passing laws and making policy. **Interest groups**, on the other hand, do not run for office; they seek to change policy and law through extra-electoral means like lobbying, issue ads, and mobilizing. They also tend to be more singular in the issues they speak about; for instance, the National Rifle Association is focused on gun rights, whereas the AARP focuses on issues related to retirement, Social Security, and health care.

Are you a member of an interest group? What about any of your friends? If you took a survey in your class, most likely, not many of your classmates are part of an interest group. This is due to a well-known phenomenon often studied by political scientists: the collective action problem. The **collective action problem**, introduced in Chapter 1, is what often happens when you work on a group project with classmates; if everybody receives the same grade, why should I do much of anything when the others will do it? The people who think like this are called free riders; they benefit from the work of others without having to do it themselves. The collective action problem afflicts interest groups of all kind. If we all benefit from the policies that interest groups espouse, why pay the money or give the time to participate in the group?

Olson was the first political scientist to tackle this issue head-on. In 1965, he published *The Logic of Collective Action: Public Goods and the Theory of Groups,* which describes collective action, the free rider problem, and how to overcome it. He postulated that in small groups, the problem of collective action is more likely to be overcome because members can utilize peer pressure to ensure that everyone participates. In larger groups, however, the costs of solving the collective action problem are much higher, and often, groups must offer selective benefits to entice people to join.[55] If you've seen the Wounded Warrior Project commercial asking you to donate money to the organization and receive a blanket in return, you know what a selective incentive is. It's something you get only if you join the group.

Other political science research has examined the role that interest groups play in government. One prominent theory has been advocated by Dahl, who published *Who Governs?* in 1961. Dahl argues that interest group **pluralism**, or a diverse array of interest groups, tends to balance each other out so that no one group or sector of society gains too much power. As different groups try to gain autonomy or power over others, when these "struggles are successful, as they often are, they result in turn in tendencies toward pluralism."[56] In many senses, this is a neo-Madisonian view of society. Just as Madison believed government needed to be structured to balance out the evils of factions, for Dahl, interest groups balance themselves out so that no one gains too much power.

But is this really the case? Since the publication of Dahl's theory (and others who have studied pluralism), other political scientists have tested whether Dahl's theory holds up. As a result, others have posited alternative theories of the nature of the interest group community, most prominently **elite theory**. Elite theorists argue that instead of a wide array of interest groups competing for power, there is in actuality a small political elite that controls the most power. Finally, a third major theory of interest groups, corporatism, argues for purposefully integrating businesses and interest groups into the government with the idea that all areas of society have a say in government policymaking.

The role of interest groups in society is not the only thing that political scientists study when it comes to this topic. What influence interest groups have over elections and influencing people to vote (and how they vote), how interest groups use campaign donations to influence politicians, how they impact not only elected officials but bureaucracies, and how interest groups alert the public to problems are just some of the ways in which political scientists look at interest groups.

Political Parties

Political parties play a key role in American politics. As discussed in Chapter 5, one of the major criticisms of the American party system is the presence of two major political parties. However, as we learned, Duverger's law holds that the electoral system a country utilizes helps to determine how many major political parties there are. With the US winner-take-all system, third parties are naturally at a disadvantage. Beyond this, however, areas of research into parties in the United States examine parties as a link between the mass population and the elites who run government. As noted before, evidence from public opinion surveys has shown that Americans display very little in the way of consistent ideological thinking and that knowledge levels tend to be rather low. Elites, on the other hand, are very ideological in thought and have high levels of knowledge.[57] If this is the mechanism through which ideas and beliefs are translated into government action, what does this relationship look like, and who influences who? What are the differences ideologically and behaviorally between elites and the mass public, and how do those differences influence and affect our politics?

The reason that these links are important is because, over time, the positions that political parties take on various issues can and do change. Who initiates those changes: the elites, the mass public, or both? For example, the Republican Party's positions on civil rights has changed dramatically between 1865 and 1965. Carmines and Stimson use racial desegregation in the 1960s to explore patterns of party change, arguing that party elites first change their positions on issues only to have those positions filter down to the mass public.[58] However, other tests of this issue evolution theory have provided mixed evidence. Souva and Rhode provide evidence that the relationship is the other way around; at least with respect to foreign policy, representatives tend to be influenced by the positions of their constituents.[59] Another mediating factor may be saliency; the importance of the issue to constituents may force representatives to be more responsive to their voters and allow them to take different positions on less important issues.[60]

This idea of issue evolution and the associated change in the stances of political parties is also intimately tied to the idea of **party realignment**. According to Carmines and Stimson, electoral realignments

> are precipitated by the emergence of new issues about which the electorate has intense feelings that cut across rather than reinforce the existing bases of support for the political parties…. [This] leads to a fundamental alteration in the party system in that the majority party can no longer command decisive electoral support. One party's previously dominant position

is ultimately usurped by a minority or third party, which becomes the ben-eficiary of the unfolding realignment process.[61]

During realignment, then, new and important issues trigger voters to change the party that they were previously attached to, leading to political parties not only changing their position on the issue but a change in leadership at the governmental level. The concept and theory of realignment have been popular with political scientists like Key, Schattschneider, and Sundquist, but others have been more critical of the theory, particularly Mayhew. While some have suggested that realignments tend to happen every generation, many are hard pressed to identify a realignment that has occurred since the 1960s. Additionally, how big of a change needs to occur? How many people need to change parties, or how many seats need to change hands? The standards of realignment theory have been rather fuzzy.

CASE STUDY
The Trump Travel Ban

The question of how active a role the courts should have in policy has been hotly contested around the issue of President Donald Trump's executive orders effectively banning immigration from several Muslim-majority countries. One week after his inauguration, President Trump issued an executive order that was to be implemented immediately that barred entry to the United States for ninety days for citizens from Iraq, Syria, Iran, Libya, Somalia, Sudan, and Yemen. Almost immediately, red flags were raised about the legality of the order because of its focus on Muslim-majority countries; protesters showed up at airports, and several organizations and states sued the Trump administration in court to halt the executive order. Judges in several states, including Hawaii, New York, and Massachusetts, soon found cause to issue temporary restraining orders, keeping the order from going into effect based on First Amendment religious bias concerns.

However, from the point of view of the Trump administration, the executive order was not only necessary for national security but legal under the president's powers to restrict immi-gration from countries deemed to be a threat to the United States. The debate that soon occurred in several courtrooms around the country, then, was whether the president's powers to protect the country and regulate immigration could be outweighed by concerns about religious discrimination. President Trump, though, recognized a related issue—whether the courts had any role to play in this whatsoever given the policy prerogatives of the executive branch. In other words, should unelected judges be in a position to strike down or uphold public policy made by other elected officials, such as the president? Immigration, after all, is a public policy issue; the question of who to allow into the country, how many, and when has historically been decided by both the Congress and the president. If the courts were to strike down the travel ban, then, they would be interfering with the policymaking process—thereby making policy themselves.

Over the course of the president's first year in office, the original executive order and a subsequent one that widened the ban to several other countries remained in legal limbo. The US

Supreme Court ultimately allowed the order to go into effect while it waited to hear an appeal on the case once its term opened in October 2017. However, by that time, the order had run out, and the Supreme Court declined to hear the case; after all, it was intended to be in effect for only ninety days. A third, less restrictive travel restriction went into effect in September 2017 with yet another challenge pending before the Supreme Court, although during oral arguments the justices appeared to side with the Trump administration. Regardless of the outcome, the clash regarding the president's power to impose such restrictions highlights several characteristics of American politics. First, the judiciary is often used to settle disputes over the extent of presidential power and how much power they have been given by the Congress. Two, the challenges to the executive orders have come from interest groups like the American Civil Liberties Union (ACLU) as well as state governments; this shows that political actors like interest groups have a number of avenues to participate in the American political process with the courts providing yet another avenue for policy change. Finally, the debate demonstrates the importance of nominations to the federal bench and the judicial philosophies of those appointed. When presidents nominate judges to the court, they most often nominate people whose judicial philosophy and ideology they agree with; since these judges then serve lifetime terms, presidents can have an impact on decisions far outlasting their term in office.

Critical Thinking Questions

1. How is the court acting as a referee between the Congress and the president?

2. How might the political culture of the United States, passed on through political socialization, impact our beliefs about the value of national security and immigration?

3. What does this case say about the powers of the president?

STUDENT STUDY SITE

Visit https://edge.sagepub.com/whitmancobb

CHAPTER SUMMARY

- Congress is made up of two very different chambers: the House of Representatives and the Senate. Their differences in terms of size, term length, and constitutional responsibilities strongly influence their behavior. Congress's responsibilities include legislating, budgeting, and oversight of the executive branch.

- Presidential power has grown over time. This has affected the president's relations with the other branches and expanded the tools they have at their disposal for the purposes of policymaking.

- The courts play an important, albeit disputed, role in policymaking in the United

States. Serving lifetime terms, they have the potential to make policy decisions that can impact the entire United States.

- As important as the institutions of governing are, how individuals act in political ways is also important. Citizens are socialized and come to believe in particular ideas based on many factors, including their upbringing. This affects whether and how people will vote and whether they will be involved with political parties or interest groups.

KEY TERMS

administrative presidency: The use of administrative and unilateral powers of the president to influence public policy

collective action problem: Describes the difficulty in getting a large number of people to work together in pursuit of a common good

continuing resolutions: Types of bills that, in the absence of a federal budget, continue funding the federal government for a defined period of time

elite theory: Theory that rather than a wide array of diverse interest groups, there is actually a small number of groups and people who control political power

executive orders: Presidential directives to government agencies to undertake a task or interpret a law in a particular way

filibuster: A legislative maneuver in the Senate to prevent a cloture vote, which would end debate on a bill

funnel of causality: A model of the different influences on a person's decision of who to vote for

gerrymandering: The redrawing of district lines for political purposes

go public: A strategy presidents may use to take their message to the public

interest groups: Political groups that represent narrow interests and attempt to influence policy through means other than running for office

partisan: To be supportive of one party or another

party realignment: A period where the electoral coalitions of political parties fundamentally change

polarization: The widening difference between the policy positions of two parties

political behavior: The actions of individuals in a political system

political parties: Political groups that represent the interests of citizens in the aggregate and run for office

pluralism: The idea that a diverse array of interest groups tends to balance each other out

signing statements: Used by presidents when signing a bill into law to praise the passage of the bill and to lay out the president's interpretation of the bill

DISCUSSION QUESTIONS

1. Who has more power in terms of influencing policymaking: Congress or the president? Why?

2. What role do you believe the courts should play in policymaking?

3. How can socialization affect an individual's political behavior?

4. What do you think can be done to increase voter turnout?

5. Why does the United States have only two major political parties?

FOR FURTHER READING

Dahl, Robert. *Who Governs? Democracy and Power in an American City*. New Haven, CT: Yale University Press, 1961.

Fenno, Richard F. *Home Style: House Members in Their Districts*. New York: Pearson, 2002.

Lewis-Beck, Michael S., et al. *The American Voter Revisited*. Ann Arbor: University of Michigan Press, 2008.

Mayhew, David. *Congress: The Electoral Connection*. New Haven, CT: Yale University Press, 1974.

Neustadt, Richard E. *Presidential Power and the Modern Presidents: The Politics of Leadership from Roosevelt to Reagan*. New York: Free Press, 1990.

Olson, Mancur. *The Logic of Collective Action: Public Goods and the Theory of Groups*. Cambridge, MA: Harvard University Press, 1971.

Stimson, James A. *Public Opinion in America: Moods, Cycles, and Swings*. Boulder, CO: Westview Press, 1999.

Theriault, Sean M. *Party Polarization in Congress*. New York: Cambridge University Press, 2008.

NOTES

1. Sean M. Theriault, *Party Polarization in Congress* (New York: Cambridge University Press, 2008); John N. Friedman and Richard T. Holden, "The Rising Incumbent Reelection Rate: What's Gerrymandering Got to Do with It?" *The Journal of Politics* 71, no. 2 (2009): 593–611.

2. Frances E. Lee and Bruce I. Oppenheimer, *Sizing Up the Senate: The Unequal Consequences of Equal Representation* (Chicago: University of Chicago Press, 1999).

3. Wendy Whitman Cobb, *Unbroken Government: Success and the Illusion of Failure in Policymaking* (New York: Palgrave Macmillan, 2013).

4. Frances E. Lee, "Senate Deliberation and the Future of Congressional Power," *PS: Political Science and Politics* 43, no. 2 (2010): 227–223.

5. David M. Primo, Sarah A. Binder, and Forrest Maltzman, "Who Consents? Competing Pivots in Federal Judicial Selection," *American Journal of Political Science* 52, no. 3 (2008): 471–489; David W. Rhode and Kenneth A. Shepsle, "Advising and Consenting in the 60-Vote Senate: Strategic Appointments to the Supreme Court," *The Journal of Politics* 69, no. 3 (2007): 664–677.

6. David Mayhew, *Congress: The Electoral Connection* (New Haven, CT: Yale University Press, 1974).

7. Lyn Ragsdale and John J. Theis III, "The Institutionalization of the American Presidency, 1924-1992," *American Journal of Political Science* 41, no. 4 (1997): 1280–1318.

8. Matthew J. Dickinson and Matthew J. Lebo, "Reexamining the Growth of the Institutional Presidency, 1940-2000," *The Journal of Politics* 69, no. 1 (2007): 206–219.

9. Richard E. Neustadt, *Presidential Power and the Modern Presidents* (New York: The Free Press, 1990).

10. Alexander Bolton and Sharece Thrower, "Legislative Capacity and Executive Unilateralism," *American Journal of Political Science* 60, no. 3 (2016): 649–663.

11. Michelle Belco and Brandon Rottinghaus, "In Lieu of Legislation: Executive Unilateral Preemption or Support during the Legislative Process," *Political Research Quarterly* 67, no. 2 (2014): 413–425.

12. Keith E. Whittington, "Presidents, Senates, and Failed Supreme Court Nominations," *The Supreme Court Review* 2006, no. 1 (2006): 401–438.

13. Timothy R. Johnson and Jason M. Roberts, "Presidential Capital and the Supreme Court Confirmation Process," *The Journal of Politics* 66, no. 3 (2004): 663–683.

14. Charles R. Shipan and Megan L. Shannon, "Delaying Justice(s): A Duration Analysis of Supreme Court Confirmations," *American Journal of Political Science* 47, no. 4 (2003): 654–660.

15. Samuel Kernell, *Going Public: New Strategies of Presidential Leadership,* 3rd ed. (Washington, DC: CQ Press, 1997).

16. George C. Edwards, *On Deaf Ears: The Limits of the Bully Pulpit* (New Haven, CT: Yale University Press, 2003).

17. Andrew W. Barrett, "Press Coverage of Legislative Appeals by the President," *Political Research Quarterly* 60, no. 4 (2007): 655–668.

18. William W. Lammers, "Presidential Press Conference Schedules: Who Hides and When?" *Political Science Quarterly* 96, no. 2 (1981): 261–278; Matthew Eshbaugh-Soha, "Presidential Press Conferences over Time," *American Journal of Political Science* 47, no. 2 (2003): 348–353.

19. Kent Tedin, Brandon Rottinghaus, and Harrell Rodgers, "When the President Goes Public: The Consequences of Communication Mode for Opinion Change across Issue Types and Groups," *Political Research Quarterly* 64, no. 3 (2011): 506–519; Amnon Cavari, "The Short Term Effect of Going Public," *Political Research Quarterly* 66, no. 2 (2013): 336–351.

20. Richard P. Nathan, *The Administrative Presidency* (New York: John Wiley and Sons, 1983).

21. B. Dan Wood and Richard W. Waterman, "The Dynamics of Political Control of the Bureaucracy," *American Political Science Review* 85, no. 3 (1991): 801–828.

22. Anthony Bertelli and Sven E. Feldman, "Strategic Appointments," *J-PART* 17, no. 1 (2007): 19–38.

23. Ian Ostrander and Joel Sievert, "The Logic of Presidential Signing Statements," *Political Research Quarterly* 66, no. 1 (2013): 141.

24. Teena Wilhelm, "The Policymaking Role of State Supreme Courts in Education Policy," *Legislative Studies Quarterly* 32, no. 2 (2007): 309–333.

25. Craig F. Emmert, "An Integrated Case Related Model of Judicial Decision Making: Explaining State Supreme Court Decisions in Judicial Review Cases," *The Journal of Politics* 54, no. 2 (1992): 543–552.

26. Jeffrey K. Staton and Georg Vanberg, "The Value of Vagueness: Delegation, Defense, and Judicial Opinions," *American Journal of Political Science* 52, no. 3 (2008): 504–519.

27. Lauren Cohen Bell, "Senatorial Discourtesy: The Senate's Use of Delay to Shape the Federal Judiciary," *Political Research Quarterly* 55, no. 3 (2004): 589–608.

28. Wendy L. Martinek, Mark Kemper, and Steven R. Van Winkle, "To Advise and Consent: The Senate and Lower Federal Court Nominations, 1977–1998," *The Journal of Politics* 64, no. 2 (2002): 337–361.

29. Glen S. Krutz, Richard Fleisher, and Jon R. Bond, "From Abe Fortas to Zoe Baird: Why Some Presidential Nominations Fail in the Senate," *American Political Science Review* 92, no. 4 (1998): 871–881.

30. Whittington, "Presidents, Senates, and Failed Supreme Court Nominations."

31. Bob Woodward and Scott Armstrong, *The Brethren: Inside the Supreme Court* (New York: Simon and Schuster, 1979).

32. Bryan Calvin, Paul M. Collins Jr., and Matthew Eshbaugh-Soha, "On the Relationship between Public Opinion and Decision Making in the US Courts of Appeals," *Political Research Quarterly* 64,

no. 4 (2011): 736–748; Micheal W. Giles, Bethany Blackstone, and Richard L. Vining Jr., "The Supreme Court in American Democracy: Unraveling the Linkages between Public Opinion and Judicial Decision Making," *The Journal of Politics* 73, no. 1 (2008): 293–306.

33. Fred I. Greenstein, "The Benevolent Leader: Children's Images of Political Authority," *American Political Science Review* 54, no. 4 (1960): 934–943.

34. Robert D. Hess and David Easton, "The Child's Changing Image of the President," *Public Opinion Quarterly* 24, no. 4 (1960): 632–644; Heinz Eulau et al., "The Political Socialization of American State Legislators," *Midwest Journal of Political Science* 3, no. 3 (1959): 188–206.

35. James W. Clarke, "Family Structure and Political Socialization among Urban Black Children," *American Journal of Political Science* 17, no. 2 (1973): 302–315; Lewis A. Froman Jr., "Personality and Political Socialization," *The Journal of Politics* 23, no. 2 (1961): 341–352; Steven A. Peterson, "Biology and Political Socialization: A Cognitive Developmental Link?" *Political Psychology* 4, no. 2 (1983): 265–288.

36. Michael J. Korzi, "Lapsed Memory? The Roots of American Public Opinion Research," *Polity* 33, no. 1 (2000): 56.

37. Angus Campbell et al., *The American Voter* (Chicago: University of Chicago Press, 1960).

38. John R. Zaller, *The Nature and Origins of Mass Opinion* (New York: Cambridge University Press, 1990).

39. James A. Stimson, *Public Opinion in America: Moods Cycles, and Swings* (Boulder, CO: Westview Press, 1999).

40. Michael S. Lewis-Beck et al., *The American Voter Revisited* (Ann Arbor, MI: University of Michigan Press, 2008).

41. Brandice Canes-Wrone and Kenneth W. Shotts, "The Conditional Nature of Presidential Responsiveness to Public Opinion," *American Journal of Political Science* 48, no. 4 (2004): 690–706.

42. Christopher J. Casillas, Peter K. Enns, and Patrick C. Wohlfarth, "How Public Opinion Constrains the US Supreme Court," *American Journal of Political Science*

55, no. 1 (2011): 74–88; Jonathan P. Kastellec, "Public Opinion and Senate Confirmation of Supreme Court Nominees," *The Journal of Politics* 72, no. 3 (2010): 767–784; Giles et al., "The Supreme Court in American Democracy."

43. Gabriel R. Sanchez, "The Role of Group Consciousness in Latino Public Opinion," *Political Research Quarterly* 59, no. 3 (2006): 435–446.

44. Alan S. Gerber, Gregory A. Huber, and Ebonya Washington, "Party Affiliation, Partisanship, and Political Beliefs: A Field Experiment," *American Political Science Review* 104, no. 4 (2010): 720–744.

45. Ronald B. Rapoport, "Partisanship Change in a Candidate-Centered Era," *The Journal of Politics* 59, no. 1 (1997): 185–199.

46. Samara Klar, "Partisanship in a Social Setting," *American Journal of Political Science* 58, no. 3 (2014): 687–704.

47. Benjamin Highton and Cindy D. Kam, "The Long-Term Dynamics of Partisanship and Issue Orientations," *The Journal of Politics* 66, no. 1 (2011): 202–215.

48. Mark Souva and David Rhode, "Elite Opinion Differences and Partisanship in Congressional Foreign Policy, 1975–1986," *Political Research Quarterly* 60, no. 1 (2007): 113–123; Helen V. Milner and Benjamin Judkins, "Partisanship, Trade Policy, and Globalization: Is There a Left-Right Divide on Trade Policy?" *International Studies Quarterly* 48, no. 1 (2004): 95–119.

49. Morris P. Fiorina, Samuel A. Abrams, and Jeremy C. Pope, "Polarization in the American Public: Misconceptions and Misreadings," *The Journal of Politics* 70, no. 2 (2008): 556–560; Morris P. Fiorina and Samuel J. Abrams, *Culture War? The Myth of a Polarized America* (London: Longman, 2010).

50. Alan I. Abramowitz and Kyle L. Saunders, "Is Polarization a Myth?" *The Journal of Politics* 70, no. 2 (2008): 542–555.

51. Michael R. Alvarez, Ines Levin, and Andrew Sinclair, "Making Voting Easier: Convenience Voting in the 2008 Presidential Election," *Political Research Quarterly* 65, no. 2 (2012): 248–262.

52. Joseph D. Giammo and Brian J. Brox, "Reducing the Costs of Participation: Are States Getting a Return on Early Voting?" *Political Research Quarterly* 63, no. 2 (2010): 295–303.

53. Ellen Quintelier, Dietlind Stolle, and Allison Harell, "Politics in Peer Groups: Exploring the Causal Relationship between Network Diversity and Political Participation," *Political Research Quarterly* 65, no. 4 (2012): 868–881.

54. Cindy D. Kam, "Risk Attitudes and Political Participation," *American Journal of Political Science* 56, no. 4 (2012): 817–836.

55. Mancur Olson, *The Logic of Collective Action: Public Goods and the Theory of Groups* (Cambridge, MA: Harvard University Press, 1971).

56. Robert Dahl, "Pluralism Revisited," *Comparative Politics* 10, no. 2 (1978): 191–203.

57. M. Kent Jennings, "Ideological Thinking among Mass Publics and Political Elites," *Public Opinion Quarterly* 56, no. 4 (1992): 419–441.

58. Edward G. Carmines and James A. Stimson, "On the Structure and Sequence of Issue Evolution," *American Political Science Review* 80, no. 3 (1986): 901–920.

59. Souva and Rhode, "Elite Opinion Differences and Partisanship."

60. Christopher Wlezien, "Patterns of Representation: Dynamics of Public Preferences and Policy," *The Journal of Politics* 66, no. 1 (2004): 1–24.

61. Edward G. Carmines and James A. Stimson, "Issue Evolution, Population Replacement, and Normal Partisan Change," *American Political Science Review* 75, no. 1 (1981): 107.

China's National People's Congress removed presidential term limits in 2018, allowing Xi Jinping to continue as president indefinitely.

Source: Nicolas Asfouri/Pool//Getty Images

CHAPTER 8

Comparative Politics

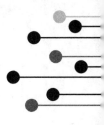

Today's China is an interesting amalgam of communist ideology and capitalist practice. In 1949, Mao Zedong established the People's Republic of China with himself as the ruler. Mao's influence on China can hardly be overstated; under his dictatorial leadership, China underwent significant social, cultural, and economic change. Mao's "Little Red Book" of communist thought and ideology was, and still is, required reading throughout China. His modernization programs quickly industrialized the country, but the Cultural Revolution decimated professional classes and easily set China back. Following his death, the Communist Party of China instituted a term limit for presidents at two five-year terms in order to limit the type of power Mao had acquired. While Chinese presidents remain quite powerful, perhaps even authoritarian, politicians since Mao have abided by these rules.

However, in March 2018, China's National People's Congress agreed to abolish term limits on China's president, which had been in place since Mao Zedong in order to allow its current president, Xi Jinping, to hold power for many years to come. In addition to his position as president, Xi also holds the positions of general secretary of the Chinese Communist Party's Central Committee and chairman of the Central Military Commission. While many in the West had hoped that economic reforms in China, allowing for some capitalist practices, would eventually lead the country to a democratic future, Xi's consolidation of power for the foreseeable time means that nothing like democratic principles appear to be at work. The challenge, then, for political scientists, is to understand the complex politics of a country as large and as complicated as China. With its long historical traditions and blending of communism and capitalism, it is a country that the West often misunderstands.

Chapter Objectives

1. Outline the comparative method.

2. Explore the meaning of the state and its key characteristics.

3. Define *democracy*, and identify ways in which it is measured.

4. Discuss patterns in postcommunist transitions and state development.

5. Define *nationalism*, and identify how it can often lead to conflict.

Comparative politics is the study of countries and politics around the world; comparativists examine the same thing political scientists do in American politics but do it in an international manner. They study institutions, political parties, public opinion, and voting all around the world. Some will compare patterns in one country to patterns in another or study the politics of an entire region. The name *comparative politics* also applies to another aspect of study: the methodology used. In comparing and contrasting countries, comparativists seek to understand why politics is different or the same around the world.

There are many ways of looking at politics around the world. We can look at different political institutions, the executives, legislatures, and court systems around the world. We can examine countries that are liberal democracies and those that are authoritarian. We can look at democracies versus monarchies versus oligarchies. We can look at health policy around the world or education policy or foreign policy. We can even look at the development of countries, from industrialized countries to developing countries, to the least developed.

So how to break up this chapter? If you were taking an introductory course to comparative politics, your professor may choose one of two main ways to organize the class: around regions and countries or around topic. In the country approach, you may study three or four countries in each of the following categories: industrialized democracies (think Europe here); communist and postcommunist countries such as Russia and China; and developing states such as those in Latin America, Africa, or the Middle East. Because patterns of politics are generally similar in countries in the same region or stage of development, by learning about the politics of some of these states, you can better understand the larger region. In the second approach, you may learn about major concepts such as the state, democracy, regime change, policy, and economics. This way, you learn not only about major concepts in comparative politics but can learn how to apply them across different countries. Either of these approaches is a valid and constructive way of learning about comparative politics.

For our purposes here, we'll be using the second approach to exploring comparative politics. We certainly will not be able to address every major topic of study in comparative politics, nor will the ones addressed be considered by everyone to be the most important. However, major topics like states, including their structure, development, economy, and democracy, are some of the most important concepts you'll come across in comparative politics. But first, we'll need to address the methodological component of comparative politics, the comparative method.

The Comparative Method

In 1971, Lijphart wrote, "Among the several fields or subdisciplines into which the discipline of political science is usually divided, comparative politics is the only one that carries a methodological instead of a substantive label. The term, 'comparative

Know a Political Scientist

Arend Lijphart

Arend Lijphart has been a significant influence on comparative politics since the mid-twentieth century. Born in 1936 in the Netherlands, he received his PhD from Yale in 1963. His article on comparative politics and the comparative method has been a required read for generations of political science students and has been a proponent of the idea of consociationalism, or the sharing of power in government. He later published *Patterns of Democracy* (1999), which is a detailed assessment of different types of government, primarily arguing for consensus democracy. Lijphart served as president of the American Political Science Association (APSA) from 1995 to 1996 and is currently research professor emeritus at the University of California, San Diego, where he spent his academic career.

politics' indicates the *how* but does not specify the *what* of the analysis."[1] Lijphart identifies the comparative method as one of the basic scientific methods that allows scientists to test out propositions and hypotheses; it is "a method of discovering empirical relationships among variables."[2]

Recall from Chapter 2 our discussion of research methods. When scientists, political scientists included, form hypotheses, they usually want to test them out. Most scientists can perform experiments where they control all possible variables that could affect their experiment. Let's say we are testing the temperature at which water boils. While we're mainly concerned about what temperature causes water to boil, there are other variables that can affect when the water does boil—air pressure and purity of the water included. In a laboratory setting, scientists can control all outside factors so as to isolate the one variable, temperature, that they are interested in. Political scientists aren't nearly as lucky. If we had a hypothesis about what causes a state to be democratic, we cannot manipulate countries and control all of the possible other variables that may influence whether a state is a democracy or not. The comparative method is one way—other than the experimental method—that political scientists can go about testing their hypotheses.

If a political scientist does wish to test a theory about the causes of democracy, they can pick a handful of countries—some that are democratic and some that are not. However, those countries should be as similar as possible in all other respects; their populations should be approximately the same, their education levels, their economic development. In this way, the political scientist can isolate the variables that are causing the democratic outcome.

One immediate thing about this process to be noted is that there are many outside variables that could affect the main relationship; Lijphart calls this the problem of many variables, small number of cases. Given the large number of characteristics that could affect any hypothesis, it will not always be possible to find enough cases, enough countries, or enough governments to properly test the hypothesis, and even then, you may not be able to get enough cases with similar

Mill's Method of Difference and Method of Agreement

John Stuart Mill was a nineteenth-century British philosopher who wrote on topics ranging from the economy and society to logic and philosophy. In a set of writings, Mill put forward five methods of induction; inductive reasoning is the process of reasoning from a specific case to more general methods of causation. Many comparativists base their methodology on Mill's method of difference, which he describes in *A System of Logic*:

> If an instance in which the phenomenon under investigation occurs, and an instance in which it does not occur, have every circumstance save one in common, that one occurring only in the former; the circumstance in which alone the two instances differ, is the effect, or cause, or a necessary part of the cause, of the phenomena.

Mill built on this and also posited the joint method of agreement and difference:

> If two or more instances in which the phenomenon occurs have only one circumstance in common, while two or more instances in which it does not occur have nothing in common save the absence of the circumstance; the circumstance in which alone the two sets of instances differ, is the effect, or cause, or a necessary part of the cause, of the phenomenon.

One easy way to illustrate this is through a matrix (see the table). On the left-hand side, there are three countries listed: the United States, France, and the United Kingdom. On the top of the matrix are a series of variables that could contribute to whether a state provides health care to its citizens or not. There are two variables of interest—government and type of political culture—that differ between the cases. However, if France and the United Kingdom differ on political culture and have the same outcome, we may be able to rule political culture out as a cause. Therefore, based on this matrix, it would appear that type of government may be linked to whether health care is government provided or not. Now, we know that there are many other variables that determine something like government provided health care, but this example illustrates how Mill's methods of difference and agreement can be used in the comparative method.

	Government	Type of Political Culture	Economy	Government Health Care?
United States	Presidential republic	Participant	Developed	No
France	Parliamentary	Participant	Developed	Yes
United Kingdom	Constitutional monarchy	Subject	Developed	Yes

enough characteristics. And further, just because a relationship may be apparent in a test of five countries, who is to say that that relationship will hold for other regions, countries, or periods of time?

One other major problem can also be confronted when using the comparative method. Because scientists are picking the cases to study and test their hypotheses with, we sometimes see something called **selection bias**, or selecting on the dependent variable. This means that scientists pick the cases to study so as to ensure that their theory is not disproved. In a more technical way, Collier and Mahoney define selection bias as selecting extreme cases that could lead to biased "estimates of causal effects."[3] To be sure, scientists may not be doing this on purpose, they may not even realize that they are biasing their own results. This just means that comparativists must pay very close attention to how they choose the cases they study to ensure that selection bias does not happen.

That being said, the comparative method, when used properly, can offer political scientists the ability to understand patterns of politics around the world—particularly for countries that are similar in region, similar in history, or similar in government. This allows every state and every government in the world to come up for examination, including America. Therefore, when one studies political science in Europe, they do not recognize a difference between comparative and American politics; for everyone else, they comprise the same thing. The comparative method can be used in any study of politics, even in America.

The State

Here in America, when we say state, we're usually referring to one of the fifty United States. While this is a legitimate use, the term *state* also refers to governments and countries around the world. In fact, when we refer to places like the United Kingdom, South Africa, China, or Chile, the proper term to use is *state*. Theorists going as far back as the Enlightenment and Thomas Hobbes have struggled with the meaning of the **state**—what it is, what defines it, what differentiates it from society or government. Social contract theorists like Hobbes and Locke theorized that the state arises from the social contract entered into by citizens. Steinberger argues that under Hobbes's social contract, not only is a sovereign created in which all powers are bestowed but a commonwealth that allows the sovereign to exist and act.[4]

Idea of the State

Early political scientists also homed in on the idea of a state, attempting to define what exactly constituted a "good" state. Weber, the same prolific German sociologist so influential in early conceptions of bureaucracy and public administration, defined the state as an entity that has a monopoly on the legitimate use of force. Force does not include only physical, military, or police, but legal coercion. For example, the state can coerce us to pay taxes or drive the speed limit by threatening us with punishment if we don't abide by the laws. No one else can legitimately use these types of threats under this definition of the state. This definition has stuck with political scientists as the study of the state began to decline moving into the twentieth century. In 1968, Nettl acknowledged this, writing, "The concept of the state is not much in vogue in the social sciences right now" and argued that "the erosion of the concept of state coincides in time with, and is clearly a functional part of, the shift of the center of gravity of social science to the United States."[5] Instead, political scientists focused on institutions and government, not the meaning of the term *state*.[6]

Krasner attributes the uptick in study of the state to a new generation of Marxist scholars who sought to establish a theory of the capitalist state that focused on the differences between the classes.[7] Out of this and other studies of the state, Krasner presents four different ways that the state has been conceptualized: the state as government, the state as the bureaucracy or administrative apparatus, the state as the ruling class, and the state as the normative order. Out of these conceptualizations, we can see just how the "state" differs from other concepts we talk about in political science. Is the state the idea, the social contract that upholds the legitimacy of government? Is it the tools and structures of government itself? Or is it something much more amorphous, representing commonly held ideas and notions about what government should be?

In research taking on these proliferating definitions of the state, Mitchell argues that many of the distinctions drawn between the state and other parts of government are not necessarily part of the nature of the state.[8] Mitchell argues that instead of trying to pin down the meaning of a state, we need to do the following:

> We need to examine the detailed political processes through which the uncertain yet powerful distinction between state and society is produced. The distinction must be taken not as the boundary between two discrete entities [state and society] but as a line drawn internally within the network of institutional mechanisms through which a social and political order is maintained.[9]

In other words, the fact that we can't specifically tell the difference between state and society means something in and of itself and that the process by which countries draw that line for themselves can inform political scientists as to the nature of the state.

State Formation

Aside from identifying what the state is or is not, political scientists also try to understand what causes states to form and why. The origins of the modern state system date back to the times of Hobbes himself with the signing of the Treaty of Westphalia in 1648. The treaty ended the Thirty Years' War in Europe and established principles of territorial sovereignty with competing states held in check by a balance of power. The Westphalian system led to a decline in traditional political authority like monarchies and feudalism, an increase in sovereignty over carefully defined land masses, and an increase in the complexity of governmental institutions.[10]

Vu takes the ideas of the state and state formation one step further, arguing that the way in which states form can tell us something about the meaning of the state itself.[11] For many European states, war and the subsequent need for rulers to acquire resources to fight wars helped lead to state formation. A homogenous civil society with competing groups also seems to be a prerequisite. These characteristics can tell us a lot about when states do or not form, which is important because the largest growth in the number of states did not occur in the early period of state formation but much later. In fact, Germany as a state did not emerge until the late 1800s! Many states in Latin America and Africa did not emerge until late because they had been colonial outposts of European nations. Even then, it was not always easy for states to form; colonial powers had no interest in seeing countries develop economically and therefore compete with their mother countries. Other former colonies had, and still have, severe ethnic conflicts because colonial masters drew lines with no thought toward historical and natural conflicts. Conflicts in the Middle East and Africa demonstrate how these two problems have intertwined to either lead to late state development or the lack of development altogether.

State Strength

This last issue leads us to concerns about the strength of states. How strong or weak states are can be used to explain why state formation does or does not occur, why revolutions do or don't happen, and how countries respond to crisis. For example, prior to the US invasion of Iraq in 2003, the state of Iraq under Saddam Hussein could be considered to be strong. Saddam was able to forcibly keep his country together despite the fact that three different ethnic groups all had reason to pull apart. And pull apart they did once Saddam's regime fell; the result has been a weak Iraqi state that has been penetrated by outside forces such as the Islamic State. It isn't easy for scholars to agree on what constitutes a strong state and what constitutes a weak state. Some have identified **state strength** as the ability of states to control political outcomes. Davidheiser identifies three criteria for a strong state: how deeply the state penetrates into society, the breadth of that penetration, and state autonomy.[12] Correspondingly, fragile states are those that "lack the capacity to discharge their normal functions and drive forward development."[13]

Fragile states can very often lead to failed states. Failed states exist where there is no entity that can exert sovereignty over their territory; this can lead to dangerous situations where no rule of law exists and chaos can reign. A prominent example of a **failed state** is Somalia, which has given safe harbor to modern-day pirates precisely because there is no legitimate authority or law in place to stop them. Piazza has come to this very conclusion; in studying 197 countries between 1973 and 2003, he finds that failed states are more likely to be home to transnational terrorist groups, giving safe haven to groups that are likely to strike outside of their home territory.[14] On the other hand, Patrick questions this link, arguing that state failure is only imperfectly related to transnational security threats. In any case, failed states have come in for as much examination as states that do exert control over their territory.[15]

What's in a name? For the Islamic State of Iraq and Syria, it is the establishment of their own country, their own sovereignty in land they believe belongs to them. For most in the West, however, the name ISIS stands for something much darker: terrorism. The movement we now know as ISIS has its roots in the late 1990s but came to play a much larger role beginning in 2013 as the Syrian Civil War raged. Taking advantage of the chaos and confusion inside Syria and the weakness of the Iraqi state, ISIS merged with several other terrorist organizations and began taking over territory in both Syria and Iran in 2014. At the same time, ISIS declared itself to be a "caliphate" with religious, political, and economic power over Muslims throughout the world—an action that most Muslims rejected. At one point, it claimed control of several large cities, including Raqqa in Syria and Mosul in Iraq. Since 2014, the United States has reengaged in Iraq and Syria to push ISIS fighters out of the territory which they claimed.

But is the name *Islamic State* accurate? Is ISIS a state, or was it ever a state? Let's think about some of the characteristics of a state (discussed previously):

1. a sovereign entity, that is, an entity that holds all power in its given territory

2. legitimacy and the ability to coerce

3. governing institutions such as bureaucracies and representative bodies

How well does, or did, ISIS stack up to these characteristics? Although this is a somewhat esoteric argument, ISIS certainly is not a state in the sense that we would recognize but a terrorist group; the question highlights the changing nature of the state system in the world today. Where the Westphalian system set up a global scene populated by states, today, there are many other actors to be aware of and concerned about. Transnational terrorist groups like ISIS and al-Qaida make calculations about how to deal with states that shelter them difficult. In a more benign manner, nongovernmental organizations and international organizations like the United Nations or the European Union force us to reconsider ideas of cooperation and power. States under the European Union, for instance, have had to give up some of their sovereignty to the European Union itself, primarily in economic areas, thereby losing individual control over certain policies. Does that make the European Union more or less of a state or the states within it more or less of a state? What does a state look like given the complexities of world politics today?

Critical Thinking Questions

1. Does the definition of a state as political scientists have traditionally conceptualized it still apply in the modern world?

2. Is there one characteristic of a state that is more important than the others?

3. What is the definition of *state*, and how is its application important in a global context?

Democracy

In America, we often take the term *democracy* for granted. We're taught that America represents the pinnacle of democracy without seriously thinking about what that means. For political scientists who study democracy around the world, the meaning of democracy is a very important thing, especially if we want to know what promotes democracy and what prevents it from taking hold.

Defining Democracy

Theories of democracy go back to ancient Greece, where we are told democracy means rule by the people. But what does rule by the people mean? Does it mean all people or just some people? Does it have to be all the time or just some of the time? And what if the majority of people act to take away important rights or rules? Does the fact that the majority says something is acceptable make it democratic? If we simply think about the history of American democracy, there were large periods in history where African Americans and women were not allowed to participate and had limited rights; does that mean America wasn't a democracy? These are just some of the basic concerns of democratic theorists in trying to understand precisely what democracy is.

In the mid-twentieth century, various definitions of **democracy** were put forward. Lipset defined *democracy* as follows:

> [It is] a political system which supplies regular constitutional opportunities for changing the governing officials. It is a social mechanism for the resolution of the problem of societal decision-making among conflicting interest groups which permits the largest possible part of the population to influence these decisions through their ability to choose among alternative contenders for political office.[16]

Lipset's definition focuses mainly on the requirement of elections, but how often do those elections need to occur? And do they need to be fair? Dahl adds to this definition by requiring that a democracy have elections that are fair, or rather, that everyone's vote count equally.[17] Downs goes one step further by saying that democratic elections should be held periodically.[18] Combining these early definitions of democracy, comparativists came to the maxim that democracies are countries that have free, fair, and frequent elections.

But what about civil liberties—things that protect citizens' rights or the structure of government itself? Bollen argues that democracy is better defined as "the extent to which the political power of the elite is minimized and that of the nonelite is maximized."[19] His definition encompasses many of the structures that would allow this to happen: elections and civil liberties, protections for citizens from government. Similarly, Muller defines democratic states as follows:

> (1) The executive must be elected or be responsible to an elected assembly, in (2) at least two consecutive and free and fair competitive elections in

which (3) at least approximately a majority of the population has the right to vote, and during which (4) the rights of freedom of speech and assembly are respected.[20]

Measuring Democracy

Knowing the definition of *democracy* is only half the battle; how do we measure how democratic a country is? There are a number of indices, or ways, of measuring democracy that have been put together in studies of comparative politics. Some measures are simply dichotomies; either a country is democratic or is not. In their study of measures of democracy, Bollen and Paxton divide measures of democracy into two traditions: one where measurements utilize voter turnout statistics, composition of legislatures, or availability of the vote, and a second that utilizes subjective determinations by a group of experts who rate how democratic a country is.[21]

One example of the later approach is the Freedom House ratings, which are released every year and widely used in comparative politics. Figure 8.1 shows how the percentage of countries rated as free, partly free, and not free have changed since 1985, according to Freedom House. Another set of measurements is the Polity data

Figure 8.1 Freedom House Rankings through the Years

After years of major gains, the share of free countries has declined over the past decade, while the share of not-free countries has risen.

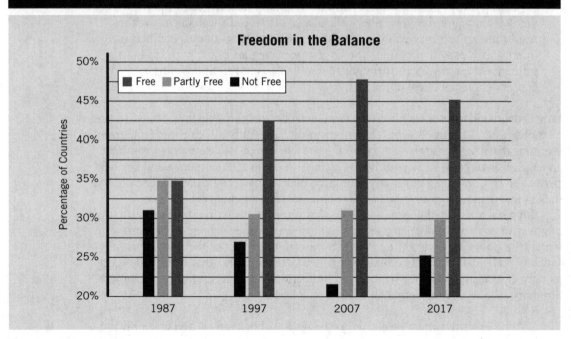

Source: www.freedominworld.com.

set, which scores states on a scale of –10 (hereditary monarchy) to +10 (democracy) (see Figure 8.2). The rankings depend on specific variables: freedom of group opposition, competitiveness of the political nomination process, election of chief executive, and effectiveness of the legislature.

So what contributes to countries becoming democratic? In a comprehensive study of civic attitudes and democracy, Muller and Seligson find that the only attitude that positively contributes to democracy is a belief in gradual rather than sudden, revolutionary reform.[22] Ross, in "Does Taxation Lead to Representation?" (which ironically appeared in the *British Journal of Political Science*), tests the idea of whether the need to raise taxes forces countries to democratize and finds support for this thesis.[23] In studying Latin America, a region where patterns of democratization have been uneven, Perez-Linan and Mainwaring demonstrate the influence of history on democratization; in states with a stronger history, a stronger experience with democracy, democratization is more likely to proceed.[24] All of these studies suggest that ideas in civil society and beliefs about what the government should or should

Figure 8.2 Polity Rankings, 1800–2014

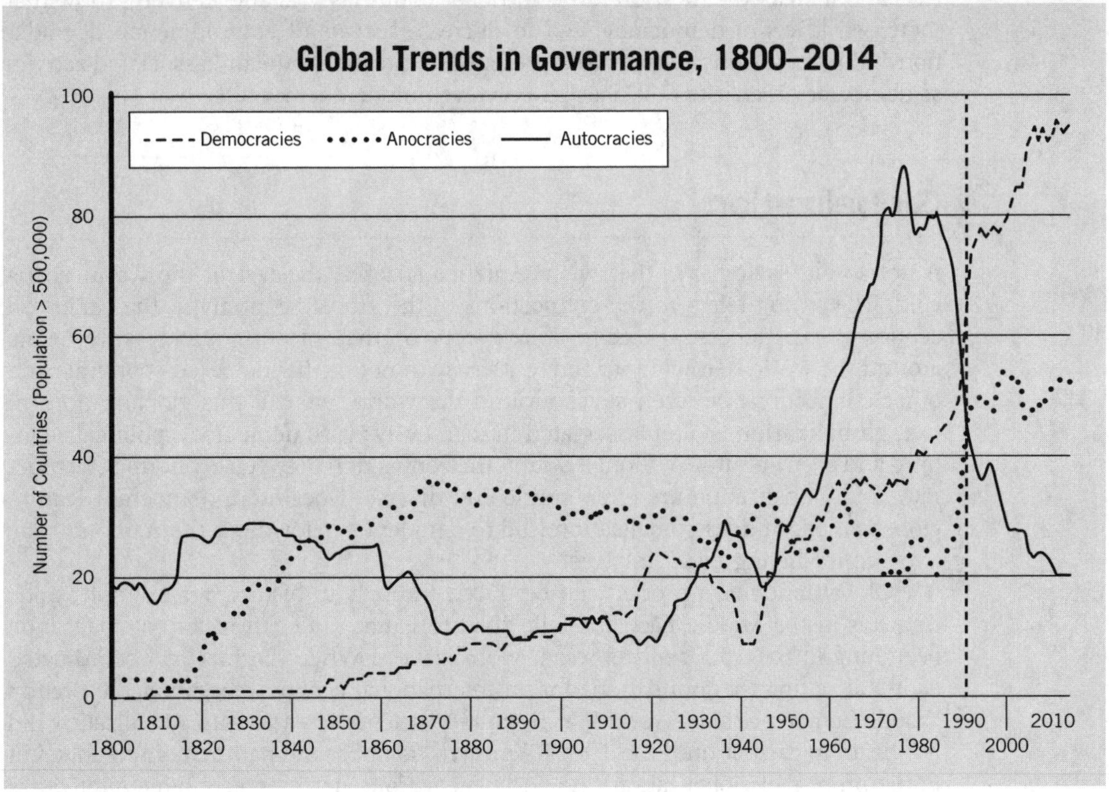

Global Trends in Governance, 1800–2014

Source: Center for Systemic Peace, 2018. Reproduced with permission.

not do contribute to the building of democracy. If we draw this line of inquiry out, democracy, then, can be very sensitive to place, time, and culture.

Culture is a concept that plays a role in a lot of comparative research. Some of the earliest research examining the relationship of culture to democracy was published by Almond and Verba in 1963 in a book called *The Civic Culture*. In examining the United States, Germany, Mexico, Italy, and the United Kingdom, Almond and Verba argue that what they call the civic culture supports a strong and vibrant democracy. Later generations of political scientists and comparativists have continued this tradition of research. Examining twenty local governments throughout Italy, Putnam identifies distinct historical legacies throughout Italy, which he argues have contributed to the strength of democracy throughout the country.[25] Putnam adapted Almond and Verba's concept of civic culture and focused on something called social capital. For Putnam, social capital represents the connections we have with one another that contribute to our resources for and abilities to contribute to a democratic life. Taken together, these two studies represent some of the major works linking culture to democracy.

Being able to measure how democratic a country is allows comparativists to study not only how democracies come about but what the effects of democracy are. Baum and Lake find that democracies lead to increased life expectancy in poor countries and increased education levels in richer countries.[26] Li and Reuveny show that increased levels of democracy lead to decreased levels of environmental degradation.[27] Boehmke finds an increased presence in interest group and associated activity as democracy increases.[28] What else do you think democracy affects?

Globalization

A not-so-old saying says that when America sneezes, the rest of the world gets a cold. The saying refers to the connections of the global economy; if the American economy experiences a hiccup, the effects of that hiccup quickly reverberate around the world. Growing up today, it's easy to notice the increased economic and other connections between states around the world; we call this globalization. In fact, **globalization** is often associated in many ways with democracy, political economy, and even culture. Without a doubt, the connection between economics, democracy, and globalization are often subtle and diverse. Does more democracy lead to globalization, or does globalization lead to democracy? How does the economy play a role in mediating these linkages?

Globalization as a process can be traced throughout history; for example, trade caravans in the Middle East, the Silk Road to China, and European colonialization beginning in the 1500s all represent globalization. While the first real coordinated efforts at setting the foundations for an international economy began at the Bretton Woods Conference after World War II, political science research into globalization did not begin in earnest until the 1980s. Kapstein describes the natural conflict inherent in the process of globalization: "how to benefit from increased economic intercourse while pursuing legitimate national objectives, such as bank safety and soundness."[29]

Countries want to take advantage of increased opportunities for trade and commerce, but if one country sneezes, others need to avoid a cold.

Economic globalization means that individual state economies are increasingly knit together, something exemplified in international trade agreements like the North American Free Trade Agreement (NAFTA) (recently renegotiated and pending ratification) and the Trans-Pacific Partnership (TPP). American critics of these sorts of trade agreements argue that by eliminating or reducing barriers to trade, companies will outsource their manufacturing to other countries where wages and costs are lower, thereby reducing employment opportunities and wages for American workers. However, Scruggs and Lange find that as far as union membership is concerned, increased economic globalization produces no effect.[30] While this may be the case for developed countries, Ha shows that among developing countries, globalization is associated with increased income inequality.[31]

Globalization does not just occur with economics but with politics; political globalization is the increasing connectedness of political institutions, particularly international organizations like the United Nations, the European Union, the International Monetary Fund (IMF), and other nongovernmental organizations. Think about the European Union in particular; the European Union is a confederation in which member states have given up some of their state sovereignty to the central political framework, especially in economics. This brings countries as different as France, the United Kingdom, Greece, and Germany together in a political and economic relationship where the actions of one affect the actions of all others.

Bretton Woods Conference

The Bretton Woods Conference was held in Bretton Woods, New Hampshire, from July 1 through 22 in 1944. The participants comprised representatives from all of the Allied states then fighting in World War II. Their purpose for meeting was to set up the foundations of the international monetary and financial system after the war ended. The primary motivation for such concerns was the realization that once the war ended, there would be a need to fund major reconstruction efforts across Japan and much of Europe. Among the institutions agreed to at Bretton Woods were the International Monetary Fund (IMF) and the International Bank for Reconstruction and Development. Agreements were also made regarding currency exchange and exchange rates, which set the stage for international trade after the war. The IMF still operates today to support currencies around the world and provide economic security to less developed states. The Bretton Woods Conference laid the foundations for a more globalized economy in the years to come.

One of the areas in which political science research has proven fruitful has been in tracing the consequences of globalization. Li and Reuveny, for instance, show that while economic changes can contribute to the spread of democracy, the more powerful factor is the spread of democratic ideas.[32] One easy way to see this finding in action is the history of the Arab Spring movement in 2011. One of the things that allowed the Arab Spring to spread across the Middle East was access to the Internet, which helped not only to organize the protestors but to familiarize them with democratic ideals. Although the effects of the Arab Spring are rather questionable, it still demonstrates the power of ideas and increased global connectedness.

Globalization also has social impacts. Gray, Kittilson, and Sandholtz as well as Richards and Gelleny find that increased globalization generally leads to the betterment of the status of women.[33] For women, globalization often means employment and educational opportunities. An example of this is in the field of microlending, where organizations lend women in developing countries small amounts of money to develop a business, which leads to increased income for the women and their families. Mukherjee and Krieckhaus show that globalization positively affects human well-being; both child and infant mortality fall, and life expectancy rises as globalization increases.[34]

Communism and Postcommunism

Perhaps no other topic in comparative politics has been as researched and discussed as the phenomenon of communism. The **Cold War**, driven by the ideological conflict between communism and democracy, was a political battle of wills between the two great superpowers of the twentieth century. As such, it was a natural topic of research for political scientists. This brief examination will be by no means a complete record or analysis of research into communism but will briefly discuss some of the more pertinent aspects of what communism is as a concept; how political scientists have studied it; and how countries, most prominently Russia, have transitioned from communism.

Communism in Practice

The first thing to understand about communism is that the brand of communism actually practiced by the Soviet Union, China, and their subsidiaries is not the theoretical construct of communism initially envisioned by Marx and Engels in *The Communist Manifesto*. Recall from Chapter 3 that Marx and Engels looked at history and saw in it a history of class struggles. The owners of the means of production, the bourgeoisie, sought to have control over the working class, the proletariat. They theorized that once a society had become industrialized and education had spread so that the proletariat came to realize how they were being used, a final revolution would occur. The proletariat would overthrow the bourgeoisie and eliminate any form of the state or government; the resulting society would be one in which all people were considered equal and shared ownership of both the means and results of production.

It's obvious why such an ideology would be attractive to those outside of the bourgeoisie. Particularly in countries where poverty and inequality were rampant, communism was easily able to gain a foothold. However, those same countries, Russia and later China, were not the theoretical hotbeds of communism that Marx and Engels envisioned. Neither were industrialized (both were incredibly agrarian in their economy), and neither country had an educated working class that had come to realize and support the communist doctrine. Instead, both countries saw revolutionary leaders emerge that took the seed of communist ideology and infused it with local flavor and characteristics that made the communism that came to be practiced unique in each country.

In Russia, the conflict between communist forces and czarist loyalists came during World War I. The Bolshevik revolution, first headed by Leon Trotsky, was soon to be taken over by Vladimir Lenin, who formed the intellectual heart of Soviet communism. Lenin, realizing that the requirements for a true communist revolution were not yet in place in Russia, modified the theory of Marx and Engels and believed that before a communist revolution could occur, there must first be a dictatorship of the proletariat to prepare the state for the coming communist movement. The leadership would ensure that conditions like industrialized and class consciousness improved such that communism could eventually be fulfilled as Marx and Engels wrote. Lenin would become the first leader of the Soviet Union to be followed by the murderous dictator Joseph Stalin. As we know today, the dictatorship of the proletariat never succeeded in preparing the way for communism; the Soviet Union disintegrated in 1991.

Much of the ideological concern and conflict would not come to a head until after World War II. Indeed, for the entirety of the war, the Allies included not only France, the United Kingdom, and the United States but also the Soviet Union. But in the absence of a common foe and the introduction of the atom bomb, the burgeoning conflict between the United States, democracy, and capitalism on one side and the Soviet Union and communism on the other blossomed into the Cold War. At that time, the forces of communism seemed stronger than ever and getting stronger by the day. Not only had the Soviet Union matched the United States in terms of the atom bomb by 1949 but more countries were succumbing to communism either by force or by choice. Many Eastern European countries that fell under the Soviet Union's purview following World War II had communist governments pushed on them from the ultimate dictator of the proletariat. And perhaps most significantly, China adopted communism in 1949.

China's road to communism, while sharing some similarities with Russia's, led to its own distinct form of communism. Like precommunist Russia, China was largely agrarian with little industrialization and little in the way of widespread education. What China did have, however, was a strong streak of nationalism that led to increased resentment as foreign powers came into China in the beginning of the twentieth century. This led to a Chinese civil war following World War II, which ended with communists, led by Mao Zedong, defeating the Nationalists led by Chiang Kai-shek.

As Lenin did for the Soviet Union, Mao did for China in adopting Marxist thought to local conditions. This eventually led to a sharp split between the Soviet Union and China. Mao acknowledged that the vast majority of Chinese citizens were, in fact, peasants, and therefore that Marxist ideology would need to be adjusted to fit the circumstances in China.[35] Writing in 1951 on the nature of Chinese communism, Littlejohn says this:

> The ultimate oracle is at present in Moscow, whence come the highest directives, but the application of all ruling is, in my opinion, a matter of local usage. In fact I have a strong suspicion that the Chinese will before long consider their Communism to be superior to the Russian brand.[36]

Studies of Communism

Most of the political science literature on communism prior to 1960 focused on communism's relation not only to individual states like Russia and China but religion and how it manifested in democratic countries like Australia. Scholar of Islam Lewis analyzed how compatible Islam would be with communism, notwithstanding Marxist communism's prohibition on religion.[37] Priestley argued that China's assault on Christian churches had not so much to do with religion as it had to do with overcoming potential obstacles to consolidation of the regime.[38] Also in regard to religion, Waddams explores the relationship between churches in Eastern Europe and the Russian Orthodox Church and the Moscow government, particularly in light of the Orthodox Church's ability to avoid complete disintegration.[39]

Regional- and country-specific studies of communism continued into the Cold War. Recognition that communism was not as monolithic as it wanted to appear became commonplace. The United States was able to exploit this shift through an opening of relations with China in the early 1970s. Recognizing these distinct differences in brands of communism, Tucker, in 1967, called for a more comparative approach to studying communism that would allow analysts to more thoroughly understand the similarities and differences in communism around the world.

By the 1980s, changes in the communist world began to take their toll. With the opening of US-Chinese relations, China was rapidly industrializing, and their economy began to become the Goliath it is today. In the Soviet Union, partly under the influence of President Ronald Reagan, political and economic reforms were instituted. Under the leadership of Mikhail Gorbachev, the twin policies of **glasnost** and **perestroika** were introduced. Glasnost led to political reforms centered around more transparency and openness while perestroika represented economic reforms allowing for greater private ownership. Then, in 1989, many of the Eastern European satellite communist states finally rebelled against their political masters, tore down (both literally and figuratively) the wall separating Eastern and Western Europe and transitioned to democracy. By 1991, the Soviet Union itself was incapable of surviving and collapsed.

One of the great failures of political scientists was their inability to predict in advance the imminent fall of communism. Therefore, in the years following the end of Soviet communism, much of the research about communism focused on why it all of a sudden failed. Schopflin identifies economic problems, a lack of government legitimacy, and shifts in public opinion as key drivers of the Eastern European transition.[40] Di Palma adds to this the existence of a civil society in Eastern European countries that survived the communist takeover.[41] Janos reexamines communist theory and the historical record to try to reconstruct patterns of political change in the communist world.[42]

Postcommunist Transitions

Other political scientists focused not only on the effects of the end of Soviet communism but on examining the transition from communism. Schopflin sees possible problems for the formerly communist Eastern European states stemming from their intolerance of economic inequalities that would naturally occur in capitalist societies, as well as a hostility toward a middle class.[43] White and McAllister looked at membership in the Communist Party in Russia and found that while it still held some sway as being the largest of the political parties to emerge after the fall of communism, younger and more religious Russians had left the party, leaving its future very much in doubt.[44] Finally, Mishler and Rose find that skepticism abounds in postcommunist countries about government, which could make consolidation of democracy more difficult to achieve.[45]

Communism continues to be an intriguing topic for political scientists because it has left marks on societies that will exist for decades to come. Many comparativists continue to investigate these legacies and the continuing changes in communist countries that still exist today such as China. At the base level of politics, the antagonism that existed between the former Soviet Union and the United States continues to play out on other levels today as both countries compete for influence around the world and, in particular, in the Middle East. Although the Cold War may be over, the possibility for research is not.

Authoritarianism

While communism was merely the theory behind the operations of governments in states like the Soviet Union, it is critical to remember that ideology and government type are distinct concepts. For many of the major communist states of the twentieth century, and for some noncommunist states, the style of government adopted was that of authoritarianism or totalitarianism. Totalitarianism and authoritarianism are related in the sense that both are forms of government where the governing authorities have almost total and complete power. However, **totalitarianism** is a type of government in which the authorities have total and complete control over their society, whereas **authoritarian** government, while still exerting almost complete control, allows for some political freedoms although there are no political protections or democratic procedures in place.[46] A good example of the difference between these two types of government is China. Under Mao in the twentieth century, China was considered a totalitarian government with Mao, as dictator, exerting near total control over the country. However, over time, China has allowed its citizens some limited political power although the state still controls the process. As such, today, China is considered an authoritarian state.

Concerns about authoritarianism naturally arise because of its lack of democratic principles and procedures but scholarly consideration of it increased greatly after World War II and the totalitarian and authoritarian governments involved in the war. In the early 1950s, Adorno and his colleagues published *The Authoritarian Personality*, which proposed that authoritarianism was a psychological trait or personality type distinguished by strict obedience to authority and oppression of diverse ideas and beliefs.[47] Although *The Authoritarian Personality* was based on a Freudian psychological analysis, scholars since the 1950s have tried to understand authoritarianism as a political attitude, its origins and causes, and its implications for democratic government. For example, if a greater number of people adopt authoritarian attitudes, they might be more willing to allow for greater government control, more limited civil liberties and civil rights, and a weakening of democratic principles.

In considering the causes of authoritarian attitudes, political scientists, sociologists, and psychologists have often linked it to beliefs in traditionalism, a need to conform to group norms, fundamentalism, a need for social cohesion, and even racial prejudice. One dominant theme in the research is the influence of parental authority when an individual was young; those with more authoritarian attitudes have been found to have had parents who imposed stricter rules during their upbringing. In turn, authoritarian individuals tend to be more intolerant of minorities, to support greater use of military force, and "to condone and even endorse illegal and blatantly undemocratic government behavior."[48]

One of the major findings since the 1950s is that authoritarian attitudes are often linked with right-wing, conservative political beliefs. This does not mean that there are no authoritarians who would be considered liberal but that there was a far higher number of authoritarians with right-wing beliefs.[49] In assessing the prevalence of authoritarian attitudes in the United States, for instance, Cizmar and her colleagues found that the number of Americans exhibiting authoritarian attitudes has risen since the mid-twentieth century with a clear impact on political polarization itself.[50] Indeed, Hetherington and Weiler make this argument explicit: that increasing polarization in the United States is most directly attributable to the rise of authoritarian attitudes.[51] The rise of authoritarian attitudes is not limited to the United States; right-wing, authoritarian groups and political parties have emerged across Europe in recent years promoting racist policies, limits on judicial independence, and anti-immigrant policies. Norris notes that the share of votes that authoritarian leaders and parties have been achieving has consistently risen over this same time period.[52]

Why authoritarian attitudes and leaders are on the rise is more complicated. Norris suggests that the shift is a result of a backlash against more progressive social norms that threaten traditionalist and conservative ideas.[53] This is further heightened by an education gap: Those with more authoritarian attitudes tend to be less educated as well as less interested in learning about politics.[54] A growing inequality between the rich and the poor and the increasing pace of social change could also contribute to these trends. While authoritarian attitudes could be a result of a changing social order, there is no doubt that these changes have implications for democratic governments worldwide. Party systems across Europe are becoming more fragmented; countries have sought more sovereignty (e.g., the United Kingdom's exit from the European Union) and economic nationalism. A key question for comparativists, then, is the extent to which authoritarianism is growing and what countries are doing as a response.

Development and Developing Countries

According to the IMF, a majority of countries in the world are considered to be less developed. What does this mean, and what consequences does being more or less developed have for a country's politics? How can international organizations aid countries that are less developed? These are just some of the topics that political scientists studying development consider.

In general, the level of **development** a country is at refers to its economy, but there is no agreed-upon definition of what is considered developed or not. In many ways, the study of development has roots in the historical patterns of colonization and imperialism. European colonial powers, historically, were able to exploit countries in what is now called the global South, comprising most of the countries in the Middle East, Africa, and South America. Many of these colonial empires had motivations to keep their colonies politically and economically dependent on the mother countries, all the while allowing the home countries to capitalize on the raw resources and captured economy of their colonies. This set into motion a global system where colonized states were purposefully kept weak and dependent. In previous years, these colonized countries were also referred to as the "third world" with Europe and America comprising the "first world." However, many critics disliked this characterization because of the inference that the people of the third world were in fact third-class peoples as compared to the citizens of the industrialized, developed first world. As a result, development theorists have preferred the term *less-developed countries* (LDCs).

Modernization and Western Bias

Evolving out of this situation was a body of theory about how states modernize. This **modernization theory** posited that LDCs would developmentally advance as they adopted more Western political and economic practices. Ideally, developed countries would assist in this practice in a paternalistic, guiding way. This early modernization theory reflected past practices of colonialization and the relationship between developed and LDCs. The ultimate stage of development according to modernization theory, however, is democracy, thereby linking development to the occurrence of democracy. This has become the implicit goal of development practices, to foster and encourage democratic governance in the LDCs, but it is not the only goal.

Development can refer to many different aspects of the human condition: social, cultural, political, and economic. However, like the terms *first world* and *third world*, there is also heavy criticism leveled at modern conceptions of development. Since the majority of political scientists, governments, and aid agencies that study and further development goals come from the developed world, they usually advocate a certain conception of development that is Western oriented. In other words, these advocates of development adhere to standards of development that may not be natural to those being targeted. For example, the Western value of equality for women is not something that is culturally believed in all parts of the world, as distasteful as it may be. What makes the Western notion of development superior or preferred to other notions of development? What about LDCs that simply do not want to develop economically, politically, or culturally? Should they be forced to? While these are what political scientists call normative concerns, we still must be aware of the meaning of many of these terms, not only to those of us in the West but to those who are being studied.

Sumner presents an excellent history of development studies in his article, appropriately titled "What Is Development Studies?"[55] He traces the origins of development studies to the mid-twentieth century as previously colonized countries tried to "catch up" with Western countries economically. Early on, development theorists and advocates focused on economic development as the primary aim. Development studies aim "to improve people's lives" with today's focus expanding from economic improvement to improvement across society.[56] This requires not only a multidisciplinary approach to development that not only involves political science but sociology, economics, and psychology along with the assistance of international organizations, both governmental and nongovernmental, in aiding LDCs.

Development Today

One of the primary international vehicles through which development is being pursued is a program under the United Nations called the Millennium Development Goals (MDGs). The MDGs were agreed to in 2000 with a goal for completing by 2015 the following eight principles:

1. Eradicate extreme poverty and hunger.

2. Achieve universal primary education.

3. Promote gender equality and empower women.

4. Reduce child mortality.

5. Improve maternal health.

6. Combat HIV/AIDS, malaria, and other diseases.

7. Ensure environmental stability.

8. Develop a global partnership for development.

While it is clear today that these goals were not wholly achieved, they have provided goals for development theorists and activists to consider. Political scientists have also taken on this challenge through research into not only the achievement of the MDGs but also how to go about achieving the goals. For example, Franklin argues that "results-based management" has been successful in achieving some of the measurable MDGs like those related to health but are not nearly as successful in achieving goals that do not necessarily have measurable outcomes.[57] Similarly, James contends that the MDGs do not distinguish between potential and actual achievements and that this may do more harm than good.[58] From the stance of actually implementing the MDGs, Bond examines how the goal to eradicate poverty has been implemented, and Clarke looks at the role of nongovernmental organizations, specifically faith-based organizations.[59]

But there are lessons to be learned as well. A strong line of research has emerged on what development activists have learned about development and what activities have shown to be successful. Chibba's article on lessons from development projects highlights some of the policies that can be adopted in other countries, such as taking culture into consideration when planning development and that market-based economic policies can help alleviate poverty and hunger.[60] Hope highlights some of the lessons of instituting governance reforms to increase capacity for development while Vonderlack and Schreiner detail the impact of microlending on women in the developing world and suggest an expansion of banking services for women in the developing world.[61]

Some of the critiques aimed at political scientists who study development relate back to the early roots of political science. Much like early political scientists, development theorists seek to improve the political, social, and economic life of those living in LDCs. This is quite similar to the early political science aim of discovering scientific, rational means of administering government and thereby improving the performance of states. With regard to development studies, Haberman and Langthaler formulate the critique in this way:

> For some, the purpose of development research is primarily to influence policies, and in order to do this development research has to reframe its whole approach, language, and methodology. Others maintain that development research needs to distance itself, maintain an analytical and even critical approach towards development practice, and become an academic discipline in its own right.[62]

This again reflects the split in political science from being academic in perspective but also being helpful to practitioners who may not find academic advice

CASE STUDY
India

India is the world's largest democracy with more than 1.3 billion people and for many years has been considered a developing country. Its economic statistics are staggering: Its growth rate has averaged 7 percent a year over the past two decades, it ranks fourth globally in gross domestic product (GDP) (after China, the European Union, and the United States), and it exports almost $300 billion worth of goods to the rest of the world.[63] Despite that, poverty remains a concern, literacy rates are low, and per capita income remains low.[64] India's history of colonial occupation by the British adds a further dimension to the puzzle as does the Hindu religious caste system.

For our purposes here, we can think about India's development from three points of view discussed previously: modernization theory and its relationship to democracy, economics, and cultural or social. Economics, as noted previously, represents a bright spot in Indian development. It has continued to work with organizations like the World Bank and the Organisation for Economic Co-operation and Development (OECD) on continuing projects, enhancing Indian infrastructure. Social and cultural development, however, is a different story; as represented by the Millennium Development Goals (MDGs), it has also been slow in coming to India. Table 8.1 lists the MDGs and how India ranks on each. In most all categories, India ranks fairly low. Aside from the cultural and religious concerns raised by the Hindu practice of castes, a large percentage of India's population remains below the poverty line, and inequality and human development rank low.

Table 8.1   Indian Progress on Millennium Development Goals

Millennium Development Goal	India's Rank
Eradicate extreme poverty and hunger	21.9 percent of population below poverty line
Achieve universal primary education	71.2 percent literacy rate; 134th in world in expenditures on education
Promote gender equality and empower women	in UN Gender Inequality Index
Reduce child mortality	47th in infant mortality (39.1 deaths/100,000 live births)
Improve maternal health	56th in maternal mortality rate (174 deaths/100,000 live births)
Combat HIV/AIDS, malaria and other diseases	3rd in people living with HIV/AIDS, 3rd in people dying from HIV/AIDS
Ensure environmental stability	4th largest emitter of carbon dioxide

Sources: CIA World Fact Book; UN Human Development Reports.

Finally, in many ways, India is a prime example for modernization theorists. A British colony, India was economically exploited by the British until the Indian independence movement, led by Mahatma Gandhi, established independence in 1947. India created and instituted a secular and democratic constitution three years later in 1950, which borrowed much from the British parliamentary system. From the perspective of modernization theory, the British were in a place not only to foster the development of India as an independent country but that the establishment of democracy was a key contributor. However, there is a significant question as to just how democratic India has been. For much of its independent history, Indian politics was dominated by one political party; while this certainly contributed to India's political stability, as discussed previously, democracy involves a number of elements that India may not fully satisfy.

Critical Thinking Questions

1. How would you classify India: as a developed state or still developing? Why?

2. Which characteristics of development do you believe are most important in determining a country's level of development?

3. Can a country be developed while still falling short of social goals?

useful at all. Nonetheless, development will continue to be a timely topic not only for the world but for political scientists—one that could be influential in helping people around the world.

Nationalism and Ethnic Conflict

One of the increasingly important concerns that has drawn attention worldwide is the phenomenon of nationalism and the consequences that flow from it. Before defining nationalism as a concept, it is appropriate to draw the distinction between state and nation. A state, while the definition is diffuse and uncertain, refers to institutions and forms of government, whereas nation refers to a social or ethnic grouping of people. Based on this, **nationalism** is a sense of group identity and belonging that often includes a desire for self-government based on national identity. For centuries, small states were generally referred to as nation-states or states that reflected national identities.

The concept of nationalism is not new; Hah and Martin note that it was identified as early as 1836.[65] Woodrow

Career Guidance

State development requires the work of thousands of people and organizations other than state governments. International nongovernmental organizations often assist less-developed states in improving their infrastructure, health and social outcomes, and economy. These organizations include the United Nations and its subsidiaries such as the World Health Organization and International Monetary Fund, the Bill and Melinda Gates Foundation, Doctors without Borders, and Oxfam International. Working for a nongovernmental organization such as one of these can be an exciting career path for those with degrees in political science and an interest in comparative politics or development studies.

Wilson made nationalism and self-determination a foundation of his Fourteen Points proposal following World War I. Yet, while the former political scientist Wilson was calling for self-determination, his erstwhile allies in Europe, France and the United Kingdom, were redrawing the borders of the Middle East. In their quest for colonial territory, France and the United Kingdom drew territorial lines with no concern for the traditional ethnic and religious concerns that dominated the Middle East. As such, somewhat artificial countries were created—for example, Iraq, that had no common history but different religious and ethnic groups that do not care to live together.

Conflicts spurred on by nationalist and ethnic identities are increasing in the modern world. The end of the Cold War and the increase of globalization has brought more groups into contact with each other, leading to the potential for more conflicts.[66] But nationalism can be a potentially valuable attitude as well; the belief in American values and ideals is a sort of nationalism that binds and knits a country together. But it "can just as plausibly be seen as a kind of particularism denying non-citizens or culturally deviant citizens full human rights and, in the extreme cases, even denying them membership in the community of humans."[67] It is this more extreme case that has led to conflict between groups such as the Hutus and Tutsis in Rwanda, between Sunni and Shia Muslims in the Middle East, and Arabs and non-Arabs in Darfur.

Nationalism can exist in many forms. **Economic nationalism** promotes a country's economy by protecting industries and businesses within the country and instituting tariffs and taxes to protect the domestic economy from outside economies. There exists a thread of black nationalism in American discourse. Then there is the ethnic nationalism that can often lead to the deadly conflict we see around the world today.

So why should nationalism necessarily lead to conflict? In many ethnic conflicts, the concern is about territory and sovereignty over a given parcel of land. If there are multiple ethnic or religious groups in one area and both believe they should have sovereignty, conflict will naturally develop. The Arab-Israeli conflict is yet another example of the types of conflicts that arise. And like the Arab-Israeli struggle, there is no easy answer to the question; there is no way to create more land and both groups want it and do not want to share it. Thus nationalism can also prevent solutions to conflicts.

Certainly, political scientists have been able to connect nationalism to a variety of consequences, most significantly war.[68] However, de las Casas suggests that the aspects of nationalism that foster a sense of group identity and pride can lead to outcomes such as a stronger economy and less government corruption.[69] It seems, then, that nationalism, like many of the concepts we've discussed thus far, isn't necessarily good or bad; it's in how it's used that creates positive or negative effects.

CASE STUDY
Yemen

Amnesty International has called the conflict in Yemen the "forgotten war." It has raged since 2014 involving many countries in the Middle East, including Saudi Arabia and Iran, yet little media attention has been paid to it, especially compared to the Syrian Civil War. At the heart of the conflict is ethnic conflict between the ruling Sunni government and Shiite rebels called the Houthi. Sunni and Shiite are two Muslim sects that have historically disagreed about who the successor to the prophet Mohammed is or should be; the Shia believed it should be a descendant of the Prophet while the Sunni believed the Muslim community should be able to decide. Interestingly enough, even though the split between the two groups took place soon after Mohammed's death, the two groups have largely lived in peaceful coexistence.[70] Conflict has emerged from time to time with the split becoming especially relevant in the twentieth century that brought with it a more "complex political dynamic involving Sunni and Shiites, Arabs and Persians, colonizers and colonized, oil, and the involvement of superpowers."[71]

In Yemen, the population is majority Sunni; Muslims as a whole make up 99.1 percent of the population with Sunnis composing 65 percent and Shiite 35 percent of that population.[72] Not untouched by the Arab Spring uprising that was felt across the Middle East, in 2011, the Yemeni government agreed to a political transition that forced its longtime authoritarian leader from power to be replaced with his deputy, Abdrabbuh Mansour Hadi. As president, Hadi struggled to deal with a number of problems facing the country, which the Shiite minority took advantage of, leading to the takeover of the capital Sanaa in 2015 by the Houthi rebels.[73] Since then, countries across the Middle East and the world have picked sides in the battle with the Houthi being joined by some Yemeni army groups loyal to the former president and backed by Iran. President Hadi has been supported by a number of other countries but most prominently Saudi Arabia, the United Arab Emirates, Bahrain, Kuwait, Qatar, Jordan, and Sudan (the United States has also provided assistance to the Sunni-led government).[74]

The cost of the conflict to the Yemeni people has been high. According to Amnesty International, more than 4,600 civilians have been killed with more than 8,000 injured, 3 million people have been forced from their homes by fighting, and 18.8 million Yemenis rely on humanitarian assistance simply to survive. Meanwhile, the chaos in Yemen has become a haven for terrorist groups including ISIS.

The ethnic conflict in Yemen has been spurred on by many of the same problems people across the Middle East have been facing for decades: lack of educational opportunity, lack of jobs, and inability to involve themselves in political affairs. The result has been a large group of young people who have become disillusioned and vulnerable to political and religious extremists. The Yemen conflict, then, is representative of ethnic conflict as a whole in the Middle East. Disaffected minorities, spurred by religious differences, have often taken their qualms to the streets with no easy answer or end in sight.

(Continued)

(Continued)

Critical Thinking Questions

1. In the case of Yemen, how does nationalism lead to conflict?

2. What role does religion play in stimulating conflict? Can it increase nationalistic attitudes or serve as a bridge between different groups?

3. What are the possible consequences for Yemen in terms of it being labeled a failed state?

STUDENT STUDY SITE

Visit https://edge.sagepub.com/whitmancobb

CHAPTER SUMMARY

- Comparative politics is not only a field of study in political science but a research method. The comparative method provides a means of testing hypotheses while controlling for potentially confounding variables.

- The idea of the state is a significant one in politics. States are key actors in the political system, and being a strong or weak state can come with significant consequences. However, given increasing globalization and the role of international organizations, the role of the state could be shifting.

- Communist countries played a key role in the twentieth century and into the twenty-first century. Political scientists have struggled to understand communist politics and patterns of developing in postcommunist countries.

- Many states around the world continue to develop in terms of politics, economics, and strength. Development studies examine best practices and help to identify key goals, but they are often hampered by pro-Western ideals that may not fit culturally elsewhere.

- Nationalistic attitudes and beliefs have contributed to both development and conflict. Ethnicity can reinforce nationalism and contribute to conflicts around the world.

KEY TERMS

authoritarian: Type of government that, while still exerting almost complete control, allows for some political freedoms although there are no political protections or democratic procedures in place

Cold War: Period of ideological conflict from the end of World War II to 1991 between the Soviet Union and the United States

comparative politics: The study of countries and politics around the world

democracy: States that have free, fair, and frequent elections and in which civil liberties are recognized and protected

development: How advanced a state is in terms of economics and social problems

economic nationalism: Attitudes in favor of protecting a country's economic independence and autonomy

failed state: No entity that can exert sovereignty over territory

glasnost: Series of Soviet political reforms in the 1980s

globalization: Increasing economic and other connections between states

modernization theory: Less-developed countries (LDCs) to developmentally advance as they adopted more Western political and economic practices

nationalism: Sense of group identity and belonging that often includes a desire for self-government based on national identity

perestroika: Series of Soviet economic reforms in the 1980s

selection bias: Occurs when the cases that are chosen to be studied are systematically skewed

state: Groups of people living under a single governmental system

state strength: The ability of states to control political outcomes

totalitarianism: Type of government in which the authorities have total and complete control over their society

DISCUSSION QUESTIONS

1. What is the comparative method? Give an example of how you can use it to study comparative politics.

2. What are some of the different ways democracy can be defined?

3. What are some ways in which democracy, globalization, and development might be related?

4. Do you believe globalization is a good or bad thing? What about nationalism? Why or why not?

FURTHER READING

Almond, Gabriel A., and Sidney Verba. *The Civic Culture: Political Attitudes and Democracy in Five Nations.* Newbury Park, CA: Sage, 1989.

Dahl, Robert A. *Polyarchy: Participation and Opposition.* New Haven, CT: Yale University Press, 1972.

Downs, Anthony. *An Economic Theory of Democracy.* New York: Harper and Brothers, 1957.

Lijphart, Arend. "Comparative Politics and the Comparative Method." *American Political Science Review* 65, no. 3 (1971): 682–693.

Putnam, Robert D. *Making Democracy Work: Civic Traditions in Modern Italy.* Princeton, NJ: Princeton University Press, 1994.

Freedom House: https://freedomhouse.org

United Nations Millennium Development Goals: www.un.org/millenniumgoals

NOTES

1. Arend Lijphart, "Comparative Politics and the Comparative Method," *American Political Science Review* 65, no. 3 (1971): 682 (emphasis in the original).

2. Ibid., 683.

3. David Collier and James Mahoney, "Insights and Pitfalls: Selection Bias in Qualitative Research," *World Politics* 49, no. 1 (1996): 59.

4. Peter J. Steinberger, "Hobbes, Rousseau, and the Modern Conception of the State," *The Journal of Politics* 70, no. 3 (2008): 595–611.

5. J. P. Nettl, "The State as a Conceptual Variable," *World Politics* 20, no. 4 (1968): 559, 561.

6. Stephen D. Krasner, "Approaches to the State: Alternative Conceptions and Historical Dynamics," *Comparative Politics* 16, no. 2 (1984): 223–246.

7. Krasner, "Approaches to the State."

8. Timothy Mitchell, "The Limits of the State: Beyond the Statist Approaches and Their Critics," *American Political Science Review* 85, no. 1 (1991): 77–96.

9. Ibid., 78.

10. David J. Samuels, *Comparative Politics* (Boston: Pearson, 2003).

11. Tuong Vu, "Studying the State through State Formation," *World Politics* 62, no. 1 (2010): 148–175.

12. Evenly B. Davidheiser, "Strong States, Weak States: The Role of the State in Revolution," *Comparative Politics* 24, no. 4 (1992): 463–475.

13. Eghosa E. Osaghe, "Fragile States," *Development in Practice* 17, no. 4/5 (2007): 691.

14. James A. Piazza, "Incubators of Terror: Do Failed and Failing States Promote Transnational Terrorism?" *International Studies Quarterly* 52, no. 3 (2008): 469–488.

15. Stewart Patrick, "'Failed' States and Global Security: Empirical Questions and Policy Dilemmas," *International Studies Review* 9, no. 4 (2007): 644–662.

16. Seymour Martin Lipset, "Some Social Requisites of Democracy: Economic Development and Political Legitimacy," *American Political Science Review* 53, no. 1 (1959): 71.

17. Robert Dahl, *A Preface to Democratic Theory* (Chicago: University of Chicago Press, 1956).

18. Anthony Downs, *An Economic Theory of Democracy* (New York: Harper and Brothers, 1957).

19. Kenneth A. Bollen, "Issues in the Comparative Measurement of Political Democracy," *American Sociological Review* 45, no. 3 (1980): 372.

20. Edward N. Muller, "Democracy, Economic Development, and Income Inequality," *American Sociological Review* 53 (1988): 54.

21. Kenneth A. Bollen and Pamela Paxton, "Subjective Measures of Liberal Democracy," *Comparative Political Studies* 33, no. 1 (2000): 58–86.

22. Edward N. Muller and Mitchell A. Seligson, "Civic Culture and Democracy: The Question of Causal Relationships," *American Political Science Review* 88, no. 3 (1994): 635–652.

23. Michael L. Ross, "Does Taxation Lead to Representation?" *British Journal of Political Science* 34, no. 2 (2004): 229–249.

24. Anibal Perez-Linan and Scott Mainwaring, "Regime Legacies and Levels of Democracy: Evidence from Latin America," *Comparative Politics* 45, no. 4 (2013): 379–397.

25. Robert D. Putnam, *Making Democracy Work: Civic Traditions in Modern Italy* (Princeton, NJ: Princeton University Press, 1994).

26. Matthew A. Baum and David A. Lake, "The Political Economy of Growth: Democracy and Human Capital," *American Journal of Political Science* 47, no. 2 (2003): 333–347.

27. Quan Li and Rafael Reuveny, "Democracy and Environmental Degradation," *International Studies Quarterly* 50, no. 4 (2006): 935–956.

28. Frederick J. Boehmke, "The Effect of Direct Democracy on the Size and Diversity of State Interest Group Populations," *The Journal of Politics* 64, no. 3 (2002): 827–844.

29. Ethan B. Kapstein, "Resolving the Regulator's Dilemma: International Coordination of Banking Regulations," *International Organization* 43, no. 2 (1989): 324.

30. Lyle Scruggs and Peter Lange, "Where Have All the Members Gone? Globalization, Institutions, and Union Density," *The Journal of Politics* 64, no. 1 (2002): 126–153.

31. Eunyoung Ha, "Globalization, Government Ideology, and Income Inequality in Developing Countries," *The Journal of Politics* 74, no. 2 (2012): 541–557.

32. Quan Li and Rafael Reuveny, "Economic Globalization and Democracy: An Empirical Analysis," *British Journal of Political Science* 33, no. 1 (2003): 29–54.

33. Mark M. Gray, Miki Caul Kittilson, and Wayne Sandholtz, "Women and Globalization: A Study of 180 Countries, 1975-2000," *International Organization* 60, no. 2 (2006): 293–333; David L. Richards and Ronald Gelleny, "Women's Status and Economic Globalization," *International Studies Quarterly* 51, no. 4 (2007): 855–876.

34. Nisha Mukherjee and Jonathan Krieckhaus, "Globalization and Human Well-Being," *International Political Science Review* 33, no. 2 (2012): 150–170.

35. Max Mark, "Chinese Communism," *The Journal of Politics* 13, no. 2 (1951): 232–252.

36. Justin Littlejohn, "China and Communism," *International Affairs* 27, no. 2 (1951): 143.

37. Bernard Lewis, "Communism and Islam," *International Affairs* 30, no. 1 (1954): 1–12.

38. K. E. Priestley, "Chinese Communism and Christianity," *Far Eastern Survey* 21, no. 2 (1952): 17–20.

39. H. M. Waddams, "Communism and the Churches," *International Affairs* 25, no. 3 (1949): 295–306.

40. George Schopflin, "Post-Communism: Constructing New Democracies in Central Europe," *International Affairs* 67, no. 2 (1991): 235–250.

41. Giuseppe Di Palma, "Legitimation from the Top to Civil Society: Politico-Cultural Change in Eastern Europe," *World Politics* 44, no. 1 (1991): 49–80.

42. Andrew C. Janos, "Social Science, Communism, and the Dynamics of Political Change," *World Politics* 44, no. 1 (1991): 81–112.

43. Schopflin, "Post-Communism."

44. Stephen White and Ian McAllister, "The CPSU and Its Members: Between Communism and Postcommunism," *British Journal of Political Science* 26, no. 1 (1996): 105–122.

45. William Mishler and Richard Rose, "Trust, Distrust, and Skepticism: Popular Evaluations of Civil and Political Institutions in Post-Communist Societies," *The Journal of Politics* 59, no. 2 (1997): 418–451.

46. W. Phillips Shively, *Power and Choice: An Introduction to Political Science* (New York: McGraw-Hill, 2014), 164; Charles Hausas and Melissa Haussmann, *Comparative Politics: Domestic Responses to Global Challenges,* 8th ed. (Boston: Wadsworth, 2013), 9.

47. Theodor W. Adorno et al., *The Authoritarian Personality* (New York: Harper and Brothers, 1950).

48. Frederick Solt, "The Social Origins of Authoritarianism," *Political Research Quarterly* 65, no. 4 (2012): 703.

49. Bojan Todosijevic and Zsolt Enyedi, "Authoritarianism without Dominant Ideology: Political Manifestations of Authoritarian Attitudes in Hungary," *Political Psychology* 29, no. 5 (2008): 767–787.

50. Anne M. Cizmar et al., "Authoritarianism and American Political Behavior from 1952–2008," *Political Research Quarterly* 67, no. 1 (2014): 71–83.

51. Marc J. Hetherington and Jonathan D. Weiler, *Authoritarianism and Polarization in American Politics.* (Cambridge, MA: Cambridge University Press, 2009).

52. Pippa Norris, "It's Not Just Trump. Authoritarian Populism Is Rising across the West," *Monkey Cage,*

March 11, 2016, https://www.washingtonpost.com/news/monkey-cage/wp/2016/03/11/its-not-just-trump-authoritarian-populism-is-rising-across-the-west-heres-why/?utm_term=.eaa80f5c2218.

53. Ibid.

54. Bill E. Peterson, Lauren E. Duncan, and Joyce S. Pang, "Authoritarianism and Political Impoverishment: Deficits in Knowledge and Civic Disinterest," *Political Psychology* 23, no. 1 (2002): 97–112.

55. Andrew Sumner, "What Is Development Studies?" *Development in Practice* 16, no. 6 (2006): 644–650.

56. Ibid., 645.

57. Thomas Franklin, "Reaching the Millennium Development Goals: Equality and Justice as Well as Results," *Development in Practice* 18, no. 3 (2008): 420–423.

58. Jeffrey James, "Misguided Investments in Meeting Millennium Development Goals: A Reconsideration Using Ends-Based Targets," *Third World Quarterly* 27, no. 3 (2006): 443–458.

59. Patrick Bond, "Global Governance Campaigning and MDGs: From Top-Down to Bottom-Up Anti-Poverty Work," *Third World Quarterly* 27, no. 2 (2006): 339–354; Gerard Clarke, "Agents of Transformation? Donors, Faith-Based Organizations, and International Development," *Third World Quarterly* 28, no. 1 (2007): 77–96.

60. Michael Chibba, "Lessons from Selected Development Policies and Practices," *Development in Practice* 19, no. 3 (2009): 365–370.

61. Kempe Ronald Hope Sr., "Capacity Development for Good Governance in Developing Societies: Lessons from the Field," *Development in Practice* 19, no. 1 (2009): 79–86; Rebecca M. Vonderlack and Mark Schreiner, "Women, Microfinance, and Savings: Lessons and Proposals," *Development in Practice* 12, no. 5 (2002): 602–612.

62. Birgit Haberman and Margarita Langthaler, "Changing the World of Development Research? An Insight into Theory and Practice," *Development in Practice* 20, no. 7 (2010): 771.

63. CIA World Factbook, "India," https://www.cia.gov/library/publications/the-world-factbook/geos/in.html.

64. *Guardian*, "Is India Still a Developing Country?," April 6, 2014, https://www.theguardian.com/global-development/poverty-matters/2014/apr/07/is-india-still-a-developing-country.

65. Chong-Do Hah and Jeffrey Martin, "Toward a Synthesis of Conflict and Integration Theories of Nationalism," *World Politics* 27, no. 3 (1975): 361–386.

66. Thomas Hylland Eriksen, "Ethnicity versus Nationalism," *Journal of Peace Research* 28, no. 3 (1991): 263–278.

67. Ibid., 265–266.

68. Gretchen Schrock-Jacobson, "The Violent Consequences of the Nation: Nationalism and the Initiation of Interstate War," *Conflict Resolution* 56, no. 5 (2012): 825–852.

69. Gustavo de las Casas, "Is Nationalism Good for You?" *Foreign Policy* 165 (March–April 2008): 50–56.

70. Mike Shuster, "The Origins of the Shiite-Sunni Split," *NPR*, Feb. 12, 2007, https://www.npr.org/sections/parallels/2007/02/12/7332087/the-origins-of-the-shiite-sunni-split.

71. Ibid.

72. CIA World Factbook, "Yemen," https://www.cia.gov/library/publications/the-world-factbook/geos/ym.html.

73. BBC News, "Yemen Crisis: Who Is Fighting Whom?" Jan. 30, 2018, www.bbc.com/news/world-middle-east-29319423.

74. Amnesty International, "Yemen: The Forgotten War," March 6, 2018, https://www.amnesty.org/en/latest/news/2015/09/yemen-the-forgotten-war/.

North Korea's leader Kim Jong-un (left) shakes hands with US president Donald Trump (right) at the start of their historic US-North Korea summit at the Capella Hotel on Sentosa island in Singapore on June 12, 2018.

Source: SAUL LOEB/AFP/Getty Images

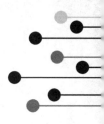

CHAPTER 9

International Relations

When Twitter was first introduced in 2006, its founders probably could not have imagined how people would potentially use it. Over the past twelve years, Twitter has expanded to more than 330 million active monthly users throughout the world. Governments have even gotten into the act: Twitter Government (@TwitterGov) even highlights how governments and politicians throughout the world use Twitter. Politicians and elected officials quickly took to Twitter, using it as a means to communicate with voters directly. Former president Barack Obama even originated a Twitter handle for presidents (@POTUS) in 2013.

The current US president, Donald Trump, has utilized Twitter to a far greater extent than his predecessor, although he does so from his own personal account (@realDonaldTrump) rather than the official @POTUS handle. In interviews, he has argued that communicating via Twitter allows him to get his message to voters without the filter of the media with the implicit argument that the media does not do a faithful and true job in reporting his actions. As such, President Trump's tweets often come directly from the president himself with no staff filtering or discussion. One area where the president's tweets have been particularly influential is in the US relationship with North Korea.

As of October 2018, President Trump has tweeted about North Korea more than 150 times since taking office. And while the tweets may not appear on the official @POTUS account or come in a statement on White House letterhead, they have played an integral role in American-North Korean relations. For example, on August 11, 2017, the president tweeted this:

> Military solutions are now fully in place, locked and loaded, should North Korea act unwisely. Hopefully Kim Jong Un will find another path!

Chapter Objectives

1. Explain the international relations theory of realism including its basic assumptions.

2. Discuss the liberal theory of international relations along with its different types.

3. Define *constructivism* and its central principles.

4. Explore feminist international relations theory and its recommendations for change.

5. Examine causes of war and peace in the international arena.

At a mere twenty-three words, the president stated what could have easily been seen as a military threat against North Korea that could have led to direct conflict. Realizing the potential implications of tweets like this from the president, US officials at the February 2018 Munich Security Conference reportedly told their counterparts not to pay attention to what the president is tweeting.[1] However, in March 2018, North Korea's leader Kim Jong-un, apparently under pressure because of the president's rhetoric, broached the idea of a summit between the two leaders. What followed was a historic meeting between the two leaders in June 2018 in Singapore as well as enhanced relations between North and South Korea.

Unlike the other subfields of political science where we were able to discuss individual concepts like public opinion, public policy, institutions of government, democracy, or so on, international relations is more organized around different theories of how states behave. This chapter summarizes and lays out the major arguments of four major theories of international relations: realism, liberalism, constructivism, and feminism. It ends by talking about one important area of research for international scholars aside from theoretical approaches, and that is the incidences of war and peace.

Before diving into the different theories of international relations, we should note here that these theories are just that—theories. Theories are built on simplified models of human behavior and as such, cannot explain all of the nuances of human action. Although it is easy to see some, or many, of the following characteristics in how states behave, we do not expect to see every characteristic. In other words, while these theories may help us explain and interpret state behavior, they probably won't explain every individual situation.

Realism

For most of the history of the world, states have sought to achieve power and expand the area in which that power can be exerted. If a state is an entity that has a monopoly on the legitimate uses of force in a given area, states have usually sought to expand that area of power and influence. This rational motivation rooted in self-interest can be traced back to the days of Athens and Sparta; the Greek historian Thucydides identified the Athenian quest for power as a key driver of the Peloponnesian War. Machiavelli, in giving advice to his patron in *The Prince,* also endorsed this idea of states acting to protect their own sovereignty, as did Thomas Hobbes. This long tradition of realism in international relations has led to a large body of work expounding on these ideas and using them to explain the actions of states around the world and throughout history. Not only has realism been influential in academia but it has also made its mark on actual international relations around the world with many practitioners of foreign policy adopting the rationale.

Basic Assumptions

While there are many variants of realism, theories of **realism** all begin from the same four assumptions. One, when it comes to actors on the global stage, states are the main players. We know in the United States that there are a lot of political variables that go into calculations of what the United States will do in the world from public opinion to the balance of power between the political parties, but as far as realists are concerned, none of that matters. Realists view states as black boxes; situations go into the black box and reactions come out, but we are never privy to what goes on inside the box that leads from situation to decision. In that sense, the people involved in making decisions or the politics in play are not areas of interest for realists—only how states react and respond to one another. What happens inside the black box is seen as the purview of policy scholars who study how states make policy, including foreign policy.

A second assumption involves the idea of rationality and argues that states act in a rational, self-interested manner. What does the idea of rationality mean? People often mistake rationality for behavior that is the best choice in a certain situation, but this is not the case. **Rationality** is acting according to an individual's (or in this case a state's) ordered preferences. As uncomfortable as it may be, the easiest way to think about rationality is the case of Hitler. Many people would argue that Hitler acted irrationally in many ways, from expanding German territory to the Holocaust of the Jews. However, rationality means that Hitler acted in accordance with his preferences; in his list of preferences, expanding German power and eliminating the Jewish population were at the top. Therefore, as difficult as it is for us to think it, Hitler was acting rationally.

In the international system, a third assumption is that there is no higher authority than states; there is nobody to tell states what they can and can't do. In realist terms, the state system is anarchic; there are no rules and nobody to enforce rules if there were any. This naturally leads to the last assumption that in a world where there are no rules, states will do anything they can to assure they survive. Survival means ensuring that they have the means to outlast threats from other states. The means by which that can be achieved is power, represented by military capability. If a state's military is strong enough and its capabilities sufficient, it will be able to outlast any challenge to its sovereignty or its territory.

Consequences of Realist Theory

From these four basic assumptions, realist theory emerges. Much like Thomas Hobbes's conception of human nature as inherently malevolent, realism accepts the same about states. The consequences, then, of state behavior do not necessarily lend themselves to a stable and peaceful international environment. If states want to ensure their security by building up military power, other states may interpret that build-up as threats to their own society; this is what's known as a **security dilemma**. The arms race may not be directed offensively, but other states may not believe one state's intentions as stated. If other countries begin to build up their own capabilities without sufficient cooperation and communication, the entire region may soon find itself in a devastating military conflict.

Arms races have happened often enough throughout history. In fact, World War I is a classic example of security dilemmas leading to war. States usually realize the futility of security dilemmas but all too often find themselves caught up in the system. This does not mean, however, that they do not try to find ways out of the conundrum. Paying close attention to a **balance of power** in a region is one of the solutions. If power is distributed roughly equally, no one state has an upper hand on any other. The Treaty of Westphalia discussed in Chapter 8 tried to enshrine a balance of power within Europe so as to avoid the devastating conflict that had pervaded Europe for centuries. During the Cold War, the Soviet Union and the United States engaged in a balance of power battle that largely led to a stalemate between the two countries directly. The balance of power can forestall the consequences of military buildups as long as all of the states in a region decide to abide by it.

There are other proposed solutions to the security dilemma posed by the search for power, one of them proposing that instead of a balance of power system wherein two or more powerful states exist so as to create a sort of equilibrium in the system; a **unipolar world** would find one country more powerful than all of the others and can police the rest of the system. This variation of realism assumes that a single hegemon or dominant actor seeking to expand their influence and power is able to amass enough power to keep other states weak. If weaker states attempt to move against others, the hegemon can strike and control the weak state's actions.

National Interest

These assumptions have led to a rich body of work examining realism in international relations. In the post–World War II period, the theorist Morgenthau achieved prominence with his writings on realism. In an era where the Cold War had yet to fully begin and new faith was placed on institutions such as the United Nations to mediate conflict (to be discussed later in this chapter), the new question became what the United States' major interests were. Morgenthau equated the US predicament with the conflict between whether man (and therefore states) is either inherently moral or immoral, the classic question of the original state of human nature.[2] Morgenthau argued that abiding by the principles of realism in foreign policy rather than trust the liberal institutions and appeals to morality would lead to far more acceptable outcomes for the United States.

If one theme runs throughout Morgenthau's writings it is that following the motivation of national interest and abiding by the principle of balance of power is the smartest strategy in foreign policy. He also endows realism with the highest of scientific principles in that realists also believe that objective laws of political science can be deduced through reason.[3] He utilizes the idea of scientific principles not only to seek out the laws of realism but as a yardstick by which to measure alternative theories of international relations.[4] Given that Morgenthau is also writing at a time where political science itself is continuing to press the idea of science and behavioralism in the study of politics, this is not at all surprising. Morgenthau thus presents realism not only as the natural and best way for a state to conduct its foreign policy but he also holds it up as a truly scientific, rational, and objective theory of international relations.

Another prominent realist theorist is Waltz. Waltz was a proponent of what he called structural realism—also known as neorealism. **Neorealism** differs from traditional realism in the emphasis on what causes states to behave as they do. For traditional realists like Morgenthau, it is the search for security in a world that is dominated by other self-interested and selfish states. Waltz and his fellow neorealists, however, recognize a more important role for the global system itself. States must respond to the conditions created by an anarchic state of international relations more than pressures from other states.

Neorealism is a natural reaction to a changing world where globalization is increasing and international organizations like the United Nations exist. The United Nations, International Monetary Fund (IMF), North Atlantic Treaty Organization (NATO), and other international organizations undoubtedly do impact the international environment. A good example of this is the passage of sanctions in the UN Security Council or going to the UN Security Council to have security actions endorsed. Therefore, neorealists are still hemming to the original assumptions of realism, but they recognize the increased importance of the international environment to the conditioning of states' actions. Even with the end of the Cold War, Waltz still argues that neorealism is essential to understanding the international system; even though the world became unipolar with the fall of the Soviet Union, it does not mean that the nature of the system changed. Instead, a changed world system "awaits the day when the international system is no longer populated by states that have to help themselves."[5]

Realism in Practice

Realism has been dominant not only in academic debates but in real-life foreign policy. A well-known proponent of realist theory, Henry Kissinger served first as national security adviser and then concurrently as secretary of state in the Richard Nixon administration. In this position, Kissinger was a constant advocate for following US interests in crafting foreign policy. This ultimately led to the reopening of relations between the United States and China in 1972. Even though the United States had foreclosed relations with China following its establishment of a communist government, Kissinger and Nixon realized that they could exploit the schism between China and its erstwhile communist ally Russia. The main interest of the United States was to reduce tension with the Soviet Union, and to do that, it reopened relations with China to make the Soviets fear a renewed friendship between China and the United States. If that happened, the Soviets were afraid that both countries would turn against Russia. Therefore, the Soviet Union was forced to moderate its policies toward the United States, and America was thus the beneficiary not only of a new relationship with China but a better relationship with the Soviet Union.

Modern research into realism generally focuses on the relevance of realism to a changed world. Not only has globalization continued to increase the importance of international organizations in moderating state activities but non–state actors like terrorist organizations have emerged as major players on the international stage. Neither traditional realism nor neorealism have a place for these non–state actors; this has been reflected in the political science literature. Walker and Morton find that despite a dominance of realism in the international relations field from the end of World War II until 1970, international relations research from 1970 to 2000 has seen a reduced role for realism.[6] Instead, liberalism (discussed in the next section) has become an integral driver of international relations research.

This is also reflected in the research that has been devoted to adopting realism to modern realities. For example, Patomaki and Wight argue for what they call critical realism, Chernoff presents a theory of scientific realism, and Sleat tries to combine liberalism and realism in a theory of liberal realism.[7] And yet the traditional tenets of realism, while not being acknowledged as frequently as during the Cold War, continue to exert an influence on American reactions to the rest of the world. This is quite apparent when crises arise in other parts of the world and when considering whether the United States should become involved or not; analysts inevitably bring up questions of the interests that the United States has in becoming involved—the stipulation becomes that if the United States has no national interest in the resolution of the crisis—we should not become involved. But what about the people who do believe we should get involved in crises around the world—particularly those of a humanitarian or moral stripe? This alternative theory is known as liberalism.

Career Guidance

Ambassadors and their support staff are the face of a state to the rest of the world. In the United States, many of these personnel are drawn from the ranks of the Foreign Service. Foreign Service officers serve throughout the world and in different functional areas, including politics, economics, and public affairs. While there is no specific educational requirement to become a Foreign Service officer, to join, you must pass the Foreign Service exam and an interview, a very selective process. For more information on the Foreign Service, visit its homepage at https://careers.state.gov/work/foreign-service/officer.

Liberalism

Recall from Chapter 3 that liberal political ideology stems directly from the Enlightenment and its rejection of the divine right of kings. In accepting that people have natural rights and that one of those rights is freedom and liberty, the liberal ideology was inaugurated. Liberal political theory posits that the best normative outcome would be a situation where states integrate democratic principles and the idea of natural rights. Of course, liberalism in international affairs is a slightly different animal, but they both share the same ideological ancestor.

Liberalism in international relations theory also rejects its international relations predecessor: realism. Proponents of liberalism argue that states pursue many more objectives than simply power—how else to explain states getting involved in conflicts that have nothing to do with their national interest? Liberalism also recognizes the growing role for international organizations and the possibility that those organizations can be used to not only mediate conflict but avoid it altogether. Particularly in an era where our global connections are increasing by the day, liberals argue that cooperation in international affairs is the only route to sustained good relations in the community of states.

Because of its focus on increased interactions between states, liberalism is really a theory of its time. The earliest formulation of liberal theory came from the German philosopher Immanuel Kant in his essay "Perpetual Peace" published in 1795.[8] In the essay, Kant argues that peace could be achieved within a region through a certain set of steps that all states would take. First among these was establishing a republican form of government and then recognizing the sovereignty of each state within its own territory. States would then proceed to establish open relationships between one another, stand down their armies, and agree to certain laws of war when conflict does emerge. Many of these ideas would later be enshrined in agreements such as the Geneva Convention and the UN treaty, but achieving peace and cooperation around the world still proves more difficult to achieve.

Basic Assumptions

As liberalism continued to develop as a theory, it too stipulated three assumptions to the theory. First, liberalism rejects the notion that states are only out for power as well as the idea that anarchy is the ultimate state of affairs. To be sure, believing that only anarchy reigns is a fairly dispiriting belief; there must be some other outcome possible than states constantly fearing the actions of another and preparing for an eventual war that must come. Liberals explicitly reject this, believing that something other than war can be a natural outcome of relations between states.

A second principle of liberalism is that international cooperation is not only possible but it can benefit the global community. If states are constantly wary of one another's search for power and military buildups, conflict might be the only possible result. But liberalism argues that states can cooperate for the betterment of not only themselves but the rest of the world. We need only look at modern cooperation between states on issues ranging from poverty and hunger to global warming. Cooperation may be difficult and states still may not trust one another, but cooperation is just as plausible as conflict.

Finally, liberalism prescribes the establishment of organizations that can grease the wheel of cooperation among states. These international organizations ease cooperation, but they can also independently change the international environment— thus, shaping states' desires and preferences. The role for international organizations also parallels the role of economic and cultural exchanges between countries. Liberal theorists propose that increased connections between states and between the peoples of free states will decrease the potential for conflict between them. For example, the extent of economic relations and ties between the United States and China greatly decrease the potential that either country would want to engage in a conflict that would disrupt the flow of goods that is so vital to each country. International organizations represent just one of the many types of ties that pull countries together and therefore encourage them to avoid conflict.

Liberalism in the Twentieth Century

Liberalism as an approach to international relations came into its own in the twentieth century. The first significant attempt at implementing liberal principles came at the end of World War I. Among Woodrow Wilson's Fourteen Points was a proposal to establish an institution called the League of Nations. The league was designed as a solution to the arms races and hostilities that led to the initiation of war in the first place. Although many countries signed on to it in the wake of World War I, the US Senate refused to ratify the Treaty of Versailles because it would obligate the United States to joining the league. At that point in American history, many in the United States were wary of continued involvement in world affairs, believing that the conflicts of other countries would only draw the United States into a continuous war.

Needless to say, the League of Nations failed in its ultimate goal of eliminating conflict. However, the failure of the league did not prevent states from trying again after World War II. This time, the United States did agree to join the new organization called the United Nations. In addition to the establishment of the United Nations, the United States and its European allies entered into an alliance: NATO. The NATO treaty specifically obligates its member states to the idea of collective security. **Collective security** is a means of discouraging conflict; it compels states to the defense of other states in the case that they are attacked. The so-called Article 5 means that if one state is attacked, the others must respond as if they were attacked as well. The idea behind collective security is that it will dissuade a state from attacking another state for fear of reprisals from others.

Types of Liberalism

A strain of liberal thinking that specifically focuses on the role of international institutions is called liberal institutionalism. Liberal institutionalists share some of the core beliefs of realists, primarily that the natural state of global affairs is anarchic. However, they depart in thinking from there. **Liberal institutionalism** argues that international organizations can be arranged in such a way as to provide order and structure in the world. These institutions can serve as a global police force that ensures states do not begin the often-deadly spiral of the security dilemma. Treaties and agreements between states can also fill the role of liberal institutions. In the process of states agreeing to certain practices or rules in areas like nuclear weapons and environmental degradation, they stipulate principles that the states must adhere to and procedures for policing the adherence to the treaties.

Another variant of liberalism is an idea called the democratic peace theory. **Democratic peace theory** posits that democratic states are much better able to avoid conflict than nondemocratic states. What is it about democracies that seem to prevent conflict? The cornerstone of modern democratic states today is that ultimately people have an opportunity to ratify the decisions of their representatives and leaders. Since leaders have to listen to the voices and opinions of their voters, liberals argue, they will be less likely to engage in a war or conflict that their countries don't support. A good example of this was the war in Vietnam and, more recently, the US war in Iraq. When public opinion turned negative on both of these conflicts, American leaders were forced to rethink their approach and end hostile engagements.

So what do democratic peace theorists believe will lessen the incidence of conflict? If democracies are less likely to go to war, then they would prescribe more democratic governments around the world. Obviously, the extent to which states around the world can enforce this idea is doubtful. While the United States and other democratized countries can support the idea of spreading democracy, actually implementing that is very difficult. Many thought that the advent of the Arab Spring heralded a new wave of democratization, but nine years after the first protests, little in the way of actual democratic government has emerged in the Middle East. While the reasons for this are many and out of the scope of this book, it demonstrates the difficulty of prescribing democracy in regions where it is not the normal order of the day.

There is also an economic corollary to the democratic peace theory that is colloquially known as the McDonald's thesis. The theory is that no two states with a McDonald's have ever gone to war with one another. As Friedman puts it, "The question raised by the McDonald's example is whether there is a tip-over point at which a country, by integrating with the global economy, opening itself up to foreign investment and empowering its consumers, permanently restricts its capacity for troublemaking and promotes gradual democratization and widening peace."[9] In other words, the more economic ties that exist between countries, the less of a chance that either of those states would want to disrupt those flows through conflict. Adding all of these ideas together leads to the theory that the more relationships that exist between the people and their governments and then between states around the world leads to decreased conflict. These relationships can be diplomatic and formal, economic, cultural, or through international organizations, but the bottom line is that when added together, they reduce conflict or the chance of conflict.

While it would seem that the establishment of liberalism would preclude further exploration of the meaning of it, current political science research into liberalism has delved back into the realm of deep theory. While some examine liberalism in modern political theory such as that of John Rawls (discussed in Chapter 3), others go back to the period of Enlightenment for insight on international relations. For example, Walker goes back to Kant and his ideas of perpetual peace and compares them to the writings of a contemporary, Thomas Paine of "Common Sense" fame.[10] Walker argues that Paine and Kant, while describing early iterations of liberalism, recommend different types of intervention thereby demonstrating Walker's overall argument that differences in liberal thought appeared early on. Ward also brings another Enlightenment thinker to bear on liberalism: this time, John Locke.[11] Rengger also notes this trend of tying international relations theory to political theory, naming it international political theory.[12]

Another stream of research into liberalism connects us with the next topic to be discussed: constructivism. As we will see shortly, constructivism argues that ideas and words hold power, and we can imbue those words and ideas with certain perspectives that bias them one way or another. This line of research, therefore, looks at the power of ideas in liberalism from uncertainty to balance of power; these scholars attempt to show the power of language and perspective in the policy prescriptions liberals advocate.[13]

Following the failure of the League of Nations in preventing World War II, President Franklin D. Roosevelt proposed, in the midst of the war, the creation of a new organization to be called the United Nations. While many of the large conceptual frameworks were worked out by the Allies during the war, representatives from fifty countries met in 1945 to write the UN charter. The charter would later be ratified by a majority of countries, and the United Nations officially became established in October 1945.

Like its predecessor, the United Nations was conceived of as an organization through which conflict could be addressed and open warfare therefore be avoided. The United Nations consists of a General Assembly; Security Council; and subsidiary councils, including the Economic and Social Council. In the General Assembly, each state has one vote, whereas the UN Security Council is made up of the five victors of World War II (United States; Soviet Union, now Russia; France; China; and the United Kingdom) who have absolute veto power and ten other rotating members. While the General Assembly is the main deliberative or legislative body of the United Nations, the Security Council has the responsibility of ensuring global peace and security; therefore, where resolutions coming out the General Assembly have little ability to be enforced, the Security Council can authorize the imposition of sanctions or other penalties or even the use of force.

The United Nations has often been criticized for being inefficient and ineffective as well as being unable to ensure global peace. Certainly, war and military conflict have continued to plague the world with the United Nations seemingly unable to stop it. The United Nations has no independent military or police force; it is reliant on member states to contribute people to peacekeeping missions. While the Security Council can authorize sanctions on states, there is no way to force states to actually impose them. The United Nations cannot even force countries to fully pay the dues that they are required to under the charter. Finally, the difficulties of the United Nations are written right into the charter: its mission is to confront global issues like conflict, human rights, disarmament, development, poverty, and health, but the charter recognizes that each member state is a sovereign entity and promises that the United Nations will not interfere within a state itself. How can the United Nations hope to fulfill its purposes with no coercive ability or the ability to mandate and ensure change?

Despite these hurdles, the United Nations has found ways to be relevant and supportive if not overwhelming. It has set overall developmental goals such as the Millennium Development Goals (MDGs) discussed in Chapter 8 about comparative politics and the Sustainable Development Goals. Its related bodies, like the World Health Organization, help to organize medical responses to health crises around the world. The World Bank assists states with development projects by providing not only funds but advice and assistance. And finally, we can always ask the counterfactual of what might have happened in the absence of the United Nations and the ongoing forum it provides for countries to communicate, talk, and discuss with one another. While there will be a distinct lack of power for the United Nations in favor of state sovereignty for the foreseeable future, the United Nations still provides powerful mechanisms through which to encourage constructive dialogue and the development of international norms.

Constructivism

Have you ever stared at a word for so long that all of a sudden it doesn't look like a word anymore? Or have you wondered why a certain word has the meaning that it does? For example, in feminist circles, there has been a controversy over the word *bitch* and whether women should try to reclaim the word for themselves instead of allowing it to be a derogatory term. These examples highlight the fact that for most ideas and concepts, society determines their meaning and whether the meanings are correct or not. This is the heart of **constructivist** theory; they reject both the ideas of liberals and realists and instead argue that all of international relations is socially and culturally constructed. What this means for international relations is that anarchy, power, or other consequences stemming from following either of these theories is not necessary nor inevitable; instead, we imbue these words with certain ideas that can be changed and often do change.

Wendt is one of the first political scientists to try to conceptualize constructivism. In his 1992 article, he attempts to explore what anarchy *means*, arguing that "anarchy is what states make of it."[14] In this basic principle, it's obvious just how radical a departure constructivism is from realism or liberalism. Both assumed that anarchy meant one thing: no structure or overriding control of the international system. If words or concepts have no exact meaning except the meaning we give them, situations are liable to change. If situations can change, then maybe anarchy is not the natural end state; perhaps states can create a situation of their own liking simply by changing their thinking about the international system.

Constructivist Concepts

Although constructivism is not constructed in the way that liberalism and realism were with assumptions and conclusions that then follow, Wendt provides some idea as to the concepts that constructivists are concerned about. The first of these is identity. "Actors acquire identities—relatively stable, role-specific understandings and expectations about self—by participating in such collective meanings."[15] Collective meanings are the definitions we give other actors and concepts; they "constitute the structures which organize our actions."[16] Thus, in a given situation, actors take on identities based on their own understanding of who they are and who others believe them to be. Wendt's example is that the way we perceive enemies and allies is affected by the identities we ascribe to them. What's key in the idea of identity is that identity can shift and change. Just because one state has taken on a particular identity does not mean that it becomes permanent and incapable of change. On the contrary, constructivists stress the idea that changing identities can lead to change in the international system.

Constructivists also emphasize in a way that would be familiar to liberals, that identity can even be shared across states. A good example of this is the European Union. Even though European states fought against each other for centuries, in recent decades, they have been able to engage in the project called the European Union, establishing broader diplomatic and economic ties, hoping to foster a European identity. This shared identity is also indicative of the way in which constructivists argue that identity can change and for the better; if peoples across multiple states identify with one another, relations between states could become more peaceful.

Identity becomes very important in defining another key concept of constructivism: that of interests. Whereas realists assume that a state's interest is stable, the pursuit of power and security, constructivists believe that the interests of a state are not at all stable and are instead capable of changing and being changed. Wendt argues that "identities are the basis of interests," states "define their interests in the process of defining situations."[17] A good example of how this may work is how the United States and the former Soviet Union changed their interest with the end of the Cold War. Because Russia no longer had the identity of a Cold War, ideological enemy, the United States became uncertain of its interests with respect to them. The ability for interests to change once again highlights constructivism's focus on the idea that concepts are socially constructed. Interests are backed by *ideas* about what is best for a country, and those *ideas* can and do change based on circumstances around the world.

While this focus on ever-changing ideas, interests, and identities demonstrates the fact that words mean only what we believe them to mean, Wendt's constructivism does allow for some entities that are stable in the international arena. Institutions are "relatively stable" sets of identities and interests.[18] These institutions are formed through norms and rules that are codified and known to all. Examples can include something as real as the United Nations or something as amorphous as the idea of self-help.[19] Institutions can still change as they are subject to what actors know or believe, but they do provide some stability in constructivist theory.

A final concept integral to constructivism is the idea of norms or beliefs about what are acceptable behaviors, institutions, or ideas in the rest of the world. An example of just such a norm would be a prohibition against torturing or killing prisoners of war. Norms set the rules for how states can or should behave in regard to one another.

The key insight of constructivism is that not every action or belief in the international system is set in stone. Just because states want one thing today does not mean that it won't change tomorrow. Just because relations between states are one way today doesn't mean that they can't get better or worse. Constructivism highlights the power of ideas and beliefs and the ability we have to change them for ourselves. Much like the saying "Behave your way to success," constructivism says we can create the world we want if we only change the way we think.

Constructivist Research

Political research into constructivism today continues to flesh out constructivism as a theory as well as discuss connections between it and other theories of international relations. For example, Barkin argues that although realism and constructivism seem diametrically opposed, they are in fact compatible in the study of power politics.[20] Similarly, Sterling-Folker argues that realism and constructivism are not only compatible but that they "need one another to correct their own worst excesses."[21] Others have examined the connections between constructivism and liberalism as well as constructivism and the feminist approach to international relations.[22] All of this research aims to flesh out the relationships between constructivism—a relatively new approach to international relations and more traditional approaches.

Since constructivism is such a new theory, other political scientists have continued to sketch out a research agenda and methodology for the field. Farrell attempts to lay out a research agenda for constructivists by laying out potential objects subject to study.[23] Farrell does note the difficulty in such a task, especially for constructivists who may not completely agree on the roles or meanings of concepts. Pouliot expands on this foundation in laying out how knowledge may be developed in constructivist theory thus allowing for theories to be generated and tested.[24]

Feminism

Much how constructivism urges us to think about international relations from a different vantage point than traditional conceptions about power and conflict, feminist international relations theory also asks us to look from another angle. For most of the history of the world, everything from business to government to social relations have been driven by men. Women have been in a historically disadvantaged position comparatively. **Feminist theory** reminds us that international politics and the international system may indeed be biased toward the view of men. If women are "brought back in" to the realm of international affairs, we can better understand state to state relations.

A Gendered Experience

Feminist international relations theory goes beyond the simple notion that the world discriminates against women to try and emphasize that ideas can be "gendered," or rather take the position of masculine ideas rather than feminine. This mirrors the constructivist idea that the ideas behind words and concepts have significance and can change. Gendered norms and concepts have the same emphasis, but feminist theorists argue that the gendered norms can have significant effects on how states get along with one another. One reason this may be important is that historically, women have been discriminated against and feminine ideals and characteristics derided. Take for instance a scenario where a world leader is caught crying; it doesn't matter if that person is a man or a woman, crying is seen as weak and feminine. But what makes crying inherently terrible? What makes it undesirable are the social norms and ideas associated with crying as a feminine characteristic.

Feminist theory also focuses on the fact that much of the world of international affairs is dominated by men. With no offense directed toward either gender, research has shown that men and women do indeed think differently. For example, research into the presence of women in state legislatures shows that legislatures that have more women in them tend to be more cooperative and pass more legislation. What if more world leaders were women? Would the way the world works change? Cohn writes about this very phenomenon in her study of the male-dominated world of defense intellectuals.[25] After spending a year immersing herself in the environment of defense studies, Cohn describes that she found her own thinking changing about nuclear strategy. From this experience, she argues that we should pay better attention to the words we use to study and describe different phenomenon because different language allows us to communicate in different ways with different people.

Following up on Cohn's piece, Enloe, one of the primary contributors to feminist international relations theory, argues that our attention to feminist issues must go beyond just the language that is used in international affairs; instead, we need to remember the role that women and girls play in the international system.[26] Women not only make up half of the world's population but they are intimately involved in the rearing and educating of children—both boy and girl. They pass on social identities and norms; they function as the heart of the family. In many countries, they are the breadwinners and supporters of their families. They are often also responsible for the care of older family members. In a way that directly ties into the international system, girls are often sold into slavery, taken across borders as slaves—sexual or otherwise—forced to carry drugs and carry out vicious attacks, and often exploited by men for their own purposes. The issues these girls and young women face are significantly tied to the international

Know a Political Scientist

Cynthia Enloe

Cynthia Enloe is a prolific feminist theorist who has taught around the world. Raised on Long Island, Enloe received her PhD in political science from the University of California, Berkeley, in 1967. Afterward, she joined the faculty at Clark University, where she spent the rest of her career. During her career, Enloe received Fulbright scholarships to study in Malaysia and Guyana and served as a guest professor in Japan, Britain, and Canada. Enloe's research has focused not just on feminism but the role that gendered variables play in international and national politics. To that end, she has published fourteen books and countless articles. She received the International Studies Association's Susan Strange Award in 2007 and the Peace and Justice Studies Association's Howard Zinn Lifetime Achievement Award in 2010.

system, and without worry or concern for the most vulnerable of participants, feminists argue that we will never really get anywhere in issues of war and peace.

Modern conflicts today also involve issues of women. Issues in the Middle East and in Islamic societies naturally bring up discussions of the role of women in society. This can be a sensitive topic. While we in the West would look at prohibitions on women driving, voting, and being full participants in society as vindictive and cruel, in many of those societies, they are culturally and socially accepted norms. This does not mean that practices such as genital mutilation, the marrying off of young girls, or harsh punishments for women who escape from marriage are any more acceptable in those societies than they would be here. But it does make relations with those countries far more difficult and nuanced. In fact, Youngs argues that understanding the role of women and gender is paramount if we are truly to understand the relationships of states.[27]

Recommendations for Change

While it would seem as if feminism lacks the concepts and assumptions of the theories that we have previously discussed, they do adopt a particular point of view about how we should *change* the way we view international relations. For example, feminist theorists have developed feminist perspectives on all types of traditional concepts examined by international relations theorists. For example, Sjoberg advances a feminist view of war in *Gendering Global Conflict*.[28] By taking traditional concepts like international organizations, anarchy, and realism, Sjoberg shows not only how these concepts are gendered but proposes how feminist theory might be constructed around them. Zalewski takes this same approach to describing a feminist approach on issues like human rights and the military.[29]

Like constructivism, a strain of feminist theory has also endeavored to not only expand feminist theory but establish a methodological foundation to studying feminist issues. Responding to the critique that feminist theory has little in the way of testable theories like realism and liberalism do, Tickner attempts to identify the possible research questions that feminists can pursue using traditional social science methods.[30] This in and of itself can be tricky; if traditional social science itself is dominated by men and potentially gendered in its own beliefs and views, why should feminists use such a standard by which to measure their academic work? Tickner notes that feminists have actually been loath to develop a methodological standard by which they can perform their research. Instead, they focus on methodological pluralism, descriptions of knowledge, discussions and critiques, and understanding how women view their lives and the world around them.[31] Partially as a response to Tickner, Caprioli argues that feminist scholarship would do well to engage multiple methodologies and goes on to show how work on gender, social justice, and quantitative methods can all be combined to create a fruitful research project.[32]

To this end, Ackerly and True take on the daunting task of developing a standard by which feminist research may be judged—something they call the feminist research ethic.[33] They argue that there are "four commitments that undergird a feminist research ethic: attentiveness to the power of epistemology, boundaries, relationships, and the situatedness of the researcher."[34] The last standard, the situatedness of the researcher, highlights a potentially dangerous flaw in how scholars engage feminist theory; if we are studying the projection of power in the world and at the same time are engaged in continuing to propagate and contribute to that structure, how can we objectively identify solutions and assumptions? Thus, Ackerly and True call for the researcher engaging in feminist scholarship to pay very close attention to their own subjectivities and bias.

War and Peace

At the end of the day, theories like realism, liberalism, constructivism, and feminism are merely theories. Real actions throughout the world actually affect the life and death of millions of global citizens. It's only natural, then, that causes of war and peace would be a topic that scholars of international relations tend to study. War is particularly amenable to study because it is a phenomenon that happens, unfortunately, all too often. It is also chronicled in histories of past periods, thereby giving scholars a bevy of information to work with in divining the causes of conflict throughout the centuries.

Defining *War*

And yet, even though political scientists have lots of information with which to avail themselves, settling on *the* cause or causes of war has eluded us. Why? Well, first of all, deciding on what specifically is a war has been difficult. While this might seem silly, defining our concepts is an important part of doing political science. Is it a war when states have fought for one day, one week, or one month? In other words, is there a timetable or length associated with it? Or is it a war when so many people have died? If that's the case, then how many people must die before a conflict is declared to be a war? Do wars differ in size and scope, and if so, how? Two political scientists took up just these questions in inaugurating what would become the Correlates of War project. Small and Singer sought to conceptualize and define what political scientists mean in invoking the terms *war* or *state*. Small and Singer defined *states* as entities with populations of more than half a million with diplomatic recognition from other states or international organizations such as the League of Nations or the United Nations.[35] With respect to the definition of wars, Small and Singer delimited wars as being conflicts with deaths of over 1,000.[36] They also identify different types of wars from interstate wars to imperial or colonial conflict.

Defining our concepts is only one barrier to understanding the patterns of war. Even though historians and political scientists have more access than ever before to information about the thoughts and actions of leaders and states, it is still difficult to dive down into the brains of the participants and to uncover exactly what was being thought about at the moment in which war is initiated. Indeed, when leaders do make statements or speeches about going to war, how can we be sure they are telling the truth about why and not playing to politics and giving the politically acceptable answer? An excellent example of this was the US intervention in Iraq, beginning in 2003. Although the George W. Bush administration claimed they were sending troops to Iraq because the Iraqis had weapons of mass destruction (WMDs) and supported terrorism, some critics argued that the Bush administration was really going to war to secure oil supplies in the Middle East. While this says nothing about ultimate causes or whether the motivation was correct or not, it does go a long way to demonstrating how and why it can be difficult to truly understand what states and their leaders are thinking in a time of war.

Causes of War

In looking at causes of war, there are a few directions at which we can come at the subject. The first approach is through the theories that we have just elaborated on. Realists argue that war is the result of power politics and states seeking out the assurances of their own security. The search for security can lead to the security dilemma and staggering arms races that ultimately lead to conflict. For realists, it is only rational that states do what it takes to stake their place in the global system and to protect their people, even if that means the result is war. Liberals, on the other hand, argue that "dissension and strife do not inhere in man and society; they arise instead from mistaken belief, inadequate knowledge, and defective governance. With the evils defined, the remedies become clear: educate men and their governors, strip away political abuses."[37] In other words, men (and women) are naturally at peace with one another; when states do enter into conflict, it is usually because of miscommunication or mistakes of one kind or another. The liberal solution, then, is to institute better forms of government and new forms of international organizations to minimize the chances of states coming to blows with one another.

These two perspectives on the causes of war are called structural theories; they represent explanations of war and conflict at the global, large-scale level. There are other ways that we can look at war, however. Realism and liberalism indict (or vindicate in the case of liberalism) the global system that all states live in. But what about causes at the lower levels? The next step down from the global level would be the state level. What is it about states, or types of states, that cause conflict? The democratic peace theory is an example of a theory that explains conflict, or the lack thereof, in states as a result of states being democratic. Are there other types of states that are more likely to engage in conflict? The research on this is wide and varied and not at all possible to fully in engage in here. However, we can think of some examples that may help to give us clues as to the types of states that may go to war more often.

In thinking back only on the twentieth century, the two most significant conflicts were World War I and World War II. World War I was triggered when Franz Ferdinand, nephew of the Austrian emperor, was shot but the major contributing cause was the arms race in Europe in the preceding years. For World War II, Germany was engaged in an imperialist project of overtaking or retaking portions of Europe that they deemed to be German territories. In both of these cases, the actions of aggressive states led to ultimate conflict. For the United States, in particular, this was not the end of war in the period. During the rest of the twentieth century, the United States engaged not only in the Korean and Vietnam Wars but countless smaller-scale conflicts and the moderately sized endeavor of pushing the Iraqi army back into Iraq from Kuwait. For Vietnam and Korea, the United States became involved because of an ideological conflict with communism—therefore suggesting that states with different types of regimes may be more likely to engage in war with one another. In the case of the first Gulf War, the United States and other countries were responding to the actions of an aggressor country: Iraq. These examples point the way toward the main explanations that political scientists have developed to explain war at the state level: imperialist aggression and conflict between states with dissimilar regimes.

The next level of analysis just below the state is that of the politics of the state. Some political scientists argue that instead of looking at states as black boxes as many realists and some liberals do, we need to peer inside the box and see what types of politics are occurring in the country. There are any number of political dramas on the big screen and television screen that demonstrate these ideas, and that is perhaps one of the best ways to describe them. First, in a little bit of art imitating life, the 1997 film *Wag the Dog* depicts an American president (fictional, of course) enduring a sex scandal. In order to take attention off the scandal, the president hires a movie producer to "produce" a war that will redirect the public's attention. Although the movie is fictional, the scenario is very real. Following the 2014 Winter Olympics in Sochi, Russia, the government of Russia began to come in for criticism aimed at the amount of money it had spent to prepare the Olympics site (approximately $50 billion). Partially as a means of disrupting such criticism, Russia invaded the country of Ukraine under the pretext of protecting pro-Russian separatists in the eastern part of the country.

Finally, we come to the lowest level of analysis, the individual level. At this level, political scientists seek to explore and understand individual behavior and how that may push countries to war. In some situations, wars could be attributed to the actions of one leader who may be off balance mentally. While we may colloquially ascribe the term *crazy* to any number of individual leaders, Hitler and Napoleon are two potential candidates for such a label who have pushed their countries to the brink. Other political scientists will argue that a leader need not be "crazy" or "insane" to take a country to war. Charismatic, well-loved leaders could influence their countries on the path to war simply because they are well liked or well spoken. In generalizing the argument, then, we could say that states that go to war may likely be influenced by significant and important leaders who have the ability to sway the opinion of the public to support engagement.

Other analysts stop short of the crazy label and argue, like Hobbes, that human aggression is natural as is the will to go to war. We can see that plain as day on our television screens most Sundays in the fall and winter as football players go helmet to helmet on the field. The desire for combat—whether it be in soldiers or athletes—could be part of the reason that states enter into conflict; the need to satisfy the desire for hard-won battles may also be part of why states go to war.

Other human characteristics can just as easily lead us down the path to war. The likelihood of individuals miscommunicating or misunderstanding each other can initiate a war. Part of international relations between leaders is being able to understand and correctly interpret the behaviors and actions of others. A good example of this was the former Iraqi dictator Saddam Hussein. Although the Bush administration claimed that Saddam had WMDs, following the American invasion, it was discovered that this claim was false. Some analysts have argued that Saddam had an interest in maintaining the idea that he possessed WMDs in order to make Iran believe that it retained the ability to fight a destructive war with them. (Iraq and Iran had previously engaged in a war in the 1980s that was fought to a stalemate.) This is just one example of how leaders may misrepresent their own actions in order to make others believe something they wouldn't otherwise. However, we can just as easily see how this can lead to war, particularly in the case of the second war in Iraq.

CASE STUDY
The United States and Iraq

Given these explanations for why countries go to war, a legitimate question can be asked regarding why the United States went to war with Iraq in 2003. At the time, the George W. Bush administration made the argument that Iraq not only harbored terrorists and sponsored terrorism but that Iraq was in possession of weapons of mass destruction (WMDs) in contravention to UN Security Council resolutions that required Iraq to disarm. In the lead-up to the American invasion, then secretary of state Colin Powell presented to the UN Security Council an array of information and intelligence that the American intelligence community claimed to show that Iraq had and was hiding WMDs. Additionally, the developing Bush doctrine held that the United States should take preemptive action to prevent an attack on the homeland if one seemed imminent. However, in the years following the invasion, it became clear that not only was the intelligence flawed but that Iraq did not, in fact, possess any WMDs at the time.

In addition to the twin arguments of terrorism and WMDs, other analysts both at the time and since have posited other theories for why the United States invaded Iraq. One, because of the vast oil reserves of the Middle East, some proposed that the US invasion was undertaken to secure oil resources for the United States in the face of a hostile Middle East. Two, and following from democratic peace theory, by toppling Saddam Hussein and installing a democratic government in Iraq, the United States could promote further peace not only in Iraq but across the Middle East. This argument was often supported by neoconservatives in the Bush administration. Finally, others have suggested that there was a connection between the 2003 invasion of Iraq and the 1991 Gulf War, led by George W. Bush's father, George H. W. Bush. Since the 1991 Gulf War did not fully topple Iraq's government but pushed the Iraqi military out of Kuwait and back into Iraq, some have interpreted the 2003 invasion as George W. Bush finishing the war that his father had started in 1991.

How do these explanations of the 2003 Iraq War comport with the different theories of war discussed previously? For one, we can view the invasion through the lens of realism—the

(Continued)

(Continued)

United States was seeking security and perceived Iraq and the WMDs we believed it possessed as a threat. In turn, the United States acted to protect its own power and safety. From a liberal perspective, there are two ways we can interpret the Iraq War. One, the United States invaded to enforce the resolutions passed by the UN Security Council. However, this neglects the fact that the UN Security Council never authorized the United States to go to war in the first place. Two, by invading Iraq and instituting a democratic government, the United States can be seen to be following the democratic peace theory: since democracies rarely go to war with one another, making sure Iraq is democratic lessens the chance of future war. Finally, the argument that the Iraq War was a personal one for George W. Bush posits an individual-level theory of war: George W. Bush wanted to get rid of the Saddam Hussein regime for personal reasons.

The models and theories discussed in this chapter and indeed throughout this book are based on ideal types and certainly abstract from the actual detail and nitty gritty of real life. In reality, a combination of these reasons probably contributed to the US decision to go to war in Iraq. Therefore, this incident is an excellent example that allows us not only to identify different perspectives on why countries go to war but the very real interaction that often happens between theories.

Critical Thinking Questions

1. Which of the major international relations theories do you believe best supports the US decision to go to war with Iraq?

2. How well do you think the individual level of analysis explains the US decision to go to war?

3. What role did the United Nations play? Does this support or detract from the position of liberal institutionalists?

STUDENT STUDY SITE

Visit https://edge.sagepub.com/whitmancobb

CHAPTER SUMMARY

- Realist international relations theory proposes that states are the main actors in international relations, that they act rationally, and that their main motivation is protecting their own power. The changing geopolitical system, however, places greater pressure on realists to respond to actors other than states.

- Liberal international relations theory does not believe that anarchy is the natural state of the world; rather, it believes cooperation among states is possible. Cooperation can be encouraged through international organizations, increased economic ties, and the spreading of democracy.

- Constructivists believe that the world as we know it can be changed by changing how we see it. In that sense, "anarchy is what we make of it." Concepts such as identify, global norms, and interests can contribute to more peaceful outcomes.

- Feminist international relations theorists argue that historically, international relations has been gendered toward men—that is, men have dominated decision making, often leaving women and their interests out of the equation altogether. They suggest that by including more women in international decision making, the issues and concerns of women will be better integrated in the global system.

- The causes of war are numerous and complicated. Scholars can use three levels of analysis to identify causes of war: systemic level, state level, and individual level.

KEY TERMS

balance of power: How evenly distributed power is across a region or the world

collective security: Compels states to defend other states if they are attacked

constructivist: Argues that all of international relations is socially and culturally constructed

democratic peace theory: Theory that democratic states are much better able to avoid conflict than nondemocratic states

feminist theory: Argues that the international system may be biased toward the view of men, systematically disenfranchising and ignoring the role and views of women

liberal institutionalism: Posits that international organizations can be arranged in such a way as to provide order and structure in the world

liberalism: An international relations theory that proposes that states pursue things other than power and can cooperate with one another; anarchy is not a natural outcome of the global order

neorealism: A variant of realism where states must also react to the anarchic state of the world in addition to the actions of states themselves

rationality: Acting in accordance with one's ordered preferences

realism: An international relations theory that posits states are the main actors in world affairs, that they act rationally, and that the world is naturally anarchic

security dilemma: Can occur when states interpret another state's arms and military buildup to be a threatening act

unipolar world: Situation wherein one country has amassed more power than any other

DISCUSSION QUESTIONS

1. Compare and contrast realist and liberal theory. If you were to pick one over the other, which one would you argue for, and why?

2. What might be some obstacles to instituting a realist foreign policy? A liberal foreign policy?

3. Where do you see feminist and constructivist theory coinciding? How are they alike?

4. What one foreign policy principle do you believe would most likely lead to an outbreak of peace around the world? Why?

FURTHER READING

Cohn, Carol. "Sex and Death in the Rational World of Defense Intellectuals." *Signs* 12, no. 4 (1987): 687–718.

Morgenthau, Hans J. *Politics among Nations: The Struggle for Power and Peace*. 5th ed. New York: Alfred A. Knopf, 1978.

Wendt, Alexander. "Anarchy Is What States Make of It: The Social Construction of Power Politics."

International Organization 46, no. 2 (1992): 391–425.

Youngs, Gillian. "Feminist International Relations: A Contradiction in Terms? Or: Why Women and Gender Are Essential to Understanding the World 'We' Live In." *International Affairs* 80, no. 1 (2004): 75–87.

Correlates of War Project: www.correlatesofwar.org

NOTES

1. Michael Birnbaum, "Donald Trump's Tweets on NATO, Russian Meddling, and North Korea Should Be Ignored, Say Top US Security Officials," *Independent*, Feb. 19, 2018, www.independent.co.uk/news/world/americas/us-politics/donald-trump-ignore-tweets-nato-europe-russia-collusion-north-korea-munich-conference-hr-mcmaster-a8217201.html.

2. Hans J. Morgenthau, "Another 'Great Debate': The National Interest of the United States," *American Political Science Review* 46, no. 4 (1952): 961–988.

3. Hans J. Morgenthau, *Politics among Nations: The Struggle for Power and Peace*, 5th ed. (New York: Alfred A. Knopf, 1978).

4. Morgenthau, "Another 'Great Debate.'"

5. Kenneth N. Waltz, "Structural Realism after the Cold War," *International Security* 25, no. 1 (2000): 39.

6. Thomas C. Walker and Jeffrey S. Morton, "Re-assessing the 'Power of Power Politics' Thesis: Is Realism Still Dominant?" *International Studies Review* 7, no. 2 (2005): 341–356.

7. Heikki Patomaki and Colin Wight, "After Postpositivism? The Promises of Critical Realism," *International Studies Quarterly* 44, no. 2 (2000): 213–237; Fred Chernoff, "Scientific Realism as a Meta-Theory of International Politics," *International Studies Quarterly* 46, no. 2 (2002): 189–207; Matt Sleat, "Liberal Realism: A Liberal Response to the Realist Critique," *The Review of Politics* 73, no. 3 (2011): 469–496.

8. Immanuel Kant (trans. Mary Campbell Smith), "Perpetual Peace," Project Gutenberg, Jan. 14, 2016, https://www.gutenberg.org/files/50922/50922-h/50922-h.htm.

9. Thomas K. Friedman, "Foreign Affairs Big Mac I," *New York Times*, Dec. 8, 1996, https://www.nytimes.com/1996/12/08/opinion/foreign-affairs-big-mac-i.html

10. Thomas C. Walker, "Two Faces of Liberalism: Kant, Paine, and the Question of Intervention," *International Studies Quarterly* 52, no. 3 (2008): 449–468.

11. Lee Ward, "Locke on the Moral Basis of International Relations," *American Journal of Political Science* 50, no. 3 (2006): 691–705.

12. Nicholas Rengger, "Political Theory and International Relations: Promised Land or Exit from Eden," *International Affairs* 76, no. 4 (2000): 755–770.

13. Brian C. Rathbun, "Uncertain about Uncertainty: Understanding the Multiple Meanings of a Crucial Concept in International Relations Theory," *International Studies Quarterly* 51, no. 3 (2007): 533–557; Deborah Boucoyannis, "The International Wanderings of a Liberal Idea, or Why Liberals Can Learn to Stop Worrying and Love the Balance of Power," *Perspectives on Politics* 5 no. 4 (2007): 703–727.

14. Alexander Wendt, "Anarchy Is What States Make of It: The Social Construction of Power Politics," *International Organization* 46, no. 2 (1992): 395.

15. Ibid., 397.

16. Ibid.

17. Ibid., 398.

18. Ibid.

19. Ibid.

20. J. Samuel Barkin, "Realist Constructivism," *International Studies Review* 5, no. 3 (2003): 325–342.

21. Jennifer Sterling-Folker, "Realism and the Constructivist Challenge: Rejecting, Reconstructing, or Rereading," *International Studies Review* 46, no. 1 (2002): 73–97.

22. Jennifer Sterling-Folker, "Competing Paradigms or Birds of a Feather? Constructivism and Neoliberal Institutionalism Compared," *International Studies Quarterly* 44, no. 1 (2000): 97–119; Birgit Locher and Elisabeth Prugl, "Feminism and Constructivism: Worlds Apart or Sharing the Middle Ground?" *International Studies Quarterly* 45, no. 1 (2001): 111–129.

23. Theo Farrell, "Constructivist Security Studies: Portrait of a Research Program," *International Studies Review* 4, no. 1 (2002): 49–72.

24. Vincent Pouliot, "'Sobjectivism': Toward a Constructivist Methodology," *International Studies Quarterly* 51, no. 2 (2007): 359–381.

25. Carol Cohn, "Sex and Death in the Rational World of Defense Intellectuals," *Signs* 12, no. 4 (1987): 687–718.

26. Cynthia Enloe, "'Gender' Is Not Enough: The Need for a Feminist Consciousness," *International Affairs* 80, no. 1 (2004): 95–97.

27. Gillian Youngs, "Feminist International Relations: A Contradiction in Terms? Or: Why Women and Gender Are Essential to Understanding the World 'We' Live In," *International Affairs* 80, no. 1 (2004): 75–87.

28. Laura Sjoberg, *Gendering Global conflict: Toward a Feminist Theory of War* (New York: Columbia University Press, 2013).

29. Marysia Zalewski, "Well, What Is the Feminist Perspective on Bosnia?" *International Affairs* 71, no. 2 (1995): 339–356.

30. J. Ann Tickner, "What Is Your Research Program? Some Feminist Answers to International Relations Methodological Questions," *International Studies Quarterly* 49, no. 1 (2005): 1–21.

31. Ibid.

32. Mary Caprioli, "Feminist IR Theory and Quantitative Methodology: A Critical Analysis," *International Studies Review* 6, no. 2 (2004): 253–269.

33. Brooke Ackerly and Jacqui True, "Reflexivity in Practice: Power and Ethics in Feminist Research on International Relations," *International Studies Review* 10, no. 4 (2008): 693–707.

34. Ibid., 694.

35. Melvin Small and J. David Singer, "Patterns in International Warfare, 1816–1965," *The Annals of the American Academy of Political and Social Science* 391 (Sept. 1970): 145–155.

36. Ibid.

37. Kenneth N. Waltz, "Kant, Liberalism, and War," *American Political Science Review* 56, no. 2 (1962): 331.

The relationship between politics and economics is clear—especially in institutions like the US Treasury.

Source: Andrew Harrer/Bloomberg/Getty Images

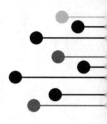

CHAPTER

10

Political Economy

The presidential election of 1992 was an interesting one. Not only did the incumbent president, George H. W. Bush, have a stunningly high approval rating coming out of the Gulf War but the election also featured a third-party candidate, Ross Perot, who received the highest percentage of votes ever in American history for a third party. The Democratic challenger, Bill Clinton, was also an anomaly. A Democrat from the solid Republican South, he had also been accused of sexual harassment. Despite what would seem an easy reelection for then president Bush, James Carville, one of Clinton's campaign advisers, summed up Clinton's message for the voters quite succinctly: "It's the economy, stupid." With America in a recession and Bush having gone back on his pledge of "no new taxes," Clinton's economic message resonated with the American people, and Clinton handily won the Electoral College that November. Political science research has consistently shown that economic concerns are a primary issue for voters—especially voters who ask themselves "Am I better off now than I was four years ago?" when deciding how to cast their vote for president. Thus, politicians are rightly concerned with a country's economy and challenged about how to respond to economic pressures.

This chapter explores the very crucial relationship between government and economy, the study of which is termed *political economy*. Although certainly not an absolute rule, a government cannot long be successful if its citizens suffer economic hardships and poor quality of life. Although there have been exceptions to this like North Korea, those states usually succeed because of their authoritarian nature. We will start first with a discussion of the connection between politics and economy and then move to discuss different types of economic systems,

Chapter Objectives

1. Describe the relationship between governments and the economy.

2. Describe different types of economic systems, including capitalism, socialism, and command economies.

3. Examine measures of economic performance.

4. Identify the fields of comparative and international political economy, including their major areas of research.

including capitalism and socialism. Although we discuss these ideal-type models, the reality is that there is no country in the world that is completely capitalist or completely socialist; rather, types of economies fall on a wide spectrum, having to do with how much each government is involved in economic activity. Following this, we will discuss the ways in which the government can be involved in the economy, primarily through the tools of fiscal and monetary policies and the types of factors that influence economic performance. Finally, the chapter discusses two subfields in this area of study: comparative political economy and international political economy.

What Does Politics Have to Do with the Economy?

Politicians care very much about how the economy is performing. One theory of how people vote is based on their experiences with the economy in previous years; if individual voters feel like they have benefited economically, they tend to vote for the person or party already in power. On the other hand, if they are feeling the economic pinch or have been hurt by the economy, people tend to vote for the person or party not already in power. In this sense, politicians must be concerned about the economy because it directly affects their chances for reelection.

Politicians are also concerned about the economy for other reasons. When the economy is humming along, governments tend to take in an increased amount in taxes. Depending on the spending priorities of the government in power, this can be a powerful incentive to shape economic dynamics. When economies are shrinking, on the other hand, governments almost always have to become involved to soften the blow for its citizens. An economist named Keynes recognized this in the twentieth century, putting forth a model of a government-economy relationship we now call Keynesian economics. In this model, during economic downturns, governments should spend money, thereby pushing funds into the economy, which can lessen the impact of recessions or depressions. According to Keynes, it would be acceptable for governments to deficit spend, or spend more than they are taking in in taxes, in order to spend more. As economic conditions improved and tax receipts increased, a government could cut its spending and pay off the debt that it had accumulated in the meantime.

Politics and government can influence the behavior and performance of the economy in various other ways. The types of **tariffs**, taxes on imported goods, implemented can encourage domestic economic growth by making foreign goods more expensive to buy. The type and amount of regulations that a government enacts and enforces can make it harder or more expensive for businesses to operate. For example, regulations restricting the amount of pollutants released into the air by factories, while good for the general health and the environment, often require those businesses to make expensive modifications to plants to reduce their emissions.

Know a Political Scientist

John Maynard Keynes

John Maynard Keynes was an influential economist who significantly affected the way in which politicians and economists think about the involvement of government in the economy. Born in England in 1883, he received a BA and MA from Cambridge in the early twentieth century. He began a career as a British civil servant by first working in India and later serving as an economic advisor to Prime Minister David Lloyd George at the Versailles Peace Conference after World War I. Deeply influenced by his experience there, Keynes criticized the economic burdens placed on Germany after the war. High British unemployment and the ensuing Great Depression caused Keynes to rethink his position supporting free market systems with relatively little government involvement. He published *The General Theory of Employment, Interest, and Money* in 1936 in which he argued that governments should deficit spend in order to promote full employment as a solution to economic depressions. Although not a political scientist by training, Keynesian economics, as these ideas would come to be called, has influenced generations of politicians, economists, and policy analysts. Keynes died in 1946 but was named to *Time* magazine's TIME 100 Persons of the Century in 1999.

Overall, however, societies cannot long survive, or survive easily, without economic success or opportunity. Take for example, the Middle East. Over the past several decades, there has been a lack of economic opportunity and growth in many countries despite the oil resources that they have. The benefits of such resources are often misdirected in these countries to ruling families or through corruption (we call this the **resource curse**) rather than distributed to all the people. As a result, the growing youth population of many of these countries have little opportunity either educationally or workwise. This has made that population vulnerable to the preaching of fringe and extremist religious groups, which have destabilized several Middle Eastern countries and whose effects have been felt across the West. Thus, governments and politicians must be concerned with and think about the state of their own economy as well as the now-globalized economy to ensure the happiness of their people and the success of their government.

Types of Economic Systems

An economic market or system is a framework of how firms produce goods and consumers buy and use those goods. In other words, an **economy** is a system of exchange. Wherever goods are exchanged between people, some sort of economy arises. However, these systems of exchange can be heavily influenced and even regulated by states and their governments. Governments can effectively institute the economic system they believe will be most effective through economic policy. This section identifies several economic systems, including capitalism and command economies.

Capitalism

As a theory, or an ideal type, economies can exist outside of a political system in what is often termed a *free market*: If there is consumer demand for a good or service, some firm will provide it with the costs of products or services determined by the amount of supply in the market and the amount of demand. When there is an excess of supply with little demand for a product, prices would go down while when supply is limited and demand is high, prices would rise. As coined by eighteenth century economist Adam Smith, the "invisible hand" would regulate the market without the need for government intervention. These basic ideas form the basis of the economic system known as capitalism. Jaeggi identifies five distinguishing characteristics of **capitalism**:

1. "Private ownership of the means of production and a separation between producers and the means of production;

2. "The existence of a free labor market;

3. "The accumulation of capital, and as a consequence;

4. "An orientation toward the exploitation of capital, thus toward gain instead of need, toward the cultivation of capital instead of the consumption of it or subsistence on it;

5. "Under capitalism the market typically functions as a coordinating mechanism for the allocation, as well as the distribution, of goods, such that capitalism and the market economy are closely bound—though not identical—to one another."[1]

However, even at the time in which Adam Smith was writing, there was widespread government involvement in the economy. For example, in medieval feudal systems, states were built around the distribution of labor by the peasants, to local landowning elites, to lords, and finally to the ruling monarchy. While loyalty and military service flowed upward, so did taxes. These taxes allowed the aristocracy and the monarchy to operate as rulers. Indeed, Adam Smith recognized that the object of the study of political economy is to provide people and the state with "plentiful revenue."[2] This revenue also allows states to overcome the deficiencies of the free market—namely the possibility of market failures. **Market failures** occur when an economic market or system fails to produce or distribute needed or wanted goods and services. Market failures tend to happen most often when the provision of public goods, or nonexcludable goods, are at play (recall the tragedy of the commons from Chapter 1).

Although the virtues and values of a free market system are often extolled, capitalism certainly has its critics. Jaeggi identifies three major critiques: functional, moral and ethical.[3] The functional critique argues that capitalism itself, as a system, is intrinsically flawed and cannot function as a social or economic system. When left unchecked, free market policies allow for the existence of monopolies, or sole providers, of a good or service that can drive up prices. Firms can also work together to control the supply of a product and therefore its prices. This sort of collusion among private firms can create profits for owners and producers but leave those at the other end of the spectrum in dire straits. This sort of economic inequality can in turn lead to social inequality or even the inability of poor people to advance in a society. In concentrating economic power in the hands of the few, a large class of people are left almost permanently "pauperized" with that population getting ever larger leading to an eventual breakdown in society.

Another critique noted by Jaeggi is an ethical one—that the type of life created by a capitalist system is in and of itself bad; "it is impoverished, meaningless, or empty, and it destroys the essential components of a fulfilled, happy, but above all, 'veritably free' human life."[4] Although this also sounds related to the Marxist critique, Jaeggi notes that Marx was but one of many people who took up this theme in the early 1800s. While Marx's solution was the abandonment of the capitalist project altogether, others saw danger in such a proposition. If all private property were abolished and people received only according to their need, what incentive would individuals have to excel, innovate, and create? In a capitalist system, the profit motive encourages people to not just to do enough to survive but do enough to thrive.

The Communist Critique

The moral critique of capitalism is that it is unjust and exploits workers:

> Capitalism exploits human beings by 'depriving' them of the fruits of their own labor in an unfair and unjust way; in other words, people are 'enslaved' by a system that in many ways defrauds them of that to which they are entitled and coerces them into social relations that are immoral and degrading.[5]

The moral critique is very similar to that made by Marx. Recall from Chapter 3 that Marx saw in capitalism not just a system that benefited private owners rather than producers but the seeds of its own eventual destruction. Marx posited that once capitalism created so much inequality, the working class, or the proletariat, will come to realize the extent to which they have been taken advantage of by the producing class, the bourgeoisie, and initiate a revolution. Realizing the capitalism and private ownership caused the severe inequality between classes, a dictatorship of the proletariat would take control, begin to abolish private ownership, and eventually transition into a system of communism. Marx's ideal form of communism envisioned no private property, no money or wealth, and a system of common ownership. In such a system, each individual would receive what they needed and no more.

In their ideal forms, neither capitalism nor Marxist communism will likely work. While communism as an ideal type has never been attempted on a large scale

Figure 10.1   Continuum of Government Economic Involvement

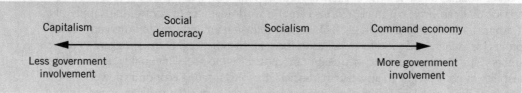

(remember from Chapter 8 that Soviet- and Chinese-style communism are modifications of Marx and Engel's original theories), capitalist systems have been attempted and have always had some sort of government involvement in order to compel the paying of taxes, provide for public goods, and avoid market failures. The obvious question, then, is this: How much government involvement is needed? To consider this, we can think of a continuum of the sort pictured in Figure 10.1. The continuum represents the extent to which the government is involved in the economic life of a country from total to none at all. Capitalism would be placed on the left side of the spectrum, representing little government involvement. Communism, you will notice, is not on the continuum at all; in its ideal form, there is no government whatsoever and therefore no exchange of goods for a government to be involved in. What is on the right-hand side of the line are types of economies that do have significant government involvement: social democracy, socialism, and a command economy.

Other Economic Systems

Command economies represent those systems in which the state controls all aspects of an economy from prices to what goods will be produced in what numbers. Command economies have existed and persisted in those countries that have attempted to establish communist states: the former Soviet Union and today's North Korea. China is an interesting mix; in the middle part of the twentieth century, they instituted a command economy but have since introduced elements of capitalism and private ownership. Despite these modest free market reforms, the Chinese government remains heavily involved in their own economy from owning hundreds of thousands of corporations and businesses to artificially setting prices low or subsidizing goods to prop up their export market. Proponents of command economies see this method as a way to ensure development and industrialization and to avoid the excesses of capitalism and the free market. However, there are also significant problems with a command economy, including the opportunity for corruption in the higher ranks of government and perhaps even the inability of the government to make sound economic decisions that reflect the needs and desires of the citizenry.

   Socialism represents a middle ground between social democracy, discussed in the next paragraph, which retains a capitalist-style market, and a command economy.

Socialism shares many of the same ideological concerns as does communism, but as Shively notes, the split between the two stems largely from the beginnings of the Russian Revolution itself. "Marx and Engels had never fully settled whether they thought the working class should take control of the state peacefully through electoral victory or violently through revolution."[6] Thus, the revolutionary elements, including Lenin's Bolsheviks, established communist parties while the other branch of socialism continued to call themselves socialist or even democratic socialists.[7] Socialists today advocate for a larger government role in the economy to include government or public ownership of key parts of the market. Added to this is a significant welfare infrastructure to provide services to citizens, including a basic wage, education, health care, and housing.

Finally, **social democracy** tries to "balance capitalist markets and private property with a greater degree of state intervention in the economy... in an effort to ameliorate the economic inequalities that the free market tends to create."[8] Social democratic systems are in wide use across Europe, where a greater degree of cooperation between the state and business is found. In fact, Germany practices something called **corporatism,** which is a formal system of cooperation between business and government. Social democratic systems supplement a capitalist-style market with a broader redistribution of wealth; taxes are higher, especially for the wealthy, but are used to more widely provide social services. The idea behind such a system is to allow for the working of a free market but to balance out the excesses and inequality of the free market with a social safety net provided by the government.

CASE STUDY
Germany

Although not directly written into Germany's constitution, businesses in Germany work closely with the federal government in determining economic policy. Though very broad, the term *corporatism* refers to formal and informal mechanisms through which businesses and business groups work and coordinate economic policy with a government. In Germany's case, corporatist practice stems back to the 1960s and 1970s when the new Federal Republic (the democratic portion of Germany that was formed post–World War II) was experiencing its first recession. The governing coalition of the Christian Democrats and Social Democrats initiated a series of "concerted

action" meetings that "brought business, government, and labor together... to reach national agreements about wage and price increases, broad macroeconomic and social policy issues," and a law on balanced growth.[9] Although business involvement in government policy occurs far more informally now, Germany's main banks have helped in coordinating economic policy.

What about the role of labor in these arrangements? In some ways, labor has a far more significant, formal role in business policies. Codetermination "gives unions half the seats on the boards of directors of all companies with more than two thousand employees."[10]

(Continued)

(Continued)

Representation in the boardroom, however, does not automatically mean a seat at the table. Kuo argues that the development of corporatist arrangements in Germany has also been due to concerted repression of labor organizations by businesses.[11] Further, as Hauss and Haussman note, other groups involved in economics issues such as women's rights, immigrant workers, and the poor are often left out entirely.[12] Finally, an argument can also be made that such coordination is an undemocratic feature of Germany's government. Although government is involved in the decision-making process, businesses, after all, are self-interested actors that do not take all sentiments into account.

The Great Recession, which the United States and the world experienced beginning in 2008, also hit Germany hard with the German government forced into bailing out one of Germany's smaller banks. Not only did this hurt the corporatist arrangement directly but it also exposed a certain element of corruption that had emerged as a result of these practices.[13] While corporatist practices may be on the wane in Germany, they are still used widely in Scandinavian countries even despite changing economic conditions.

Critical Thinking Questions

1. Why might cooperation between business and labor be helpful in economic terms?

2. Who do you believe would have more advantages in negotiating in a corporatist system, business, labor, or government?

3. Given this arrangement in Germany, where would the German economy fall on the continuum seen in Figure 10.1?

Government Involvement and Economic Performance

Some of the means through which governments can influence the economy were mentioned at the beginning of this chapter: taxes, spending, tariffs, regulations. Broadly, however, there are two main types of government policy that affect the economy: fiscal policy and monetary policy. The directions in which states decide to go with both fiscal and monetary policy can significantly affect the performance of an economy.

Fiscal Policy

Fiscal policy includes the mix of taxing and spending that a state chooses to undertake. Taxes, although often seen and portrayed as an all-around negative, can be used to both encourage and discourage economic behavior. To understand this, we can consider some different categories of taxes. The types of taxes you are probably most familiar with include the income tax and sales tax. In the United States, the federal income tax is a **progressive tax**, meaning that the more money you make, the more money you are supposed to pay. Sales taxes are used by states and localities to generate revenue for their actions and are often placed on goods and services. While a sales tax on a haircut probably isn't going to discourage you from getting that haircut, there are other types of taxes that are imposed for the specific reason of discouraging people from using them. **Sin taxes** are taxes placed on "sinful" behavior like alcohol, tobacco and cigarettes, marijuana, or even gambling. When used as such, the higher tax is meant to discourage people from partaking in the activity.

Taxes levied on businesses have a direct effect on an economy. Particularly in a globalized world, businesses will seek out locations in which they have to pay the least amount of taxes. Governments would like to, then, create a mix of taxes that is not just low but attractive to businesses and corporations to bring them to their state or locality. For instance, if state A offers a business tax of 20 percent and state B offers a tax of 35 percent, all else being equal, businesses are likely to choose state A. With more businesses in state A come more jobs; more economic investment; and, ideally, more taxes. This concept is often called trickle-down economics, referring to the idea that although businesses and richer people will benefit from lower taxes, the economic benefit may trickle down to other people in the community and the economy as a whole. Critics of the idea, however, claim that businesses and those with higher incomes will not reinvest the money they save via tax cuts and will instead keep the economic benefits for themselves. Economic research on whether tax cuts to businesses and others with a higher income is mixed; on the whole, however, it has not been supportive of the idea that tax cuts to the rich will filter down to others.

Tax expenditures, or tax breaks, are another way in which the government can influence economic behavior. Tax expenditures include money that is foregone by the government because people are allowed to claim a reduction in their overall tax bill. In the United States, one major example is the home mortgage interest deduction. Homeowners are allowed to deduct the interest they pay on their home mortgage from the income taxes that they owe each year; while the government loses out on that money, they encourage people to buy homes, which can provide other benefits to the economy. Tax expenditures can be used to stimulate investment in certain areas of the economy by encouraging individuals and businesses to partake in certain activities so that they can deduct from their overall taxes.

Governments can also use tax penalties to encourage particular behaviors. In the United States, one recent prominent example is a tax that is enforced on people who do not have health insurance in a given year. The 2010 Patient Protection and Affordable Care Act imposed a requirement on individuals to have health insurance. One of the rationales behind requiring people to do so is because of the basic concept of insurance itself. People buy insurance in general *in case* certain scenarios happen like car accidents, home damage, or problems with one's health. If those bad things do not happen, the money paid into the insurance pool is lost, but if you run into one of those problems, the insurance policy will pay for damages or costs. Insurance companies, therefore, will often charge those at higher risk more money and those at lower risk less money. In the case of health insurance, health insurance for everyone will be more expensive if only those who are at high risk of having medical problems join the insurance pool; if, on the other hand, all people are required to have insurance regardless of their health situation, the costs for everyone will go down. While there were a number of other reasons for enacting the Affordable Care Act, this was the general philosophy behind the individual mandate. In order to enforce this requirement, the law requires people to pay a tax penalty if they do not have insurance.

Many people complain about taxes in general; they don't like paying them, they think they can do better if they keep the money themselves, or they don't like what the government is doing with the money that it takes in. Others believe that the imposition of taxes or the usage of tax expenditures on certain activities is in essence the government choosing who wins and who loses in economy activity. Governments take in nearly all of their revenue via taxes with that revenue used on things many people cannot imagine going without using, including basic infrastructure like roads, bridges, and ports; schools; military and police protection; and other public goods from which no one can be excluded.

Career Guidance

As the career of John Maynard Keynes demonstrates, economists can have a great impact on politics as well. For those interested in economics, this career field has a number of exciting opportunities—particularly in the business world where economic analysis, forecasting, and planning are vital. For political science students interested in economics and finance, consider a minor in economics or business and look into opportunities on campus to enhance your education, such as investing clubs.

Monetary Policy

Where fiscal policy determines a country's taxing and spending policies, **monetary policy** determines how much money is actually available in a country. Restricting or enlarging the money supply in an economy is done to control and affect economic performance in terms of inflation, interest rates, and unemployment. **Inflation** refers to a situation in which prices in general go up, making currency worth less than it was previously. It can happen for a number of reasons, but in general, it happens "when consumers and governments have a large amount of money to spend, relative to the supply of things they want to buy."[14] Situations such as government deficit spending, a shortage in significant goods, monopolies, and trade restrictions can all cause inflation to increase. Although some inflation in an economy is good, too much can cause severe economic downturns and depressions. Thus, central banks, or government organizations, which are in charge of setting and determining monetary policy, endeavor to keep inflation low.

Monetary policy can involve several different tools. One way is through the buying and selling of short-term government bonds. When a government or central bank intervenes to *buy* government bonds, they are putting money into the economy; when they *sell* bonds, they are taking money out of the economy. A second way is central banks can set benchmark interest rates that can raise or lower the cost of borrowing funds. When interest rates are low, borrowing money is cheaper and can encourage more spending in the economy; when interest rates are high, it can discourage borrowing and economic activity. One way to think about this is in terms of one of the most expensive purchases people tend to make: a house. When interest rates are low, you will spend less money to get a mortgage loan for the house, thereby encouraging people to go out and buy houses. But when it costs more to get a mortgage, when interest rates are higher, people are less inclined to go out and make large purchases. Interest rates, then, have the ability to encourage or discourage economic activity to help keep inflation in check.

Another issue that is involved in monetary policy is unemployment. Unemployment is not just a difficult policy problem to tackle but it can be difficult to define. As of January 2019, the unemployment rate in the United States is 4 percent; however, this unemployment rate includes only those who are actively looking for jobs and do not have one. People not included in this figure are those who have dropped out of the job market for reasons including inability to find a job within a specific time frame. It also does not include people not actively looking for a job. Therefore, the percentage of people in the United States without a job is usually some percentage points higher than the official unemployment rate. A second related issue is underemployment, or those who would like to be employed full-time but are working only part-time. This has been a growing problem for the United States in the wake of the 2008 Great Recession. Finally, some unemployment is to be expected in any economy; therefore, an unemployment rate below 5 to 5.2 percent is considered full employment by the US Federal Reserve.

Governments must be concerned with the unemployment rate for a number of reasons. One reason is that when there are high numbers of unemployed, more government assistance, even if temporary, will be required. This will increase the need for governments to spend money on social welfare programs. Secondly, high unemployment is simply inefficient in an economy; "the economy would benefit if everyone who wanted to work productively could do so."[15] A final reason is more political: if people are unemployed and therefore unsatisfied with the current economic situation, they are likely to take out their frustration on those in political office, perhaps voting them out. Research demonstrates that economic performance is a significant predictor of incumbent success; when the economy does well, incumbent parties tend to be reelected, whereas when the economy is on a downswing, incumbent politicians and parties are punished.

Where interest rates and the availability of money in an economy can directly affect inflation, unemployment is a more difficult problem to tackle. When interest rates go up and economic activity declines, unemployment is likely to go up as well. Central banks could decrease interest rates to assist in countering unemployment, but then the risk is that the pace of inflation will increase. Other government policies can be used to combat unemployment as well including the provision of government jobs. When government spending increases, the number of government jobs usually increases as well. Other policies can encourage job creation—such as lower taxes or the use of tax breaks specifically designed to reward employers for creating more jobs.

In all of these scenarios, central banks play key roles in making decisions. Because of the political implications that these decisions are likely to have, an important decision for states is how independent a central bank should be. Central banks that are more independent, or have more autonomy, can insulate economic decisions from very real day-to-day political considerations. However, one question that ultimately arises from an independent central bank is how accountable they are in general and especially to political leaders and the public. While the ideal would be to have an independent central bank that makes decisions based on economic situations and applicable theory and experience, there is very real fear that central banks will begin to operate without any sort of accountability. In a democratic society, especially, this accountability to elected officials and ultimately to the public is an important consideration to keep in mind.

Take the US Federal Reserve as an example. The Fed, as it is also known, consists of twelve regional Federal Reserve Banks, each overseen by a governor. Collectively, the governors make up the Federal Reserve Board, which is headed by the chair of the Federal Reserve. The Fed chair is a position appointed by the president and confirmed by the Senate with a five-year renewable term. The five-year term makes it so that Fed chairs go beyond a single four-year term of the president and therefore insulates them to some degree from presidential politics. The Fed is subject to oversight from Congress and gives annual testimony and reports to Congress on American economic performance. Central banks in other countries can have more or less oversight and relationship to state governments.

Gross Domestic Product

Economies are generally talked about in terms of size, growth, and stability; unemployment and inflation, discussed previously, are simply two elements of an overall assessment of a state's economy. But how do we know when an economy is growing? Or when it is contracting? The most commonly used measure is a country's economic strength is the **gross domestic product (GDP).** GDP represents the sum total of all economic activity in a state; the higher the GDP, the more economic activity there is. However, GDP on its own can be somewhat misleading; China's GDP in 2017 was $12.01 trillion, while the US GDP was $19.49 trillion. The GDP in the United States is clearly higher, but think about the number of people involved in economic activity in China versus the United States. That the United States is doing that much better with far fewer people is a more impressive feat. Therefore, in order to account for the differing sizes of states in terms of populations, GDP is often calculated in a per capita manner. To get to this calculation, a country's GDP is divided by its population, making China's GDP per capita $16,700 and $59,800 for the United States.[16]

True free market, capitalist economies have natural cycles that are referred to as boom and bust. Over time, economies grow as unemployment is low, and central banks keep inflation low. With money plentiful and as interest rates grow, money to invest is widely available. Sometimes, however, people do not invest the money well, and "bubbles" begin to form. Bubbles represent increased investment in certain segments of the economy and perhaps not the best ones. For example, in the late 1990s, people overinvested in dot-coms: new Internet companies that then could not produce any economic benefits or profits. At a certain point, the bubble bursts and people begin to pull back from investment. As money comes out of the market, economic activity shrinks and inflation rises—and so does unemployment. The bust cycle can turn into an economic recession if there are three consecutive quarters of negative economic growth and a depression if the GDP growth rate becomes at least a negative 10 percent over a sustained period of time. As the economy shrinks, panic and fear among consumers and investors can inspire further withdrawals from the market and banks, leading to an even more dangerous and damaging depression. All of these factors were apparent in the lead-up to the Great Depression. While recognizing that boom and bust cycles are natural characteristics of free market economies, monetary and fiscal policy is used to smooth out the highs and the lows.

Inequality

Unfortunately, the benefits of a growing economy do not always accrue equally. As was noted previously regarding critiques of capitalism, the rich do tend to reap the most economic rewards in a free market system. Thus, another way of measuring economic success in an economy is examining how it affects everyone—particularly in terms of economic inequality. High economic inequality can have significant effects not just on the economy but on people themselves: states with a high degree of economic inequality "have greater infant mortality, higher rates of obesity, and lower life expectancy."[17] Higher economic inequality also means that governments will be expected to step in more and perhaps spend more to assist those with a lower socioeconomic status.

Economic inequality can be measured in a number of ways, including percentage of people in a country below the poverty line or the difference in percentage of income earned by the top 10 percent of wage earners and the bottom 10 percent of wage earners. Measuring inequality via percentage under the poverty line is difficult as the poverty line, or the income level that is considered adequate, differs by country. Table 10.1 displays some of these inequality measures for a selection of countries in different regions around the world.

One way we can measure economic inequality is through the Gini index. The index is a statistical measure of dispersion of income across a country. Depending on how the index is calculated, it can be measured either on a scale of 0 to 1 or 0 to 100; the basic logic, however, is 0 represents perfect equality and 1 or 100 represents perfect inequality, where one person would have all the wealth. Figure 10.2 displays how the Gini index varies across the world with high levels of inequality in South America and Africa. Although the United States compares favorably to the developed world, economic inequality has been on the rise. The Gini index for the United States in 1979 was 34.6 while, more recently, it has risen to 45.

Income inequality can often be dealt with through a set of government policies collectively known as redistribution. Redistribution policies provide special subsidies and assistance for the poor—usually using tax revenues drawn from the more wealthy. While redistribution policies can provide a valuable and helpful social safety net for

Table 10.1   Inequality across the World

Country	Percent below the Poverty Line	Percent of Income Earned by Poorest 10% of Population	Percent of Income Earned by Richest 10% of Population	Difference in Wages between Top and Bottom 10%	Gini Index
France	14%	3.6%	25.4%	21.8	29.2
United Kingdom	15%	1.7%	31.1%	29.4	32.4
Norway		3.8%	21.2%	17.4	26.8
Italy	29.9%	2.3%	26.8%	24.5	31.9
Belarus	5.7%	3.8%	21.9%	18.1	26.5
Iraq	23%	3.6%	25.7%	22.1	
Israel	22%	1.7%	31.3%	29.6	42.8
Saudi Arabia					45.9
India	21.9%	3.6%	29.8%	26.2	35.2
Pakistan	29.5%	4%	26.1%	22.1	30.7
China	3.3%	2.1%	31.4%	29.3	46.5
Russia	13.3%	2.3%	32.2%	29.9	41.2
Indonesia	10.9%	3.4%	28.2%	24.8	36.8
Australia		2%	25.4%	23.4	30.3
South Africa	27.6%	1.2%	51.3%	50.1	62.5
Zimbabwe	72.3%	2%	40.4%	38.4	50.1
Egypt	25.2%	4%	26.6%	22.6	30.8
Sierra Leone	70.2%	2.6%	33.6%	31	34
United States	15.1%	2%	30%	28	45
Mexico	46.2%	2%	40%	38	48.2
Costa Rica	21.7%	1.5%	36.9%	35.4	48.5
Brazil	3.7%	1.2%	41.6%	40.4	49.7
Argentina	32.2%	1.6%	30.8%	29.2	42.7

Source: CIA World Factbook.

Figure 10.2 Gini Index Globally

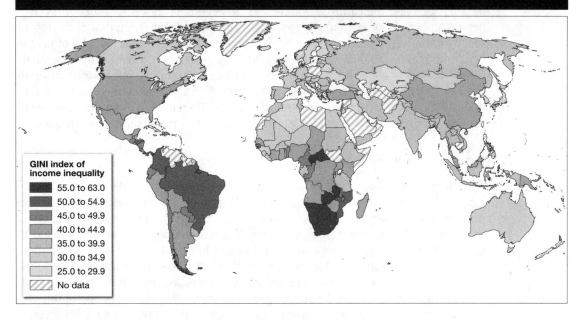

GINI index of
income inequality

55.0 to 63.0
50.0 to 54.9
45.0 to 49.9
40.0 to 44.9
35.0 to 39.9
30.0 to 34.9
25.0 to 29.9
No data

Source: Data from World Bank.

those left out of the economy for whatever reason, critics often argue against them for reasons similar to the arguments against progressive taxes: people should work for what they receive and be able to reap the benefits of working hard, and you may discourage people from working and bettering themselves if they know they will receive government assistance in any case. The question of what redistributive policies, then, to employ, is clearly a very political one with everything from the state of the economy to a country's culture and beliefs about responsibility for the less fortunate playing a role.

International Political Economy

As stated at the beginning of this chapter, the study of political economy examines the relationship between politics and the economy. The broader study of this can also be broken down into two further subfields: international political economy and comparative political economy. While related, the two are used to examine two distinct questions. **International political economy** examines the "two-way relationship between international politics and international economics."[18] While we have thus far discussed economies at the state level, the global economy is also a relevant and important area of study, which is what international political economy studies.

Dickins notes that the origins of international political economy as a field came from "the failure of International Relations scholars to engage with the international economy. International political economy emerged as the international economy developed apace in the 1960s."[19] Recall from Chapter 8 that globalization represents the increased and increasing economic ties between countries across the world. It is nearly impossible today to totally isolate a country's economy from that of the rest of the world; in fact, it is almost necessary to produce the goods that millions of people use around the world. For example, the widely popular Apple iPhone utilizes precious metals, including gold; silver; palladium; platinum; aluminum; copper; and rare earth metals like lanthanum, terbium, and gadolinium.[20] While most of these can be found in the United States, the rarer earth metals are not. Therefore, in order to create one of the products Americans use the most, trade—in some form or another—is required.

Comparative Advantage

The theory of **comparative advantage** supports the idea that trade can be mutually beneficial to both partners that engage in it. If it is cheaper to produce product A in country X and cheaper to produce product B in country Y, both countries are better off trading with one another *even if* country X could produce both products A and B. Comparative advantage works well in the scope of free market policies as well; if there is limited to no government involvement in the economy or in the setting up of trade barriers, then trade across countries can occur unimpeded, and the overall economy will benefit. However, in the domestic sphere, increased international trade of this sort can have serious impacts. For example, if China can produce steel in a greater amount and more cheaply than in the United States, there is no economic incentive to actually make steel in the United States. This would cause steel mills to go out of business and steel workers to lose their job. In some cases, China actually subsidizes the cost of certain products, thereby making them cheaper and therefore more competitive on a global market. Further, imagine a scenario where relations between China and the United States deteriorate to such a degree that China refuses to let the United States buy any of their steel. The US economy would be significantly hurt, not to mention the potential national security implications of not being able to build any military infrastructure that uses steel.

Free and Fair Trade

It is for these reasons that economic protectionists support limits on free trade through the imposition of trade barriers such as import taxes and tariffs. Tariffs are a type of tax that are imposed on certain goods coming from other countries that essentially raise the prices of those goods. This can make it more cost effective for the good to be produced domestically, thereby protecting the domestic economy and domestic jobs. However, the levying of tariffs and other import taxes can lead to retribution by the countries the tariffs are aimed at with those countries often imposing their own set of taxes on imports from a country. When taken to extremes, the result is a trade war that progressively increases trade barriers, eventually harming the economies of both countries involved. It is for these reasons that the concept of "fair trade" is often invoked. Where free trade is the lowering of trade barriers and little government involvement in trade and the economy, fair trade is an approach that "advocates retaliation against states that are perceived as 'cheating' on free trade by using various barriers to trade to stimulate their economies."[21]

The politics involved in these sorts of international trade disputes are quite easily seen in the politics of the North American Free Trade Agreement (NAFTA). NAFTA originated in the early 1990s as a trade agreement among Mexico, the United States, and Canada that would limit trade barriers among the three countries and create a free trade zone across North America. While Republicans, who have traditionally supported free trade and limited government involvement in the economy, were supportive of the plan, Democrats, who feared for the jobs that might be lost, were not. The situation changed as Bill Clinton became president in 1993 and broke with Democratic orthodoxy and supported the joining of NAFTA. In the short term, some jobs were indeed lost. Many manufacturing companies left the United States and relocated to Mexico where labor was cheaper; with labor at a lower cost, the goods produced would cost less. Since there were no tariffs on goods coming from Mexico into the United States, goods could be produced more cheaply in Mexico and sold at a lower price in the United States. The overall effect on the US economy was positive even though some manufacturing and other sectors lost jobs and capacity.

Debates over the value of NAFTA and other free trade agreements continue. In the 2010s, the United States engaged in negotiations with several other Pacific countries to create the Trans-Pacific Partnership (TPP), a free trade agreement that would lower trade barriers among the countries that signed on to the deal. Like Democrat Bill Clinton, then president Barack Obama also supported the TPP; however, it became an issue in the 2016 presidential election when then candidate Donald Trump came out against TPP and even against NAFTA. Then candidate and now president Donald Trump's arguments stemmed very much from these criticisms of fair trade: that free trade agreements of this sort took jobs away from American industry and that other countries were "cheating" the system and creating conditions that favored their own goods and products at the expense of the United States. When he became president, Trump pulled the United States out of the TPP and renegotiated NAFTA with Mexico and Canada. The president has repeatedly used arguments including unfair trade and trade imbalances to bolster protectionist policies such as the imposition of tariffs on steel and aluminum imports in March 2018.

Exchange Rates

One additional element that can affect the international economy is that of exchange rates. **Exchange rates** represent the price of one currency in terms of another. In other words, how much, in US dollars, does one euro cost? Exchange rates typically float and change based on currency markets; when the US dollar is expensive to buy, the currency can be said to be strong, and when it is inexpensive, it is weak. Exchange rates can affect international trade because how strong or weak a currency is can affect how expensive products are to buy from a given country. While the United States and many Western countries allow their currency and exchange rates to be governed by the market, some states, such as China, subsidize and control their currency so that they can keep it artificially low. This makes products cheaper to buy and can increase their exports relative to their imports. This can become a diplomatic sticking point between countries and can contribute to the idea that countries are not trading fairly.

Comparative Political Economy

Comparative political economy utilizes many of the methods of comparative methods to examine the connection between a country's policies and its economy. "Contributions to this field of inquiry have emphasized institutional differences between countries and the way that such differences have refracted political and economic responses to common economic shocks or opportunities."[22] For example, Pontusson, Rueda, and Way examine the effects of differing institutions on wage distribution, finding that "unionization, centralization of wage bargaining and public sector employment primarily affect the distribution of wages by boosting the relative position of unskilled workers."[23] They add that the effect of partisanship in a government is contingent on how centralized wage bargaining is. Iversen and Soskice examine the role of unions and political coalitions in determining why some states have high exchange rates along with a large number of exports.[24] Finally, Urbatsch suggests that the distribution of occupations and jobs affects public opinion on trade policy, which can ultimately affect a state's trading policies themselves.[25]

The focus on the role of states is important. Schmidt identifies four ways in which the structure of a state can impact an economy. First, the state determines what kind of economy a state is going to have, whether it is more liberal and free market in its posture or whether there will be more government involvement. Second, states can affect the "substantive content of policies," not just determining the type of economy but specific fiscal and monetary policies that will affect the economy directly.[26] Third, "as a polity, the state constitutes the political institutions that frame the interactions between political and economic actors."[27] In other words, the state forms the context in which political and economic actors interact. And finally, institutional change and the mechanisms through which that occurs can have direct impacts on the economy.

Women and the Economy

Women also play a key role in studies of political economy and economic development. Women comprise more than half of the people globally who live in impoverished situations.[28] And although studies have shown that globalization generally enhances the status of women, "feminist scholars argue that the international political economy has particular effects on women, because women often are assigned specific (disadvantageous) economic roles around the world."[29] These roles are either left behind or forgotten about as economic development continues. In some countries, women are left out of economic improvement altogether. For example, even though free market theorists argue that a continuously growing economy will benefit all, many women who are homemakers, stay-at-home caretakers (for children or other dependent individuals), or who pursue other "domestic" labors are left out of the wage market altogether. In some economies, women may be disadvantaged from the start: they may be denied educational opportunities that would allow them to advance economically, or they are not allowed to enter the market at all. These conditions combine to keep women systematically disenfranchised from the market, dependent (on men, governments, or families), or severely impoverished.

Inequality and poverty often hit women and children the hardest.[30] Inequality can even strike in highly developed economies, including the United States. Depending on profession, women on average in the United States earn 78 to 82 percent of what men earn. Around the world, however, that percentage is much larger, with the World Economic Forum finding that globally women earn only 68 percent of what men earn.

Despite these disadvantages, women can be very important in stimulating economic development. To demonstrate this on a small scale, we can look at the effect of microlending programs. *Microlending* is a term referring to programs that provide small loans to people in impoverished situations—in many cases, women—that allow them to buy livestock such as goats or chickens or that allow them to start a small business. If a woman buys a goat, they not only have a source of milk and cheese with which to feed their family but can sell the excess milk and cheese in the local area and therefore establish an income stream, which can be used to assist with the educational goals of their children or improve the living situations of their families. As women are able to economically develop, this has strong benefits for the family and in particular children in a family.[31] Because of the success of microlending programs in stimulating economic development, Muhammad Yunus, who pioneered the theories and practices of microlending, won the Nobel Peace Prize in 2006.

Because of the benefits that can accrue in economic development through women, many development agencies purposefully focus on women in development efforts. Beath, Christia, and Enikolopov report on a field experiment in Afghanistan where, in some villages, women were required to participate in economic development programs.[32] Although they found that such programs did not necessarily transform entrenched views on the status of women, the programs did enhance female economic mobility and income generation. Studying small communities in Ghana, Opare finds that the lack of political opportunity for women in community affairs severely restricts their ability to develop socioeconomically.[33] Nongovernmental organizations have also been key in promoting women's economic development, with Chowdhury showing the importance of nongovernmental organizations in very rural and remote areas of Bangladesh and their ability to promote the economic outcomes of women.[34]

Democracy and the Economy

The relationship between economic and political opportunity highlighted by studies of women's opportunity discussed previously are a key element in discussions of the relationship between free market, liberal economic policies and democracy. Some scholars propose that democracy can hamper economic development because of the need to appease multiple audiences. If the goal of legislators is to be reelected, then they must listen to and satisfy the concerns of interest groups and voters; if those groups and individuals agitate for more resources at the cost of spending on other activities to promote economic development or to the point where taxes must be raised, then economic growth may stall out. In more authoritarian-type governments, like China, leaders do not have to listen to public opinion when making significant policy decisions, freeing them from reelection concerns and allowing them to make decisions that can foster economic growth.

However, there are just as good theoretical reasons to believe that democracy can encourage economic growth. One, authoritarian leaders are not guaranteed to be public minded—in other words, the decisions they make do not automatically have to benefit the citizenry. In fact, one of the biggest problems of authoritarian regimes, often, is the amount of corruption, which wastes economic potential. Additionally, the threat of being thrown out of office is nonexistent, meaning that authoritarian leaders do not have to worry about public opinion at all, so if they make bad economic decisions, there is no way to either take the leader out of office or make them conform to public desires through the voting mechanism. Two, democracies can promote economic development through their protections for private property and property rights, which can affect the incentives workers have to take part in the economy. If individuals know that the fruits of their labor, their property, will be protected and will be theirs, there is more incentive for them to work harder, whereas in authoritarian style states, there is no guarantee that what workers earn will be theirs to keep.

There is one further argument about the relationship between democracy and economic development, and that is that economic development can cause a growth in democracy. The arguments for this proceed along many of the same lines as those noted previously. When an economy is growing, developing, and producing, workers will want to keep the benefits they receive and thus their own property. This can encourage more authoritarian states to begin to institute protections for private property and the legislative and judicial systems needed to enforce them. Further, as a state establishes more global economic ties, its people are exposed to new ideas and attitudes, perhaps stoking their desire for a more democratic type government. As the people begin to advance economically and reap the benefits that that entails, including education, they will be in a better place to demand democratic reforms. This hypothesis has been put to the test in states like China, where theorists hoped to see democratic reforms as the country increased its global ties and economic development (discussed further in the next section). Despite solid economic growth, China has continued to lag behind in terms of democracy.

When the Maoist revolution took over China in 1949, the United States and most of the rest of the Western world cut off diplomatic and economic ties with it in line with the foreign policy of containment, or the idea of keeping communism in the countries it was in and not allowing it to spread. Spearheaded by then president Richard Nixon and his national security adviser (and later secretary of state), it would not be until the early 1970s when the United States began to open up relations with China. By that time, although China had undergone a period of rapid industrialization, it still faced severe economic headwinds, and its people had just undergone the Cultural Revolution, which had purged many high-ranking government officials and put a stop to modernizing efforts within the government. Following Mao's death and the reopening of relations with the United States, China's leaders undertook a series of economic reforms to foster development and growth across China.

In 1972, just prior to Mao's death, Zhou Enlai, another of the country's communist leaders, announced a series of policy changes aimed at modernization: one, private property could be allowed and given a role to play in a socialist system; two, market forces should be used to allocate goods and determine prices; and three, "material incentives, including higher wages, personal profit, and the accumulation of wealth, should be the main way to boost productivity and efficiency."[35] While these reforms have certainly contributed to the spectacular growth of the Chinese economy over the past few decades, the growth has been relatively uneven and has largely benefited those in power. There is still a large Chinese agricultural population that is quite poor, and many of the "private companies" in China are owned by the state. Additionally, the state subsidizes many economic activities and artificially keeps the price of its currency low to stimulate trade.

What effect have these changes had on the nature of Chinese government, however? Beginning in the late 1970s and into the 1980s, some dissent did appear in China. These dissent movements reached their apex in 1989 when the democracy movement organized protests in Tiananmen Square in response to the death of a reformist government official. The protests continued to grow over a number of days, eventually leading the Chinese government to send in the army (with their tanks) to disperse the protest, resulting in the deaths of many protesters. Although democratic movements continue to exist in China, state leadership has long repressed it and kept dissent to a minimum by controlling the media as well as the Chinese Internet. Prospects for democracy in China took another hit in March 2018 when the National Congress of the Communist Party voted to remove presidential term limits—essentially allowing the current Chinese president Xi Jinping to serve as president for as long as he would like.

The case of China demonstrates that the relationship between democracy and free market economics, whichever direction the relationship runs, is not clear cut. The Chinese Communist Party has allowed certain free market reforms but has maintained strong political control over the country.

(Continued)

(Continued)

Critical Thinking Questions

1. Is it possible to have a capitalist system without democracy?

2. Do you believe greater economic freedom will lead to greater demands for political freedom?

3. What tools can the Chinese government utilize to limit political freedom?

STUDENT STUDY SITE

Visit https://edge.sagepub.com/whitmancobb

CHAPTER SUMMARY

- There is a complicated relationship between politics and the economy with politics influencing economic growth and trends and the economy influencing political developments.

- States can choose which economic system to utilize through the types of policies and regulations that they enact. These can include free market systems like capitalism, social democracy, socialism, and command economies.

- Governments can utilize fiscal policy (taxing and spending) and monetary policy (affecting the supply of money in an economic system) to influence an economy. Economies can be measured in terms of growth of GDP or even assessed in terms of how much inequality is produced.

- International political economy examines the interaction of international politics on the global economy while comparative political economy focuses on how states can and do affect economics.

KEY TERMS

capitalism: An economic system in which there is a free market wherein supply and demand regulates the availability and price of goods and labor

command economies: Systems in which the state controls all aspects of an economy

comparative advantage: Theory that proposes the idea that trade can be beneficial to all states involved

comparative political economy: A field of study using the methods of comparative politics to examine the relationship between politics and economics across a range of states

corporatism: A formal system of cooperation between business and government

economy: A system of exchange of goods

exchange rates: The price of one currency in terms of another

fiscal policy: The mix of taxing and spending policies that a state enacts

gross domestic product (GDP): The sum of all economic activity in a state

inflation: The general increase in prices, causing money to be worth less than it previously was

international political economy: Field of study examining international politics and its relationship with the international economy

market failures: Occurs when an economic system fails to produce or distribute needed goods and services

monetary policy: Determines how much money is available in an economic system

political economy: A field of study examining the connections between economies and politics

progressive tax: The more you make, the more you pay

resource curse: Countries that have vast mineral resources and often misdirect the benefits toward ruling families and corruption

sin taxes: Taxes placed on goods and services to discourage people from buying them

social democracy: Economic system that utilizes government intervention to balance out the excesses of a free market system

socialism: Economic system that envisions a greater role for the state in controlling the negative aspects of capitalism and providing significant welfare benefits

tariffs: Taxes on imported goods

tax expenditures: Taxes foregone by a government because people are allowed to claim a reduction in their overall tax bill

DISCUSSION QUESTIONS

1. Through what methods and policies can politics affect economies?

2. Compare and contrast capitalism, social democracy, and command economy.

3. What is the best method for measuring economic inequality in a country?

4. What is the difference between fiscal and monetary policy?

5. How much accountability should central banks have to their governments?

FOR FURTHER READING

Jaeggi, Rahel. "What (if Anything) Is Wrong with Capitalism? Dysfunctionality, Exploitation, and Alienation: Three Approaches to the Critique of Capitalism." *The Southern Journal of Philosophy* 54, Spindel Supplement (2016): 44–65.

Schmidt, Vivien A. "Putting the Political Back into Political Economy by Bringing the State Back in Yet Again." *World Politics* 61, no. 3 (2009): 516–546.

World Bank: https://www.worldbank.org

NOTES

1. Rahel Jaeggi, "What (if Anything) Is Wrong with Capitalism? Dysfunctionality, Exploitation, and Alienation: Three Approaches to the Critique of Capitalism," *The Southern Journal of Philosophy* 54, Spindel Supplement (2016): 46.

2. Gustav Cohn, Joseph Adna Hill, and Edmund J. James, "Supplement: A History of Political Economy," *The Annals of the American Academy of Political and Social Sciences* 4, supplement 6 (1894): 11.

3. Jaeggi, "What (if Anything) Is Wrong with Capitalism?"

4. Ibid., 60.

5. Ibid., 53.

6. W. Phillips Shively, *Power and Choice: An Introduction to Political Science*, 14th ed. (New York: McGraw-Hill, 2013), 37–38.

7. Ibid.

8. David J. Samuels, *Comparative Politics* (Boston: Pearson, 2013), 299–300.

9. Charles Hauss and Melissa Haussman, *Comparative Politics: Domestic Responses to Global Challenges*, 8th ed. (Boston: Wadsworth, 2013), 165.

10. Ibid.

11. Alexander G. Kuo, "Explaining Historical Employer Coordination: Evidence from Germany," *Comparative Politics* 48, no. 1 (2015): 87–106.

12. Hauss and Haussman, *Comparative Politics*

13. Wolfgang Munchau, "Two Nails in the Coffin of German Corporatism," *Financial Times*, Feb. 17, 2008, https://www.ft.com/content/cafc5320-dd77-11dc-ad7e-0000779fd2ac.

14. Shively, *Power and Choice,* 105.

15. Ibid., 106

16. CIA World Factbook, "China," March 1, 2019, https://www.cia.gov/library/publications/the-world-factbook/geos/ch.html; CIA World Factbook, "United States of America," March 1, 2019, https://www.cia.

gov/library/publications/the-world-factbook/geos/us.html.

17. Ibid., 109.

18. Paul D'Anieri, *International Politics: Power and Purpose in Global Affairs* (Belmont, CA: Wadsworth, 2010), 245.

19. Amanda Dickins, "The Evolution of International Political Economy," *International Affairs* 82, no. 3 (2006): 479.

20. Bianca Nogrady, "Your Old Phone Is Full of Untapped Precious Metals," *BBC*, Oct. 18, 2016, www.bbc.com/future/story/20161017-your-old-phone-is-full-of-precious-metals.

21. D'Anieri, *International Politics,* 251.

22. Lucio Baccaro and Jonas Pontusson, "Rethinking Comparative Political Economy: The Growth Model Perspective," *Politics and Society* 44, no. 2 (2016): 176.

23. Jonas Pontusson, David Rueda, and Christopher R. Way, "Comparative Political Economy of Wage Distribution: The Role of Partisanship and Labour Market Institutions," *British Journal of Political Science* 32 (2002): 281.

24. Torben Iversen and David Soskice, "Real Exchange Rates and Competitiveness: The Political Economy of Skill Formation, Wage Compression, and Electoral Systems," *American Political Science Review* 104, no. 3 (2010): 601–623.

25. R. Urbatsch, "Industries, Occupations, and Trade Policy Preferences," *Political Behavior* 35, no. 3 (2013): 605–620.

26. Vivien A. Schmidt, "Putting the Political Back into Political Economy by Bringing the State Back in Yet Again," *World Politics* 61, no. 3 (2009): 517.

27. Ibid.

28. Olusola Olufemi, "Women and the Burden of Unsustainable Development: Practice and Policy Contradictions," *Development in Practice* 14, no. 3 (2004): 428–432.

29. David L. Richards and Ronald Gelleny, "Women's Status and Economic Globalization," *International Studies Quarterly* 51, no. 4 (2007): 855–876; D'Anieri, *International Politics: Power and Purpose in Global Affairs*: 263.

30. Olufemi, "Women and the Burden of Unsustainable Development."

31. D'Anieri, *International Politics*, 264.

32. Andrew Beath, Fotini Christia, and Ruben Enikolopov, "Empowering Women through Development Aid: Evidence from a Field Experiment in Afghanistan," *American Political Science Review* 107, no. 3 (2013): 540–557.

33. Service Opare, "Engaging Women in Community Decision-Making Processes in Rural Ghana: Problems and Prospects," *Development in Practice* 15, no. 1 (2005): 90–99.

34. Nusrat Jahan Chowdhury, "A Journey towards Development: The Impact of Local NGO Programmes on Women Living in the Char Lands of Bangladesh," *Development in Practice* 18, no. 1 (2008): 117–124.

35. Hauss and Haussman, *Comparative Politics*, 290.

Immigrants' rights activists opposed moves by the Trump administration in the summer of 2018 to separate children and their parents who entered the country illegally at the Mexico-US border.

Source: Spencer Platt/Getty Images News/Getty Images

CHAPTER

11

Public Policy and Public Administration

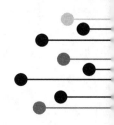

At the beginning of 2018, one of the biggest policy areas under consideration by Congress and the president was immigration policy and specifically how to deal with people who were brought illegally to the United States as children. These individuals are commonly known as "Dreamers," after legislation that was proposed to address the issue—the Development, Relief and Education for Alien Minors Act, or DREAM Act. In 2014, then president Barack Obama signed an executive order giving legal protection to children who were brought to the United States illegally by their parents, often called Dreamers. With many calling such an order unconstitutional, President Donald Trump rescinded the order in September 2017, calling on Congress to come up with a permanent legislative solution. In January 2018, after months of negotiating with no solution, congressional Democrats refused to vote on a short-term continuing resolution to continue funding the government without a deal on Dreamers, thereby shutting it down for three days, in order to push the issue of DACA, or the Deferred Action for Childhood Arrivals. In this instance, Democrats utilized their leverage in the Senate to force Republicans to finalize a policy that could be passed and adopted by Congress. Portrayed in the media, the issue has become embroiled in repeated recriminations between Democrats and President Trump, strong language, and tough negotiations. However, all of this obscures different analytical tools that political scientists use to examine the politics of policy areas like immigration.

While DACA and Dreamers deals with a small slice of immigration policy, a basic conundrum is why the United States has not been able to engage in comprehensive immigration reform for over two decades despite several

Chapter Objectives

1. Identify the stages of the policymaking process.

2. Compare patterns of policy change, specifically budgetary incrementalism and punctuated equilibrium.

3. Discuss the various actors involved in making public policy and the different types of policy.

4. Examine the role of bureaucracies in policymaking and the politics involved.

tries in the US Congress. This chapter introduces some of the many ways through which political scientists may attempt to answer such a question. Why has it gotten stuck in the policy formulation and adoption stages? What actors are involved, and what do they want out of immigration policy? How does immigration policy compare with other policy areas in terms of achievement or even difficulty? In attempting to answer these questions, political scientists can begin to understand the policy dynamics of immigration specifically and public policy in general.

Looking at the immigration debates of early 2018, most of the attention has been devoted to the roles of the president and Congress. However, other actors are equally involved in the setting and carrying out of policy—in particular, bureaucracies like the Department of Homeland Security, which oversees agencies like the Border Patrol and the US Citizenship and Immigration Services. Not only do bureaucracies have a significant amount of input in the making of laws but the way they implement and carry out laws are a continuation of policymaking. As such, to fully understand all aspects of policy studies, we also need to think about bureaucracies and the dynamics involving public administration.

If politics is defined as deciding who gets what, when, and where, then **public policy** is the vehicle through which that is done. The ultimate goal of politics is the solving of problems through the creation of public policies. Public policy, both its creation and administration, is also the area in which early political scientists believed that a scientific method could provide the most guidance and assistance to policymakers. Through scientific, objective study, political scientists would be able to identify the best approaches to solving social problems and would be able to critically analyze their potential consequences. This information could then be provided to decision makers who would be able to use it to inform their ultimate choices.

This chapter examines public policy, stages of the policymaking process, the people involved, the theories regarding its creation, and even the various types. Because of how the federal government has grown, particularly since the twentieth century, there is practically a policy for most every aspect of modern life. This can certainly complicate matters for political scientists seeking to understand broader patterns about public policy, but the diversity of policy areas also makes it exciting and interesting to study.

Stages of the Policymaking Process

There are five general stages of the public policy process: agenda setting, policy formulation, policy adoption, policy implementation, and policy evaluation. While this process isn't strictly followed in every situation with every policy, when looking broadly at the political and policy process, we can usually see each of these stages when examining individual public policies. As such, political scientists take this as a helpful framework for evaluating, analyzing, and understanding the formation of public policy.

Agenda Setting

Agenda setting, as stage one in the process, is often the hardest; how do you get a policy problem on the agenda of the most powerful people in the world? One of the classic treatises on agenda setting in public policy is *Agendas, Alternatives, and Public Policies* by Kingdon.[1] Kingdon argues that three "streams" must combine together in order for a policy problem to make it onto the political agenda: the problem, the existence of a solution, and the political will to deal with it. When these three things coincide, a policy window opens when it is the easiest for political institutions to consider an issue. Oftentimes, it takes willing and able policy entrepreneurs to prepare the groundwork, to work to make sure the three streams coincide.

While it might appear strange at first to think that problems and solutions can be so easily separated by Kingdon, this distinction is actually very important. Some members of Congress may seek changes to particular policy areas absent a crisis or problem simply because of an ideological belief about what the policy should be doing. For example, some Republicans have sought for years to reduce the amount of money being spent on entitlement programs like the Supplemental Nutrition Assistance Program, or SNAP (commonly known as welfare), Medicaid, Medicare, and Social Security. However, if there is no major problem with any of these areas and the policies are operating relatively well, why would anyone see a need to change them, other than ideologically based reasons, of course? On the other hand, it is easy to see where policy problems may arise suddenly that have no existing solutions; if there is no agreed-upon way of solving a crisis, there may be stopgap policies but no longer term way of fixing the problem in the first place. Therefore, Kingdon's policy streams theory highlights how circumstances must come together just right in order for policy changes to be successfully made.

Others have examined the role that political actors play in agenda setting. Perhaps one of the most powerful agenda setters is the president. Presidents, by focusing time and energy on a topic, can influence the media and Congress to pick up on problems as well.[2] Given all of the things that a president may choose to focus on in a given term, let alone week or month, a president's choice in focusing the nation's attention on certain issues sends a strong signal that an issue is important. When making these decisions, presidents are likely to take into consideration the makeup of Congress and the status of the federal budget when deciding what issues to take up.[3] Presidents then can use the resources of their office, such as the bully pulpit and even the State of the Union address, to highlight policy issues they wish to focus on. Especially in the run-up to election periods, presidents must be seen to be responding to public concerns and therefore may use this agenda setting power to help their own reelection efforts.[4]

If any institution, however, would be predicted to be concerned with election and reelection the most, it would be Congress. Walker describes the importance of choosing issues as such: "By deciding what they will decide about, legislators also establish the terms and the most prominent participants in the debate, and ultimately, the distribution of power and influence in the society."[5] Research on agenda setting in Congress has mostly focused on the role of parties and partisanship. For example, Cox tests the role of party in agenda setting in the House of Representatives and finds it to be a significant predictor of support.[6] In other words, the majority party so strongly controls the agenda that majority party members rarely dissent in committee or on the floor. While the House lends itself to being a majoritarian institution, the Senate, on the other hand, requires minority participation in setting the agenda. This would suggest that the minority party can more easily set the agenda in the Senate; however, Gailmard and Jenkins find evidence of just the opposite.[7] Thus, when setting the agenda in Congress overall, majority parties appear to have the most power to influence what issues will be taken up.

Despite the best efforts of agenda setters throughout politics, the contingent nature of crises and focusing effects are also important in helping legislators and citizens decide what is important or not. For an example of this, we can look no further than 9/11, which brought home the issue of terrorism. Although terrorism is an ancient tactic, and many terrorist acts had been carried out against the United States prior to 9/11, it took the drastic events of that day to focus the attention of the American public and its lawmakers on the problem that was al-Qaeda, Osama bin Laden, and their brand of Islamic terrorism. Policy failures like those of the Department of Veterans Affairs (VA) in treating the health problems of the nation's veterans similarly brought the attention of politicians and the public to systemic problems at the VA. Outside events and policy failures, then, also have inordinate agenda setting power and the power to override many other issues that might have previously been on the political radar.

Policy Formulation

Once a policy problem is acknowledged to be such, the next step in the process is to formulate a solution. This doesn't mean that the solution will be perfect; more often than not, it isn't. But policymakers bargain and negotiate among one another to devise a solution that makes the largest number of people the happiest. The propriety of doing that versus doing what is right is a debate that politicians have all the time and will not be answered with any certainty here. But what we do know is that formulating a policy response is not the same as solving the policy problem.

One way to think about policy formulation is whether elected officials are crafting policy in a top-down manner or whether the policy is being designed from the bottom up. If policy is being driven in a **top-down** manner, Congress, the president, or both acting together can draw on their staffs and bureaucratic officials to design a broad piece of legislation or executive order that can be considered. In Congress, for example, members are assisted in this not only by their own legislative staff but committee staff and leadership as well. Members may receive outside help from interest groups and other organizations; although this may appear distasteful, these groups can provide valuable experience, knowledge, and insight especially when crafting complex legislation. Similarly, the president can draw on their own advisers along with the bureaucracies of the federal government that have the knowledge and expertise to assist the president.

While top-down policy formulation seems to be the type that we hear the most about, many policies are also driven from those lower down the government hierarchy. However, these bureaucrats are usually closely placed to where policy is actually being carried out, allowing them to understand the ins and outs and details of what policies are actually working and what policies aren't. New policy, then, can also be driven by these experiences, allowing bureaucrats to build on their experience and knowledge to develop policy that is then presented to the president and Congress to decide on. One clear example of the difference between top-down and **bottom-up** policy formulation comes to us from NASA, an agency that is discussed later in the chapter. In 1961, President John F. Kennedy directed NASA to send men to the moon by the end of the decade in pursuit of Cold War goals. This top-down formulation left it to NASA to determine the means and the how of carrying out the policy, but it was clearly designed at the executive level. On the other hand, the NASA space shuttle program developed out of an internally designed process with NASA taking the idea for the program to the Nixon White House to decide upon.

Policy Adoption

What is far easier for political scientists and the public to understand is the policy adoption stage. This part of the process deals with decision makers and elected politicians deciding to adopt one policy over another. One of the most prominent means through which this is done is legislation, and because it is easy to quantify and examine votes in Congress, this is one area of fruitful research for political scientists. In fact, the number of analyses of congressional roll call votes grows every year. One of the biggest determinants, if not the biggest, of how members of Congress vote on bills is party; Democrats tend to support Democratic proposals, Republicans tend to support Republican proposals. While this is not an ironclad law, it happens more often than not.

Other factors that influence members of Congress include the salience, or importance, of the issue—in particular, the salience of the issue to their constituents. When the issue is important and visible, members of Congress will often defer to the opinion of their voters; when the issue is not so visible, members of Congress will often vote based on other factors. Other times, members may engage in a process called **logrolling**; one member will vote for bill A if another member votes for what the first member wants on bill B. This sort of horse trade is common but very difficult to track and therefore analyze.

Policy adoption has become more difficult in Congress as party polarization has grown. The problem is particularly acute in the Senate, which often requires a supermajority to end debate on legislation to clear the way for a vote to be held. For regular pieces of legislation, the Senate requires sixty votes to end debate and move on to vote on a bill; with the margins between parties closer than ever, the majority party often needs the support of several minority party members to move on to votes. As a result, Congress has turned to an option known as **budget reconciliation** to overcome the sixty-vote Senate. Reconciliation is a procedural move that instructs committees in Congress to create legislation that accomplishes a certain budgetary objective. The resulting piece of legislation is then considered privileged, and a cloture vote, the vote to end debate, is not needed in the Senate, and only a simple majority is required to pass a bill.

Budget reconciliation has been used to pass major pieces of legislation in recent years, including the Patient Protection and Affordable Care Act and Tax Cuts and Jobs Act of 2017. What is interesting about both of these bills is that when they were adopted by Congress, public approval was upside down: more people disliked the bills than were in favor of them. In the case of the Affordable Care Act, lack of public support led to years of attempts by Republicans to repeal parts of the law if not the whole law itself. This highlights the need for a policy to be seen as legitimate in addition to its being adopted. If a policy lacks a broad base of support or a broad section of people who believe it to be legitimate, it can easily be changed, amended, or repealed in the years following. Thus, in addition to the Congress adopting policy, the public must be willing to adopt it as well.

Legislation is not the only avenue to policy adoption. Presidents can use their executive powers to unilaterally adopt policy initiatives—whether it's through executive orders, their power as commander in chief, or through administrative powers in the bureaucracy. However, presidents' abilities to do this are severely constrained by both the Constitution and congressional powers. A good example of this is gun control. President Barack Obama wanted to enact stricter regulations on gun sales and ownership, but without broad-scale legislation from Congress, not much movement can be made on the issue. What the president did was to utilize executive orders to clarify the interpretation of previous laws to make guns harder to buy. While this is making policy, it is making policy on the margins on a small issue within the confines of presidential power.

Policy Implementation

Once policies have been adopted, it is up to the bureaucracy to implement them. More often than not, the legislation that gets passed is vague—bare bones. While it might not seem like it, given that modern legislation is often hundreds of pages long, it will take hundreds more pages of regulations to put that law into practice. Bureaucracies must decide the meaning of nebulous words and phrases and how particular policies will be put into practice. An example of this was the Affordable Care Act, passed in 2010. Although the bill itself was 906 pages long, some elected officials have claimed that the regulations issued to support its implementation have surpassed 20,000 pages!

Research on policy implementation has generally occurred along two lines of inquiry: what policy researchers call top-down and bottom-up. The difference in these two theories is a discussion of who should be in charge of deciding how to implement policy: those at the top who have a broad view of the agency, the policy, and what can be done, or those at the bottom who have the most experience and knowledge of how things actually work on the front lines. Top-down scholars have argued that looking at policy implementation from this vantage point has led to breakthroughs not only in understanding the process but in being able to compare and contrast across policy areas.[8] However, bottom-up researchers counter this by saying that the top-down approach neglects the vast majority of bureaucrats who actually do the hard work of making a policy work at the lower levels. These "street-level bureaucrats," bottom-up researchers contend, have myriad ways of working in and around the system that often counter the intent and will of the administrators at the top.[9] Compared to top-down research, it is harder to compare and contrast across policy areas because the policy network of important actors may be completely different from policy to policy. In reality, both sides in the debate are correct about many of their arguments; because many of the things the federal government does are so large and broad in nature, it is very difficult to comprehensively trace and study the actions taken to implement policy. As a result, like policy formulation, many of the studies performed have focused on individual policies—particularly at the state and local level, which are easier to identify, trace, and explain.

Policy Evaluation

The final and oft-neglected stage of policymaking is that of evaluation. Evaluation pertains to the assessment of whether the policy is working or not, whether the way a policy was implemented was appropriate or not, and what can be done to improve not only the policy but the way it has been implemented. There are many different types of policy evaluation—from formative evaluation (how well do the inputs of a policy match its outputs) to summative evaluation (is the policy working or is it working better than other alternatives)—with other stages in between.

But why don't we hear more about policy evaluation? Part of the reason is after a policy is adopted, public attention to the issue naturally fades. We trust that the government can implement policy and that the policy will work, but often we're not entirely sure. Evaluation research can also be difficult to perform; people on the inside of a bureaucracy may not have the appropriate objectivity to report on a policy's progress, people on the outside may not have all of the information and may be kept at arm's length for fear of severe criticism of what the agency had been doing.

Theoretically, the evaluation stage should lead back to agenda setting, to an opportunity for policymakers to adjust the policy they've adopted to make it perform better. This rarely happens until a major policy failure occurs, bringing the issue back into the public eye. This brings the cycle back around to Kingdon's theory of agenda setting: only when a problem is recognized will the policy streams begin to open a window of change.

This explanation has laid out the policymaking process in a rational, step-by-step way. However, the reality is that policymaking is far messier than can often be described, and the stages aren't often clearly delineated. Agenda setting can flow into formulation, and formulation can be tied with adoption; concerns about implementation will sometimes be addressed as the bill is being written. The policymaking process is an excellent example of how political scientists often must simplify very complicated processes to be able to understand, study, and explain them, but we must also be careful not to lose sight of how byzantine the things we study sometimes are.

Patterns of Policy Change

Theories of policy change are just that—theories. What do real-life patterns of policymaking actually look like? Because it would be really difficult to compare, say, foreign policy to something like agriculture policy in terms of the activities that each undertakes, one way political scientists examine patterns of policy change is through the budgets allocated to each policy area. Budgets are good representations of policy activity because everything the government wants to do requires money and resources to do it. Since money doesn't grow on trees (not even for the government), the government can't simply manufacture money to do everything it wants. It must make choices: which areas to fund more or less, whether it's worth raising taxes to allocate more money to something. Budgets, therefore, become a representation of dedication on the part of the government toward particular policy directions.

Take a look at the budget allocated to NASA in Figure 11.1. In general, we notice two things: first, when NASA began, the money allocated to it skyrocketed through the mid-1960s, and two, following a large decline in the late 1960s, the NASA budget has been relatively stable. We can use these patterns to help explain two major theories of policy change: incrementalism and punctuated equilibrium.

Budgetary Incrementalism

The theory of incrementalism dates back to the 1950s and 1960s with work by Lindblom and Wildavsky.[10] **Incrementalism** is the idea that an agency's or entity's budget in a given year is based on its budget in the previous year and that the budget will generally go up or go down by only a small amount. One of the assumptions that underlie this theory is the idea that rational lawmakers limit their attention to a policy or agency in a given year by basing its next year's activities on what they had done previously with few, if any, large jumps or changes in its activities. Berry summarizes the common conceptions that have come along with budgetary incrementalism—among them being the restriction of the number of alternatives, limited assessment of policy consequences, simple decision rules, and the smallness of the ultimate change.[11]

Although Berry argues that the term *incrementalism* has lost its meaning because it has been used in so many different ways, we can still use it to examine and explain the budget for NASA, especially after the 1960s. For the most part, the NASA budget has stayed relatively steady except for a post-1986 increase (partially due to the explosion of the shuttle *Challenger*); in fact, the budget for 2015 was actually $2 billion less than

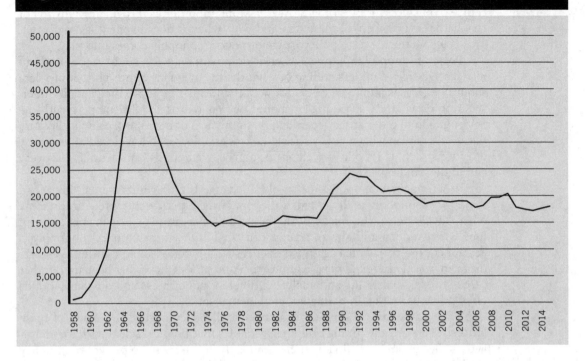

Figure 11.1   NASA Budget, 1958–2015 (in millions of constant 2014 dollars)

the budget in 1970. In this sense, their budget is an excellent example of incrementalism; for the most part, the budget goes up or down in small percentages. Over time, those small percentages may add up to an overall increase or decrease in funding.

Why would policymakers make policy in this way? Think of all the different policy areas that just 535 members of Congress and one president have to consider every year; there's just not enough time in the day or the year to thoroughly consider every agency's budget on a thorough basis every year. Because of this, Congress and the president will usually rubber-stamp a small increase in an agency's budget with little oversight since there are so many other things for them to do. Larger increases are much harder to get by Congress because that would call for a more comprehensive and time-consuming decision process.

Punctuated Equilibrium

This doesn't mean, however, that policies and their budgets never change drastically; just looking at the NASA budget disproves this. Incrementalism as a theory cannot explain the sudden changes such as what NASA experienced in the early 1960s or late 1980s. For that, we turn to a different budgetary theory, something called **punctuated equilibrium**, proposed by Baumgartner and Jones. In looking at the entire history of the NASA budget, we can see that it is marked by periods of great change followed by periods of stability; Baumgartner and Jones argue that this is the normal course of business for most policy areas.[12] More important is recognizing why major change doesn't happen all that often and why, when it does happen, it's so abrupt. This is where the idea of a policy image or policy monopoly comes into play.

Policy monopolies happen when a dominant actor or set of actors can put into place a shared understanding of what the major policy approach to a problem should be. For example, when NASA was first formed in 1958, the general understanding of what US space policy should be was that it should compete with the Soviet Union in outer space—particularly in the area of human spaceflight. Because this monopoly on what a policy should be was established, it foreclosed other policy directions such as robotic spaceflight or a greater emphasis on scientific discovery and understanding.

When policy monopolies are in place, change is rather incremental, but when the policy monopoly is disrupted, either by crisis, a policy entrepreneur, or some other outside force, the image of the policy becomes in play. It is at this point in time when sudden and abrupt change can occur. Once a new policy monopoly is developed, the policy area again experiences a long period of equilibrium—hence, the term *punctuated equilibrium*. Baumgartner and Jones's theory has been used rather successfully in explaining and analyzing different policy areas and obviously builds off of previous work—in particular, incrementalism.

It would be far too simplistic to say that all policy change is a result of these factors. There are any number of other variables that political scientists have identified as affecting budgets. In an article from early 2009, trying to predict what policy changes America would experience as a result of the Obama election, Woon demonstrates that something as basic as elections and polarization affect the types of policies that are capable of being enacted.[13] This is an easily understood relationship; if there are more Republicans or Democrats in office, more conservative or liberal policies, respectively, will be able to be passed. Swedlow argues that cultural changes can be precursors for major political change and can be used in conjunction with punctuated equilibrium to specify when conditions might be ripe for large-scale policy change.[14] Even changes in the neighboring state, community, or country can lead to policy change in government.[15] This is the idea of policy diffusion, when one government enacts policy change, those physically around it might be more inclined to adopt the change as well.

How do both of these ideas—smaller, policy-dependent variables and larger theories of policy change—fit together to explain how and why policy changes? We can again return to our example of NASA as an illustration. The NASA budget is obviously very well-explained by punctuated equilibrium; there are long periods of stability with shorter periods of major change. But what leads to those changes specifically? In the case of NASA, it is often factors like international competition (first from the Soviet Union and later from Russia and China), the gross domestic product (GDP) of the United States (in good economic times, it's easier to fund discretionary items like NASA), and the overall US budget (it restricts the amount of money available for NASA in the first place). In the case of the two punctuations, the first one, during the 1960s, is largely explained by the international competition of the Cold War. For the second, it was the policy crisis brought about by *Challenger* in 1986.

Policy Actors and Types of Policies

Most every political actor you can think of is involved in setting policy somehow. The president and the Congress are only the two most obvious institutions we can think of as well as the bureaucracy. But who else is involved? The media, interest groups, political parties, businesses and corporations, voters, and even academics can be involved at some point or another. It would be a far longer chapter if we were to consider each in turn, so for our purposes here, we will focus on two models of policy actors, the iron triangle and the policy network.

Iron Triangles

Perhaps one of the oldest of such models in political science is the idea of an **iron triangle,** which brings together congressional committees, interest groups, and bureaucracies. The theory behind the iron triangle is that policy is often truly formulated at the committee level in Congress rather than by Congress as a whole; members of a standing committee often have expertise and experience in dealing with a given policy area and more often than not have some sort of constituent connection with it as well. For example, many members of both the House and Senate committees who deal with agriculture have significant agricultural and farming interests in their districts and states. Therefore, these members become the most important in making policy.

In addition to constituent concerns and their own policy knowledge, congressional committees also heavily rely on the relevant bureaucracy that oversees a policy area to provide further expertise in developing policy. In turn, bureaucracies act in a rational, self-interested manner; in other words, bureaucracies would like to see their budgets and bureaus grow, so they have an incentive to work with the committees who are writing the policy. Finally, interest groups provide yet another policy perspective along with constituent connections. Interest groups can represent policy interests of consumers, advocates, and even manufacturers who have a distinct interest in policy. Interest groups, in attempting to influence policy in a particular direction, seek to influence not only the bureaucracy but congressional committees. This can be done through direct lobbying of either the bureaucracy or the committee or even through campaign support for members of Congress. Thus, the iron triangle represents a policymaking relationship where each partner has an incentive to create policy and work together in some way or another.

The classic example of an iron triangle is in military and defense policy (see Figure 11.2). Obviously, the armed services committees in both the House and the Senate realize the importance of determining defense policies and programs for the

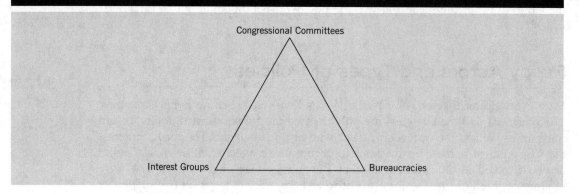

Figure 11.2   Iron Triangle

Congressional Committees

Interest Groups

Bureaucracies

country, but in this instance, both the Department of Defense, which carries out military policy, and military contractors have significant interest and influence in what the committees decide. Because members of the committee may not be entirely sure of the Department of Defense's or the military's capabilities and needs, they must rely on the Department of Defense to recommend programs and policies to them. Further, military contractors who often provide equipment and personnel have a vested interest in seeing certain programs succeed. Thus, the iron triangle represents the influence that the Department of Defense can have on both congressional committees and the military-industrial complex as well as the influence defense-oriented interest groups can have on the Department of Defense and Congress.

Issue Networks

Just as important for what is included in the iron triangle model is what is not— policy actors like the president or even the public directly are excluded from this type of idea. Further, the iron triangle describes a segmented and closed-off decision-making process, allowing for no other input into the system. While all theories are necessarily simplistic accounts of the phenomena they are trying to describe, some policy analysts have rejected the iron triangle concept for a more open policymaking process with different types of actors involved. As a result, Hugh Heclo introduced the idea of a **policy or issue network** in the 1970s:

> Issue networks are much more fluid coalitions in which sometimes anonymous participants from both inside and outside of government coalesce around a particular issue on an ad hoc basis. Issue networks, unlike iron triangles, are temporary coalitions whose members are motivated by passion and ideals as much as by the chance of some economic gain from involvement in the policy process.[16]

Where the idea of an iron triangle may be applied to multiple policy areas, the policy network concept would vary across policies. Different policy areas might have different participants; for example, the president may be very interested in the direction of military policy but not so much in agricultural policy. Policy network theory would be able to accommodate a varying and often shifting variety of actors involved in the policymaking process. In his review of domestic policy in the United States, Grossman identifies 790 "notable" policy enactments with the involvement of over 1,300 different actors![17] However, if there are so many different policy areas with so many different people involved, is there any utility in making broad generalizations? In other words, is there any usefulness in the idea of policy networks? Grossman argues that policy networks can be used to create generalized knowledge if scholars are "attentive to the few ways that each issue area differs from the others."[18] In other words, scholars can use policy networks to examine broad policy areas such as agriculture, civil rights, energy, education, labor, and social welfare and generate useful differences between policy areas.

Additionally, since policymaking is not always accomplished at the congressional level, policy networks better describe who is making policy and where. Golden highlights this difference in her study of administrative rulemaking.[19] When policy is being implemented, bureaucracies often have to craft a number of rules and regulations to put into effect the vague laws that Congress has passed. These rules have the effect of setting policy—sometimes quite consequentially. Golden notes that this aspect of policymaking is often ignored, so her study aims to identify which model—the iron triangle or policy network—better describes the process of agency rulemaking. She finds that policy networks are far more prevalent in rulemaking with groups moving in and out of the policy process, even within the same agency, communication among groups, and identifiable winners and losers.[20]

Policy Typologies

Since political scientists seek to explain in as parsimonious a manner as possible, the conclusion that all policy areas are unique and therefore unable to be explained as a whole is a difficult pill to swallow. What's the middle ground between one general theory that doesn't explain individual policy shifts and no theory and only individual policy explanations? One middle-of-the-road approach to this is to look at different categories or types of policies. Policy typologies go beyond individual policy areas like homeland security, education, or agriculture; they are categories underneath which multiple, but similar, policy areas might fall.

The benefit of breaking policies up by subject type is that the same political factors might be involved in similar types of policy. For example, partisan differences could help explain changes in multiple social policies, including Social Security and welfare. If Democrats are in charge of the government, we might expect to see actions to strengthen those types of policies. Republicans, on the other hand, might seek to change and modify military policy when they are in charge. All economic policies might be intimately affected by global economic conditions, or sharp upturns or downswings in the stock market. In this way, we can explain changes across more policy areas leading to more parsimonious theories. Smith sums up this argument, saying, "Typologies draw their theoretical strength from the idea that public policies can be systematically classified and that associated with each policy category are distinct and predictable patterns of political behavior."[21]

Another way of thinking about different types of policy is by those that are frequently on the political agenda and those that are not. Handberg presents a type of fluctuating policy typology based upon what issues presidents perceive as important to the success of their administration.[22] In this view, primary issue items, such as the economy and international relations, receive increased attention compared to secondary or tertiary items. This suggests that policy change or the type of policy change may be different in policy areas that are considered frequently or on top of the president's agenda. If the president pays little attention to an agenda item lower on the scale, the type of change may be inherently different.

One of the most influential policy typologies in political science was put forward by Lowi in 1972.[23] He bases this categorization on the premise that government carries out policy through coercion—through making people or systems behave in a particular way for fear of the consequences if they do not. Therefore, on one axis is the likelihood of coercion (remote or likely), and on the other is the method through which coercion is exercised (through individual behavior or through the environment). The resulting four types of policy are shown in Table 11.1.

What do these four policy areas consist of? Distributive policies are characterized by low levels of conflict where many different people can benefit from projects. Lowi's examples include tariffs and subsidies along with land use policies. Regulatory policies consist of policies aimed at eliminating things like unfair competition or fraudulent advertising; these are policies that protect individual citizens. Lowi includes policies like reapportioning or creating new bureaucracies as examples of constituent policy while redistributive policy includes things that redistribute benefits, Social Security, taxes, welfare, etc.

Despite, or perhaps because of, the various typologies policy analysts have proposed, some political scientists are critical of their usefulness. Smith summarizes several of these critiques, including the fact that some policies do not fit neatly into whatever typology is being used, some policies overlap several categories, and some

Table 11.1 Lowi's Policy Typology

		Applicability of Coercion	
		Individual	Environment
Likelihood of Coercion	**Low**	Distributive policy	Constituent policy
	High	Regulatory policy	Redistributive policy

policies may even shift categories over time.[24] Smith writes that "the key obstacle in addressing this issue was identified as the ambiguity of policy as a concept, that its status as a particular type was a mental construct and not an observable and measurable empirical quality."[25] In other words, different policy scholars may categorize and classify policy areas differently depending on subjective criteria that can change from person to person. In some ways, this critique is reminiscent of the larger debate within political science between qualitative and quantitative scholars. Those who prefer quantitative methods would be skeptical of such classification schemes precisely because there is no objective empirical standard that causes one policy area to fall into one category or another. On the other hand, qualitative scholars might argue that not everything can be quantified, and this debate is representative of that. Despite these drawbacks, policy typologies continue to be used and are still useful in order to "understand variation across issue areas in the venues where policymaking takes place and the factors responsible for policy change."[26]

Public Administration

It's one thing to talk about the policies themselves; it's another to discuss the people who actually carry them out. Mention the word *bureaucracy* to most people, and you'll probably get a negative reaction. Who doesn't have a terrible story about waiting in line for hours for a driver's license or having the post office lose their mail? Who hasn't heard about the immigration backlogs or difficulties with Social Security checks? For most, the negative reaction to bureaucracy is only natural due to their experiences with it, but when we take a step back and look at all of the activities that bureaucracies undertake, you'll see a much more nuanced perspective. Most of the 2.6 million Americans who make up the executive branch bureaucracies serve to carry out public policy to the best of their ability, but it's not always the easiest thing to do.

Growth of the Federal Bureaucracy

For much of the first 100 years of American history, the size of the federal bureaucracy was quite small. Receiving a job as a postman or government official usually came as a result of someone you knew; party supporters were rewarded with patronage jobs. However, the demands on government steadily began to grow, and as they grew, government had to respond with new agencies and organizations to carry out solutions to public problems. The Department of the Interior was created in 1849 to deal with issues surrounding American Indians, land management, and wildlife conservation. During the Civil War, Lincoln created the Department of Agriculture with the responsibility of farm and agricultural policy. These two federal bureaucracies are only two large examples of the growth of the federal bureaucracy as well as the growth of the number of people working in it.

By the late 1800s, the problem of patronage began to rear its ugly head in America. Every time a new president would enter office, he would be besieged by the pleas of job seekers looking for a job in the new administration. Often called the **spoils system**, presidents and their partisans were able to reward supporters with any number of jobs. Like many other presidents, James A. Garfield was also hounded by job seekers including one named Charles Guiteau, who would eventually assassinate him in 1881. As a result of the Garfield assassination, a series of civil service reforms were initiated with the goal of ending the spoils system and making civil service employment a result of merit and not patronage. As a result of this and other progressive era reforms, the people who make up the majority of the bureaucracy today get and keep their job based on what they know and their ability to do the job; top posts in the executive agencies are handed out by the president and could be a reward for patronage, but this is also the main method through which presidents get and maintain control of the executive branch as well.

The early twentieth century also brought with it a new focus on bureaucracy. Not only did early political scientists see administration as an area in which they could make a significant contribution, but the German sociologist Max Weber wrote extensively on bureaucracies. As an ideal type, "To Weber, a bureaucracy was an organization with specified functional attributes: large size; a graded hierarchy; formal rules; specialized tasks; written files; and employees who are salaried, technically trained, career-appointed, and assigned state duties requiring expert knowledge."[27] Based on this description, we can think of bureaucracies as technical organizations designed to carry out policy and design effective mechanisms through which government can operate.

Bureaucracies do not simply carry out policy, however. Bureaucracies can interpret law to change and modify policy on a regular basis. An example of how this operates in a negative sense is the case of the Clean Air Act of 1970. The Clean Air Act gives the Environmental Protection Agency (EPA) the ability to set emission standards for "any air pollutant"; up until the early 2000s, the EPA had not interpreted that to include carbon dioxide. In 2003, twelve states sued the EPA, arguing that under the Clean Air Act, carbon dioxide should be regulated. Although the Supreme Court eventually backed the states, the point is that the EPA, in how the law was interpreted, or rather not interpreted, was able to make a significant effect on the overall policy. Bureaucracies do this all the time. Depending on how they interpret legal statutes and findings, the way policy is actually carried out may be significantly different from what Congress and the president originally intended.

Bureaucracies also help to shape policy as it is being formed. Many policies that eventually make it into law or regulations that are put into effect have their start with career bureaucrats. Why might this be the case? Well, compared to members of Congress or even those in the White House, bureaucrats know far more about their area than anyone else. We call this an information asymmetry. Bureaucrats can use this expertise and knowledge to put together packages of policy, propose them to the White House and Congress, and persuade politicians to back them. At the end of the day, ideally, all policy will get the stamp of approval from political, elected leaders, but the bureaucracy can be a significant source of policy information and ideas.

Congressional Control

Despite criticisms, real or imagined, of bureaucratic personalities, another major criticism leveled at bureaucracies is that unelected bureaucrats have too much control over public policy. In a democracy, they argue, shouldn't elected officials, the representatives of the citizens, direct and make public policy? And given the power noted previously that bureaucrats have to make and influence policy, this could be a fair critique. However, there are a number of elements of control over bureaucratic actions that must also be taken into consideration. We will consider these restraints by branch: legislative, executive, and judicial.

With respect to Congress, they do have the ultimate tool at their disposal to control bureaucracies: the threat of dissolving those agencies to begin with. However, it is very unlikely for government bureaucracies to ever "die"; therefore, the next ultimate sanction is the ability to make laws. Members of Congress can make those laws very explicit and direct, thereby cutting down on the discretion left to bureaucrats. Given the current status of Congress, though, it would prove to be very difficult to pass legislation at all, especially explicit legislation. That said, sometimes the simple threat of legislation can influence bureaucratic behaviors.

Short of passing a law, members of Congress have at their disposal another powerful tool: the budget. Ideally, Congress would construct and pass a budget for the federal government every year; this gives members of Congress the opportunity to review public policy on a regular basis and determine how much money to appropriate for it, as discussed earlier in the chapter. These appropriations controls have the ability to significantly affect the policy process as well as bureaucrats.[28] For example, if the EPA is given less money, it would not be able to engage in as many regulatory actions—thereby limiting their impact on policy.

And even if members of Congress don't change the budget or even increase it, the use of another legislative tool in the appropriations process gives them an opportunity to crack down on bureaucratic activities: the policy rider. **Policy riders** are portions of legislation that are used to restrict bureaucratic actions, particularly in regulations. For example, policy riders may be used to forbid the EPA from regulating carbon dioxide. MacDonald has found that between 1993 and 2002, over 4,000 policy riders were introduced by the House Committee on Appropriations.[29] Policy riders are often attached to appropriations bills because they are generally looked at as "must pass" legislation; unless members of Congress would like the government to shut down, they have to pass the budget—even if there is a so-called poison pill attached to it in the form of a policy rider.

Another form of control is through congressional hearings and investigations. These oversight activities give members of Congress the opportunity to question bureaucrats and learn about the activities of various bureaucracies. Other participants can include interest groups or even critics of the bureaucracy who can give varying opinions on the activities being undertaken. Often, the oversight hearings are called in response to investigations that members have requested. The nonpartisan Government Accountability Office provides investigative services to members who request information on particular programs, policies, or actions, and these reports can then serve as a basis for examination in a hearing.

Although hearings are held almost every day on Capitol Hill, there is not much data that shows they make a difference. Weingast and Moran conclude that hearings do not provide much of an effective means at agency control and that Congress can influence agency activities through many other means.[30] Certainly, there is a ring of truth to that. If you ever watched a hearing on C-SPAN, or a hearing of a particular topic that has made it on the general news, you'll notice that members seem to be talking more at themselves than the bureaucrats, instead grandstanding and making personal points rather than trying to influence the policy process. However, what limits the influence of these types of hearings is that no one is usually watching.

A final means of influencing agency action is through changes in party control or makeup in the Congress.[31] When party control changes—for example, from Democratic to Republican—agencies are alerted to changing desires on the part of their political masters. In their study of regulatory changes following the 1994 Republican revolution that led to Republicans in charge in both the House and the Senate, Hedge and Johnson find that the EPA actually decreased its regulatory activities temporarily following the change in party control.[32]

Executive Control

If these controls weren't enough to keep the bureaucracy in line, the president has in his or her power another set of controls. Nathan argues that the primary means through which a president can control bureaucracies is through the administrative presidency—a set of tactics that can be used outside of Congress to control what the bureaucracy does.[33] These tactics include the use of the appointment power, the process of budget review through the Office of Management and Budget (OMB), civil service reorganizations, and regulatory control.

By far, the most effective means presidents have to control bureaucratic behavior is through the appointment power.[34] Although presidents used to focus solely on the top leadership at agencies, beginning with the Nixon administration, presidents began to take more care with appointments further down the agency totem pole, thereby helping to ensure that the president's wishes would be carried out.[35] Of course, part of Nixon's motivations in doing this was a fear that the bureaucracy had turned against him, but the practice of also being concerned with lower appointees continues as a result.

The OMB is a powerful but less well-known office within the White House that holds the power to affect many areas of policy. One of the most significant things that it does is that it acts on behalf of the president to oversee the budgets of executive agencies and departments. When bureaucracies are putting together budget proposals for the next fiscal year, before they are transmitted to Congress, the OMB must approve the budget requests. This allows the president, through the OMB, to place his own stamp on a bureaucracy's activities before Congress even gets the opportunity. Logsdon in *After Apollo?* provides an excellent case study of how influential the

OMB can be.[36] He studies in detail the creation of the NASA space shuttle program following the moon landings in the late 1960s and early 1970s. Time and again, the major players in shaping the policy were often analysts within the OMB who were looking out for President Nixon's budget priorities. While conflicts would eventually make it to the president for him to decide, Nixon often came down on the side of the OMB.

The OMB also provides clearance for any regulation government bureaucracies may be proposing. Before an agency like the Food and Drug Administration or the Federal Communications Commission publishes or proposes a rule implementing a law, the OMB, again acting on behalf of the president, must approve it. This gives the White House an opportunity to check the actions of bureaucracies to ensure they are in line with the president's objectives. Presidents can also request that agencies make regulations in certain areas that the president desires. President Obama requested that the EPA issue more stringent regulations with regard to regulating carbon dioxide, for example. Presidential requests, then, are direct policy actions that the bureaucracy must then carry out.

Finally, while a president cannot necessarily hire and fire civil service bureaucrats at will, he or she can reorganize the federal bureaucracy within certain parameters. **Reductions in force (RIFs)** can also be utilized to practically eliminate some areas of the bureaucracy. When presidents issue a RIF, bureaucrats can be forced out of agencies, thereby reducing capabilities. President Reagan utilized this tactic to reduce the civil service at the EPA in the 1980s, which was keeping with his policy of reduced regulations.[37] Again, this allows presidents to shape bureaucracies to their liking.

Judicial Control

In addition to the controls placed on the bureaucracy by the president and Congress, the judiciary also has a hand in ensuring that bureaucracies are on their best behavior. Under the 1946 Administrative Procedure Act, there are certain rules and procedures that bureaucracies must follow when they enact rules and regulations. They must first publish a proposed rule, allow time for comment, and then publish the final rule all in advance of when the rule goes into effect. Administrative law courts and judges can review the legality and procedures of bureaucracies to ensure that due process has been followed. Laws also give citizens the opportunity to appeal certain bureaucratic decisions such as Social Security disability decisions and decisions on benefits through the VA. Overall, the role of the court is to ensure that agencies follow all appropriate rules, interpret law correctly, and afford every citizen due process procedures.

Bureaucratic Politics

If you combine the knowledge and specialized expertise that bureaucrats have, along with their desire to create policies in a way they would prefer and the political controls offered through the Congress and the president, you create a world of politics central to the operations of bureaucracies. Bureaucrats and politicians will more often than not work in concert to not only create policy but shape how it is carried out. It is easy to recognize this in the actions of people like the secretary of state or the secretary of defense. If the country is faced with a military or international relations crisis, the secretary of defense will most likely try to convince the president to respond in a certain way, as will the secretary of state. Once a president makes their decision through the give-and-take of advice and consideration, those bureaucrats will have to act to carry out the decision. This back-and-forth doesn't only occur at the top levels of government; it happens all the way down the chain of command.

The term **bureaucratic politics** encompasses the actions of bureaucrats being involved in politics and policy. 't Hart and Rosenthal call the study of bureaucratic politics "one of the last remaining taboos in government. Everybody knows it occurs, but insiders are reluctant to speak about it frankly."[38] As mentioned before, this is often criticized as many believe the role of the bureaucracy is to competently carry out policy, not make it. But bureaucratic politics heavily influences the eventual policies that are decided upon. The most well-known example of how this has worked in practice is Allison's account of the Cuban missile crisis, *Essence of Decision*.[39] In it, Allison, along with Zelikow, argue that the best way to understand the actions of the Kennedy administration during the crisis was through the lens of bureaucratic politics, or what they call governmental politics: "What happens is understood as a *resultant* of bargaining games among players in the national government."[40] In other words, different actors, including bureaucrats, are engaged in bargaining and negotiations, and policy results from this give-and-take. The positions that bureaucrats take on issues are a result of the interests of their agency; for instance, when

Know a Political Scientist

Graham Allison

Graham Allison was only an undergraduate in college when the Cuban missile crisis occurred, but like the rest of the country, the experience of living through the closest the country has come to nuclear annihilation made an impact on his studies. Allison completed his undergraduate studies at Davidson College, Harvard, and Oxford University before receiving his PhD from Harvard in 1968. He published the first edition of *Essence of Decision* in 1971, thereby introducing the model of bureaucratic politics that would come to dominate studies of the bureaucracy. Not only was he a scholar but

he served as dean of the Kennedy School of Government at Harvard and served as a defense analyst and consultant to the Pentagon. Allison is a member of the Council on Foreign Relations and later served in government as the assistant secretary of defense for policy and plans from 1993 to 1994. President Bill Clinton later awarded Allison the Department of Defense Medal for Distinguished Public Service. Graham Allison's career demonstrates how political scientists can serve to impact governmental thinking on policy and just one of the ways that political scientists can perform valuable governmental work.

the Department of Defense is consulted on a policy problem, they will advocate the solution that their agency wants, not what might be in the best interest of the president or the United States. In the same vein, the Department of State will advocate the response that they want. It is up to the major players, including most of all the president and the Congress, to negotiate across agencies to come to a policy decision.

In another study of decision making during the Vietnam War, Preston and 't Hart argue that the way in which presidents surround themselves with advisers and the organization of the advisers greatly impacts the decisions that are made.[41] If presidents cut some parts of the government out, the positions of those agencies might not be included in the decision-making process. In this sense, policymaking is a result of horizontal processes—negotiations among players at similar levels of government—not a hierarchical process.[42] The problem with studying bureaucratic politics isn't just that some people do not believe in its legitimacy but that it is a difficult process to understand, see, and therefore analyze. As 't Hart and Rosenthal mentioned, no one really wants to talk about it, and no records are usually kept. As such, if we can't understand the exact behaviors of all the players involved, it is hard to understand the rationales and explanations that are taking place.

In any case, bureaucratic politics—the negotiating, talking, backroom deal making—does indeed happen throughout Washington. Bureaucrats have information and expertise as well as a desire to do good for their agency. Politicians want to be reelected and must listen not only to their constituents but to the information and advice given from not only bureaucrats but interest groups, political action committees, and other interested parties. Presidents must listen not only to bureaucrats but Congress and the nation of constituents. If we don't look deeper at politics, we might not see the bureaucratic politics happening, but looked at with a microscope, it is certainly there.

CASE STUDY
Guns, Bump Stocks, and Regulatory Fixes

Since 2000, there have been, on average, more than four mass shootings a year, where mass shootings are defined as the killing of four or more people by a single individual.[43] This significant historical increase has been blamed on multiple factors, but one of the major variables that increased the lethality of the mass shooting in Las Vegas, Nevada, on October 1, 2017, was the shooter's usage of something known as a bump stock. Bump stocks are an accessory that can be added to a semiautomatic rifle with the purpose of speeding up the weapon so that it fires in nearly an automatic style. Twelve such devices were found in the hotel room of the Las Vegas shooter. Following the incident, a number of people, including President Donald Trump and the National Rifle Association, announced that they would support the banning of bump stocks. Despite these pronouncements, no major policy changes were made in the months that followed.

While not used in the attack that killed seventeen people at Marjory Stoneman Douglas High

(*Continued*)

(Continued)

School in Parkland, Florida, in the aftermath of that shooting, President Trump announced administrative measures to ban the bump stock. In ordering the Bureau of Alcohol, Tobacco, Firearms and Explosives (ATF) within the Department of Justice to issue a regulation that would make owning a bump stock illegal, President Trump was using one of his administrative powers to make gun control policy. While it might have appeared to be an easy move, ATF had been previously unsure about whether it had the legal ability to carry out such an action. "Under the Obama administration, the bureau had determined it could not regulate them. Given that prior position, ATF officials had indicated privately in the months after the Las Vegas massacre that any ban of bump stocks would require new legislation."[44]

The president's action to ban bump stocks administratively highlights several important questions and lessons from this chapter. First, even though there might be widespread agreement that policy changes are needed, the challenges of the policy formulation and adoption stages make it so that changes are all but guaranteed. Second, presidents do have certain administrative capabilities, but they are limited to those that are granted to them by the Constitution or Congress. Finally, the ATF—the bureaucracy most closely involved—has been influential in influencing the types of policy and regulatory choices that have been made. The ATF regulation banning bump stocks was challenged in the courts, and as of February 2019, a US district judge ruled that the ban is not only legal but that the ATF followed all applicable procedures in issuing it.[45] However, other court challenges are still pending, further demonstrating the interconnectedness of the policymaking process.

Critical Thinking Questions

1. Who are the different policy actors involved in gun policy? Which model better describes them: the iron triangle or policy network?

2. If you were placing gun policy in Lowi's typology, in which category would it fall? Why?

3. Administratively, why is it difficult for the ATF and other bureaucracies to undertake and implement significant public policy decisions?

STUDENT STUDY SITE

Visit https://edge.sagepub.com/whitmancobb

CHAPTER SUMMARY

- There are five stages of the policymaking process: agenda setting, policy formulation, policy adoption, policy implementation, and policy evaluation.

- Typically, policy, as expressed by a budget, changes incrementally over time. However, there are periods in which change can come swiftly, and the policy is significantly overhauled.

- Most everyone is involved with the policy process at some point, but two different models of policy actors highlight the most important: iron triangles and policy networks, which can shift depending on the policy. Policy typologies can be helpful in analyzing public policy and the actors that are involved.

- Bureaucracies are critical actors in policymaking, and the federal bureaucracy has grown extensively since the twentieth century. Despite criticisms of too much bureaucratic involvement, all three branches of government have at their disposal tools through which they can control the actions taken by bureaucracies.

KEY TERMS

bottom-up: Policymaking that is driven by bureaucrats who then seek approval from higher political actors

budget reconciliation: A procedural move in Congress that directs committees to revise a budget to meet a specific target

bureaucratic politics: The involvement of bureaucracies and bureaucrats in policymaking decisions

incrementalism: The idea that an agency's budget will be based on its budget in the previous year and that the budget will generally only go up or go down by a small amount

iron triangle: Describes a policymaking relationship among interest groups, congressional committees, and relevant bureaucracies

logrolling: Agreements among members of Congress to vote for bills that other members favor so that other members will vote for bills a member wants

policy monopolies: A dominant understanding of the nature and direction of a particular policy

policy or issue network: Describes a fluid coalition of actors involved in policy on an ad hoc basis

policy riders: Portions of legislation that restrict the ability of bureaucracies to spend money on certain actions

public policy: Government-defined solutions to societal and governmental problems

punctuated equilibrium: Theory that policies generally exhibit long periods of stability with short periods of significant change

reductions in force (RIFs): Presidential order that can serve to shrink federal bureaucracies

spoils system: Presidents appointing their supporters to bureaucratic positions to reward their support

top-down: Policymaking that is driven by political actors such as the president or Congress

DISCUSSION QUESTIONS

1. In addition to the actors involved in agenda setting described in this chapter, who else can influence the government's policy agenda?

2. Compare and contrast iron triangles and issue networks. Which do you think is the better descriptor of the actors involved in policymaking?

3. What are the benefits to categorizing public policies?

4. What are some different ways in which bureaucracies can influence public policy?

5. Based on the chapter and what you know, who do you think has more control over the bureaucracy: the president or Congress? Why?

FOR FURTHER READING

Allison, Graham, and Philip Zelikow. *Essence of Decision: Explaining the Cuban Missile Crisis.* 2nd ed. New York: Longman, 1999.

Eshbaugh-Soha, Matthew. "The Politics of Presidential Agendas." *Political Research Quarterly* 58, no. 2 (2005): 257–268.

Goodsell, Charles T. *The Case for Bureaucracy: A Public Administration Polemic.* 4th ed. Washington, DC: CQ Press, 2004.

Lowi, Theodore J. "Four Systems of Policy, Politics, and Choices." *Public Administration Review* 32, no. 4 (1972): 298–310.

American Evaluation Association: https://www.eval.org

CDC's Policy Analytical Framework: https://www.cdc.gov/policy/analysis/process/analysis.html

NOTES

1. John W. Kingdon, *Agendas, Alternatives, and Public Policies*, 2nd ed. (New York: Pearson, 2002).

2. Jeffrey S. Peake, "Presidential Agenda Setting in Foreign Policy," *Political Research Quarterly* 54, no. 1 (2001): 69–86.

3. Matthew Eshbaugh-Soha, "The Politics of Presidential Agendas," *Political Research Quarterly* 58, no. 2 (2005): 257–268.

4. Jeff Yates and Andrew Whitford, "Institutional Foundations of the President's Issue Agenda," *Political Research Quarterly* 58, no. 4 (2005): 577–585.

5. Jack L. Walker, "Setting the Agenda in the US Senate: A Theory of Problem Selection," *British Journal of Political Science* 7, no. 4 (1977): 423.

6. Gary W. Cox, "Agenda Setting in the US House: A Majority Party Monopoly," *Legislative Studies Quarterly* 23, no. 2 (2001): 185–210.

7. Sean Gailmard and Jeffrey A. Jenkins, "Negative Agenda Control in the Senate and the House:

Fingerprints of Majority Party Power," *The Journal of Politics* 69, no. 3 (2007): 689–700.

8. Paul A. Sabatier, "Top-Down and Bottom-Up Approaches to Implementation Research: A Critical Analysis and Suggested Synthesis," *Journal of Public Policy* 6, no. 1 (1986): 21–48.

9. Ibid.

10. Robert A. Dahl and Charles Lindblom, *Politics, Economics, and Welfare* (New York: Harper and Row, 1953); Charles Lindblom, "The Science of Muddling Through," *Public Administration Review* 19 (1959): 79–88; Aaron Wildavsky, *The Politics of the budgetary Process* (Boston: Little, Brown, 1964); Otto A. Davis, M. A. H. Dempster, and Aaron Wildavsky, "A Theory of the Budgetary Process," *American Political Science Review* 60 (1966): 529–547.

11. William D. Berry, "The Confusing Case of Budgetary Incrementalism: Too Many Meanings for a Single Concept," *The Journal of Politics* 52, no. 1 (1990): 167–196.

12. Frank R. Baumgartner and Bryan D. Jones, *Agendas and Instability in American Politics* (Chicago: University of Chicago Press, 1993).

13. Jonathan Woon, "Change We Can Believe In? Using Political Science to Predict Policy Change in the Obama Presidency," *PS: Political Science and Politics* 42, no. 2 (2009): 329–333.

14. Brendon Swedlow, "Cultural Surprises as Sources of Sudden, Big Policy Change," *PS: Political Science and Politics* 44, no. 4 (2011): 736–739.

15. Sarah M. Brooks, "Interdependent and Domestic Foundations of Policy Change: The Diffusion of Pension Privatization around the World," *International Studies Quarterly* 49, no. 2 (2005): 273–294.

16. E. Sam Overman and Don F. Simanton, "Iron Triangles and Issue Networks of Information Policy," *Public Administration Review* 46 (Nov. 1986): 584.

17. Matt Grossman, "The Variable Politics of the Policy Process: Issue-Area Differences and Comparative Networks," *The Journal of Politics* 75, no. 1 (2012): 65–79.

18. Ibid., 65.

19. Marissa Martino Golden, "Interest Groups in the Rule-Making Process: Who Participates? Whose Votes Get Heard?" *Journal of Public Administration Research and Theory: J-PART* 8, no. 2 (1998): 245–270.

20. Ibid., 265.

21. Kevin B. Smith, "Typologies, Taxonomies, and the Benefits of Policy Classification," *Policy Studies Journal* 30, no. 3 (2002): 379–395.

22. Roger Handberg, "The Fluidity of Presidential Policy Choice: The Space Station, the Russian Card, and US Foreign Policy," *Technology in Society* 20 (1998): 421–439.

23. Theodore J. Lowi, "Four Systems of Policy, Politics, and Choices," *Public Administration Review* 32, no. 4 (1972): 298–310.

24. Smith, "Typologies, Taxonomies."

25. Ibid., 380.

26. Grossman, "The Variable Politics," 66.

27. Charles T. Goodsell, *The Case for Bureaucracy: A Public Administration Polemic,* 4th ed. (Washington, DC: CQ Press, 2004), 6.

28. Lawrence C. Dodd and Richard L. Schott, *Congress and the Administrative State* (New York: Macmillan, 1979).

29. Jason A. MacDonald, "Limitation Riders and Congressional Influence over Bureaucratic Policy Decisions," *American Political Science Review* 104, no. 4 (2010): 766–782.

30. Barry R. Weingast and Mark J. Moran, "Bureaucratic Discretion or Congressional Control? Regulatory Policymaking by the Federal Trade Commission," *The Journal of Political Economy* 91, no. 5 (1983): 765–800.

31. Ibid.; Terry M. Moe, "Control and Feedback in Economic Regulation: The Case of the NLRB," *American Political Science Review* 79, no. 4 (1985): 1095–1116; B. Dan Wood and Richard W. Waterman, "The Dynamics of Political Control of the Bureaucracy," *American Political Science Review* 85, no. 3 (1991): 801–828; David Hedge and Renee J. Johnson, "The Plot That Failed: The Republican Revolution and Congressional Control of the Bureaucracy," *J-PART* 12, no. 3 (2002): 333–351.

32. Hedge and Johnson, "The Plot That Failed."

33. Richard P. Nathan, *The Administrative Presidency* (London: Macmillan, 1983).

34. Wood and Waterman, "The Dynamics of Political Control"; Moe, "Control and Feedback"; Marissa Martino Golden, *What Motivates Bureaucrats? Politics and Administration during the Reagan Years* (New York: Columbia University Press, 2000).

35. Nathan, *The Administrative Presidency.*

36. John Logsdon, *After* Apollo? *Richard Nixon and the American Space Program* (New York: Palgrave Macmillan, 2015).

37. Golden, *What Motivates Bureaucrats?*

38. Paul 't Hart and Uriel Rosenthal, "Reappraising Bureaucratic Politics," *Mershon International Studies Review* 42, no. 2 (1998): 233.

39. Graham Allison and Philip Zelikow, *Essence of Decision: Explaining the Cuban Missile Crisis*, 2nd ed. (New York: Longman, 1999).

40. Ibid., 6 (emphasis in the original).

41. Thomas Preston and Paul 't Hart, "Understanding and Evaluating Bureaucratic Politics: The Nexus between Political Leaders and Advisory Systems," *Political Psychology* 20, no. 1 (1999): 49–98.

42. Thomas H. Hammond, "Agenda Control, Organizational Structure, and Bureaucratic Politics," *American Journal of Political Science* 30, no. 2 (1986): 379–420.

43. Bonnie Berkowitz, Denise Lu, and Chris Alcantara, "The Terrible Numbers That Grow with Each Mass Shooting," *Washington Post*, June 15, 2017, https://www.washingtonpost.com/graphics/2018/national/mass-shootings-in-america/?utm_term=.b7dfda4c78cb.

44. Michael D. Shear, "Trump Moves to Regulate 'Bump Stock' Devices," *New York Times*, Feb. 20, 2018, https://www.nytimes.com/2018/02/20/us/politics/trump-bump-stocks.html.

45. Meagan Flynn, "Bump-Stock Ban Enacted by Trump Administration Can Stand, Federal Judge Rules," *Washington Post,* Feb. 26, 2019, https://www.washingtonpost.com/nation/2019/02/26/bump-stock-ban-enacted-by-trump-administration-can-stand-federal-judge-rules/?utm_term=.0952fc78db54.

Index

Baumgarten, Frank R., 265, 266
Beath, Andrew, 249
Becker, Lee B., 122
Bedi, Sonu, 69
Behavioralism, 8, 9
Bejan, Teresa M., 69
Belco, Michelle, 150
Benchmark interest rates, monetary policy and, 240–241
Benefits
  of using qualitative methods, 38–39
  of using quantitative methods, 35
Bennett, Andrew, 36
Bentham, Jeremy, 60
Berlusconi, Silvio, 103
Bernstein, Carl, 121, 155
Berry, William D., 264
Bertelli, Anthony, 151
Bias
  case studies and, 36
  media, 124, 136
  in media, 129
  media and potential for, 126–128
  selection, 38, 179
Bicameral legislature, 100, 104, 144
Bill and Melinda Gates Foundation, 197
Bill of Rights, 20, 77, 80–81
bin Laden, Osama, 260
Black nationalism, 198
Blankenship, Don, 3
Bloomberg, Michael, 124
Bloomberg L.P., 124
Boehmke, Frederick J., 186
Boleyn, Anne, 57–58
Bollen, Kenneth A., 183, 184
Bolsheviks, 237
Bolton, Alexander, 150
Bond, Jon R., 155
Bond, Patrick, 195
Boom and bust cycles, 242–243
Bork, Robert, 155
Bottom-up policy formulation, 261
Bottom-up policy implementation, 262–263
The Brethren (Woodward and Bernstein), 155
Bretton Woods Conference, 186, 187
British Journal of Political Science, 185
Brown v. Board of Education, 153
Brox, Brian J., 163

Bryan, William Jennings, 113
Bubbles, 242–243
Budget
  Congress and, 147
  congressional control of bureaucracy and, 273
  executive control of bureaucracy and review of, 274–275
  NASA, 264–267, 275
  punctuated equilibrium and, 265–267
Budgetary incrementalism, 264–265
Budget reconciliation, 143, 261–262
Bully pulpit, 259
Bump stocks, regulation of, 277–278
Bundesrat, 100, 101, 104
Bundestag, 101, 104
Bureaucracy
  administrative law and, 83
  French, 108
  growth of federal, 271–272
  policy implementation and, 262–263
  policymaking and, 258, 267–268
  president and, 151–152
  rulemaking and, 269
Bureaucratic politics, 275–277
Burr, Aaron, 119
Bush, George H. W., 113, 225–226, 231
Bush, George W., 113, 126, 128, 129, 152, 155, 162
Bush, George W. administration, war in Iraq and, 223, 225–226
Businesses, taxes on, 239

Cabinet
  in parliamentary system, 99
  in presidential systems, 104
Campbell, James E., 12
Capitalism, 234–235
  communist critique of, 235–236
  critique of, 234–236
  relationship to democracy, 251–252
Caprioli, Mary, 221
Carmines, Edward G., 165
Carville, James, 231
Case law, 83–84
Case studies
  comparative method, 37–38
  defined, 36
  democracies and conflict, 46
  democracy and capitalism, 251–252

Tyranny, 6, 54
Tyranny of the majority, 6

Ukraine, Russian incursion into, 36, 37, 44, 45, 224
Unanimous consent agreement (UCA), 147
Unemployment, monetary policy and, 241
Unified government, 112
Unipolar world, 210
Unitary states, 79
United Kingdom
    constitutional monarchy in, 15, 99
    judicial independence in, 88
    Parliament, 100, 101
United Nations, 210
    constructivism and, 218
    diplomatic recognition of states by, 222
    establishment of, 214
    globalization and, 187, 211
    Security Council, 216, 226
    state development and, 197
    strengths and weaknesses of, 216–217
    United Nations treaty, 213
    Universal Declaration of Human Rights, 21, 92
United States
    exchange rate and, 247
    GDP in, 242
    Gini index for, 243
    intervention in Iraq, 223, 224, 225–226
    involvement in twentieth-century wars, 224
    judicial independence in, 88
    mandatory minimum sentencing in, 91
    relationship with North Korea, 207–208
    reopening of relations with China, 211, 251
    state of political parties in, 111
    steel production in, 246
    unemployment rate in, 241
United States of America, origin of term, 14
Universal Declaration of Human Rights (UDHR), 21, 92
University of Michigan, 158
Urban-Brookings Tax Policy Center, 70
Urbatsch, R., 248
USA Today (newspaper), 127
US Federal Reserve, 242
US tax code, Trump and overhaul of, 143
Utilitarianism, 60
Utopia (More), 6

Vanberg, Georg, 154
Van Winkle, Steven R., 154
Variables, 31–33
    dependent, 32, 38
    independent, 32
    problem of many, 177, 179
Veil of ignorance, 64
Verba, Sidney, 22, 42–43, 186
Versailles Peace Conference, 233
Vertical equity, 70
Vietnam War, 224, 277
Vonderlack, Rebecca M., 195
Voter mobilization, 163
Voter turnout, media effects on, 130
Voting, 162–163
    experience with economy and, 232
    by mail, 162
    new methods of, 162
Vu, Tuong, 181

Waddams, H. M., 190
Wag the Dog (film), 224
Walker, Jack L., 259
Walker, Thomas C., 211–212
"Wall of separation" policy, 129
Wall Street Journal (newspaper), 127
Waltz, Kenneth N., 210–211
War, 222–226
    causes of, 223–226
    defining, 222–223
    democracy and, 46
    United States and Iraq, 224, 225–226
Warnement, Megan K., 122
The War of the Worlds (Wells), 134
Washington, Ebonya, 160
Washington, George, 103, 109, 152, 157, 163
Washington Post (newspaper), 121, 127
Watchdog function of the press, 121, 122
Watergate, 121, 156
Waterman, Richard W., 151
Way, Christopher R., 248
Weapons of mass destruction (WMDs), US intervention in Iraq and, 223, 225
Weber, Max, 179–180, 272
Websites, fake news, 134
Weiler, Marc J., 192
Weingast, Barry R., 274
Weisberg, Herbert F., 158